Further Requirements

by Philip Larkin

poetry

THE NORTH SHIP

THE LESS DECEIVED (Marvell Press)

THE WHITSUN WEDDINGS

HIGH WINDOWS

COLLECTED POEMS

(*edited by Anthony Thwaite*)

SELECTED LETTERS OF PHILIP LARKIN 1940–1985

(*edited by Anthony Thwaite*)

THE OXFORD BOOK OF

TWENTIETH-CENTURY ENGLISH VERSE (ed.)

fiction

JILL

A GIRL IN WINTER

TROUBLE AT WILLOW GABLES AND OTHER FICTIONS

(*edited by James Booth*)

non-fiction

ALL WHAT JAZZ: A RECORD DIARY 1961–71

REQUIRED WRITING:

MISCELLANEOUS PIECES 1955–82

LARKIN'S JAZZ: ESSAYS AND REVIEWS 1940–84

Further Requirements

Interviews, Broadcasts, Statements and Book Reviews

PHILIP LARKIN

Edited and with an Introduction by

ANTHONY THWAITE

faber and faber

First published in 2001
by Faber and Faber Limited
3 Queen Square London WC1N 3AU
This paperback edition, with two additional chapters,
first published in 2002

Photoset by Wilmaset Ltd, Birkenhead, Wirral
Printed in England by Bookmarque Ltd, Croydon

A CIP record for this book
is available from the British Library

ISBN 0–571–21614–5

2 4 6 8 10 9 7 5 3 1

Contents

Introduction, xi
Acknowledgements, xvii

I · STATEMENTS AND INTERVIEWS
The Writer in His Age, 3
Not the Place's Fault, 6
On Publishing *The Less Deceived*, 12
Context, 14
Poet's Choice 17
Louis MacNeice, 18
A Conversation with Ian Hamilton, 19
A Conversation with Neil Powell, 27
The True Voice of Feeling, 35
The State of Poetry, 38
Let the Poet Choose, 39
W. H. Auden, 40
The Sanity of Lawrence, 42
An Interview with John Haffenden, 47

II · BROADCASTS
'New Poetry', BBC Third Programme, 13 April 1956, 65
'How or why I write poetry . . .', BBC Overseas Service, 20 August 1958, 78
'The Living Poet', BBC Third Programme, 3 July 1964, 79
Larkin at Fifty, BBC Radio Three, 9 August 1972, 92
On *The Oxford Book of Twentieth-Century English Verse*, BBC Radio Three, 12 April 1973, 94

Desert Island Discs, BBC Radio Four, 17 July 1976, 103
Meeting Philip Larkin, BBC Radio Four, 29 March 1984, 112

III · FOREWORDS

Operation Manuscript, 119
Adventures with the Irish Brigade by Colin Gunner, 127
Fen Country: Twenty-Six Stories by Edmund Crispin, 131
The Arts Council Poetry Library Catalogue, 133
A Rumoured City: New Poets from Hull, 136
An Unsuitable Attachment by Barbara Pym, 137
The Condemned Playground by Cyril Connolly, 142
Earth Memories by Llewelyn Powys, 147

IV · REVIEWS

Afternoon Men by Anthony Powell, 155
Not Literary Enough: John Heath-Stubbs, 158
Beyond a Joke: John Betjeman, 160
Abstract Vision: Kathleen Raine, 165
Shem the Penman: Hugh Kenner on Joyce, 167
No More Fever: W. H. Auden, 168
Chosen and Recommended: W. S. Merwin and Kathleen Nott, 174
Separate Ways: Kingsley Amis, Lawrence Durrell, Siegfried Sassoon, 176
You Do Something First: Gertrude Stein, 179
Mrs Ridler and Miss Millay: Anne Ridler, Edna St Vincent Millay, Ezra Pound, 181
Poetry at Present: John Bayley and Babette Deutsch, 183
Recent Verse – Some Near Misses: John Holloway, Charles Causley, Richard Wilbur, Louis MacNeice, 185
Ideas about Poetry: Frank Kermode, Robert Langbaum, 188
Thomas Hardy and the Cosmic Mind by J. O. Bailey, 190
Reports on Experience: Elizabeth Jennings, Alan Ross, R. S. Thomas, 192

No Fun Any More: John Press, 195
Graves Superior (with a note by Robert Graves), 197
Poetry Beyond a Joke: John Betjeman, 200
West Britons and True Gaels: *The Oxford Book of Irish Verse*, 203
The Industrial Muse by Jeremy Warburg, 205
Betjeman En Bloc, 206
Keeping Up with the Graveses: Robert Graves, Robert Lowell, John Berryman, Christopher Logue, Rex Taylor, 217
Look, No Kangaroos: Randolph Stow, Geoffrey Dutton, 221
Texts and Symbols: Vernon Watkins, Anne Ridler, Andrew Young, 226
Down among the Dead Men: *Georgian Poets*, Sir John Squire, Ralph Hodgson, 229
Imaginary Museum Piece: Donald Davie, P. J. Kavanagh, 233
Lies, Fleas and Gullible Mayflies: Vernon Scannell, Peter Redgrove, 236
Collected Poems by Roy Campbell, 239
Gleanings from a Poor Year for Poetry: *The Guinness Book of Poetry*, Edwin Muir, Peter Levi, 240
Exhumation: C. Day Lewis, 243
Last-but-one Round-up: William Plomer, 245
Open Your Betjemans, 248
Groupings: The Powys brothers, Ronald Firbank, John Betjeman, 251
Christina Rossetti, 253
Bond's Last Case: Ian Fleming, 256
Poets in a Fine Frenzy and Otherwise: Geoffrey Grigson, 259
Hardy's Mind and Heart: F. R. Southerington, Michael Millgate, 261
Stevie, Good-bye: Stevie Smith, 263
Archibald MacLeish, 266
The Hidden Hardy: Hardy's letters, 269

Articulate Devotion: *The Faber Book of Love Poems, The Penguin Book of Love Poetry*, 274
The Puddletown Martyr: *Young Thomas Hardy*, 277
Shelving the Issue: *Books for the People*, 282
In the Seventies: Hardy's Collected Letters, 285
Amis and Auden: The Oxford anthologies of light verse, 291
The Ascent of WHA: *W. H. Auden: The Life of a Poet*, 296
'A decent minor poet': C. Day-Lewis, 299
Chatterbox without Charity: *The Letters of Evelyn Waugh*, 301
Castigations: *The Oxford Book of Satirical Verse*, 304
Four Legs Good: Dick Francis, 307
The Life under the Laurels: *Tennyson: The Unquiet Years*, 310
Words for Music Perhaps: *Britten and Auden in the Thirties*, 317
Horn of Plenty: Gavin Ewart, 320
A Late Bonus: John Betjeman, 325
A Slackening of the Reins: Dick Francis, 328
Under a Common Flag: *The Penguin Book of Contemporary British Poetry*, 330
Brief for Betjeman: *John Betjeman: His Life and Work*, 334
The Powys Pantomime: *The Brothers Powys*, 338
Bubble Reputation: *W. H. Auden: The Critical Heritage*, 342
Point of No Return: *The Oxford Book of Death*, 345
Inner Horizons: *Cyril Connolly: Journal and Memoir*, 348
On Familiar Ground: *The Middle of My Tether*, Joseph Epstein, 353
Lost Content: *A. E. Housman: A Critical Biography*, 355
Bridey and Basil: *The Essays, Articles and Reviews of Evelyn Waugh*, 358
David Lodge's Period Piece: *Small World*, 361
Lover-Shadows in the Flesh: H. G. Wells, 364
An Unofficial Life: T. S. Eliot, 372
Solitary Walker: Andrew Young, 376

The Missing Thou: *With Friends Possessed: A Life of Edward FitzGerald*, 378

Index, 383

Introduction

Required Writing ('a ragbag of fugitive scribblings', as he characteristically described it in a letter to a friend) was the last book to be published by Philip Larkin in his lifetime. It was a gathering of Larkin's 'miscellaneous' prose, from 1955 to 1982, was much praised when it appeared in 1983, and was given the W. H. Smith Award. But it was a highly selective gathering. In a long and handsome review of the book (*Encounter*, February 1984), Blake Morrison commented that Larkin's phrase in his foreword ('the pieces collected here') 'leaves it open to the careless reader to infer that this is the Collected Prose'. Morrison went on to itemize important omissions: interviews, statements and reviews which he believed should have been included.

The present book attempts to make good those omissions, and also to assemble later pieces, after Larkin had made his selection for *Required Writing*. It carries Larkin's first published review, from an indeed 'fugitive' source. Published in the autumn of 1952, in *Q*, the literary magazine of Queen's University, Belfast, where he was Sub-Librarian at the time, it immediately establishes one of Larkin's enthusiasms, for the fiction of Anthony Powell. It does so with assurance and authority, as if Larkin had been doing this sort of thing for years. Much later, in his foreword to *Required Writing*, he commented: 'I have heard it said that anyone who has spent three years writing a weekly essay for his tutor finds literary journalism easy: I didn't.' Larkin's apparent ease in the Powell review belies this. He had nothing of a literary reputation at the time. At thirty, he had published two novels, *Jill* and *A Girl in Winter*, the first of which had gone totally unnoticed in 1946; the second had received a few good notices in 1947 (including one by Anthony Powell), but it was out of print and largely forgotten.

He had earlier, in 1945, published *The North Ship*, his first book of poems. It too went unnoticed. In 1951, a year before the *Q* piece on Powell, he had paid a Belfast printer to produce a hundred copies of a pamphlet, *XX Poems*, for private distribution. There was one review, by the then equally unknown D. J. Enright, in a Catholic periodical, *The Month*.

So the confident address of Larkin's review did not spring from a firm place in the literary world. Nor did Larkin's equally confident review of his former Oxford contemporary and acquaintance, John Heath-Stubbs, in another fugitive organ, *Poetry and Audience*, in June 1954. *Poetry and Audience* was a cyclostyled magazine emanating from the Department of English Literature at Leeds University. It began in 1953, appeared once a week during term at a penny a time, and is notable for having carried early work by poets associated with Leeds University such as Geoffrey Hill, Jon Silkin and Tony Harrison. Larkin's poem 'Triple Time' first appeared there on 28 January 1954, to be followed in the 10 June issue with both the first printing of 'Poetry of Departures' and the review of Heath-Stubbs's *A Charm Against the Toothache*. Heath-Stubbs was at that time Gregory Fellow in Poetry at Leeds University, and his name is blazoned as 'Editorial Adviser' on the title page of the magazine. That being so, it was generous of him to allow Larkin's trenchant and funny strictures to go by. It is an amazingly self-assured notice by a Nobody of a Somebody.

The Marvell Press's publication of Larkin's book *The Less Deceived* in November 1955 marked what can now be seen as the transition from Nobody to Somebody. It was a little later picked out by *The Times* as one of the books of the year. Some literary editors pricked up their ears, and before long one of them (Bill Webb of the *Guardian*, or rather the *Manchester Guardian*, as it then was) made his approaches to the new poet.

Larkin's first review for Webb (17 April 1956) was of a book of poems by someone few would associate with him, Kathleen Raine; and it is, one could say, judicious rather than warm – even cautious. His BBC 'New Poetry' broadcast, on the other hand, was rather more enthusiastic about her and he was perhaps feeling his way into this new milieu of metropolitan journalism. But he soon got into his stride, producing between 1956 and his death many more reviews than could be guessed from reading *Required Writing*. Though his remarks in the foreword to that book about being 'reluctant' in response are no doubt accurate, it was a reluctance he surprisingly often overcame.

One area of reviewing in which he was less reluctant was jazz – jazz records, and books about jazz and jazz musicians. He took his own initiative, at first (as he admits in *Required Writing*), in gathering together the many jazz record reviews he wrote for the *Daily Telegraph* between 1960 and 1968. These appeared in his book *All What Jazz* (1970). Later, towards the end of *Required Writing*, he collected more from that original source. Earlier, first in the weekly magazine *Truth* in 1957, later in the *Manchester Guardian* and other papers, he published many reviews of books about jazz. None of these appear in the present book, for the good reason that all have already been collected in *Reference Back: Philip Larkin's Uncollected Jazz Writings 1940–84*, expertly edited by Richard Palmer and John White (University of Hull Press, 1999; reissued as *Larkin's Jazz* by Continuum in 2001). As is well known, jazz was supremely important to Larkin; but with *Required Writing*, *All What Jazz* and *Reference Back* available, there is no need to duplicate their contents.

In spite of his reiterated complaints ('minor tasks of literary journalism ... foolishly undertaken, fatiguingly completed', in a letter to Barbara Pym, 8 April 1963), Larkin seems to have allowed himself to take up many such tasks well beyond the call of duty, or even of making a reputation. And, in spite of his insistence in the foreword to *Required Writing* that he had 'never proposed to an editor that I should write this article or review that book', there is the evidence of his first letter to Barbara Pym (16 January 1961) in which he wrote:

> Dear Miss Pym,
>
> I wonder if you are preparing to publish another novel soon? I ask because, if you are, I should like to give further consideration to an idea I had of a general essay on your books, which I might persuade *The Spectator* to publish in the form of a review of the next. (It would, of course, be written from the standpoint of one who much enjoys them.)
>
> At this stage I know neither whether I could do it to my own satisfaction (let alone yours), or whether *The Spectator* would be interested. However, I thought it worth raising in a preliminary way at least.

As Larkin observed in a follow-up to this letter (22 February), the move of Karl Miller as literary editor from the *Spectator* to the *New Statesman*, and the fact that *No Fond Return of Love* had just been published as he wrote, overtook his question. But he had at least asked it. What followed, of course, was the long period of Pym's rejection, until her triumphant reappearance in 1977, in which Larkin played a vital part.

At least in the earlier days, a lot of work must have been done for little or no money. His *Modern Language Review* piece on J. O. Bailey's *Thomas Hardy and the Cosmic Theme* (January 1958) is, as usual, succinct; and it gives a clear picture of how he regarded Hardy's *The Dynasts*. But it can have brought few rewards, beyond those of a job well done. And when he contributed a 'Short Notice' of Jeremy Warburg's *The Industrial Muse* to the same academic journal (April 1959) his by-line ('P. A. Larkin') seems not only a sign of his own down-grading in performing such a task, but an almost deliberate acknowledgement of how 'minor' it was. (To be just, though, one might notice that 'P. A. Larkin' was the librarian's normal signature.)

Now and then he perhaps took on such jobs out of sheer professionalism. His contribution to the March 1972 *Journal of Documentation* (a specialist librarians' journal) is not only an indication of his high regard for the Larkin-like tenaciousness of Archibald MacLeish, poet drafted into being Librarian of Congress (1939–44), but a tacit acknowledgement of how an amateur such as MacLeish might put in perspective the concerns of professionals: 'There is not so much well-written and forthright praise of our profession about that we can afford to disregard them.'

Early and late, Larkin was sometimes prepared to contribute to 'little' magazines: not only *Q* in Belfast or *Poetry and Audience* in Leeds but George Hartley's *Listen*, out of which the Marvell Press grew. Later, he wrote for the *New Review* (Autumn 1978) a rather less than enthusiastic piece about his old friend Kingsley Amis's *New Oxford Book of Light Verse;* and much more warmly about Gavin Ewart in *Quarto* (May 1982). But how he was inveigled into reviewing Randolph Stow and Geoffrey Dutton in *Australian Letters* (June 1959) remains obscure to me.

In the pieces brought together here, there is inevitably some repetition, of views and even of phrases. One way of looking at this is that it underlines Larkin's consistency: he said what he meant to say, and went on saying it, about himself and about other writers. The qualities of Tennyson, Hardy, Betjeman, Auden, Waugh – all are considered, and then reconsidered, over a long period of years. And they should be put alongside what he says in the pieces in *Required Writing*.

The present book begins with three sections not made up of reviews, but of, first, what I call 'Statements and Interviews', then 'Broadcasts', and then 'Forewords'. Over the years, Larkin was invited by literary magazines to be interviewed or to answer questionnaires. B. C. Bloomfield, his bibliographer, acknowledges that 'Larkin at one time granted interviews fairly readily and the reports by the interviewers are often the surest way of ascertaining his opinions on various topics at those times.' The present book excludes those pieces which are, substantially, and with whatever degree of accuracy, renderings-down of recorded meetings with Larkin, from 'Four Young Poets: I' (*Times Educational Supplement*, 13 July 1956) to Dan Jacobson's 'Philip Larkin – a Profile' (*New Review*, June 1974), or any in between or since.

What the book does include are the direct responses that Larkin made to questionnaires/interviews, together with the 'statements' (there should be a better word, but I can't think of one) he made when approached by a journal; or when he chose to write some sort of prefatory or explanatory material, as in his sleeve-notes to the Marvell Press recording of *The Less Deceived* – two different notes (1959 and 1968) to the same recording.

Apart from the transcripts of recorded and (sometimes) published interviews, there are the commissioned tributes to MacNeice and to Auden immediately after their deaths; the brief notes he contributed to anthologies; and – I think most importantly – the autobiographical essay he wrote in 1959 for a short-lived Coventry arts magazine, *Umbrella*, 'Not the Place's Fault'. When the present editor put this forward for a place in *Required Writing*, Larkin responded: 'You plead very ably for it, but I still can't bring myself to include it. It gives me small profound inexplicable shudders' (30 November 1982). It has since been published (in Harry Chambers's collection, *An Enormous Yes*, 1986), but deserves its place in this book.

The 'Forewords', in Section III, are various. Colin Gunner was an old Coventry school friend of Larkin's: they had grown up disgracefully together through King Henry VIII School in the city, and when, after many years apart, Gunner made contact again with Larkin, the response was generous. Their relationship can be glimpsed in the *Selected Letters*. Of the other forewords, two (to *A Rumoured City* and to the Arts Council Poetry Library Catalogue) were perhaps dutiful rather than full-hearted; the others (to

'Edmund Crispin', Barbara Pym, Cyril Connolly and Llewelyn Powys) were acts of allegiance.

This is not a totally exhaustive collection of Larkin's non-fictional prose pieces: for example, it excludes some published judgements on various student poetry competitions, mainly in Hull, and it also excludes some letters to the press. There may, one day, be a place for these, too, in some Complete Works. For the time being, this book – together with James Booth's edition of Larkin's unpublished fiction (Faber and Faber) – goes as far as the literary executors feel it useful or appropriate to go at the present time.

ANTHONY THWAITE

Acknowledgements

I thank the following for help with material, advice, and support: Jonathan Barker; Bruce Bennett; B. C. Bloomfield; John Bodley (Faber and Faber); Charles Boyle (Faber and Faber); British Library Newspaper Library, Colindale; BBC Written Archives Centre, Caversham; Brian Dyson (Archivist, Brynmor Jones Library, University of Hull); Brian Hulan; Mary Kelly (Special Collections, Main Library, Queen's University, Belfast); Michael Millgate; Blake Morrison; Andrew Motion: Richard Palmer; Peter Porter; Neil Powell; Judith Priestman (Bodleian Library, Oxford); C. D. W. Sheppard (Brotherton Collection, Leeds University); Ann Thwaite; John White.

Acknowledgements, and in some cases permissions, are due to the following: John Haffenden (editor, *Viewpoints*, Faber and Faber); Ian Hamilton; George Hartley; Estate of Randall Jarrell; Vicki Mitchell (BBC Copyright); Estate of Edwin Muir; Kathleen Raine; Estate of E. J. Scovell; A. N. Wilson; April Young (Roy Plomley Estate). Also to: *Daily Telegraph*; *Guardian*; *London Magazine*; *New Statesman*; *Observer*; *Spectator*; *The Times Literary Supplement*. Philip Larkin's poems 'Absences', 'I Remember, I Remember', 'Coming' and 'Church Going' are reprinted from *The Less Deceived* by permission of The Marvell Press, England and Australia.

A.T.

I · STATEMENTS AND INTERVIEWS

The Writer in His Age

My only criticism of a writer today, or any other day, is that he writes (as I think) badly, and that means a great many things much more certainly than it means 'non-engagement': being boring, for instance, or hackneyed, pretentious, forced, superficial, or – the commonest – simply leaving me flat cold. Therefore, if I find a novel or poem the reverse of all these things – gripping, original, honest, and so on – I shall be much too grateful to take up a quarrel with its author over motives or material.

Therefore my answer to each of your questions is no, though not always at the same volume. I am quite happy to agree with the implication, for instance, that good writing is most likely to deal with present-day situations in present-day language, but only because good writing is largely a matter of finding proper expression for strong feelings, and those feelings are most likely to arise from the writer's own experiences and will be most properly expressed in his own language, both of which will spring from his ordinary life. But I should not like to make rules prohibiting fantasies of the past or future, or 'experimental' writing, though I don't much like them myself. I am less sure about changes in social structure and recent discoveries in the sciences. These, if they are not what the work is about, are no more than background, and as such should be implicit rather than stated. A writer must have regard for the negative truthfulness necessary to sneak his poem or story past the reader's logical threshold. But otherwise it should not be there without artistic justification. As for the last question about dating, I was brought up to think that the better a work was, the less you thought about its period: the highest praise you could give was to say that it was not of an age, but for all time. Perhaps I was brought up wrongly. But if I were shown a work written 'today' that could be placed only somewhere within the last fifty years, I should wonder if I were not in the presence of a considerable talent.

Surely a writer's only 'necessary engagement' is with his

subject-matter, which is not primarily a conscious choice at all, but is what generates in his imagination the peculiar excitement that draws intellect, feeling and expression readily and appropriately into service until the subject has been realized. I should say that this is the only way to write well. Answering yes to all your questions leaves a concept of good writing far too dependent on the intellect and the social conscience to be acceptable, for the imagination is not the servant of these things, and may even be at variance with them. A man may believe that what we want at present is a swingeing good novel on the state of this or the fate of that, but his imagination remains unstirred except by notions of renunciation or the smell of a certain brand of soap. Less improbably, the intellect (assuming for the moment that such a thing exists) may be so busy handling the imagination's excitement over the natural world, or the way things turn out, that it will just be too tired to read the papers.

In other words, good social and political literature can exist only if it originates in the imagination, and it will do that only if the imagination finds the subject exciting, and not because the intellect thinks it important; and it will succeed only in so far as the imagination's original concept has been realized. To say more than this seems possible only if you are prepared to postulate and compare two equal concepts equally realized, and to argue that the one about factories is better than the one about fairyland, and I don't think you can do this as long as you are talking about literature and not about something else.

London Magazine, May 1957

NOTE: The headnote by the editor, John Lehmann, states: '*The London Magazine* has invited nine authors to answer the questions printed below. They were asked not to consider themselves obliged to answer the questions in order or precisely point by point, but to give their views as a general statement.'

> During the Thirties it was a widely-held view that poets, novelists and playwrights should be closely concerned *in their writing* with the fundamental political and social issues of their time. Since then, the degree of an imaginative writer's necessary engagement with the age in which he lives has been the subject of constant debate with very varied conclusions. Do you think that today, in 1957, it is a valid criticism of such a writer to say that (1) he appears indifferent to the immediate problems of human freedom involved in, say, the Rosenberg case and the Hungarian revolution; (2) he shows no awareness (a) of the changes that have been caused in our social structure and our way of life by, for instance, the development of

> atomic weapons and the levelling down of classes through discriminatory taxation, nor (b) of the challenges to our conception of human existence caused by recent discoveries in such sciences as biology, astronomy and psychology; (3) his novel, play or poem could, *judged on internal evidence only*, have been written at any time during the last fifty years.

The other eight authors were Maurice Cranston, D. J. Enright, Roy Fuller, William Golding, John Osborne, Stephen Spender, John Wain and Colin Wilson.

Not the Place's Fault

In January 1954 I wrote a poem called 'I Remember, I Remember' (included in *The Less Deceived*, Marvell Press, 1955) after stopping unexpectedly in a train at Coventry, the town where I was born and lived for the first eighteen years of my life. The poem listed, rather satirically, a lot of things that hadn't happened during the time, and ended:

> 'You look as if you wished the place in Hell,'
> My friend said, 'judging from your face.' 'Oh, well,
> I suppose it's not the place's fault,' I said.
>
> 'Nothing, like something, happens anywhere.'

This poem was not of course meant to disparage Coventry, or to suggest that it was, or is, a dull place to live in, or that I now remember it with dislike or indifference, or even can't remember it at all. It is true that I could not today direct anyone to Binley or Hearsall Lane or Wyken or Stoke Park. But then I never could, even in my schooldays. And of course the inside of the railway station of one's home town is never very familiar, and I was certainly not likely to recognize mine. If I disregard journeys under supervision, a pawn in the hands of fate, I can remember taking only one journey by train – to Berkswell, to see John Greenwell – before I left for Oxford in 1940, and I really doubt if many others occurred. I am not a natural traveller: a place has to be pretty intolerable before it enters my head that somewhere else might be nicer. As I get older, for instance, I grow increasingly impatient of holidays: they seem a wholly feminine conception, based on an impotent dislike of everyday life and a romantic notion that it will all be better at Frinton or Venice; few men want a holiday, or work hard enough to need one. And I can discern this view in embryo in my reaction to the family annual holiday during the first ten years of my life. It seemed hard to be separated from my playmates and the series of complicated cricket games I was holding by means of cards and dice between the counties and the visiting touring team, and to be set down in a strange place without any of one's belongings. We usually went to Devon or Cornwall. I cannot remember details of any such excursions until the year when with what I now suspect to have been a kind of despairing malice my father arranged the family summer holiday at a holiday camp. This was long before the days of Butlin, but the essential characteristics were already in existence – the chalets, the communal meals, the forfeits and weekly initiation rites for 'new campers', the dances, beauty parades, baby-sitting and campfire sing-songs. Personally I enjoyed it – there was billiards all day, and no nonsense about walks – but it marked the break-up of our yearly holiday as a group. After that, we tended to go away in couples or with other people: my father in particular liked going abroad, at least to Teutonic and Scandinavian areas, and rarely agreed that more than one of us should accompany him. As far as I was concerned, holidays relapsed into tiresome interruptions of my precious summer freedom.

I should have recognized the outside of the station better, for I passed and repassed it daily on my way to and from school. Coming up the short, somehow rather unofficial road that joins Warwick Road by the Station Hotel took me past the line of station horses in their carts outside the Goods Office. When I went back at lunch-time they were wearing their nosebags, and on my return at a quarter to two there was a scatter of chaff on the ground where they had stood. I liked this corner best at summer teatime, when in addition to the man selling the *Midland Daily Telegraph* there was frequently a white Eldorado box-tricycle that sold lime-green or strawberry-pink ices at a penny each. In those days newspaper placards bore properly-printed posters that today would look depressingly un-urgent. Beside the paperseller was a cigarette-machine, which gave ten cigarettes for sixpence and twenty for a shilling (but with the twenty you got a halfpenny back under the cellophane): one of my fantasies was to unlock it and rifle the packets for cigarette cards. I sometimes think the slight scholarly stoop in my bearing today was acquired by looking for cigarette cards in Coventry gutters. There seemed to be a 'Famous Cricketers' series every summer then: Woolley, A. W. Carr, R. E. S. Wyatt (who went to my school), Kenneth Farnes, Freeman, Ames, Duckworth, Chapman, Hammond, all on green fields against cloudless blue skies; and then the Australians, the bland Woodfull in his blue Victorian cap, burly Ponsford, swarthy Wall, and Bradman, with his green Australian cap and crisp white shirt-collar, enclosed in a legend that grew bigger daily, like a gigantic indestructible crystal.

In childhood friends are necessary: you cannot bowl to yourself. I had none I remember until we moved to Manor Road; then I got to know Peter in St Patrick's Road, and his cousin Arthur in Stoney Road. Arthur, a shadowy figure now, was a gentle, slightly older boy in whom I recognized for the first time the power to create and sustain private worlds. I can remember now his distress when our games did not tally with his imagined anticipation of them; the hours he spent playing rugger matches, enacting not only both teams but the referee and the crowd as well, with no other property than a clothes-peg; his construction of a complete chart of programmes for all the cinemas in the city, including mid-week changes, and his willingness to render any one we cared to pick. It was Arthur who with a kazoo and a battery of toffee tins, lids, pens and a hair-brush first introduced me to 'dance music', sitting buzzing and tapping his way through pre-selected programmes of current hits and standard hot numbers (how I now appreciate the artistic sensibility that drove him to render 'Ever so Goosey, Goosey, Goosey, Goosey' as lengthily as 'Temptation Rag'!). Once a friend left a tenor saxophone at Arthur's house, and together we reverently handled its heavy silver-plated intricacy and depressed the numerous cork-padded keys. What became of him I do not know. I think he was apprenticed to a butcher.

Later, Peter must also have introduced me to Tom and Jim, who lived further off in the Earlsdon area. We all went to the same school, and continued to meet for several years at Jim's house in Beechwood Avenue that had a tennis court and a sunk ornamental pond and two garages. Behind the tennis court was a line of poplars. I suppose it was not a really big house, but it was the first I had known where people could be completely out of earshot of each other indoors, and which had a spare room or two that could be given over to a Hornby lay-out or a miniature battlefield that need not be cleared up at the end of the day. I always supposed Jim's family to be richer than mine – at one time it must have been – but this was less because of Jim's many boxes of soldiers and Dinky Toys from Haddon's basement, and his frequent visits to the Astoria, than because of the airy hospitality informing his parents' house. The careless benevolence that produced Chelsea buns and Corona at eleven, and ignored the broken window and excoriated furniture seemed to me eloquent of a higher, richer way of living. The family were natural hosts. They had not to school themselves into accepting that a certain amount of noise and damage was inevitable if their son and his friends were to enjoy themselves: they took it as a matter of course. Looking back I can see that we were a great nuisance. I can only plead that we were very happy. One of my strongest memories of their house is of its long attic, that ran the length of the house, and which contained among many other things the debris of a hat-shop the family had once owned. There was a forest of hat-stands, small plush hemispheres on long metal stalks, like depetalled flowers, and cardboard boxes full of receipted invoices, wads of them, bearing dates of 1928, 1929 and 1930.

Before long Peter and Tom went to Tettenhall College, which threw Jim and myself more into each other's company. He was a year older than I, and left after taking Matric to become a master-builder's apprentice, but he had somehow got interested in painting. Together we took our education in hand: I lent him Lawrence, he retaliated with Cézanne. On Saturday afternoons we sat, frowning intently, in the glass cubicles at Hanson's, trying to decide whether both sides of the latest Parlophone Rhythm-Style Series or Vocalion Swing Series were sufficiently good to justify expenditure of the record's stiffish price of three shillings.

Our standards were very high in those days. The idea of paying nearly two pounds for an LP containing only three tracks of real interest would have appalled me. Jim's family took him away for their usual Bournemouth holiday, and we began to write – real letters, that is, not dependent on time or place: a correspondence to be continued, on and off, for the next ten years.

It now seems strange to me that all the time I lived in Coventry I never knew any girls, but it did not at the time. I had grown up to regard sexual recreation as a socially remote thing, like baccarat or clog dancing, and nothing happened to alter this view. None of my friends knew any girls either (or if they did they never produced or spoke of them) which seems even stranger. Perhaps strangest of all was that no girls so to speak appeared on the threshold of my life as a natural part of growing up, like beer and cigarettes, as novels say they do. Surely life should not have been discouraged simply because I did not dance and had no love of parties (I once retired to bed in the middle of the celebration of my own birthday)? How I reconciled this with my total acceptance of Lawrence I have no idea.

The first writing of mine ever to be printed appeared in the school magazine when I was twelve. It was a short facetious paragraph or two, reminding me that all my early contributions were in the manner of 'The Humourist', and all excruciating. I don't know why I can't be funny on paper but it has been proved too often to need further demonstration. I can only say that when friends of mine had promoted to their own pages things I have said or written to them privately I have not felt that my jokes sounded unworthy of their reputations.

I never knew anyone in Coventry who was interested in writing. There may have been little groups who met and discussed each other's work, but I never came across them; nor was there at school any literary society where talent might try itself out. No pipe-lighting dominie (I am afraid I am falling into the style of my poem) casually slipped a well-worn volume into my hands as I was leaving his book-lined den ('by the way, you might care to have a look at this'): I did not much like the senior English master, and I do not think he much liked me. Of course none of this mattered. Thanks to my father, our house contained not only the principal works of most main English writers in some form or other (admittedly there were exceptions, like Dickens), but also nearly-complete collections of authors my father favoured – Hardy, Bennett, Wilde, Butler and Shaw, and later on Lawrence, Huxley and Katherine Mansfield. Not till I was much older did I realize that most boys of my class were brought up to regard Galsworthy and Chesterton as the apex of modern literature, and to think Somerset Maugham 'a bit hot'. I was therefore lucky. Knowing what its effect would be on me, my father concealed the existence of the Central Public Library as long as he could, but in the end the secret broke and nearly every evening I set off down Friar's Road with books to exchange. Many were returned unfinished, chosen because I had liked the thought of myself reading them. But for quite long periods I suppose I must have read a book a day, even despite the tiresome interruptions of morning and afternoon school.

Reading is not writing, though, and by then my ambition had

pretty well deserted jazz drumming to settle upon a literary career. Apart from the school magazine I had still not got into print. I wrote ceaselessly, however; now verse, which I sewed up into little books, now prose, a thousand words a night after homework, resting my foolscap on Beethoven's Op. 132, the only classical album I possessed. Both were valueless, but I wish I could command that fluent industry today.

When the war broke out, I decided to go up to Oxford a year earlier than I had intended, since despite the Government's assurance that the 18 and 19 age groups would be registered last of all, no one knew when this would be once the fighting started in earnest. I felt it was imperative to have made some mark on the world before I did so, and during the cloudless summer of 1940 I sent four poems to *The Listener*. I was astonished when someone signing himself J. R. A. wrote back, saying that he would like to take one (it was the one I had put in to make the others seem better, but never mind). As I had hoped, it had not appeared before I nervously left for Oxford (changing trains, and stations, at Leamington), delaying until the issue of 28 October, just when I was ready for an injection of self-esteem. I remember buying several copies at Smith's in Cornmarket Street, and making sure that it was actually in each copy. Within a fortnight Coventry had been ruined by the German Air Force, and I never went back there to live again.

Umbrella, 1:3, Summer 1959

On Publishing *The Less Deceived*

When George Hartley had been editing and publishing the magazine *Listen* for a year from the Hull suburb of Hessle, he thought it would be an interesting experiment to publish books of poems by individual authors. (This was in 1954, when he was 21.) He accordingly wrote to Philip Larkin, whose work he had seen and admired, and asked if he had enough poems for a book. Larkin, who was working in Belfast, replied amiably, and early in 1955 Hartley received the typescript of a collection called *Various Poems*.

Little of Larkin's poetry had at that time been published. He was 32, and his last publication had been 100 copies of a privately-printed pamphlet called *XX Poems* in 1951. These had been sent to many well-known people, whose failure to respond may have been due to the fact that the envelopes bore penny stamps at a time when three-halfpenny ones would have been more appropriate. Before this, he had published no poetry since *The North Ship* in 1945. On the other hand, he had been writing regularly in Belfast, so that Hartley's invitation came at an opportune moment.

The book took nearly the whole of 1955 to print and bind. By a coincidence, work had no sooner been put in hand than Larkin got a job in Hull, and author and publisher were able to meet for the first time. Hartley disliked the title *Various Poems*, so Larkin gave one poem a new title, 'Deceptions' and took its old one, 'The Less Deceived', for the book. By the end of June subscription forms were distributed announcing publication in October with a list of pre-publication subscribers' names at the end. (Some subscribers were confused by a request to indicate whether or nor they wished their names to be included in this list: Larkin had thought there might be people who, while wanting the book, would prefer not to be publicly associated with it.) Neither author nor publisher had any idea what response the forms would provoke. In fact the first subscription came by return of post (from Mr Richard Hoggart), and others followed until by the closing date (15 September) more than 100 had been received. Copies of the book at length went out to subscribers at the end of November 1955, and rather surprisingly *The Times* mentioned it in a review of the year's literature on 22 December.

The first sign that it was going to be a success was the quick sale of the remainder of the subscription issue. This, for the bibliographical record, numbered 300, with a flat spine and the misprint *floor* for *sea* on page 38, which is still occasionally the subject of discussion between Larkin and Hartley. Another 400 were quickly bound up (this time with round spines), but none the less the book was out of print by April 1956, and another printing was ordered. This was delayed by the necessity of re-setting the type (the original setting had been dismantled in mistake for an American poetry magazine), and did not appear until August, now in soft covers to keep the price down to six shillings, at which many unfulfilled orders had been entered. These had asked for *Alas! Deceived*, *A Lass Deceived*, *The Less Received*, *The Kiss Deceived*, *The Less Desired*, *The Ilex Deceived*, and *The Gay Deceivers*, by Carkin, Lartin, Lackin, Laikin and Lock, all of which the Marvell Press had identified without difficulty. More orders were patiently forwarded by the Harvill Press. In January 1958 another edition in hard covers was issued at half a guinea, and during the summer copies were imported into the United States for sale by the St Martin's Press. The signs are that the book will be as kindly received in America as it has been in England.

Has all this a moral? 'Commercial publishers are so awfully unenterprising,' George Hartley told the *News Chronicle* in 1957, and Larkin has said that it is rather nice to have a publisher who publishes your poems because he likes them and not because you are somebody's aunt or may one day write a novel. Nevertheless, neither really believes that they have changed the pattern of British publishing. The book remains an accident, an odd flowering of the unpredictable element in life that is most likely to appear just when it seems firmly established that things (such as the publishing of successful poetry) are done in a certain way.

Sleevenote from LP of *The Less Deceived* (Listen Records, 1959)

Context

One of the pleasures of writing actual poems is the final and honourable release it bestows from worrying about poetry in the abstract. In an age that sees poetry as syllabus rather than menu this is luxury of the thickest pile. Another similar release is from reading poems by other people. In youth – say up to twenty-five – inarticulacy compels one to accept the expression of feeling second-hand, and inexperience ranks literature equally with life. Later, all poetry seems more or less unsatisfactory. Inasmuch as it is not one's own, and experience makes literature look insignificant beside life, as indeed life does beside death. Such reasons may contribute to the growing disinclination that I find in myself to keep up with poetry. Within reach at the moment are collections by Hopkins, Whitman, Wordsworth, Frost, Barnes, Praed, Betjeman, Edward Thomas, Hardy, Christina Rossetti, Sassoon and Auden, but the living writers I order before publication are not (with the exception of Betjeman) primarily poets: Waugh, Powell, Amis, Gladys Mitchell, Barbara Pym. I should say my mind was now immune from anything new in poetry. Whether this represents saturation, anaestheticism, or purposeful exclusion of distraction I could not say.

Although the admission seems natural enough to me, I can see it might be taken as damaging. There is a theory that every new poem, like an engineer's drawing, should sum up all that has gone before and take it a step further, which means that before anything worthwhile can be written everything worthwhile must be read. This seems to me a classroom conception. Reading is a normal part of early life, as I have said, but all it can really do for a poet is to develop such poetic muscles as he possesses and to show him what has been done already (with the implication, at least to my mind, that it should not be done again). A style is much more likely to be formed from partial slipshod sampling than from the coherent acquisition of a literary education.

What one is not released from is the constant struggle between mind and imagination to decide what is important enough to be written about. I suppose that most writers would say that their purpose in writing was to preserve the truth about things as they see it. Unfortunately to write well entails enjoying what you are writing, and there is not much pleasure to be got from the truth about things as anyone sees it. What one does enjoy writing – what the imagination is only too ready to help with – is, in some form or other, compensation, assertion of oneself in an indifferent or hostile environment, demonstration (by writing about it) that one is in command of a situation, and so on. Separating the man who suffers from the man who creates is all right – we separate the petrol from the engine – but the dependence of the second on the first is complete. Again, the imagination is always ready to indulge its fetishes – being classic and austere, or loading every rift with ore – with no responsible basis or rational encouragement. Very little that catches the imagination, in short, can get its clearance from either the intelligence or the moral sense. And equally, properly truthful or dispassionate themes enlist only the wannest support from the imagination. The poet is perpetually in that common human condition of trying to feel a thing because he believes it, or believe a thing because he feels it.

Except when springing from those rich and narrow marches where the two concur, therefore, his writing veers perpetually between the goody-goody-clever-clever and the silly-shameful-self-indulgent, and there is no point in inclining towards one kind of failure rather than another. All he can do is hope that he will go on getting flashes of what seems at the time like agreement between their opposed impulses.

London Magazine, February 1962

NOTE: This issue of the *London Magazine*, which also contained Larkin's poem 'Nothing To Be Said', carried a feature, 'Context', with a headnote from the editor, Alan Ross:

> The following questions were sent to a number of poets, for them to answer individually or to use as a basis for a general statement about the writing of poetry today.
>
> (a) Would poetry be more effective, i.e. interest more people more profoundly, if it were concerned with the issues of our time?
>
> (b) Do you feel your views on politics or religion influence the kind of poetry you write? Alternatively, do you think poetry has uses as well as pleasure?

(c) Do you feel any dissatisfaction with the short lyric as a poetic medium? If so, are there any poems of a longer or non-lyric kind that you visualize yourself writing?
(d) What living poets continue to influence you, English or American?
(e) Are you conscious of any current 'poeticization' of language which requires to be broken up in favour of a more 'natural' diction? Alternatively, do you feel any undue impoverishment in poetic diction at the moment?
(f) Do you see this as a good or bad period of writing poetry?

Others who replied were: Robert Graves, George Seferis, Stephen Spender, C. Day Lewis, Lawrence Durrell, Roy Fuller, Robert Conquest, Laurie Lee, Thomas Blackburn, Derek Walcott, Judith Wright, D. J. Enright, Thom Gunn, Charles Causley, Bernard Spencer, Vernon Watkins, Ted Hughes, Sylvia Plath, Edwin Brock, Hugo Williams, John Fuller, Julian Mitchell, Elizabeth Jennings, Anthony Thwaite and Norman Nicholson.

Poet's Choice

Absences

Rain patters on a sea that tilts and sighs.
Fast-running floors, collapsing into hollows,
Tower suddenly, spray-haired. Contrariwise,
A wave drops like a wall: another follows,
Wilting and scrambling, tirelessly at play
Where there are no ships and no shallows.

Above the sea, the yet more shoreless day,
Riddled by wind, trails lit-up galleries:
They shift to giant ribbing, sift away.

Such attics cleared of me! Such absences!

I suppose I like 'Absences' (a) because of its subject matter – I am always thrilled by the thought of what places look like when I am not there; (b) because I fancy it sounds like a different, better poet rather than myself. The last line, for instance, sounds like a slightly unconvincing translation from a French symbolist. I wish I could write like this more often.

Incidentally, an oceanographer wrote to me pointing out that I was confusing two kinds of wave, plunging waves and spilling waves, which seriously damaged the poem from a technical viewpoint. I am sorry about this, but do not see how to amend it now.

Poet's Choice, edited by Paul Engle and Joseph Langland (Dial Press, 1962)

NOTE: Engle's Introduction to *Poet's Choice* concludes with the statement:

> 'When we had collected our poems and the poets' explanations, we thus found that we had a double revelation: the poem, telling us what a man or woman felt about a lived-through experience, and the comment, telling us what the poet felt about the experience of writing the poem or the experience of returning to it after some time and deciding that he liked it enough to let it stand for all of his work. And in these accounts of the lives of poets are all our lives.'

Louis MacNeice

When we were young, the poems of Louis MacNeice were not recommended to us in the same breath as those of Eliot and Auden. Perhaps for this reason the secret taste we formed for them was all the stronger. He was, as his photograph in Grigson's *New Verse* showed, a town observer: his poetry was the poetry of our everyday life, of shop-windows, traffic policemen, ice-cream soda, lawn-mowers, and an uneasy awareness of what the newsboys were shouting. In addition he displayed a sophisticated sentimentality about falling leaves and lipsticked cigarette stubs: he could have written the words of 'These Foolish Things'. We were grateful to him for having found a place in poetry for these properties, for intruding them in 'the drunkenness of things being various'.

Now we are older, some of these qualities have faded, some seem more durable. Against the sombre debits of maturity that his later poetry so frequently explores – the neurosis, the crucifying memory, the chance irrevocably lost – he set an increased understanding of human suffering, just as against the darkening political skies of the late Thirties he had set the brilliantly quotidian reportage of *Autumn Journal*. In what will now be his last collection, *The Burning Perch*, the human condition is shown as full of distress. If it is described not too solemnly, the chances are, he seems to be saying, it will become easier to bear.

New Statesman, 6 September 1963

A Conversation with Ian Hamilton

IAN HAMILTON: *I would like to ask you about your attitude to the so-called 'modernist revolution' in English poetry; how important has it been to you as a poet?*
PHILIP LARKIN: Well, granted that one doesn't spend any time at all thinking about oneself in these terms, I would say that I have been most influenced by the poetry that I've enjoyed – and this poetry has not been Eliot or Pound or anybody who is normally regarded as 'modern' – which is a sort of technique word, isn't it? The poetry I've enjoyed has been the kind of poetry you'd associate with me, Hardy pre-eminently, Wilfred Owen, Auden, Christina Rossetti, William Barnes; on the whole, people to whom technique seems to matter less than content, people who accept the forms they have inherited but use them to express their own content.

You don't feel in any way guilty about this, I imagine; would you see yourself as rebelliously anti-modern – you have talked about the 'myth-kitty' and so on ...
What I do feel a bit rebellious about is that poetry seems to have got into the hands of a critical industry which is concerned with culture in the abstract, and this I do rather lay at the door of Eliot and Pound. I think that Eliot and Pound have something in common with the kind of Americans you used to get around 1910. You know, when Americans began visiting Europe towards the end of the last century, what they used to say about them was that they were keen on culture, *laughably* keen – you got jokes like 'Elmer, is this Paris or Rome?' 'What day is it?' 'Thursday.' 'Then it's Rome.' – you know the kind of thing. This was linked with the belief that you can order culture whole, that it is a separate item on the menu – this was very typically American, and German too, I suppose, and seems to me to have led to a view of poetry which is almost mechanistic, that every poem must include all previous poems, in the same way that a Ford Zephyr has somewhere in it a Ford T Model – which means that to be any good you've got to

have read all previous poems. I can't take this evolutionary view of poetry. One never thinks about other poems except to make sure that one isn't doing something that has been done before – writing a verse play about a young man whose father has died and whose mother has married his uncle, for instance. I think a lot of this 'myth-kitty' business has grown out of that, because first of all you have to be terribly educated, you have to have read everything to know these things, and secondly, you've got somehow to work them in to show that you are working them in. But to me the whole of the ancient world, the whole of classical and biblical mythology means very little, and I think that using them today not only fills poems full of dead spots but dodges the writer's duty to be original.

You are generally written up as one of the fathers of this so-called Movement; did you have any sense at the time of belonging to a group with any very definite aims?
No sense at all, really. The only other writer I felt I had much in common with was Kingsley Amis, who wasn't really at that time known as a writer – *Lucky Jim* was published in 1954 – but of course we'd been exchanging letters and showing each other work for a long time, and I think we laughed at the same things and agreed largely about what you could and couldn't write about, and so on. But the Movement, if you want to call it that, really began when John Wain succeeded John Lehmann on the BBC programme; John planned six programmes called *First Readings* including a varied set of contributors – they weren't all Movementeers by any means. It got attacked in a very convenient way, and consequently we became lumped together. Then there was an article in *The Spectator* actually using the term 'Movement' and Bob Conquest's *New Lines* in 1956 put us all between the same covers. But it certainly never occurred to me that I had anything in common with Thom Gunn, or Donald Davie, for instance, or they with each other and in fact I wasn't mentioned at the beginning. The poets of the group were Wain, Gunn, Davie and, funnily enough, Alvarez.

To what extent, though, did you feel consciously in reaction against Thomas, the Apocalypse, and so on?
Well, one had to live through the forties at one's most impressionable time and indeed I could show you, but won't, a lot of poems I

wrote that you wouldn't – well, that were very much of the age. I wrote a great many sedulous and worthless Yeats-y poems, and later on far inferior Dylan Thomas poems – I think Dylan Thomas is much more difficult to imitate than Yeats – and this went on for years and years. It wasn't until about 1948 or 9 that I began writing differently, but it wasn't as any conscious reaction. It's just that when you start writing your own stuff other people's manners won't really do for it.

I would like to ask you about reviews of your work; do they bore you, do you find any of them helpful? In general, how do you react to what is said about you?

Well, one can't be other than grateful for the kind things that are said. They make you wish you wrote better. Otherwise one tries to ignore it – critics can hinder but they can't help. One thing I do feel a slight restiveness about is being typed as someone who has carved out for himself a uniquely dreary life, growing older, having to work, and not getting things he wants and so on – is this so different from everyone else? I'd like to know how all these romantic reviewers spend their time – do they kill a lot of dragons, for instance? If other people do have wonderful lives, then I'm glad for them, but I can't help feeling that my miseries are over-done a bit by the critics. They may retort that they are over-done by me, of course.

You usually write in metre, but now and then you have rather freer poems. I wonder if you have any feeling of technical unrest, of being constricted by traditional forms. Do things like syllabics, projective verse, for instance, have any interest for you?

I haven't anything very original to say about metre. I've never tried syllabics; I'm not sure I fully understand them. I think one would have to be very sure of oneself to dispense with the help that metre and rhyme give and I doubt really if I could operate without them. I have occasionally, some of my favourite poems have not rhymed or had any metre, but it's rarely been premeditated.

I'd like to ask you about the poem, 'Church Going', which has been taken fairly generally as a kind of 'representative attitude' poem, standing for a whole disheartened, debunking state of mind in post-war England. How do you feel about that poem, do you think that the things that have been said about it are true? How do you feel about its enormous popularity? In a way I feel what Hardy is supposed to have said about *Tess*; if I'd known it was going to be so popular I'd have tried to make it better. I think its popularity is somewhat due to extraneous factors – anything about religion tends to go down well; I don't know whether it expresses what people feel. It is of course an entirely secular poem. I was a bit irritated by an American who insisted to me it was a religious poem. It isn't religious at all. Religion surely means that the affairs of this world are under divine superveillance, and so on, and I go to some pains to point out that I don't bother about that kind of thing, that I'm deliberately ignorant of it – 'Up at the holy end', for instance. Ah no, it's a great religious poem; he knows better than me – trust the tale and not the teller, and all that stuff.

Of course the poem is about going to church, not religion – I tried to suggest this by the title – and the union of the important stages of human life – birth, marriage and death – that going to church represents; and my own feeling that when they are dispersed into the registry office and the crematorium chapel life will become thinner in consequence. I certainly haven't revolted against the poem. It hasn't become a kind of 'Innisfree', or anything like that.

I have the feeling about it – this has been said often enough, I suppose – that it drops into two parts. The stanza beginning 'A serious house on serious earth it is' seems significantly different in tone and movement to the rest of the poem and it is almost as if it sets up a rejoinder to the attitudes that are embodied in the first part. And that the first part is not just about religious belief or disbelief, it's about the whole situation of being a poet, a man of sensibility, a man of learning even, in an age like ours – that it is all this exclusiveness that is being scoffed at in the first half – it is seriousness in general. Somehow the final stanzas tighten up and are almost ceremonial in their reply to the debunkery; they seem to affirm all that has been scoffed at, and are deliberately more poetic and dignified in doing so. In this sense it seems a debate between poet and persona. *I'd like to know if you planned the poem as a debate.*
Well, in a way. The poem starts by saying, you don't really know about all this, you don't believe in it, you don't know what a rood-loft is – Why do you come here, why do you bother to stop and look round? The poem is seeking an answer. I suppose that's the

antithesis you mean. I think one has to dramatize oneself a little. I don't arse about in churches when I'm alone. Not much, anyway. I still don't know what rood-lofts are.

A number of poems in The Less Deceived *seem to me to carry a final kick in the head for the attitudes they have seemed to be taking up. In a poem like 'Reasons for Attendance', say, where you have the final 'Or lied'; somehow the whole poem doubles back on itself. What I want to know is how conscious you are of your poems plotting a kind of elaborate self-imprisonment. Do you feel, for instance, that you will ever write a more abandoned, naïve , kind of poetry where you won't, as it were, block all the loopholes in this way? I think this is why I prefer* The Whitsun Weddings *book, because it doesn't do this anything like as confidently.*
Well, I speak to you as someone who hasn't written a poem for eighteen months. The whole business seems terribly remote and I have to remember what it was like. I do think that poems are artificial in the sense that a play is artificial. There are strong second act curtains in poems as well as in plays, you know. I don't really know what a 'spontaneous' poem would be like, certainly not by me. On the other hand, here again I must protest slightly. I always think that the poems I write are very much more naïve – very much more emotional – almost embarrassingly so – than a lot of other people's. When I was tagged as unemotional, it used to mystify me; I used to find it quite shaming to read some of the things I'd written.

I didn't mean that there is not strong personal feeling in your poems, or that they don't have a strong confessional element. But what I do rather feel is that many of them carry this kind of built-in or tagged-on comment on themselves, and I wonder if you will feel able to dispense with this. I can see how this might mean being less alert, in a way, less adult and discriminating even. It's probably a stupid question.
It's a very interesting question and I hadn't realized I did that sort of thing. I suppose I always try to write the truth and I wouldn't want to write a poem which suggested that I was different from what I am. In a sense that means you have to build in quite a lot of things to correct any impression of over-optimism or over-commitment. For instance, take love poems. I should feel it false to write a poem going overboard about someone if you weren't at the same time marrying them and setting up house with them, and I should feel bound to add what you call a tag to make it clear

I wasn't, if I wasn't. Do you see what I mean? I think that one of the great criticisms of poets of the past is that they said one thing and did another, a false relation between art and life. I always try to avoid this.

I would like to ask you about your novels, and why you haven't written any more.
Well, because I can't. As I may have said somewhere else, I wanted to be a novelist. I wrote one, and then I wrote another, and I thought, This is wonderful, another five years of this and I'll be in the clear. Unfortunately, that was where it stopped. I've never felt as interested in poetry as I used to feel in novels – they were more theatrical, if you know what I mean, you could do the strong second-act curtain even better. Looking back on them, I think they were over-sized poems. They were certainly written with intense care for detail. If one word was used on page 15 I didn't re-use it on page 115. But they're not very good novels. A very crude difference between novels and poetry is that novels are about other people and poetry is about yourself. I suppose I must have lost interest in other people, or perhaps I was only pretending to be interested in them.

There was a review recently in the Times Literary Supplement *which gave this portrait of you as being some kind of semi-recluse, almost, deliberately withdrawing from the literary life, not giving readings, talks, and so on. I wonder to what extent this withdrawal from literary society is necessary to you as a writer; given that it is true, that is.*
I can't recall exactly what the *TLS* said, but as regards readings, I suppose I'm rather shy. I began life as a bad stammerer, as a matter of fact. Up to the age of 21 I was still asking for railway tickets by pushing written notes across the counter. This has conditioned me against reading in public – the dread that speech failure might come back again. But also, I'm lazy and very busy and it wouldn't give me much in the way of kicks. I think if there is any truth in this rumour or legend, it's because I do find literary parties or meetings, or anything that considers literature, in public, in the abstract rather than concretely, in private, not exactly boring – it is boring, of course – but unhelpful and even inimical. I go away feeling crushed and thinking that everyone is much cleverer than I am and writing much more, and so on. I think it's important not to feel crushed.

Following on, really, from the last question, I was going to ask you about that poem, 'Naturally the Foundation Will Bear your Expenses' ...
Well, that was rather a curious poem. It came from having been to London and having heard that A had gone to India and that B had just come back from India; then when I got back home, happening unexpectedly across the memorial service at the Cenotaph on the wireless, on what used to be called Armistice Day, and the two things seemed to get mixed up together. Almost immediately afterwards *Twentieth Century* wrote saying that they were having a Humour number and would I send them something funny, so I sent that. Actually, it's as serious as anything I have written and I was glad to see that John Wain has picked this up, quite without any prompting from me, in an article in *The Critical Quarterly*. Certainly it was a dig at the middleman who gives a lot of talks to America and then brushes them up and does them on the Third and then brushes them up again and puts them out as a book with Chatto. Why he should be blamed for not sympathizing with the crowds on Armistice Day, I don't quite know. The awful thing is that the other day I had a letter from somebody called Lal in Calcutta, enclosing two poetry books of his own and mentioning this poem. He was very nice about it, but I shall have to apologize. I've never written a poem that has been less understood; one editor refused it on the grounds, and I quote, that it was 'rather hard on the Queen'; several people have asked what it was like in Bombay! There is nothing like writing poems for realizing how low the level of critical understanding is; maybe the average reader can understand what I say, but the above-average often can't.

I wonder if you read much foreign poetry?
Foreign poetry? *No!*

Of contemporary English poets, then, whom do you admire?
It's awfully difficult to talk about contemporaries, because quite honestly I never read them. I really don't. And my likes are really very predictable. You know I admire Betjeman. I suppose I would say that he was my favourite living poet. Kingsley Amis I admire very much as a poet as well as a novelist; I think he's utterly original and can hit off a kind of satiric poem that no-one else can (this is when he is being himself, not when he's Robert Graves). Stevie Smith I'm very fond of in a puzzled way. I think she's

terribly good but I should never want to imitate her. Anthony Thwaite's last book seemed very sensitive and efficient to me. I think one has to be both sensitive and efficient. That's about as far as I can go. I don't mean I dislike everyone else, it's just that I don't know very much about them.

What about Americans?
I find myself no more appreciative of Americans. I quite liked Lowell's *Life Studies* but his last book was all about foreign poets – well, I think that is the end; versions of other people's poems are poor substitutes for your own. Occasionally one finds a poem by Donald Justice or Anthony Hecht, but I don't know enough about them to comment. Actually, I like the Beat poets, but again I don't know much about them. That's because I'm fond of Whitman; they seem to me debased Whitman, but debased Whitman is better than debased Ezra Pound.

Do you have many poems you haven't collected? Are you more prolific than you seem to be?
I'm afraid not. There was a whole period between *The North Ship* and *The Less Deceived* which produced a book with the portentous title of *In the Grip of Light*, which went round the publishers in the middle and late forties, but thank God nobody accepted it. Otherwise I hardly ever finish a poem that I don't publish.

One final, rather broad question. How would you characterize your development as a poet from The North Ship *to* The Whitsun Weddings*?*
I suppose I'm less likely to write a really bad poem now, but possibly equally less likely to write a really good one. If you can call that development, then I've developed. Kipling said somewhere that when you can do one thing really well, then do something else. Oscar Wilde said that only mediocrities develop. I just don't know. I don't think I want to change; just to become better at what I am.

London Magazine, November 1964

Three other interviews by Ian Hamilton were included in this issue of the *London Magazine*, with Thom Gunn, Christopher Middleton and Charles Tomlinson.

A Conversation with Neil Powell

NEIL POWELL: *Do you think that it's possible for our society to produce a poet of the same scale as, say, Yeats?*
PHILIP LARKIN: You mean that poets thirty years ago, and novelists too, took on the whole of the world and tried to render it in terms of art? There could be several explanations why this may not be possible now. Of course, perhaps you haven't got any really great writers; another reason is that it's just been done, and one tends always not to do things that have just been done. If you've had a period of epic verse, then you get a period of lyric verse; a period of satire is followed by a period of romanticism. We've had a period of rather intellectual verse, we may now be experiencing a period of unpretentious personal poems. I'm a great believer in waves of fashion – it's rather like having a Conservative government, and then having a Labour government for no real reason except that you got sick of it.

You don't think there's some reason like increasing urbanization or the increasing focus of poetry on universities; one looks at post-war poets, and they're mostly connected in some way with the academic world.
Strictly speaking, that ought to produce the more intellectual kind of poetry.

But poetry on a smaller scale?
Well, I shouldn't have thought so. I'd have thought that when you get men whose approach to literature is intellectual, they're much more likely to produce work in which the intellectual scale perhaps overweighs the emotional content. I can think of one or two poets who are very clever intellectually, and who are trying to integrate all sorts of influences, but they don't really make it emotionally. And poetry is a matter of emotion. I think you're really trying to say nicely that the stature of poets today is undeniably smaller than it was fifty years ago.

Not so much the stature as the pretensions of poetry.

I suppose one felt that poetry *was* pretentious. I think we all find the poetic attitude irritating – though there's quite a lot of people who don't I suppose – but in any case it has to be backed up by hellish good poetry not to grate on your nerves.

Poetry, in fact, has become very much a spare-time occupation. Poets aren't – can't be – solely poets.
Some people try to make a living out of it – I don't just mean a financial living; but you can't write poetry all the time, and you can't live on the proceeds of it, and therefore you must do something else. The question is whether you do something as like poetry as possible or as unlike it. And that depends on your temperament. You can earn your money talking about poetry in universities or hopping from one foundation to another or one conference to another – or you can go away and be something very different like an accountant – I believe Roy Fuller is something like that, Wallace Stevens was an insurance man; I'm a librarian, I never see a book from one year's end to another. It depends on your temperament.

Your first collection, The North Ship, *was, as you say in your introduction to the recent edition, heavily influenced by Yeats. Is this something that you have consciously tried to shake off?*
I'm sure I did. I think I left off reading him because I began to read Hardy more. But it wasn't a reaction: the reaction seemed to come later, I think, because when I did get back to Yeats I found I couldn't read him without impatience. It seemed so very artificial compared with what I'd moved on to. The awful thing about Yeats is that you just cannot conceal him – I think I mentioned garlic in that introduction. He *is* like garlic: one touch of Yeats and the whole thing stinks of it. You think of someone like Theodore Roethke: you remember he began writing poems about plants; in the end he moved on to very Yeatsian things; or Vernon Watkins who has never lost his admiration for Yeats; or Thomas Blackburn; even Auden – once you fall into that particular three-stress beat, it's very difficult not to sound like Yeats.

Apart from Yeats, what poets do you think have most influenced your own writing?
Well, I began reading old poets at school – people like Keats; for some reason Keats was much more in favour thirty years ago than

he is now. There was a terrific pro-Keats drive, largely centred on Middleton Murry – they tried to convince you that Keats was the poet who was most like Shakespeare, negative capability and all that kind of thing; and for a time one believed this, though he isn't, as far as I can see, really like Shakespeare at all. And then there was Housman and people that come in little squashy leather books; even Rupert Brooke, I suppose; and I was very fond of Edward Dowson. Then suddenly you discover modern poetry, Eliot and Auden, Yeats not for a long time. And Dylan Thomas. But after Yeats and Hardy, I don't think anyone has seriously influenced me, except Betjeman.

I'm probably well known for my admiration for Betjeman. I think this irritates some people, but I do admire him. I think he is a remarkable figure, not only a remarkable poet. He's somebody like William Morris, who creates a whole climate of taste, and gives people new eyes and new ears. His knowledge is enormous: it may be a bit sketchy but its range is colossal. I don't know whoever could write a really good book about Betjeman when the time comes. And in poetry he has simply made it possible to write about all sorts of things that you thought it wasn't possible to write about: things which seemed outrageously sentimental or trivial.

An almost Eliot-like extension of the frontiers of poetry.

Eliot took poetry away from the tradition, and Betjeman brought it back. I think it's significant that a lot of Betjeman's poems are funny – quite often there are things that you can only say as jokes. He is rather like the fool that speaks the truth through jokes, though that's a horribly literary way of putting it. I see Betjeman very much in the English tradition that some people like and some people don't – if one *can* talk of an English tradition; it has always been under the influence of somebody or other, Italians or French. There's a kind of underground tradition in this century: Hardy, I suppose, begins it, then there are the Georgians, and the poets who didn't survive the war, Owen, Rupert Brooke, then nobody really, except Betjeman.

And someone like Auden, earlier Auden at least.

Early Auden seems to me much more English than later Auden. Something very peculiar happened to Auden when he went to America, I think – I'm not sure what – but for one thing he must have begun to read a lot more. One gets the impression that he hardly read anything before that, then suddenly, instead of the occasional reference to Marx and Freud, you get every kind of writer stuffed in. He became very much an intellectual and eclectic poet.

What is it about Betjeman that makes him sell to such a mass market?
He is very *original* – paradoxically, because his stanzas are usually lifted from other people, mainly Victorians. But his subject-matter is original; and I think he conveys much stronger *feeling* than most modern poets. It is difficult to read a Betjeman poem without being moved, I think; other people may be moved to spew, but I'm moved in the way I'm meant to be moved. There is a sentence or two of Leslie Stephen, which Hardy used to be very fond of, I can't remember it exactly, but it's something like 'The poet's task is to move our feelings by showing his own, and not to display his learning, or mimic the fine notes of his predecessors . . .' I've always thought it is a magnificent motto, for me anyway, it is the kind of thing I should like to think I did.

That's where I think Betjeman's popularity resides, in that he is completely original, and very moving, and thirdly he is fairly easy to understand, though I don't think he is simple. He is complex without being difficult, if you know what I mean.

To return to your own work: there is an enormous increase in precision and economy between the poems in The North Ship *and those in* The Less Deceived *and* The Whitsun Weddings.
To some extent. I don't think I had anything serious to write about in *The North Ship*; or at least if I had I couldn't see it. I think that's perhaps one of the baneful influences of Yeats. The worst thing about a poetic influence that is alien to you is not so much that it dominates the words you pick, it dominates your view of what you can write about. As long as I was looking at the world out of the eyes of Yeats, vague melancholy was all right, inspiration and clouds were all right; the real world was all right providing you made it pretty clear that it was a symbol. But Yeats really prevented me from writing poems about the things I could see, and which I should have been writing about, much dingier and less glamorous things. Yeats presumably couldn't write about a mucked-up seaside poster on a railway station; but as soon as you begin to see your own subject, then the style is nothing. You find

your style. The influence of another poet is not primarily on the choice of words but on the choice of subject.

The Less Deceived *seems to be a book with a lot of negatives in it: there is a tendency almost to deny what you are writing about, which perhaps is just a form of extreme caution.*
Ian Hamilton once said that whenever I said anything I gave a little twist to show that I didn't really mean it. People say I'm very negative, and I suppose I am, but the impulse for producing a poem is never negative; the most negative poem in the world is a very positive thing to have done. The fact that a poem makes a reader want to lie down and die rather than get up and sock somebody is irrelevant. Perhaps my negation is my subject-matter: it doesn't seem like negation to me, but like daffodils to Wordsworth.

It's a cutting-down to life-size of subject-matter – 'Nothing, like something, happens anywhere.' Nothing is more likely to happen than something.
I don't think that's a negative poem, I think it is a very funny poem. I can't read it without laughing, or almost laughing. Auden was chivvied into writing a short thing for members of a book club in America of which he was one of the panel of judges – it was The Egg-heads' Book Society or something. One month they issued two books of poetry, one of which was *The Less Deceived*, and Auden did pick on 'I Remember, I Remember' and said how much he liked the rhyme-scheme, the rhyme-scheme is a nine-line thing whereas the stanza is a five-line thing. When you get to the end there's one line left over, which you must have for the rhyme, and it comes in very neatly. That was the only thing that Auden had noticed about *The Less Deceived*, but I was very pleased though it was quite accidental really.

There is a desire to stress the ordinariness of life in a poem like 'I Remember, I Remember', phrases like 'where my childhood was unspent'. It's a tendency not to glorify things which other people are always glorifying.
Really that poem started off as a satire on novels like *Sons and Lovers* – the kind of wonderful childhoods that people do seem to have. I was thinking how very peculiar it was that I myself never experienced these things, and I thought one could write a funny

poem about it. So I did. It wasn't denying that other people did have these experiences, though they did tend to sound rather clichés: the first fuck, the first poem, the first this that and the other that turn up with such wearisome regularity.

Which might perhaps bring us to your novels, which don't seem to have had the attention they deserve.
No, I don't think they have; I don't think they deserve it either. The thing about the novels is that they were written about the same time as *The North Ship*. I went down from Oxford in 1943; I immediately began *Jill*, finished it in 1944, and then began *A Girl in Winter*, which I finished in 1945. So they are not, perhaps, very mature. I wanted to be a novelist. I thought novels were a richer form of literature than poetry; I suppose I was influenced by the kind of critical attitude that you used to get in *Scrutiny* – the novel as dramatic poem. I certainly saw novels as rather poetic things, perhaps too poetic. When I stopped writing novels it was a great disappointment to me; I went on trying in the 1945–50 period. Why I stopped I don't really know, it was a great grief to me. And one *could* live as a novelist – if you write 500 words a day for about six months you've got your novel, and you've got another six months to correct the proofs in and spend your advance.

I think that Jill *is probably rather a better novel than* A Girl in Winter.
Many people think that it is, it's certainly got more direct feeling in it, but it is a good deal less polished. *A Girl in Winter* is terrifically polished, rewritten and rewritten; I took great care not to use particular words too often and so on. I was very keen on Virginia Woolf, and also on Henry Green, who was having a great creative period in the forties, producing an extraordinary set of novels – a combination of realism with the aesthetic approach, an avant-garde approach to things like dialogue.

Jill was written too, under the influence of a book that nobody's heard of, except Kingsley Amis (because I lent it him), and that was a book about Eton called *The Senior Commoner* by Julian Hall. I don't know who Julian Hall is – I think he's the son of some titled person – but I'm sure he is still alive; he was very young when he wrote it, and it was published in 1932. It was the most extraordinary book I had ever read, and I still re-read it with fascination, although I'm ashamed to say that I stole the copy I possess from a public library: it seemed the only way of getting hold of it, and they had another copy anyway. I think if you look at *The Senior Commoner* you would find certain echoes of it in *Jill*: it was an account of life at Eton, written immediately after the man left Eton. It was extremely dry, extremely mature, a collection of little linked scenes – mostly dialogue – involving everybody from the headmaster and vice-provost down to the boys. What was remarkable about it was the deliberate use of irrelevant detail in setting a scene. I showed it Kingsley, and he was equally amused by it – parts of it were very funny – and we searched for Hall's other books. I found one called *Two Exiles* on a market stall in Leicester, but it wasn't as good as *The Senior Commoner*.

I don't know about my novels. I think someone once said – I did, actually – that poems were about yourself, novels about other people. The fault of the novels is that they're about me. They're not really about other people, they don't have the sympathy with other people and interest in them, so I suppose that, when I'd written them, I'd said all there was to say about me in that form.

And yet they're very consciously non-autobiographical, attempts not to write the traditional early novel which, as John Wain said somewhere, is simply a catalogue of your experiences to date. Wain also said that the main characters are both equally removed from yourself; and you yourself have said, I think, that the only autobiographical thing about it is the setting.

Yes, there's a bit more than that, it's a tremendous mixture of truth and fiction. I certainly went up to Oxford, I certainly shared a room with a chap, I certainly rushed home to Coventry when it was bombed in my first term; on the other hand, I was not poor, I liked the chap I shared rooms with, and I didn't make up a fantasy about a younger sister. Similarly, in *A Girl in Winter*: I certainly was very miserable towards the end of the war, I certainly was feeling lonely and working in a library, but I wasn't a girl and I wasn't foreign.

There's this conscious distancing that is so often in your work.

Oscar Wilde said, 'Give a man a mask and he will tell you the truth.' (I think it was Wilde, it may have been Yeats.) I think that's what I was doing: fiction enables you to tell facts, but they're so wound up together that it's difficult to disentangle them.

I always remember Kingsley getting a copy of *A Girl in Winter*. He looked at it; 'I can't think why you want to write a book like this,' he said. He never thought anything of it, but it just wasn't his sort of thing. You would be surprised how little I knew about people in those days. I didn't know how they lived or anything: if you read the parts where Katherine goes to where she lives in the first and third parts of the book, you'll find they are most uncertain. She seems to have a flat in the centre of the town, which is a very unusual thing to have; the flat itself is hardly described. The extent of one's ignorance of the ordinary carry-on of life was fantastic.

I think that when I began to write more characteristic poetry, I'd found how to make poems as readable as novels, if you see what I mean. And, of course, it's much quicker to write poems.

Tracks, 1, Summer 1967

The True Voice of Feeling: an Auto Interview

INTERVIEWER: *Despite this record, I believe you say somewhere that you're against poetry being read aloud?*
LARKIN: Very likely: that's rather sweeping, of course. In fact there are only three legitimate things anyone can do with poetry – write it, read it, or publish it. Writing reviews, or holding seminars, or reading it in public – even making records of it – well, this is secondary activity, unimportant at best, meretricious at worst. But I suppose that an actual reading of a poem by its author can be helpful: you can hear where he puts the stresses, whether he sounds ironic or flippant or serious. You go back to the text with a firmer grasp on what he meant. I can see you're about to say that a poem doesn't fully exist except in terms of sound, and I agree, but any adult reader ought to be able to imagine that as he reads with the eye. A vocal rendering alone, particularly of a poem you're not familiar with, misses so much that the eye picks up naturally – punctuation, stanza-shape, where one *is* in the poem, how far from the end, that kind of thing. Mind you, one doesn't always know that from the text. I remember once a man showing me a poem he had written about his wife. He was sitting on one side of me, she was sitting on the other. It was a pretty dramatic moment. When I got to the end of the sheet I racked my brains for some suitable comment, but none came. I wondered if I dare faint, or go into a trance, or something: anything to end that awful silence. At last the husband broke it. 'It goes on over the page,' he said. It did, too.

So this is how you intend your reading to be taken – as a help to understanding the sense?
Yes. I think tone of voice does something for the colloquial ones, 'Poetry of Departures' for instance. And it's surprising how many people misread the end of 'Toads', as if there were a comma or something at the end of the first line of the last stanza. Then in 'Coming' the repeated line is supposed to suggest the bird call – that kind of thing.

Were you used to reading your poems when you made this record?
As a matter of fact I'd done it only once, for the British Council. They shut you up alone in a room with a live microphone and tell you to read, talk, anything you like. One man went to sleep. But this record was made in a very busy and rather noisy commercial studio: it was probably all right for making a private record for your New Zealand cousins of your daughter singing 'Over the Rainbow', but with a quiet thing like the speaking voice there were all sort of extra noises that were upsetting – people going upstairs, and pulling lavatory chains, and so on. You can't hear them on the record, but they were there.

They didn't put you off?
No more than I was put off already, by simple nervousness.

Were you satisfied with your reading?
I think generally speaking I read very fast, comparatively, and sometimes too fast – I believe 'Maiden Name' suffers from this. On the other hand, I wanted the readings to sound like someone talking, rather than that laboured snail's-pace style some people have, full of breathing. Kingsley Amis has an imitation of Dylan Thomas reciting the last two lines of Yeats's 'Lapis Lazuli'. They're thirteen words long and take him about a minute and a quarter to get through. Another thing I dislike rather is my voice – I come from Coventry, between the sloppiness of Leicester and the whine of Birmingham, you know – and sometimes it comes out.

Would you sooner have someone else read them?
Well, that's the funny thing – in fact, although I'd be the first to admit that I'm not a particularly good reader in any sense, I always have a sneaking preference for these versions.

I'm not at all surprised – I think your voice follows every shade of meaning and variation of emotion in a way a professional reader never could. –
(*inaudible*)

– simply because they are your *poems.*
I suppose you could say that. There's a book[1] that argues that every poet writes for his own voice, and that if you listen carefully

1 Francis Berry: *Poetry and the Physical Voice* (1962)

you can actually hear their voice in their poems – people like Milton and Shelley. Consequently they would be their own poems' ideal reader. I think the trouble with actors is that they often come to a bit they don't understand, and think they'll ham it up a bit to cover the fact. Beautifully, of course, but then you never get everything.

Sleevenote from LP of *The Less Deceived* (Listen Records, 1968)

The State of Poetry

I find it difficult to say anything in reply to your questions, because I never think of poetry or the poetry scene, only separate poems written by individuals. These, to the best of my admittedly-sketchy knowledge, prompt the reflection that the most encouraging features of the last decade have been the good poems, and the most discouraging etc., the bad poems, and that one hopes in the next decade that there will be more good and less bad ones. But this isn't very helpful. I think that the contemporary poetry scene is rather like the thirties – vernacular, political and anti-establishment (of course, there are exceptions): on the whole, however, I find this encouraging. Whether one finds the recent emphasis on violence and insanity discouraging depends, I suppose, on what your view of poetry is. If these are genuinely what a writer finds poetic, then of course he must deal with them. For some, I fear, they have become simply fashionable properties.

As regards the next decade, I hope a really big talent will arise that will make the business of reading poetry exciting once more.

the Review, 29–30, Spring–Summer 1972

NOTE: Under the title 'The State of Poetry – A Symposium', a headnote by the editor of *the Review*, Ian Hamilton, read:

> The following questions were sent to a wide-ranging selection of poets, critics and editors, both English and American.
> 1. What, in your view, have been the most (a) encouraging, (b) discouraging features of the poetry scene during the past decade?
> 2. What developments do you hope to see during the next decade? We print below, in full, all the answers we received.

The other replies came from: Dannie Abse, A. Alvarez, John Bayley, Jon Silkin, Kingsley Amis, Richard Eberhart, Martin Dodsworth, Clive James, Douglas Dunn, Peter Levi, Elizabeth Jennings, Richard Wilbur, Julian Symons, John Fuller, Anthony Thwaite, Roy Fuller, George MacBeth, David Harsent, Donald Hall, Vernon Scannell, Peter Porter, Alan Dugan, Gavin Ewart, Michael Longley, Charles Tomlinson, Alan Brownjohn, Edwin Morgan, Hugo Williams, Jonathan Raban, Patricia Beer, Jeff Nuttall, John Carey, Peter Redgrove, Adrian Henri, and Colin Falck.

Let the Poet Choose

I looked through my three books of poems, and after some time came to the conclusion that I was subconsciously looking for poems which did not seem to me to have received their due meed of praise. Of course, there were quite a lot of them, and selection was difficult, but in the end I picked 'MCMXIV' and 'Send No Money', both from *The Whitsun Weddings*.

Looking at them, I see that they have a certain superficial resemblance: they are both, for instance, in more or less the same metre. On the other hand, they might be taken as representative examples of the two kinds of poem I sometimes think I write: the beautiful and the true. I have always believed that beauty is beauty, truth truth, that is not all ye know on earth nor all ye need to know, and I think a poem usually starts off either from the feeling How beautiful that is or from the feeling How true that is. One of the jobs of the poem is to make the beautiful seem true and the true beautiful, but in fact the disguise can usually be penetrated.

Let the Poet Choose, edited by James Gibson (Harrap, 1973)

NOTE: This anthology was the result of the editor inviting '44 poets to select and introduce two favourite poems of their own'.

W. H. Auden

No poet's life fell more decisively in two. What was English Auden's game *about*, that tended to become like a war – was it capital and labour, communism and fascism, life and death? It hardly mattered: what rang true was that inimitable Thirties fear, the sense that something was going to fall like rain, on the other side of which, if we were lucky, we might build the Just City. English Auden was a superb, magnetic, wide-angled poet, but the poetry was in the blaming and warning.

American Auden, on the other hand, was a walking readers' digest: names – Rilke, Kierkegaard, Goethe, James – clung to him like Coney Island confetti. He spread easily into longer works, their themes our civilization, the Christian story, the relation of life and art. Now part academic, part journalist, part international man of letters, his genius decreased in impact while maintaining, or even increasing, its productivity.

What held the two together, and us to both of them? First, his unique blend of dedication and irreverence: poetry is a fine thing, but the poet – even one of Auden's stature – mustn't give himself airs ('in the end, art is small beer'). Secondly, a love of the English language ('I believe in the OED') that was still far from subservience (he sat on Volume X at meals). Thirdly, a personal toughness and isolation that, scouting self-pity in himself and others, recalled the life-style of his Anglo-Saxon ancestors. It's hard not to read the Malebolgian 'On the Circuit' in this spirit; indeed, the last lines of his last collection have something of the same resonance, when he instructs his flesh at their moment of parting to

> ... pay no attention
> To my piteous *Don'ts*, but bugger off quickly.

It is a Stoic aspiration. It is good to know it was granted.

New Statesman, 5 October 1973

NOTE: The other contributions published by the *New Statesman* under the heading 'W. H. Auden (1907–1973)' were by Stephen Spender, Charles Monteith, Frank Kermode, William Coldstream, and a quatrain by John Betjeman.

The Sanity of Lawrence

I am greatly honoured to be asked to open this exhibition. In this year that marks the fiftieth anniversary of Lawrence's death there will be Lawrence exhibitions in libraries all over the world. But a Lawrence exhibition in Nottingham is something special, like a Hardy exhibition in Dorchester or even a Shakespeare exhibition in Stratford. Over and above natural homage to a great writer is the pride of being able to claim him as a fellow-citizen, of sharing to some small extent the local spirit that gave initial shape to his original and independent genius.

A few weeks ago, when I was looking among my Lawrence books to find something to say on this occasion, I came across Professor de Sola Pinto's Lawrence lecture he gave here in 1951. It is interesting that Professor Pinto, who did so much to initiate the study of Lawrence in this university, should have had to begin by apologizing that at that time Nottingham had paid so little attention to him.

He points out in extenuation that Lawrence has been dead for scarcely twenty years, and that the university as such is only three years old, but he goes on to mention the promising start that has been made in building up a Lawrence collection in the university library, adding, 'which, I hope, will one day be the great D. H. Lawrence collection in this country'. The exhibition we have before us today has been supplemented by loans from a number of friendly sources, but even so it shows what excellent progress has now been made towards fulfilling this ideal, and I think we should pay tribute to all those in the university who over the last three decades have kept it steadily in view. For the collector, Lawrence is a diverse and expensive field, but we can see how far generosity and diligence combined have already taken the university, and I hope it will be possible even in these difficult days

Opening speech at D. H. Lawrence exhibition 'A Phoenix in Flight' (Nottingham University Library, 1980)

for its library, under the enterprising guidance of my old friend Peter Hoare, to continue to increase its holdings in commemoration of one whom Professor Pinto called 'perhaps the one truly literary artist who can be claimed in any true sense as the product of this part of England'.

As the *Notes* to the exhibition make clear – and I am sure you will agree that we owe Mrs Welch our special thanks and praise not only for these notes but for assembling and mounting the entire display – its theme is not Lawrence and Nottingham but Lawrence and the world. This is a valid approach: Lawrence was always on the move, and he was never happier than when packing up to go. Among the scores of books about him is one entirely devoted to establishing where he was on any given day of his life, and I believe it is far from complete. Some have taken this constant travelling as a defect in his personality, a view Frieda Lawrence rejected when she wrote: 'He travelled because he wanted to see what the world was like in other places, not because he was a hunted, haunted man running away from himself.' While I am sure this is true, I doubt whether it is the whole truth. *Sea and Sardinia*, you will remember, begins abruptly: 'Comes over one an absolute necessity to move.' There *was* an element of compulsion. Lawrence admitted this, but he did not see it as anything to be ashamed of. In *Aaron's Rod* he rather disarmingly likens himself in this respect, not to a phoenix, but to a cuckoo, that migrates from Africa to Essex and back again simply because that is its nature.

While there may have been other more mundane factors involved such as his own wretched health and even in earlier years the exchange rate of sterling, this peripatetic streak in Lawrence is entirely characteristic. No writer of this century aimed himself more at the world, no writer took it on more completely, its countries and continents, its peoples and philosophies, everything down to its smallest birds, beasts and flowers. It is this universality that is one of Lawrence's most compelling qualities, the sense he gives that, in his own words, this is not only a world of men, but a vivid epiphany of life in all its alternatives, of which humanity is only one, and perhaps not the best one at that. This variousness was his element, and it was natural for him to move freely in it.

I think if we are honest we must admit that Lawrence would not have approved of this exhibition. He hated keeping things: that was why he liked the Etruscans, because they left no great buildings, no great literature, no glorious national history. As he wrote: 'Give us things that are alive and flexible, which won't last too long and become an obstruction and a weariness.' In fact, I doubt whether he would not find his own present reputation, of which this exhibition is so eloquent, more than a little absurd. If he could see the thousands of term papers on *Women in Love* being handed in all over the world, or watch the film we have made of it, or look at a few issues of the *D. H. Lawrence Review*, he might think he was well on the way to becoming an obstruction and a weariness himself.

But if he did, it would be a pity, because this reputation has been made up of two great waves of admiration; the first for the man, that produced all the personal accounts of him after his death, and the second for his works, originating in the pages of *Scrutiny* in Leavis's study of the novels in the mid-1930s and culminating in Leavis's study of the novels in 1956. And each in its own way was genuine and justifiable: Lawrence was both a wonderful man and a wonderful writer, and he was recognized as such right from the start. No doubt there were elements of self-interest in both waves: some of the people who had known him were anxious to show that they had known him better than anyone else, and Leavis tended at times to see him as a fellow-sufferer at the hands of the literary establishment, someone he could use to attack T. S. Eliot and *The Times Literary Supplement*. But between them they brought about the post-war Penguin Lawrence explosion, the ten titles published to celebrate the twentieth anniversary of his death in 1950, and of course the unsuccessful prosecution in 1960 for publishing *Lady Chatterley's Lover*, which unwittingly installed Lawrence as something like the patron saint of the permissive society, a canonization he would certainly have viewed with the utmost repugnance.

All this may have been more than some of his advocates bargained for, and I think that we are now in the middle of a third, more dispassionate, wave of Lawrence studies. The other week I was reading one of the books on him that nowadays seem to come out every month or so. It was well-researched and deeply interesting, and for a while I could not think what made it different from other similar books I had read in the past. Then I realized that the author was trying neither to make me like Lawrence nor dislike him; in fact I could not tell whether he liked or disliked him himself. And I had to realize that the age of proselytizing is over. We are all Lawrence converts nowadays, or at least converted to the fact that he is there, like Wordsworth or Hardy. We have entered the age of Lawrence scholarship, with Professor Boulton's magnificent first volume of the *Letters*, and the promised exciting new texts of the novels from Cambridge University Press.

It will be interesting to see what effect this has. In theory, of course, it may well be time for a more balanced assessment, a sorting out of the acceptable from the unacceptable, the readable from the unreadable. I should certainly welcome fewer term papers on the turgid and hypertensive *Women in Love*, and a few more on, say, *Kangaroo*. But as E. M. Forster said fifty years ago, Lawrence 'is not a creature of compartments. You cannot say, "Let us drop his theories and enjoy his art", because the two are one.' Therefore I do not think we can ever have a consistent, critically-approved Lawrence, fitting in neatly somewhere between Arnold Bennett and Graham Greene. This is what Frieda Lawrence meant when she wrote that it was very kind of Dr Leavis to put Lawrence on the shelf beside George Eliot, but that he was *not* a classic, he was an *experience*. He is a writer of such abounding creative energy, of such wilful assertions and counter-assertions, that, like his own St Mawr, he is liable to kick to pieces any critical stall we try to put him into. His genius thrived on self-contradiction, just as in his essay the crown is upheld by the opposition of the lion and the unicorn. I suspect that as long as Lawrence's writings are real to us we can only hate him or love him, and that balanced assessment will in the end have to retire to a safe distance and leave us to it.

The great virtue of an exhibition such as this one is that it puts us back in touch with Lawrence in a way that criticism cannot. Criticism, after all, is bound to take its subjects seriously, and while Lawrence should be taken seriously it is all too easy to take him solemnly. We need to remember the casual mockery and vividness of his letters, the lack of pretension with which he managed the whole business of 'being a writer'. It is refreshing to be reminded that in the intervals of writing his prophetic books Lawrence sent chatty postcards, and painted pictures he was rather proud of, but which, to be honest, are not very good. We sometimes forget that behind the ecstasies and the exhortations was a man who scrubbed floors and darned his own socks and was not a bad cook. And we should remember such things, because they demonstrate that at the heart of his writing lay a sane and healthy spirit. Let us today when looking at this exhibition acknowledge that spirit with homage and affection.

Times Literary Supplement, 13 June 1980

An Interview with John Haffenden

JOHN HAFFENDEN: *You once wrote that if you were to try your hand at autobiography you'd have to begin at the age of twenty-one, or even thirty-one ...*

PHILIP LARKIN: Yes. Next question? (*Laughs*) Whenever I read an autobiography, or even a biography, I tend to start half-way through, where the chap's grown-up and it becomes interesting. Some writers seem to stop at twenty-one rather than start there: Betjeman, Day Lewis. Still, there's probably a good physiological reason for this: old people remember what happened forty years ago but not last week. Goethe says somewhere that what is distant seems to him immediate, and vice versa. No doubt when I get to my dotage all those dusty motor-car filled days in Coventry will seem vivid and delightful, but just now they're far away. My childhood wasn't unhappy, just boring.

Does your feeling imply a regret that you can't attach more significance to your childhood – no traumas, no villainous mother?

Well, it would have been nice to have more technicolor, so to speak.

You've reviewed a number of biographies – Christina Rossetti, for example, Owen and Housman – and have always held that it's some sort of aberration to take childhood, in the way of Walter de la Mare, as the great beneficent lap of the world.

I think it is. If you're more interesting as a child than as a grown-up, what's the point of growing up? I think grown-ups are nicer than children. I hated everybody when I was a child, or I thought I did. When I grew up, I realized that what I hated was children.

You've written that children have been devalued – we don't think of them any more as holy innocents ...

I think that since the middle class was reintroduced to its offspring by the disappearance of servants a good many people feel this. Of course I speak as a childless person: I've never lived in hideous contact with them, having toast flung about at breakfast and so on. Perhaps worse than toast. The whole doctrine of original sin implies that children are awful, don't you think? The nearer you are to being born, the worse you are. I wasn't a happy child: I stammered badly, and this tends to shape your life. You can't become a lecturer or anything that involves talking. By the time you cure yourself – which in my case was quite late, about thirty – all the talking things you might have done are lost. If you catch me tired or frightened, I still stammer.

Was that why you became a librarian?
I tried twice for the Civil Service, during the war of course, but even in those days they had some standards. I'm glad now that they didn't take me, though I was a bit surprised then. I've been much happier as a librarian.

Did you find Oxford a nourishing experience? You did make some close friends there, such as Kingsley Amis.
I made some very good friends and enjoyed being there, but I never had the *Brideshead Revisited* feeling about it. I could never write there. Although I love the place, I feel a pressure at the back of my neck at being surrounded by about six thousand people who are cleverer than I am. When I left I felt a great upsurge of – well, since it's so long ago I'll call it creative relief. I wrote *The North Ship*, *Jill* and *A Girl in Winter* in about two years, straight off.

Was Jill *in fact close to your own experience, and if so does it now embarrass you?*
It embarrasses me a bit by being so very much a first novel, but apart from the air-raid – that was in Coventry in November 1940, just after I'd gone to Oxford – it's not my own experience. I shared rooms with an old school friend; and had plenty of good times. I certainly didn't have any fantasies about a schoolgirl sister. But at the same time a lot of it is what I felt. The incidental details are mostly imaginary, but the feeling is absolutely true.

And yet the book explores a mentality that is uncomfortable there.
It's all rather paradoxical really. John Kemp is uncomfortable because he's working class, but I made him working class to give him some inadequacy, some equivalent of my stammer. I was sort of professional middle class. *Jill* has always had the edge over *A Girl in Winter* as far as sales go, which surprises me because

that's a much more sophisticated book – written, shaped, a Virginia Woolf–Henry Green kind of novel. I took much more trouble over it. But I don't think either of them is any good.

You've said somewhere that, in your view, novelists are interested in other people, but you're not …
I don't think my books were novels, they were more kinds of prose poems. I spent about five years trying to write a third novel, but couldn't. When I lapsed back into poetry, it was so much easier, so much quicker. It's not characters that are the trouble in writing a novel, it's finding a background for them, knowing what they do.

In reviewing biographies of writers, you've taken pains to analyse what gives each one his or her particular emphasis, what provokes their work, and to define any crisis or shift in their lives as if it were a cause of their writing. That's to say, your reviews tend towards a biographical interpretation of a writer's work …
I think we *want* the life and the work to make sense together: I suppose ultimately they must, since they both relate to the same person. Eliot would say they don't, but I think Eliot is wrong.

I think you've said that a writer must write the truth – presumably the truth of his experience?
I was probably lying. A more important thing I said was that every poem starts out as either true or beautiful. Then you try to make the true ones seem beautiful, and the beautiful ones true. I could go through my poems marking them as one or the other. 'Send No Money' is true. 'Essential Beauty' is beautiful. When I say beautiful, I mean the original idea seemed beautiful. When I say true, I mean something was grinding its knuckles in my neck and I thought: God, I've got to say this somehow, I have to find words and I'll make them as beautiful as possible. 'Dockery and Son': that's a true one. It's never reprinted in anthologies, but it's as true as anything I've ever written – for me anyway.

At the end of that poem you have what amounts to a statement:

> *Life is first boredom, then fear.*
> *Whether or not we use it, it goes,*
> *And leaves what something hidden from us chose,*
> *And age, and then the only end of age.*

Do you think that sort of enunciation is imaginatively justified within the poem, or did you feel it true-as-true?
Both. I'm very proud of those lines. They're true. I remember when I was writing it, I thought this is how it's got to end. There's a break in the metre; it's meant as a jolt.

A number of critics have commented on the fact that, even as early as The North Ship, *you seem to have decided that life is a matter of regretfulness, of unfulfilment. Many of the poems in the book are kinds of lucubration, thoughts on love, and the paradox whereby one only values something when it's past . . .*
I can't really go back to *The North Ship*: it was so very young, born of reading Yeats and so on. Remember Yeats's early poems were wan and droopy, very unlike the later Yeats. I can't explain *The North Ship* at all. It's not very good, though your courtesy will prevent you from agreeing. It's popular with musicians, they like setting it. Musicians like things that don't mean too much.

But there is meaning in the book.
Do you think so? I have to make a tape-recording for America, and I'm putting in three *North Ship* poems – 'X', 'XIII' and 'XXX' – only because I think they're fairly acceptable as poems: they're not meant to be what I think good nowadays. I don't particularly like 'XXX' except for the last quatrain. There are some pieces in the book I hate very much indeed.

I quite like number XXV.
It's not very sharp, is it? I distinctly remember the dream and what it was about, but it's quite unimportant.

Do you believe that the poet can best explain his own work?
As to what it was about or what it's supposed to mean, yes, not as to whether it's any good.

But what if a critic construes a poem in a way you felt you didn't mean?
I should think he was talking balls. I get endless trouble about 'Dry-Point'. Schoolgirls write to me about it, and I have to explain that originally it was one of two poems about sex, and that modesty forbids me to say any more. They were written in the late forties: Kingsley called the first one my Sanders of the River poem – that was the first one, whooping it up – and I was so

dashed that I dropped it. 'Dry-Point' is the other, saying how awful sex is and how we want to get away from it.

Do you still feel, as you told Ian Hamilton many years ago, that critics can hinder your work?
Yes. A critic can never help you. He can say you should be writing like someone else, which is like water off a duck's back. But if he says, 'Larkin, you're crumby, anti-life, defeatist' and so on, you may get so depressed that you pack it up – if you read him, that is.

You think of yourself as an emotional poet, and it must strike you as ironic when some critics describe you as 'neutral', especially when you've spoken of some poems as being almost shamefully self-revealing?
Well, there are many types of emotion. I've said that depression is to me as daffodils were to Wordsworth. But a poem isn't only emotion. In my experience you've got the emotion side – let's call it the fork side – and you cross it with the knife side, the side that wants to sort it out, chop it up, arrange it, and say either thank you for it or sod the universe for it. You never write a poem out of emotion alone, just as you never write a poem from the knife side, what might be a letter to *The Times*. I can't explain it: don't want to.

Can we speak a little about your response to Hardy? You remarked in one review about Hardy's sense of time as being a necessary ingredient of spiritual growth ...
This goes back to what we were saying about children, doesn't it, who know nothing about life. I think that until you're about thirty you really haven't got things into perspective: the term 'young poet' seems a contradiction in terms to me.

If one extends what you're saying to the practice of writing poetry, what do you say to your critics who imply or infer that at some point you pre-determined what you felt about life, that you made up your mind once and for all, for example, about the occasions of suffering that people endure?
They've got it the wrong way round. I don't decide what I think about life: life decides that, either through heredity or environment, what you're born with or what happens to you. If I'd been born a different person and different things had happened to me, I might have written differently. I didn't invent age and death and failure and all that, but how can you ignore them? Hardy or someone said that life was a comedy to those who think, but a tragedy to those who feel. Good stuff.

Do you actually share Hardy's feeling for what you've called the 'passive apprehension of suffering' and the capacity for spiritual growth it can bring?
The more sensitive you are to suffering the nicer person you are and the more accurate notion of life you have. Hardy had it right from the start: his early poems are wonderful – 'She, to Him', for example. As I tried to say in 'Deceptions', the inflicter of suffering may be fooled, but the sufferer never is.

I suppose what I'm asking is why you've felt that suffering is the real thing in life, and haven't expressed more of what other people find fulfilling?
I just think it is. The really happy moments of my life, such as when I caught the captain of the other side in the deep or passed my driving test first go, aren't really subjects for poetry. And they don't stay with you.

Do you feel that you've carried out Wordsworth's dictum that a great poet must create the taste by which he is to be enjoyed and understood?
Please don't think that I'm great. If I'm noticeable, it's because we're in a trough at the moment. Forty years ago we had Yeats, Eliot, Graves, Auden, Spender, MacNeice, Betjeman, Dylan Thomas; and who have we got now? If I seem good, it's because everyone else is so bad. Well, almost everyone. Well, anyway ...

You don't think of yourself as didactic at all?
Not really. One of the minor mistakes people make about me is thinking that I'm a sort of cut-price Betjeman. Now he *is* didactic: a real protest poet – 'Come, friendly bombs, and fall on Slough' and that kind of thing. He's always against uglification, greed, vulgarity and the rest of it. I just accept them for the most part.

You've observed in writing that 'poetry is an affair of sanity', which does seem to imply the view that it must be level-headed, can't admit anything that doesn't seem tolerable and can't tax the reader ... but perhaps you made the remark against experimentalism or the oddness you found in Emily Dickinson?
There certainly is a cult of the mad these days: think of all the boys who've been in the bin – I don't understand it. Chaucer, Shakespeare, Wordsworth, Hardy – it's the big, sane boys who get the medals. The object of writing is to show life as it is, and if you don't see it like that you're in trouble, not life. Up to you, of course.

What answer do you make to those who find your work defeatist?
I don't find anything defeatist about being sane, do you? I know Lawrence said tragedy ought to be a great big kick at misery, but then Lawrence was Lawrence, a man I've always admired. I love *Lady Chatterley's Lover*, just because it doesn't come to a happy ending, or any sort of ending: Mellors is like everyone else, he wants to have his end away and then forget about it. It's a very equivocal ending.

Isn't there a danger in adducing one's own temperament as the truth about life?
A danger who for? Nobody pays any attention to what you write. They read it and then forget about it. There may be a lunatic fringe who believe that life is what writers say, not what they experience themselves, but most people just say, 'Oh well, that's what it's like to be Larkin', and start thinking about something else.

And yet, to go back to the sort of statement you make at the end of 'Dockery and Son': you see it as true, but others might dispute it.
It's a bit simplified, I suppose, but I think it's all perfectly true. I can't see how anyone could possibly deny it, any of it.

If I can raise one further criticism: Raymond Gardiner wrote in 1973 that 'Philip Larkin's poetry represents an art of desolation ... it lacks the humanity of comfort ...'[1] I've rather unfairly extrapolated from his comments, but can you bear such appraisals or do they provoke you?
The drift of these questions seems to be that I shouldn't be myself, I should be somebody else. Well, there may be something to be said for that, but it's not a thing I can do anything about. I don't want to turn other people into me, I'm only saying what I feel. It's very difficult to write about happiness. 'Happiness writes white,' as Montherlant says somewhere; in other words, you can't read it afterwards. It would be fun to be a novelist and write about imaginary happiness: I suppose lots of people do. Wonderful weathers and landscapes, and a new girl in every chapter.

I want to ask you why you resist going abroad. Betjeman said that he feels frustrated by his ignorance in foreign countries, but that's something different from what you said in your speech to the FVS Foundation in Hamburg when you won the Shakespeare Prize in 1977 – that a poet who

1 *Guardian*, 31 March 1973, p. 12.

goes from country to country might find that 'his sense of cultural identity becomes blurred and weakened.'
Perhaps I was unlucky. My father liked going to Germany, and took me twice, when I was fourteen or so. I found it petrifying, not being able to speak to anyone or read anything, frightening notices that you felt you should understand and couldn't. My father liked the jolly singing in beer-cellars, three-four time to accordions – Schiffer Klavier, did they call them? – think of that for someone who was just buying the first Count Basie records! Perhaps if I'd been younger, or older, or with people my own age even, it would have been different, but I doubt it. It's a language thing with me: I can't learn foreign languages, I just don't believe in them. As for cultural identities, that sounds a bit pretentious, but I think people do get pallid if they change countries. Look at Auden. But people must suit themselves.

But it might be said that in not exposing yourself to European cultures or literature, you're possibly cultivating a sort of narrow-mindedness or chauvinism ...
But honestly, how far can one really assimilate literature in another language? In the sense that you can read your own?

Yet, by not trying, one might be courting a social, personal or national security, an insularity ...
I don't think poetry is like that. Poems don't come from other poems, they come from being oneself, in life. Every man is an island, entire of himself, as Donne said. This American idea – it is American, isn't it? Started with Pound and Eliot? – that somehow every new poem has to be the sum of all old poems, like the latest Ford, well, it's the sort of idea lecturers get, if you'll excuse my saying so. Makes sense and so on: only it's not how poetry works. You remember that wonderful remark of Sidney Bechet when the recording engineer asked if he'd like to hear a playback: 'That don't do me no good.' That's what I think about foreign literature.

Would you actually accept Donald Davie's view of your philosophy of life as being 'patiently diminished'?
Funny sort of phrase. I don't think I understand it. I didn't invent old age and death and failure and disillusion: they're there, and I don't see why I shouldn't write about them if they seem writeable-

about. No, it all comes down to what I said before: people don't want you to be yourself. It's really not so very far from being told, 'Now, comrade, let's have a poem about this month's steel production. None of this bourgeois personalism, unless you want to see the inside of Downing College.' You write a poem because it's something you've got to get done, not because it's a philosophy of life.

Do you take great care in ordering the poems in a collection?
Yes, great care. I treat them like a music-hall bill: you know, contrast, difference in length, the comic, the Irish tenor, bring on the girls. I think 'Lines on a Young Lady's Photograph Album' is a good opener, for instance; easy to understand, variety of mood, pretty end. The last one is chosen for its uplift quality, to leave the impression that you're more serious than the reader had thought.

Within The Less Deceived *you have a group of three poems basically about mortality – 'Next Please', 'Going' and 'Wants' – before providing a counter-movement in 'Maiden Name', which is about a sense of preservation from time...*
I used to be quite original in those days. As far as I know, nobody else has written about maiden names, and yet they are very powerful things. I often wonder how women survive the transition: if you're called something, you can't be called something else. Like I was saying about foreign languages.

I wonder if you could say something about a poem I like called 'If, My Darling', or perhaps somebody's asked you that before?
Never, nobody's paid the slightest attention to it. I like it very much too. It was the first poem that made Kingsley think I was some good: he loved it when I sent it to him. I wanted, in the last line, to change 'unpriceable' to 'unprintable', but he said no: 'unprintable' would just mean cunt, whereas 'unpriceable' *probably* meant cunt but could mean all sorts of other things too.

It's a fantastically self-derogatory poem, telling the girl that if she really knew me she'd know what a terrible person I am ...
Well, I think we all think that, with girls. It's funny rather than self-derogatory. I'm surprised it hasn't been anthologized more.

Do you value as highly a poem such as 'Spring', another one in which you look at yourself deprecatingly, but with a difference in tone?

I don't think that's a particularly good poem, though there are some nice things in it. I like the last few lines.

The mood certainly takes off in those lines, but perhaps you can explain your feeling about the last passage:

> *And those she has least use for see her best,*
> *Their paths grown craven and circuitous,*
> *Their visions mountain-clear, their needs immodest.*

Isn't it clear? It means that these people, these indigestible sterilities, see rebirth and resurrection most vividly and imaginatively, but it isn't for them; their way through life isn't a gay confident striding. What they *see* is clear and wonderful, but their needs are immodest in the sense that they want more girls and Jaguars than the normal amount other people get, because they get none.

Are you distinguishing yourself from that type of person?
No, that's me all right. Or was: you must remember it's all about thirty years ago.

Do you feel the poem 'Church Going' has been rather too much evaluated?
Over-valued, do you mean? Or analysed? I don't think I've seen much about it, except one chap who said it was too long. I think it all develops naturally enough. It came from the first time I saw a ruined church in Northern Ireland, and I'd never seen a ruined church before – discarded. It shocked me. Now of course it's commonplace: churches are not so much ruined as turned into bingo-halls, warehouses for refrigerators or split-level houses for architects.

It's not clear in the poem that you began with a ruined church.
No, it wasn't in the poem, but when you go into a church there's a feeling of something ... well ... over, derelict.

Some critics have discerned in it a yearning for a latter-day Christian or religious sanction. Is that so?
I suppose so. I'm not someone who's lost faith: I never had it. I was baptized – in Coventry Cathedral, oddly enough: the old one – but not confirmed. Aren't religions shaped in terms of what people want? No one could help hoping Christianity was true, or at least the happy ending – rising from the dead and our sins forgiven. One longs for these miracles, and so in a sense one longs for

religion. But 'Church Going' isn't that kind of poem: it's a humanist poem, a celebration of the dignity of ... well, you know what it says.

Could you comment on what one of your critics has said about The Less Deceived *as a whole: 'What saves [Larkin] from the limitations of the Movement is his occasional transcendence, without inappropriateness, of the commonplace'?*
I never thought the Movement commonplace, if that's what's implied. Not like *Lyrical Ballads*. It was much wittier and more cerebral. I don't want to transcend the commonplace, I love the commonplace, I lead a very commonplace life. Everyday things are lovely to me.

If I can move on to The Whitsun Weddings, *which one of your less favourable critics has called 'a sad and even bitterly cynical book' ...*
Eh? You can't say 'The Whitsun Weddings', which is central to the book, is a sad poem. It was just the transcription of a very happy afternoon. I didn't change a thing, it was just there to be written down.

Did you intend to give an unqualified assent to hopefulness at the end of the poem, where you seem to be flirting with a romantic visionary quality?
Yes. You couldn't be on that train without feeling the young lives all starting off, and that just for a moment you were touching them. Doncaster, Retford, Grantham, Newark, Peterborough, and at every station more wedding parties. It was wonderful, a marvellous afternoon. It only needed writing down. Anybody could have done it.

Elsewhere in your poems you've tended to moderate any hopefulness ...
The Greeks used to spill a few drops of wine in propitiation of the Fates, didn't they. Perhaps it's like that. But it wasn't necessary in 'The Whitsun Weddings'. There's nothing to suggest that their lives won't be happy, surely? I defy you to find it.

Could one say the same about 'An Arundel Tomb'?
Well, that is rather a romantic poem; there's even less reservation in that. I don't like it much, partly because of this; technically it's a bit muddy in the middle – the fourth and fifth stanzas seem trudging somehow, with awful rhymes like voyage/damage.

Everything went wrong with that poem: I got the hands wrong – it's right-hand gauntlet really – and anyway the hands were a nineteenth-century addition, not pre-Baroque at all. A friend of mine who visited the tomb in Chichester Cathedral told me that the guide said, 'A poem was written about this tomb by Philip Spender.' Muddle to the end.

But did you feel sceptical about the faithfulness that's preserved for us in stone?
No. I was very moved by it. Of course it was years ago. I think what survives of us is love, whether in the simple biological sense or just in terms of responding to life, making it happier, even if it's only making a joke. I was delighted when a friend asked me if I knew a poem ending 'What will survive of us is love.' It suggested the poem was making its way without me. I like them to do that.

I want to relate that to what you say about our sense of love in 'Faith Healing' – 'across most it sweeps/As all they might have done had they been loved' – which does sound like a projection of one's own experience which might not match others' . . .
Well, people want to be loved, don't they. The sort of unconditional love parents give if you're lucky, and that gets mixed up with the love of God – 'dear child', and so on. The poem came after seeing faith-healing in a film. 'At Grass' was a film too, about Brown Jack. You wouldn't remember him, a famous flat-racer and jumper, I think: there he was, completely forgotten and quite happy.

Is 'Naturally the Foundation will Bear Your Expenses' meant to be just a funny poem in which the speaker is the butt of the joke?
It's both funny and serious. The speaker's a shit. That's always serious.

It's seemed to some reviewers that you suffered from problems of identification with Mr Bleaney in 'Mr Bleaney', but it seems to me that perhaps they're missing the grammatical construction of the last two stanzas – 'But if he . . . I don't know' – which both ventures a judgement and refuses it at the same time.
The first two-thirds of the poem, down to 'But if', are concerned with my uneasy feeling that I'm becoming Mr Bleaney, yes. The last third is reassuring myself that I'm not, because he was clearly quite content with his sauce instead of gravy, and digging the

garden and so on, and yet there's doubt lingering too, perhaps he hated it as much as I did.

But to that extent you're not being presumptuous, judging him by what you sense yourself?
I don't think so. Unless you think it's presumptuous to judge anyone.

Do you think the poem has been given a false emphasis in your work?
Well, no, not a false one. Excessive, perhaps. I've never understood why it's so popular: I thought the subject was peculiar to me, and yet everybody seems to understand it and like it. When you're an only lodger, your relation with your landlady is very delicate: she's constantly urging you to do what she wants – dig the garden, or sit with her in the evenings, instead of sloping off to your own room.

The Whitsun Weddings *starts with the poem 'Here', which is sometimes read as a brief for retirement, the simpler life. Is that what you intended?*
Oh no, not at all ... well, it all depends what you mean by retirement. If you mean not living in London, I suppose it might be interpreted along those lines. I meant it just as a celebration of here, Hull. It's a fascinating area, not quite like anywhere else. So busy, yet so lonely. The poem is frightful to read aloud: the first sentence goes on for twenty-four-and-a-half lines, which is three-quarters of the poem, and the rest is full of consonants.

I've read one article which speaks of a growing disenchantment in High Windows ...
Just me getting older, I suppose. What's disenchanted about describing a hospital, or a nursing home?

I think the poem called 'High Windows' is slightly perplexing, since it starts on a vulgar level and shoots beyond it in the last stanza.
I think the end shows a desire to get away from it all, not unlike 'Dry-Point' in a way, or 'Absences'. I don't think it very good: I called the book after it because I liked the title. It's a true poem. One longs for infinity and absence, the beauty of somewhere you're not. It shows humanity as a series of oppressions, and one wants to be somewhere where there's neither oppressed nor oppressor, just freedom. It may not be very articulate.

Is it to be associated with the poem that stands before it in the book, 'Forget What Did', where you propose that a diary might be filled with 'observed/Celestial recurrences'?
Yes, that's about getting away from the miseries of life as well. It's about a time when I stopped keeping a diary because I couldn't bear to record what was going on. I kept a diary for a long time, more as a kind of great grumble-book than anything else. It's stopped now.

Would you acknowledge that there's in fact more compassion and generosity in High Windows *as a whole ...*
I should like to think so.

... as in poems like 'To the Sea', where you conclude with a sentiment about people 'helping the old, too, as they ought'?
My father died when my mother was sixty-one, and she lived to be ninety-one. We used to take a week's holiday in the summer. That poem came when we were in Southwold, when I realized that I hadn't had a 'seaside holiday' for years, and remembered all the ones when I was young.

It reminds me of what you wrote about William Barnes back in 1962 – you rebuked him for being almost too gentle, too submissive and forgiving, and yet in a sense you seem to have arrived at that position yourself. You had reservations about the fact that Barnes didn't show Hardy's bitter and ironical despair.
He doesn't have Hardy's cutting edge, does he? The rhythms are so regular, and it's all a bit cosy. I'm glad if you do find the poems in *High Windows* more compassionate: I don't know that they are. But one must be more aware of suffering as one grows older, as we said earlier. I thought the poems were more of the same, you know. There are some quite nasty ones in it. 'They fuck you up, your mum and dad' doesn't sound very compassionate.

It's very funny, though.
It's perfectly serious as well.

In some poems you're taking the risk of sentiment brimming over into sentimentality.
Am I? I don't understand the word sentimentality. It reminds me of Dylan Thomas's definition of an alcoholic: 'A man you don't like who drinks as much as you do.' I think sentimentality is

someone you don't like feeling as much as you do. But you can't win, can you?

Several of the poems can be docketed with your word 'beautiful', such as 'Cut Grass' or 'Solar' ...
Yes, 'Solar' was the first poem I wrote after *The Whitsun Weddings*. Nobody's ever liked it, or mentioned it. It was unlike anything I'd written for about twenty years, more like *The North Ship*.

I suppose critics find it doesn't comport with the general run of what your poems say.
So much the worse for them. It's a feeling, not a thought. Beautiful.

Was it your intention, in using bad language in one or two poems, to provide a shock tactic?
Yes. I mean, these words are part of the palette. You use them when you want to shock. I don't think I've ever shocked for the sake of shocking. 'They fuck you up' is funny because it's ambiguous. Parents bring about your conception and also bugger you up once you are born. Professional parents in particular don't like that poem.

How did you come to write 'The Explosion', the last poem in the book?
I heard a song about a mine disaster; a ballad, a sort of folk song. I thought it very moving, and it produced the poem. It made me want to write the same thing, a mine disaster with a vision of immortality at the end – that's the point of the eggs. It may be all rather silly. I like it.

Looking back over all your work, what do you feel is the imaginative note that is peculiarly your own?
I don't know. You see, you don't write the poems you really want to write. I should like to write poems about how beautiful the world is and how wonderful people are, but the words somehow refuse to come. I don't think any of my poems are more typical of me than the rest. 'The Whitsun Weddings', 'The Explosion', 'Show Saturday', 'Coming', 'Absences' – no, I can't pick and choose. 'Send No Money' is the one I repeat to myself. Don't judge me by them. Some are better than me, but I add up to more than they do. One does one's best, and lets the result stand or fall by itself.

Viewpoints: Poets in Conversation with John Haffenden
(Faber and Faber, 1981)

NOTE: The other poets in conversation with John Haffenden were Douglas Dunn, Thom Gunn, Seamus Heaney, Geoffrey Hill, Thomas Kinsella, Paul Muldoon, Richard Murphy, Tom Paulin, and Craig Raine. Four of the interviews – with Heaney, Dunn, Murphy and Larkin – first appeared in the *London Magazine*, and that with Thom Gunn in an abbreviated version in *Quarto*.

II · BROADCASTS

'New Poetry'

I am always very puzzled when I hear a poem condemned as 'mere personal emotion'. It seems to suggest that emotion can be impersonal, can exist in the abstract with nobody to feel it, which of course can't possibly be true. Or does it perhaps refer to what the feeling is about – matters usually called personal affairs, that are noticed in the personal column of newspapers? But these are just what is most universal about us, not personal at all: and in any case, why 'mere'? Do we call the sonnets of Shakespeare 'mere personal emotion'? No: the only meaning I can attach to the phrase is this: mere personal emotion is emotion which, despite all the poet's efforts, remains personal to him without becoming personal to us. We understand him to be in the grip of some emotional experience, because he tells us so, but his poem fails to bring it home to us, and we therefore register this failure by saying 'mere personal emotion'. Well, all right, but I think it enormously important for us to recognize that what has failed is not the poet's emotion but his technique. What we should be saying, in other words, is 'mere incompetent writing'.

I say 'enormously important' because I strongly object to the implication that feeling is in some way suspect as a basis for poetry nowadays. To me, now as at any other time, poetry should begin with emotion in the poet, and end with the same emotion in the reader. The poem is simply the instrument of transference. No matter what else we ask of poetry, or what methods we choose to bring it about, it must fulfil this first function, or cease to be an art at all. I say this because it is very much in danger of being forgotten nowadays, and if it is forgotten, then it will be the fault of phrases like 'mere personal emotion'.

Broadcast review of Randall Jarrell, *Selected Poems* (Faber and Faber, 1956), E. J. Scovell, *The River Steamer* (Cresset Press, 1956), Edwin Muir, *One Foot in Eden* (Faber and Faber, 1956) and Kathleen Raine, *Collected Poems* (Hamish Hamilton, 1956)

I say it also because it lies behind my present choice of poems, and even to some extent poets. I am predisposed to like Mr Randall Jarrell, for instance, because in the introduction to his *Selected Poems* he goes to great trouble to remove any obscurities that might stand between the reader and his meaning. I like him also because he refuses to give up the subject-matter of character and situation which has in this century been handed over more and more to the novel and the film. He is not afraid to dramatize an emotion, either, so that some of his poems need almost to be acted rather than read, like this one, called 'The Face'.

Not good any more, not beautiful –
Not even young.
This isn't mine.
Where is the old one, the old ones?
Those were mine.

It's so: I have pictures,
Not such old ones, people behaved
Differently then ... When they meet me they say:
You haven't changed.
I want to say: You haven't looked.

This is what happens to everyone.
At first you get bigger, you know more,
Then something goes wrong.
You are, and you say: I am –
And you were ... I've been too long.

I know, there's no saying no,
But just the same you say it. No.
I'll point to myself and say: I'm not like this.
I'm the same as always inside.
– And even that's not so.

I thought: if nothing happens ...
And nothing happened.
Here I am.
But it's not *right*.
If just living can do this,
Living is more dangerous than anything:

It is terrible to be alive.

Yes, Mr Jarrell is an emotional poet, but his poems are sometimes founded on what I might call 'mere public emotion': that is, he has all the feelings of the Good American – he is angry about war, indignant about refugees, romantic about Europe and children –

but his poetry is so friendly and discursive that they rarely build up sufficient emotional pressure to avoid sounding conventional.

Here however is an original, concentrated success, an astonishing and painful poem called 'La Belle au Bois Dormant'. He explains that this is about a murdered woman whose body has been put in a trunk and checked in at a railway station; he assumes we know that the title refers to the French legend of the sleeping beauty, and perhaps it is unnecessary for me to do more than indicate the overtones he draws from this idea.

> She lies, her head beneath her knees,
> In their old trunk; and no one comes –
> No porter, even, with a check
> Or forceps for her hard delivery.
> The trains pant outside; and she coils breathlessly
> Inside his wish and is not waked.
>
> She is sleeping, but, alas! not beautiful.
> Travellers doze around; are borne away;
> And the thorns clamber up her stony veins.
> She is irreparable; and yet a state
> Asks for her absently, and citizens
> Drown for an instant in her papery eyes.
>
> Yet where is the hunter black enough to storm
> Her opening limbs, or shudder like a fish
> Into the severed maelstrom of her skull?
> The blood fondles her outrageous mouth;
> The lives flourish in her life, to alienate
> Their provinces from her outranging smile.
>
> What wish, what keen pain has enchanted her
> To this cold period, the end of pain,
> Wishes, enchantment: this suspending sleep?
> She waits here to be waked – as he has waited
> For her to wake, for her to wake –
> Her lips set in their slack conclusive smile.

I mentioned earlier Mr Jarrell's use of character and situation, and in this he stands in line with Robert Frost and the whole nineteenth century, but often he uses the dramatic monologue not only to present a character but to present a period, as in this next poem, 'Money'. The speaker, an old American self-made man who is now a philanthropist because it is the only thing left to him, is not a particularly original conception, but the background of the nineteen-twenties when Big Business pretended it was a kind of social service in order to foil the attacks of the socialists, is excellently sketched in – too well, perhaps, for English readers to pick up all the allusions, but most people will be able to translate them into the English equivalents of the period. Here is the poem, 'Money':

> I sit here eating milk-toast in my lap-robe –
> They've got my night-shirt starchier than I told 'em ...
>   Huh! ...
> I'll tell 'em ...
>   Why, I wouldn't have given
> A wooden nickel to a wooden Indian, when I began.
> I never gave a soul a cent that I could help
> That I remember: now I sit here hatching cheques
> For any mortal cause that writes in asking,
> And look or don't look – I've been used to 'em too long –
> At seven Corots and the Gobelins
> And my first Rembrandt I outbid Clay Frick for:
> A dirty Rembrandt bought with dirty money –
> But nowadays we've all been to the cleaners'.
> (Harriet'd call Miss Tarbell Old Tarbaby –
> It none of it will stick, she'd say when I got mad;
> And she was right. She always was.)
> I used to say I'd made my start in railroads
> – 'Stocks, that is,' I'd think and never say –
> And made my finish in philanthropy:
> To think that all along it'uz Service!
> I could have kicked myself right in the face
> To think I didn't think of that myself ...
> 'There isn't one of you that couldn't have done what I did –'
> That was *my* line; and I'd think: 'If you'd been me.'
> SEES U.S. LAND OF OPPORTUNITY,
> A second-page two-column headline,
> Was all I got, most years ...
>
>   *They never knew a thing*! ...
> Why, when I think of what I've done, I can't believe it!
>
> ... A Presbyterian'd say it's Providence.
> In my time I've bought the whole Rhode Island Legislature
> For – I disremember how much; what for too ...
> Harriet'd have Nellie Melba in
> To entertain our friends – it never entertained *me* none –
> And I'd think: 'Birdie, I could buy you
> The way you'd buy a piece of Melba toast.'
>
> I had my troubles – nothing money wouldn't cure.
> A percentage of the world resented me

There on my money bags in my silk hat.
(To hear Ward I'd still straw stuck in my fur.)
But in the end the money reconciled 'em all.
Don't someone call it the Great Reconciler?
When my boys dynamited thirteen trestles
On the New York Central, I went against my custom then
And told the papers: 'Money's a *responsibility*.'

I'd talk down money if I hadn't any. As it was,
The whole office force could hear me through two doors.
E.J. said they said: 'Listen to the Old Man go!'

Why, it was money
That got me shut of my poor trusting wife,
And bought my girl from her, and got me Harriet –
What else would Harriet've married *me* for? ... She's gone now
And they're gone too, but it's not gone ...
You can take it with you anywhere *I'm* going.

... While I was looking up my second son-in-law
In Dun and Bradstreet, the social secretary
Came on him in the *Almanach de Gotha*.
It was like I figured, though: he didn't take.

You couldn't tell my grandson from a Frenchman.

And Senators! ...
I never saw the man I couldn't buy.

When my Ma died I boarded with a farmer
In the next county; I used to think of her,
And I looked round me, as I could,
And saw what it added up to: money.
Now I'm dying – I can't call this living –
I haven't any cause to change my mind.
They say that money isn't everything: it isn't;
Money don't help you none when you are sighing
For something else in this wide world to buy ...
The first time I couldn't think of anything
I didn't have, it shook me.
But giving does as well.

Miss E. J. Scovell's new book, *The River Steamer*, contains in addition to poems previously unpublished work reprinted from her scarce earlier volumes, and so gives a good perspective of her progress over ten years. At first sight, her poems are rather reminiscent of the utterances of the character Susan in *The Waves* – meditations on domestic and country themes, slow in tempo, each word having all the time it needs to make its full contribution.

But Susan was rather a dull girl, and one cannot read far in Miss Scovell without recognizing an extremely alert intelligence and perception.

Her poems are full of the actuality of daily life and observation, and while the impression they make is pleasing rather than powerful, this is a fair achievement when most poems make no impression at all. This poem 'The Swan's Feet' shows how adroitly she can build a poem on a single observation – namely that swans' feet are like big black leaves.

Who is this whose feet
Close on the water
Like muscled leaves darker than ivy
Blown back and curved by unwearying wind?
They, that thrust back the water,
Softly crumple now and close, stream in his wake.

These dank weeds are also
Part and plumage of the magnolia-flowering swan.
He puts forth these too –
Leaves of ridged and bitter ivy
Sooted in towns, coal-bright with rain.

He is not moved by winds in air
Like the vain boats on the lake.
Lest you think him too a flower of parchment,
Scentless magnolia,
See his living feet under the water fanning.
In the leaves' self blows the efficient wind
That opens and bends closed these leaves.

We tend to think of poems about childhood always in terms of the poet's own childhood, but children, like times of day and times of year, are part of Miss Scovell's natural subject-matter, and she is adept at conveying the curious blend of selfishness and vulnerability that makes up childhood. Here is one example: 'Sorrows of Childhood'.

Your griefs lie where they fall to earth.
Do you remember now your hamster's death? –
That died at night, no one to know,
Claiming at last its lost wild status so.

That death was altered when you cried.
Now it is in your hands the hamster died;
And in my head your fondling moan,
Though it was brief in time, sounds on and on.

Your griefs lie where they fall to ground.
You on your forward way do not look round.
Slighter, and yet incurable,
Your griefs in me, the ground on which they fall.

I find that many of Miss Scovell's poems divide into two parts: the original perception, which is good, and a kind of pushing forward to reach some sort of conclusion, which sometimes confuses rather than clarifies it. Her title-poem 'The River Steamer' does not suffer from this fault: she simply sets the scene – her favourite scene, it seems to me, of evening in summer – and is content to evoke in us the same almost-religious expectancy it evoked in her.

Waiting for a spirit to trouble the water,

Waiting for a spirit from beneath or over
To trouble the surface of the river
From which the hours like clouds reflected gaze
White, and the daylight shines of all earth's days,

Waiting for a spirit to dissolve the glass,
I see, in the unbreaking wave that fans from us,
Incline and circle the reeds and sedges;
And see the ripples on the under sides of bridges

And under the dark green leaves of deepest summer
And the green awning of the river steamer,
The secondary ripple, the shadow's shadow,
Abstract and pure appearance, follow and follow;

And see the roan banks flecked with rose and seed
Of willow herb, and fields beside the river-bed
Freshened by total light in day's decline,
And the elms standing in the heart of the sun;

And hear the passengers telling the day's praises,
And the tired wildness of their children's voices
Too young for the journey's hours; and all of these
Clear in the river's glass, I also praise,

Waiting for a spirit to transpierce the glaze.

Mr Edwin Muir's new book *One Foot in Eden* has already been the subject of a separate radio programme, but I cannot resist including a poem I find very charming and also rather outside Mr Muir's usual way of writing. It is called 'A Late Wasp', and shows Mr Muir taking a holiday from allegory and myth, for it is I think simply about a late wasp.

You that through all the dying summer
Came every morning to our breakfast table,
A lonely bachelor mummer,
And fed on the marmalade
So deeply, all your strength was scarcely able
To prise you from the sweet pit you had made, –
You and the earth have now grown older,
And your blue thoroughfares have felt a change;
They have grown colder;
And it is strange
How the familiar avenues of the air
Crumble now, crumble; the good air will not hold,
All cracked and perished with the cold;
And down you dive through nothing and through despair.

Perhaps the most important book of verse that has appeared recently is Miss Kathleen Raine's *Collected Poems*. For something like twenty years Miss Raine has inflexibly pursued in her poetry the most abstract of universal themes: time, the nature of reality, the life of man: and now she stands apart, almost a by-word for faithfulness to a personal vision, a purity of language and a seriousness of purpose. While I think that the failure-rate is bound to be high in this kind of abstract poetry, it is still hard to show in one or two poems the range of Miss Raine's success.

Here at any rate is one of the rather less abstract ones, called 'Night Thought':

I lie alone, in love
In a room that no one enters but myself,
Outside, in the world, I see the trees wave
In the sky in the rain, filled with their own life.

Inmate and prisoner of human walls,
Chairs, books and pictures, a red rose in a glass
Are real for me, built in surrounding space,
For out of life, no living creature fails.

Only desire, like radium, or the grail
Pierces the lead of sleep, the casket of the world,
All doors before its beams crumble and fall,
And the dense trees to quench it have no shade.

In its cup carrying my life, my heart passes
Through walls, through houses, through the stone of London,
Through dreams and real places –
O never, I pray my heart, come back again,

But go in peace, and enter my loves' rest,
Farther than sight can travel, and past thought –
O but there is no way, my heart is lost,
And tired returns, empty and crying to my breast.

In my dark room I weep that human love is so,
Blindly must go, and blindly still return,
Lost in the self it knows, and lost in the unknown,
Lost for beyond its life, no living heart can go.

One of Miss Raine's most characteristic ways of writing a poem is to build up a chain of images, each of which expresses a different facet of her subject, so that the poem has in fact no development at all. The effect is paradoxically both static and exciting, as may be seen from this poem, called 'The Unloved':

I am pure loneliness
I am empty air
I am drifting cloud.

I have no form
I am boundless
I have no rest.

I have no house
I pass through places
I am indifferent wind.

I am the white bird
Flying away from land
I am the horizon.

I am a wave
That will never reach the shore.

I am an empty shell
Cast up on the sand.

I am the moonlight
On the cottage with no roof.

I am the forgotten dead
In the broken vault on the hill.

I am the old man
Carrying his water in a pail.

I am light travelling in empty space.

I am a diminishing star
Speeding away
Out of the universe.

In her later poetry, the success of this incantatory method has led Miss Raine to experiment with a kind of pastiche of Old English and Celtic spell-poetry, and some of these – 'Spell against Sorrow', 'Spell to Bring Lost Creatures Home' – are remarkably fine. It is curious how well Miss Raine's intellectual abstractions combine with the strong rhythms of this primitive mode. This last poem is not strictly one of this group, but is allied to it both in rhythm and mind: it is called 'Two Invocations of Death', though I feel it does in fact make up one poem, the first half expressing an almost-ethical desire for annihilation, the second asking whether death will bring not only this, but also the lost meaning of life we are all continually seeking.

I

Death, I repent
Of these hands and feet
That for forty years
Have been my own
And I repent
Of flesh and bone,
Of heart and liver,
Of hair and skin –
Rid me, death,
Of face and form,
Of all that I am.

And I repent
Of the forms of thought,
The habit of mind
And the heart crippled
By long-spent pain,
The memory-traces
Faded and worn
Of vanished places
And human faces
Not rightly seen
Or understood
Rid me, death,
Of the words I have used.

Not this or that
But all is amiss
That I have done,
And I have seen
Sin and sorrow
Befoul the world –

Release me, death,
Forgive, remove
From place and time
The trace of all
That I have been.

II

From a place I came
That was never in time,
From the beat of a heart
That was never in pain,
The sun and the moon,
The wind and the world,
The song and the bird
Travelled my thought
Time out of mind.
Shall I know at last
My lost delight?

Tell me, death,
How long must I sorrow
My own sorrow?
While I remain
The world is ending,
Forests are falling,
Suns are fading,
While I am here
Now is ending
And in my arms
The living are dying.
Shall I come at last
To the lost beginning?

Words and words
Pour through my mind
Like sand in the shell
Of the ear's labyrinth,
The desert of brain's
Cities and solitudes,
Dreams, speculations
And vast forgetfulness.
Shall I learn at last
The lost meaning?

Oh my lost love
I have seen you fly
Away like a bird,
As a fish elude me,
A stone ignore me,

In a tree's maze
You have closed against me
The spaces of earth,
Prolonged to the stars'
Infinite distances,
With strange eyes
You have not known me,
Thorn you have wounded,
Fire you have burned
And talons torn me.
How long must I bear
Self and identity –
Shall I find at last
My lost being?

And lastly, just as a tailpiece, I should like to include a poem written by a young man of twenty-six and published a few months ago, called 'The Unplanted Primrose'. I shouldn't say it is an unforgettable poem, but I wonder whether you will feel, as I do, that despite its clumsiness of expression its author has a firm grip of the principle that the primary purpose of poetry is to convey emotion, and that this emotion should be no different in kind from that found in the novel, or indeed for that matter in human life itself. Here is the poem, 'The Unplanted Primrose'. Its author, by the way, is Thomas Hardy.

'A pink primrose from the plant he knows
Let me send him in his far spot,
From the root I brought to his garden-knot
When he dwelt herefrom but a little mile;
A root I had reared at that time of love,
And of all my stock the best that throve,
Which he took with so warm a smile.'

Such she sang and said, and aflush she sped
To her Love's old home hard by
Ere he left that nook for the wider sky
Of a southern country unassayed.
And she crept to the border of early stocks,
Of pansies, pinks and hollyhocks,
Where their vows and the gift were made.

'It has not bloomed!' And her glances gloomed
As she missed the expected hue.
'Yet the rest are in blow the border through;
Nor is leaf or bud of it evident.
Ah, can it have died of an over-care

In its tendance, sprung of his charge to spare
   No pains for its nourishment?'

She turned her round from the wrong ones found
   To the seat where a year before
She had brought it him as the best of her store,
And lo, on a ledge of the wall she neared,
Lay its withered skeleton, dry and brown,
Untouched since there he had laid it down
   When she waved and disappeared.

BBC Third Programme, 13 April 1956

'How or why I write poetry'

I have never claimed to know fully how or why I write poetry: it seems to me a skill easily damaged by self-consciousness, and poetic theory is not much good if it hinders the poet. If I must account for it, I think it would be best described as the only possible reaction to a particular kind of experience, a feeling that you are the only one to have noticed something, something especially beautiful or sad or significant. Then there follows a sense of responsibility, responsibility for preserving this remarkable thing by means of a verbal device that will set off the same experience in other people, so that they too will feel *How beautiful, how significant, how sad*, and the experience will be preserved. This does not mean it will always be a simple and non-intellectual thing. It may be complex, like perceiving the whole drift of a society. But the reaction is the same.

Does this mean my poetry is over-personal, in the sense of being narrow or shallow? Certainly the poems I write are bound up with the life I lead and the kind of person I am. But I don't think this makes them superficial; I think it improves them. If I avoid abstractions such as are found in politics and religion it's because they have never affected me strongly enough to become part of my personal life, and so to cease being abstractions. I suppose the kind of response I am seeking from the reader is, Yes, I know what you mean, life *is* like that; and for readers to say it not only now but in the future, and not only in England but anywhere in the world.

BBC Overseas Service, 20 August 1958

The Living Poet

When I look at my own poems, I can't help feeling that they are not altogether what I should have written had I had the chance. By this I don't mean, or don't only mean, that I should have written a good deal more a great deal better. That goes without saying. My point is that because what one writes depends so much on one's character and environment – either one writes about them or to escape from them – it follows that, basically, one no more chooses what one writes than one chooses the character one has or the environment one has. And further, one no more *likes* what one writes than the character one has or the environment one has. Critics who are about to censure a poet for the kind of poetry he writes might reflect that the chances are that he would agree with them.

Fortunately, there are always the subjects of one's poems to restore the balance and let in some fresh air. I quite realize that they too are chosen by our own natures no less than the tone one adopts with them and the moral one draws, but blessedly the links are for the most part out of sight and the subjects themselves free to expand. I sometimes think that the most successful poems are those in which subjects appear to float free from the preoccupations that chose them, and to exist in their own right, reassembled – one hopes – in the eternity of imagination. But I am frequently reminded of a story Forrest Reid tells about himself as a boy, lying in bed and watching the swallows nesting in the eaves of University Street, Belfast. Realizing they had flown all the way from Africa, he was astonished that with the whole world to choose from they should have picked University Street, Belfast. Well, I lived in Belfast myself for five years – not far from University Street – and one poem I wrote there was a kind of comic catalogue of the kinds of character and environment I *hadn't* had. It started as a satire on the 'artist's childhood' sort of novel, but ended by expressing something I realized I felt deeply. It's called 'I Remember, I Remember'. The journey mentioned, of course, was the journey up to Liverpool to get the Belfast boat.

Coming up England by a different line
For once, early in the cold new year,
We stopped, and, watching men with number-plates
Sprint down the platform to familiar gates,
'Why, Coventry!' I exclaimed. 'I was born here.'

I leant far out, and squinnied for a sign
That this was still the town that had been 'mine'
So long, but found I wasn't even clear
Which side was which. From where those cycle-crates
Were standing, had we annually departed

For all those family hols? ... A whistle went:
Things moved. I sat back, staring at my boots.
'Was that,' my friend smiled, 'where you "have your roots"?'
No, only where my childhood was unspent,
I wanted to retort, just where I started:

By now I've got the whole place clearly charted.
Our garden, first: where I did not invent
Blinding theologies of flowers and fruits,
And wasn't spoken to by an old hat.
And here we have that splendid family

I never ran to when I got depressed,
The boys all biceps and the girls all chest,
Their comic Ford, their farm where I could be
'Really myself'. I'll show you, come to that,
The bracken where I never trembling sat,

Determined to go through with it; where she
Lay back, and 'all became a burning mist'.
And, in those offices, my doggerel
Was not set up in blunt ten-point, nor read
By a distinguished cousin of the mayor,

Who didn't call and tell my father *There*
Before us, had we the gift to see ahead –
'You look as if you wished the place in Hell,'
My friend said, 'judging from your face.' 'Oh well,
I suppose it's not the place's fault,' I said.

'Nothing, like something, happens anywhere.'

Most people would agree that we don't, nowadays, believe in poetic diction or poetic subject-matter. All the same, I think there are certain received opinions still very much operative which the poet flouts at his peril. Take advertisements, for instance – like most people, I have always lived in towns, and am constantly seeing enormous pictorial billboards. When I was young, I condemned them as ugly and corrupting – that is the 'poetic' attitude. Later I learned to ignore them. Recently I've grown quite fond of them: they seem to me beautiful and in an odd way sad, like infinitely-debased Platonic essences. Now this is quite the wrong attitude: unfortunately, it was the only one that produced a poem. I called it, obviously enough, 'Essential Beauty'. You will be able to judge whether or not it comes off.

In frames as large as rooms that face all ways
And block the ends of streets with giant loaves,
Screen graves with custard, cover slums with praise
Of motor-oil and cuts of salmon, shine
Perpetually these sharply-pictured groves
Of how life should be. High above the gutter
A silver knife sinks into golden butter,
A glass of milk stands in a meadow, and
Well-balanced families, in fine
Midsummer weather, owe their smiles, their cars,
Even their youth, to that small cube each hand
Stretches towards. These, and the deep armchairs
Aligned to cups at bedtime, radiant bars
(Gas or electric), quarter-profile cats
By slippers on warm mats,
Reflect none of the rained-on streets and squares

They dominate outdoors. Rather, they rise
Serenely to proclaim pure crust, pure foam,
Pure coldness to our live imperfect eyes
That stare beyond this world, where nothing's made
As new or washed quite clean, seeking the home
All such inhabit. There, dark raftered pubs
Are filled with white-clothed ones from tennis-clubs,
And the boy puking his heart out in the Gents
Just missed them, as the pensioner paid
A halfpenny more for Granny Graveclothes' Tea
To taste old age, and dying smokers sense
Walking towards them through some dappled park
As if on water that unfocused she
No match lit up, nor drag ever brought near,
Who now stands newly clear,
Smiling, and recognizing, and going dark.

From time to time, however, one writes something that seems to have no bearing on one's character or environment at all. I can't for the life of me think why I should have wanted to write about Victorian drawing-room ballads: probably I must have heard one on the wireless, and thought how terrible it must be for an old lady to hear one of these songs she had learned as a girl and reflect how different life had turned out to be. Here is 'Love Songs in Age'.

She kept her songs, they took so little space,
 The covers pleased her:
One bleached from lying in a sunny place,
One marked in circles by a vase of water,
One mended, when a tidy fit had seized her,
 And coloured, by her daughter –
So they had waited, till in widowhood
She found them, looking for something else, and stood

Relearning how each frank submissive chord
 Had ushered in
Word after sprawling hyphenated word,
And the unfailing sense of being young
Spread out like a spring-woven tree, wherein
 That hidden freshness sung,
That certainty of time laid up in store
As when she played them first. But, even more,

The glare of that much-mentioned brilliance, love,
 Broke out, to show
Its bright incipience sailing above,
Still promising to solve, and satisfy,
And set unchangeably in order. So
 To pile them back, to cry,
Was hard, without lamely admitting how
It had not done so then, and could not now.

The most difficult kind of poem to write is the expression of a sharp uncomplicated experience, the vivid emotion you can't wind yourself into slowly but have to take a single shot at, hit or miss. Some fifteen years ago, in February, I heard a bird singing in some garden when I was walking home from work: after tea I tried to describe it, and after supper revised what I had written. That was the poem, and I must say I have always found it successful. It is called 'Coming' – what is coming, I suppose, is spring.

On longer evenings,
Light, chill and yellow,
Bathes the serene
Foreheads of houses.
A thrush sings,

Laurel-surrounded
In the deep bare garden,
Its fresh-peeled voice
Astonishing the brickwork.
It will be spring soon,
It will be spring soon –
And I, whose childhood
Is a forgotten boredom,
Feel like a child
Who comes on a scene
Of adult reconciling,
And can understand nothing
But the unusual laughter,
And starts to be happy.

But usually the experience is much more complicated. One Sunday afternoon in Ireland when I had cycled out into the country I came across a ruined church, the first I had seen. It made a deep impression on me. I had seen plenty of bombed churches, but never one that had simply fallen into disuse, and for a few minutes I felt the decline of Christianity in our century as tangibly as gooseflesh. The poem I subsequently wrote, called 'Church Going', did not seem altogether successful to me, and indeed the paper I eventually sent it to procrastinated about publishing it and finally lost it. In the end they did publish it, after about a year, and I immediately had a request from a publisher to send him a collection. I also had a letter from one of the paper's subscribers enclosing a copy of the Gospel of Saint John. In fact it has always been well liked. I think this is because it is about religion, and has a serious air that conceals the fact that its tone and argument are entirely secular.

Once I am sure there's nothing going on
I step inside, letting the door thud shut.
Another church: matting, seats, and stone,
And little books; sprawling of flowers, cut
For Sunday, brownish now; some brass and stuff
Up at the holy end; the small neat organ;
And a tense, musty, unignorable silence,
Brewed God knows how long. Hatless, I take off
My cycle-clips in awkward reverence,

Move forward, run my hand around the font.
From where I stand, the roof looks almost new –
Cleaned, or restored? Someone would know: I don't.
Mounting the lectern, I peruse a few

Hectoring large-scale verses, and pronounce
'Here endeth' much more loudly than I'd meant.
The echoes snigger briefly. Back at the door
I sign the book, donate an Irish sixpence,
Reflect the place was not worth stopping for.

Yet stop I did: in fact I often do,
And always end much at a loss like this,
Wondering what to look for: wondering, too,
When churches fall completely out of use
What shall we turn them into, if we shall keep
A few cathedrals chronically on show,
Their parchment, plate and pyx in locked cases,
And let the rest rent-free to rain and sheep.
Shall we avoid them as unlucky places?

Or, after dark, will dubious women come
To make their children touch a particular stone;
Pick simples for a cancer; or on some
Advised night see walking a dead one?
Power of some sort or other will go on
In games, in riddles, seemingly at random;
But superstition, like belief, must die,
And what remains when disbelief has gone?
Grass, weedy pavement, brambles, buttress, sky,

A shape less recognizable each week,
A purpose more obscure. I wonder who
Will be the last, the very last, to seek
This place for what it was; one of the crew
That tap and jot and know what rood-lofts were?
Some ruin-bibber, randy for antique,
Or Christmas-addict, counting on a whiff
Of gown-and-bands and organ-pipes and myrrh?
Or will he be my representative,

Bored, uninformed, knowing the ghostly silt
Dispersed, yet tending to this cross of ground
Through suburb scrub because it held unspilt
So long and equably what since is found
Only in separation – marriage, and birth,
And death, and thoughts of these – for which was built
This special shell? For, though I've no idea
What this accoutred frowsty barn is worth,
It pleases me to stand in silence here;

A serious house on serious earth it is,
In whose blent air all our compulsions meet,
Are recognized, and robed as destinies.
And that much never can be obsolete,

Since someone will forever be surprising
A hunger in himself to be more serious,
And gravitating with it to this ground,
Which, he once heard, was proper to grow wise in,
If only that so many dead lie round.

I have always tried to keep literature out of my poems as a subject, but I did once amuse myself by trying to describe the normal man's gradual abandonment of reading as a source of pleasure. When we are young, we identify ourselves with the hero; during adolescence, with the villain; but when we are grown up we see that our true likeness is to some minor and even contemptible figure, and this puts us off the whole business. I called it 'A Study of Reading Habits'.

When getting my nose in a book
Cured most things short of school,
It was worth ruining my eyes
To know I could still keep cool,
And deal out the old right hook
To dirty dogs twice my size.

Later, with inch-thick specs,
Evil was just my lark:
Me and my cloak and fangs
Had ripping times in the dark.
The women I clubbed with sex!
I broke them up like meringues.

Don't read much now: the dude
Who lets the girl down before
The hero arrives, the chap
Who's yellow and keeps the store,
Seem far too familiar. Get stewed:
Books are a load of crap.

The next poem is about the First World War, or the Great War as I still call it; or rather about the irreplaceable world that came to an end on 4 August 1914. It is called '1914', but written in roman numerals, as you might see it on a monument. It would be beyond me to write a poem called '1914' in arabic numerals. After finishing it, I found it had no main verb, but this was entirely accidental, not a piece of daring experimentalism.

Those long uneven lines
Standing as patiently
As if they were stretched outside

The Oval or Villa Park,
The crowns of hats, the sun
On moustached archaic faces
Grinning as if it were all
An August Bank Holiday lark;

And the shut shops, the bleached
Established names on the sunblinds,
The farthings and sovereigns,
And dark-clothed children at play
Called after kings and queens,
The tin advertisements
For cocoa and twist, and the pubs
Wide open all day;

And the countryside not caring:
The place-names all hazed over
With flowering grasses, and fields
Shadowing Domesday lines
Under wheat's restless silence;
The differently-dressed servants
With tiny rooms in huge houses,
The dust behind limousines;

Never such innocence,
Never before or since,
As changed itself to past
Without a word – the men
Leaving the gardens tidy,
The thousands of marriages
Lasting a little while longer:
Never such innocence again.

I said a few minutes ago that I tried to keep literature out of my poems: what I should have said is that I believe that art which takes its origin in other art is less likely to be successful than art founded in unsorted experience. I am ashamed, therefore, to have to admit that the next poem, 'Faith Healing', was written after seeing a film in which such a scene occurs. Still, it was a documentary film – the actors were real people who did not know that they were being photographed. This I hope mitigates the offence somewhat.

Slowly the women file to where he stands
Upright in rimless glasses, silver hair,
Dark suit, white collar. Stewards tirelessly
Persuade them onwards to his voice and hands,
Within whose warm spring rain of loving care

Each dwells some twenty seconds. *Now, dear child,*
What's wrong, the deep American voice demands,
And, scarcely pausing, goes into a prayer
Directing God about this eye, that knee.
Their hands are clasped abruptly; then, exiled

Like losing thoughts, they go in silence; some
Sheepishly stray, not back into their lives
Just yet; but some stay stiff, twitching and loud
With deep hoarse tears, as if a kind of dumb
And idiot child within them still survives
To re-awake at kindness, thinking a voice
At last calls them alone, that hands have come
To lift and lighten; and such joy arrives
Their thick tongues blort, their eyes squeeze grief, a crowd
Of huge unheard answers jam and rejoice –

What's wrong! Moustached in flowered frocks they shake:
By now, all's wrong. In everyone there sleeps
A sense of life lived according to love.
To some it means the difference they could make
By loving others, but across most it sweeps
As all they might have done had they been loved.
That nothing cures. An immense slackening ache,
As when, thawing, the rigid landscape weeps,
Spreads slowly through them – that, and the voice above
Saying *Dear child*, and all time has disproved.

Every now and then you will see some happening or situation that prompts you to think that if only you could get that down, in a kind of verbal photography, you would have a poem ready-made. This was what I felt some years ago when I happened to see a series of wedding parties at a succession of stations on the way to London one hot Saturday afternoon. Their cumulative effect produced an emotion so strong that I despaired of ever getting it under control; in the end, however, it produced 'The Whitsun Weddings'.

That Whitsun, I was late getting away:
  Not till about
One-twenty on the sunlit Saturday
Did my three-quarters-empty train pull out,
All windows down, all cushions hot, all sense
Of being in a hurry gone. We ran
Behind the backs of houses, crossed a street
Of blinding windscreens, smelt the fish-dock; thence
The river's level drifting breadth began,
Where sky and Lincolnshire and water meet.

All afternoon, through the tall heat that slept
  For miles inland,
A slow and stopping curve southwards we kept.
Wide farms went by, short-shadowed cattle, and
Canals with floatings of industrial froth;
A hothouse flashed uniquely: hedges dipped
And rose: and now and then a smell of grass
Displaced the reek of buttoned carriage-cloth
Until the next town, new and nondescript,
Approached with acres of dismantled cars.

At first, I didn't notice what a noise
  The weddings made
Each station that we stopped at: sun destroys
The interest of what's happening in the shade,
And down the long cool platforms whoops and skirls
I took for porters larking with the mails,
And went on reading. Once we started, though,
We passed them, grinning and pomaded, girls
In parodies of fashion, heels and veils,
All posed irresolutely, watching us go,

As if out on the end of an event
  Waving goodbye
To something that survived it. Struck, I leant
More promptly out next time, more curiously,
And saw it all again in different terms:
The fathers with broad belts under their suits
And seamy foreheads; mothers loud and fat;
An uncle shouting smut; and then the perms,
The nylon gloves and jewellery-substitutes,
The lemons, mauves, and olive-ochres that

Marked off the girls unreally from the rest.
  Yes, from cafés
And banquet-halls up yards, and bunting-dressed
Coach-party annexes, the wedding-days
Were coming to an end. All down the line
Fresh couples climbed aboard: the rest stood round:
The last confetti and advice were thrown,
And, as we moved, each face seemed to define
Just what it saw departing: children frowned
At something dull; fathers had never known

Success so huge and wholly farcical;
  The women shared
The secret like a happy funeral;
While girls, gripping their handbags tighter, stared
At a religious wounding. Free at last,

And loaded with the sum of all they saw,
We hurried towards London, shuffling gouts of steam.
Now fields were building-plots, and poplars cast
Long shadows over major roads, and for
Some fifty minutes, that in time would seem

Just long enough to settle hats and say
I nearly died,
A dozen marriages got under way.
They watched the landscape, sitting side by side
– An Odeon went past, a cooling tower,
And someone running up to bowl – and none
Thought of the others they would never meet
Or how their lives would all contain this hour.
I thought of London spread out in the sun,
Its postal districts packed like squares of wheat:

There we were aimed. And as we raced across
Bright knots of rail
Past standing Pullmans, walls of blackened moss
Came close, and it was nearly done, this frail
Travelling coincidence; and what it held
Stood ready to be loosed with all the power
That being changed can give. We slowed again,
And as the tightened brakes took hold, there swelled
A sense of falling, like an arrow-shower
Sent out of sight, somewhere becoming rain.

My next poem, 'Sunny Prestatyn', is rather difficult to describe: like the last one, the scene is a railway station, only this time I am looking at one of those cheerful posters okayed by some seaside town's publicity manager, showing the most convenient shorthand for happiness, a beautiful girl. Unfortunately, some travellers have been at work and the result is funny or terrifying, whichever way you look at it. If you are like me, it is both.

Come to Sunny Prestatyn
Laughed the girl on the poster,
Kneeling up on the sand
In tautened white satin.
Behind her, a hunk of coast, a
Hotel with palms
Seemed to expand from her thighs and
Spread breast-lifting arms.

She was slapped up one day in March.
A couple of weeks, and her face
Was snaggle-toothed and boss-eyed;

Huge tits and a fissured crotch
Were scored well in, and the space
Between her legs held scrawls
That set her fairly astride
A tuberous cock and balls

Autographed *Titch Thomas*, while
Someone had used a knife
Or something to stab right through
The moustached lips of her smile.
She was too good for this life.
Very soon, a great transverse tear
Left only a hand and some blue.
Now *Fight Cancer* is there.

The last poem brings me back full circle to the character and environment business. A year or two ago I was visiting my college, and in conversation the don who had been Dean in my day remarked that a man who had been some years behind me now had a son at the place. This led me to reflect how very different our lives must have been, so different as to suggest different concepts of life behind them, and I wondered where these concepts came from. This is what 'Dockery and Son' is about. It is the last poem I wrote, and so I have a particular affection for it. There is always the chance, after all, that one's last poem may turn out to be just that.

'Dockery was junior to you,
Wasn't he?' said the Dean. 'His son's here now.'
Death-suited, visitant, I nod. 'And do
You keep in touch with —' Or remember how
Black-gowned, unbreakfasted, and still half-tight
We used to stand before that desk, to give
'Our version' of 'these incidents last night'?
I try the door of where I used to live:

Locked. The lawn spreads dazzlingly wide.
A known bell chimes. I catch my train, ignored.
Canal and clouds and colleges subside
Slowly from view. But Dockery; good Lord,
Anyone up today must have been born
In '43, when I was twenty-one.
If he was younger, did he get this son
At nineteen, twenty? Was he that withdrawn

High-collared public-schoolboy, sharing rooms
With Cartwright who was killed? Well, it just shows

How much ... How little ... Yawning, I suppose
I fell asleep, waking at the fumes
And furnace-glares of Sheffield, where I changed,
And ate an awful pie, and walked along
The platform to its end to see the ranged
Joining and parting lines reflect a strong

Unhindered moon. To have no son, no wife,
No house or land still seemed quite natural.
Only a numbness registered the shock
Of finding out how much had gone of life,
How widely from the others. Dockery, now:
Only nineteen, he must have taken stock
Of what he wanted, and been capable
Of ... No, that's not the difference: rather, how

Convinced he was he should be added to!
Why did he think adding meant increase?
To me it was dilution. Where do these
Innate assumptions come from? Not from what
We think truest, or most want to do:
Those warp tight-shut, like doors. They're more a style
Our lives bring with them: habit for a while,
Suddenly they harden into all we've got

And how we got it; looked back on, they rear
Like sand-clouds, thick and close, embodying
For Dockery a son, for me nothing,
Nothing with all a son's harsh patronage.
Life is first boredom, then fear.
Whether or not we use it, it goes,
And leaves what something hidden from us chose,
And age, and then the only end of age.

BBC Third Programme, 3 July 1964

Larkin at Fifty

Really one should ignore one's fiftieth birthday. As anyone over fifty will tell you, it's no age at all. All the same it is rather sobering to realize one has lived longer than Arnold of Rugby or Porson, the eighteenth-century Professor of Greek. It's hard not to look back and wonder why one hasn't done more or forward and wonder what ... what if anything, you'll do in the future. I seem to have spent my life waiting for poems to turn up. That's probably a negative attitude, but writing isn't an act of the will, all you can do is try to make sure that when something does arrive, you aren't too tired or too busy or anything else to do it justice. As regards the future, I doubt if writers get better after they're fifty and I don't suppose I shall be any exception. Can one find fresh things to say, or fresh ways of saying them? Will one 'develop'? There's a great pressure on writers to 'develop' these days. I think the idea began with Yeats and personally I'm rather sceptical of it. What I should like to do is to write different kinds of poems that might be by different people. Someone once said that the great thing is not to be different from other people but to be different from yourself. That's why I've chosen to read now a poem that isn't especially like me, or like what I fancy I'm supposed to be like. It's called 'The Explosion'.

On the day of the explosion
Shadows pointed towards the pithead:
In the sun the slagheap slept.

Down the lane came men in pitboots
Coughing oath-edged talk and pipe-smoke,
Shouldering off the freshened silence.

One chased after rabbits; lost them;
Came back with a nest of lark's eggs;
Showed them; lodged them in the grasses.

So they passed in beards and moleskins,
Fathers, brothers, nicknames, laughter,
Through the tall gates standing open.

At noon, there came a tremor; cows
Stopped chewing for a second; sun,
Scarfed as in a heat-haze, dimmed.

The dead go on before us, they
Are sitting in God's house in comfort,
We shall see them face to face –

Plain as lettering in the chapels
It was said, and for a second
Wives saw men of the explosion

Larger than in life they managed –
Gold as on a coin, or walking
Somehow from the sun towards them,

One showing the eggs unbroken.

BBC Radio Three, 9 August 1972

NOTE: This birthday tribute, introduced by George MacBeth, included W. H. Auden, Kingsley Amis, John Betjeman, Robert Conquest, Douglas Dunn, Roy Fuller, Ted Hughes and Anthony Thwaite. Each spoke about, and then read, a favourite Larkin poem. The programme ended with Larkin's own contribution.

On *The Oxford Book of Twentieth-Century English Verse*

ANTHONY THWAITE: *Philip, you're not generally regarded as somebody who keeps up in any very strict sense with what is going on in contemporary verse. Some people might think it surprising that you were asked to edit this anthology. What were your own feelings when you were asked to do so?*

PHILIP LARKIN: I was very honoured. I don't think it's the kind of invitation that many people would refuse, and I liked the idea of the challenge. You're right in saying that I'm not somebody who's forced by his job, for instance, to know what they think about twentieth-century English verse. I haven't got all my ideas sorted out and laid in neat rows. I hoped they would emerge.

Once you'd accepted the idea, how did you go about it?

Well, in simplistic terms, I read all the poetry produced in this century, which took about four and a half years, and then picked out the bits I liked the best.

How physically did you do this?

First of all, having decided what the title meant, which wasn't altogether easy – what 'twentieth-century' means, where you begin, where you end, what 'English' means – I then made a list of about three hundred poets who seemed to qualify: it finished up by being about four hundred and fifty. I then tried to get hold of their collected works if they had them, or all their books if they hadn't. As a librarian, I was well placed to do this. Of course, I possess books myself. My library possesses books, and I could borrow books from other libraries perhaps more easily than some people. But in the end I increasingly felt the need for a copyright library that really would have everything and that would show me what I didn't know, and that was why I was so glad at the end to go to Oxford and spend four months in the Bodleian actually handling the stuff and picking up things I'd never heard of.

And once you'd got down to the Bodleian grind, how did you go about it then? Did you work through chronologically or alphabetically, starting with Abercrombie and working down to Yeats?
It was more or less chronologically. The Bodleian were very kind: they let me into their stacks, and I used to go there every morning at ten o'clock and go down into the depths and work along the shelves, physically handling all the books. I didn't try to read them then and there: in the afternoons I would sit in the Upper Reading Room, having had them sent up to me, and read them in comparative peace.

Did you have some notion from the beginning that certain poets had to be in it, and very fully represented?
I think anybody would have thought that: that wasn't a difficulty.

I've done some statistical work on the anthology and some of the representation at the top end of the scale – that is, people that you rather heavily represent in terms of numbers of poems and numbers of pages – strikes me as surprising. I'm wondering whether it now strikes you as surprising or whether it's what you intended from the beginning? The poet who is most fully represented in terms of numbers of pages is Eliot with 29 pages; Hardy and Auden, 24 pages each; Yeats, 21 pages; Kipling 19 – I begin to wonder here – Betjeman 18; Basil Bunting 11; Dylan Thomas 10½.
You're counting pages: I didn't have the advantage of seeing the thing in terms of pages until the proofs arrived. I tended to work more in terms of poems. The people you've mentioned, with one possible exception, I gave no limit to. I just wanted to represent them fully. I thought I had given the maximum representation to Hardy: he certainly got more poems than anyone else. You must remember that some people write longer poems than others, which tends to step up their page count. With others – Eliot, for instance – you are limited by publishers. The fact that Bunting, for one, has a high page count only means that I did want to put in one of his long poems, and, you know, long poems are long.

One thing that strikes me very forcibly about the book is how strongly the Georgians come through in the earlier part of the anthology. There has, it's true, been a certain amount of rehabilitation work on the Georgians in recent years, but I don't know of any anthology that makes them come across as strongly as this one. J. C. Squire comes across with 9½ pages

and Wilfrid Gibson with 6½, and if one looks at the cold statistics, I, at any rate, might have thought: what is Larkin up to? But when I actually read the poems – and in many cases I hadn't read the Squire and Gibson poems before – I was very, very struck. You have resuscitated these poets for me. Did you feel that the Georgians needed to be thought about again in this really rather radical way?
I did want to look at them. I think it's true to say I read them, which some people, I think, haven't done for a long time. I had in my mind a notion that there might have been what I'll call, for want of a better phrase, an English tradition coming from the nineteenth century with people like Hardy, which was interrupted partly by the Great War, when many English poets were killed off, and partly by the really tremendous impact of Yeats, whom I think of as Celtic, and Eliot, whom I think of as American. And I wondered whether, if one looked for them, there hadn't been some quite good poems which had become unfashionable which had never been dug up again and looked at. I certainly had this in mind when reading. But, quite honestly, the Georgians didn't resuscitate themselves in my mind. I like the poems I've included, but there are only two poems by Squire: true, one of them is very long.

But they do take up a lot of space. The stockyard one is very, very good.
I'd never read that before. I thought it extremely good. But a lot of the others I was disappointed in, and the worst thing about the Georgians as a class was, I am afraid, what has already been said by so many people: that their language was stale. It was Eliot and Yeats, and perhaps even Pound, who sharpened up the language.

Another thing that comes through to me very strongly reading the anthology is that it keeps pace with history. It can be read, in fact, as a kind of social history, so that if one reads it chronologically from the beginning to the end, one has a sense of tracing the events of the time as if through documents. You get the changing countryside, and the Depression, and the two world wars. I don't know of any other anthology that does this so firmly and often so movingly. Is this something that you were aiming for quite consciously?
Possibly. I did want to put in a number of poems which I felt couldn't have been written in any other century: poems about the H-Bomb, for instance, are an obvious example, and poems about the wars. But there is also a poem about having cancer, a poem about being a homosexual. There is a poem – or a part of a poem –

about strikes. These things I did want to put in for local colour, as you say. But of course poets as a class are not terribly good at social scenes. I don't think the nineteenth-century poets were very good at the Industrial Revolution. But I'm glad it came off, if it did.

It comes across very often in the single poem by a single poet. There was a very good poem by somebody I've never heard of before called May Wedderburn Cannan, 'Rouen 1915'.
Oh, I loved that. I found that in the Bodleian in the depths of the stacks, and immediately knew that this was something that had to go in. It seemed to me to have all the warmth and idealism of the VADs in the First World War. I find it enchanting.

I don't know what else she wrote: I can't imagine there was anything else as good as this. I can see precisely why that poem is there, it makes its point. Another one from somebody I did know, and indeed a poem I'd read before, was the single poem by John Pudney from the Second World War called 'Missing'. Again, it has a kind of resonance which goes beyond anything else Pudney has written, and pretty well had to be there in your scheme of things, to represent one kind of attitude to the Second World War. Is this why you chose it, or do you simply say: 'Oh well, I liked the poem and put it in for that reason'?
I begin to wonder how old you are, Anthony, because during the war Pudney's poems were very, very popular, and that poem, and the other one about 'Johnny Head-in-Air', seemed to express the fighter pilot generation completely.

I am aware of that. In fact, I saw the movies in which those were part of the script. My point is this: that many anthologists of our time would say that these Pudney poems are not very good poems. I wouldn't argue from a strictly literary point of view that Pudney's poems, including 'Missing', are good, but in the context of the anthology I can see very well indeed why it's there: it makes its point, and it makes it movingly. Can you see the kind of distinction I'm trying to make between a poem that really makes sense in an anthology like this and a poem which must be judged nakedly, and apart from anything else that is going on around it, as a good poem?
I made that distinction myself, I think, when I was assembling my final collection. I found that I had three groups of poems. First, the representation of the big names who had to be there, and who I agreed had to be there, and who everybody else agreed had to be

there. Secondly there were the poems not necessarily by people who had to be there but which I thought ought to be there in their own right as poems. Thirdly, there was the group you're talking about – or poems which were good essential twentieth-century poems, which show you what the twentieth-century was like: 'Ah yes, that's typically twentieth-century, it couldn't have been any other century.' These three groups overlap a bit, of course.

I think they do. We all know what you mean by the first group: about thirty names who are the big guns, and they're going to be there and they are there and they're very fully represented. But there is an overlap between the second and third group, the second group being the single-poem merchants – that is almost what it amounts to – where you don't think that X or Y is really worth putting in very fully but X or Y has written one poem which is so good that it must be there. Let's take the single-poem merchants in your book: the poem by F. Pratt Green which I knew already and like very much called 'The Old Couple', and there's a poem by Laurence Lerner called 'A Wish' about the idea of being a woman. Now these two seem to me extremely good poems – far, far better than anything else that these two poets have written. But then there is this third group, which merges into the second one, and it can include slightly eccentric things like the Noel Coward poem you've included, 'The Boy Actor', the Christopher Isherwood about his queerness, but also the May Wedderburn Cannan and the John Pudney. They're all, in a way, poems of their century: do you see what I mean?
Yes.

And yet they're making very different points.
This would to some extent have been overemphasized and spoiled if the poems had been in a kind of logical order. The kind of order they are in is the date of birth of the poet, and so you get the most extraordinary confrontations and inconsistencies. You get A. P. Herbert's poem about help for Russia, Stalin and all that sort of thing, coming before Wilfred Owen just because Herbert was born before Owen. I think the contrast gains from this jumbling. If it had all been arranged so that Pudney was next door to Herbert, it would have been less striking.

Do you feel at all vulnerable about what might be considered to be eccentricities in your anthology? I'm not suggesting that your anthology is as eccentric as your predecessor Yeats's Oxford Book of Modern

Verse. *You haven't done anything as obviously crazy as his inclusion of 16 pages of Dorothy Wellesley and 16 pages of Sturge Moore and of W. J. Turner. But are you aware, now that you see the whole book bound together, that it might be thought odd or eccentric in any possible Yeatsian sort of way?*
This is something I look to the reviewers to point out. If I did it all over again, which heaven forfend, I doubt if I would make any major changes. I can't think of anybody substantial that isn't represented, though they may not be represented properly. One or two poems are in I would prefer not to see in. One or two people might have been more fully represented. The difficulty with doing an anthology of poems of your own time, and particularly when you get up to the terminal date, which in my case was 1965 – I began it in 1966 so I thought I'd go up to the last year – is that you haven't got the help of that greatest anthologist, time. You're really just bashing away by instinct. The people who are going to be good are not yet fully good: their time will come. The little poems you see and like you can't be sure whether they're flashes in the pan or not. I think the anthology tends to tail off a bit, but that was an impression I gained from reading the whole period – that in the Sixties we were in a bit of a trough.

You did, in fact, relax this 1965 ruling, didn't you? In the last few pages there are people who started publishing their work in book form after 1965.
It would have meant an awfully unrepresentative end otherwise. The Liverpool boys really hadn't been published by 1965.

You felt they had to be in.
I did, yes. I like them.

I myself can see something like a dozen omissions, complete omissions of poets who really had some right to be in there if X and Y and Z and the Liverpool poets are included, but I don't think this is a very profitable line to follow. I would agree with you that there is a tailing-off towards the end, and in your preface you remark: 'Looking at what I have chosen, I see that it represents a much greater number of poets than are to be found in the volumes corresponding to this one for the nineteenth and eighteenth centuries. To some extent, this is due to the kind of book I wanted to produce, but it also prompts the conclusion that once the anthologist has to deal with poets born after 1914 his loyalty turns perforce to poems rather than to individuals.' Is 1914 the crucial birth-date: is it with poets

born after that that things tend to fall away? Are you saying that after Dylan Thomas there is no commanding poet?
Yes, really. And this is a popular point of view. I'm not Dylan Thomas's greatest admirer, but I do feel that he was the last person to produce a corpus of work that really was worth arguing about and obtained an international reputation. Plenty of people were born after Dylan Thomas and wrote quite nicely, but I don't think, to be quite honest, that we have had his equal.

There are two points one can make about Dylan Thomas, apart from the fact that he was very good. The first is that he's dead, and the second is that he was eight years older than you by birth-date. Is it possible for you, a poet, to judge your contemporaries and juniors fairly?
I tried throughout my selection to put my own taste reasonably in the background. One was also looking for the number of books, the number of articles, about a poet, which poets are set for A levels and that sort of thing, and in saying or implying that about Dylan Thomas, I think I was doing no more than saying what is generally thought at sixth form level.

I don't think that's entirely so, because, for one thing, if one's taking what one might call the standard-English-schoolmaster-of-1973 line, his thinking might run something like this ... One poet per decade, as it were. We have Dylan Thomas, and after Dylan Thomas there's the decade of people born in the Twenties: who is there? Philip Larkin. Then there is the decade of people born in the Thirties: who is there? Ted Hughes. Now I don't think that's quite the way that Larkin and Hughes come out in the anthology. I can see how difficult it must have been to represent yourself in the book. I myself would have given more space to you: I would have included not only 'The Whitsun Weddings' but 'Church Going', I'd have included 'Mr Bleaney'. As for Ted Hughes, though he has quite a reasonable amount of representation as far as pages go, he doesn't emerge as quite the dominating figure he has seemed to many people in the last 15 years. I would have put in perhaps one from 'Crow', though this is not a work that either of us admire as much as many people do. I would certainly have put in more of his first two books. Here are two post-Dylan Thomas poets, yourself and Hughes, whom many people would have thought should have emerged more strongly from the book.
As an anthologist, one is very shy and fearful about seeming to over-represent oneself. About Ted Hughes, I said earlier that I was a little remorseful about not representing some poets more fully

than I had, and he's one of them. I really ought to have put in one from *Crow*. *Crow* itself came out late in 1970, when I had more or less wrapped up the selection except for the top dressing, so to speak, and I was uncertain of it myself. Now I would certainly put something in from there. You can put this down as a failure of taste or a failure of nerve or whatever you like. One tended, in dealing with one's contemporaries and with people younger than oneself, to say: right ho, five or six of each and let time do the sorting out. I think I was holding back a little from putting my money down on any particular people, and, for all we know, the poets of the Fifties and Sixties may not be Larkin and Hughes at all: they may be Davie and Brian Patten.

My feeling with your book is that after Thomas it's not a matter of five or six poems from so-and-so, but the singletons: we have this great parade of single poems, which starts up just about then with poets born from 1920 onwards. I think it's this that makes me concur with your feeling that perhaps there's a slight falling-off towards the end. There's a great splatter of the target with single poems: many of them are good, but there's a feeling that the whole thing somehow disintegrates into a lot of nice amiable small poets.
That's just what I think English poetry does.

You talk in your preface about wide rather than deep representation, and I've been comparing your anthology with other Oxford anthologies, and have come to, not conclusions, but again statistics. You include 207 poets – let's call it 200-odd.
That seems a terrible lot. I'd be interested to know how many of them are singly represented. Quite a lot of things I put in because I wanted to know where to find them myself in the future. Humbert Wolfe's 'You cannot hope to bribe or twist, thank God, the British journalist': everybody knows that, but nobody knows where to put their finger on it.

What do you mean by wide rather than deep representation? Is it, in fact, inevitable with an anthology of one's own day that one's going to have a wide scatter?
I think if you are producing an anthology you've got to compromise to some extent. You could produce a purely historical anthology: this is what poetry in this century was like – it may not be the best poetry, it may not be the most enjoyable poetry, but

this is what it was like. Well, that's one way of doing it. The other way, or *an* other way, is the critical approach: this is the best poetry of the century. And there would be about thirty names in it, and it would be full of poems that everybody already possesses, and it would be critically irreproachable. But it wouldn't be historically true, and it might not always be as enjoyable as it might have been if you'd let in a few little strays. The third way is to pick just the poems you personally find enjoyable, but that would have been too personal: it would have left out things that were critically accepted, it would have left out people who, like Everest, were there. In the end, you have to compromise. Sometimes you are acting historically, sometimes you are acting critically, sometimes you're acting just as a reader who reaches out to his bedside table and picks up a book and wants to have a quick change of mood and enjoy himself. I tried to cater for all these people.

What you've just been saying is the sort of thing which you might have said in an extended preface. Your own preface to this book is very brief. Were you ever tempted to try a full-length preface like Yeats?
Not really, because very early on the Press said that although they would like an introduction, it need not be a manifesto, and they added quickly that they would prefer it not to be. That was a pretty fair direction, and it accorded with my own feelings. I'm not a theorist, I'm not a critic, I'm not an academic. In a sense, the selection itself is my preface, if that's not too metaphysical. I have no real desire to lay down the law about anything. I hope it's a broad-minded anthology.

I would support that. On the whole, my feeling is that it's a very original anthology, and that it has a distinct personal flavour without being eccentric – and that, I think, is what you were aiming at.

BBC Radio Three, 12 April 1973

Desert Island Discs

ROY PLOMLEY: *On our desert island this week is the poet Philip Larkin. Mr Larkin, are you a gregarious man?*
PHILIP LARKIN: I never think of myself as a gregarious man but having thought about your island for a few weeks I've come to the conclusion that I probably am. I should be very happy there for about twenty-four hours, and fairly happy for another forty-eight hours, but after that I suspect that I should miss people and society in general.

What would you be happiest to have got away from?
Well, as I say I don't think I'd be happy to get away from anything. The instant answer is work – but over the years I've come to think that I rather like work.

What was your plan in choosing your eight records?
Well, either records that I have known and liked for a long time simply because they seem to me marvellous musical experiences, or else music that reminds me of probably rather imaginary things that I like thinking about, but they are not as you would say nostalgic.

What's the first one?
The first one is a Louis Armstrong record. I suppose any jazz lover has to decide which Louis Armstrong record he is taking, because there are so many and Louis is such a combined Chaucer and Shakespeare of jazz. I've chosen 'Dallas Blues' from 1929 because I've been playing it for about forty years and never got tired of it. It is a blues, and Armstrong plays it in a beautiful warm and relaxed way that he doesn't always achieve on his later more showmanship sides.

[Record: Louis Armstrong, 'Dallas Blues']

Louis Armstrong – 'Dallas Blues'. You're a jazz lover, you've been playing that record for forty years, do you play an instrument yourself?

I don't, no. I wish I'd been taught, forcibly if necessary when I was young. The only musical instrument, if you can call it musical, I tried to play was the drums, but I never got very far with them and of course in those days there were no friends around the corner with whom you could form a group.

You wrote about jazz for a number of years didn't you?
I had the job of reviewing jazz records in the *Daily Telegraph* for ten years, which I enjoyed very much. But there came a point when I felt that, not only had I said all I had to say, but I was losing sympathy with the kind of jazz that was coming out and I thought it proper to close down.

Let's have your second record, what's that to be?
This is a Newcastle street song, I think dating from the 1790s, sung by Louis Killen. It's called 'Dollia'; it's about one regiment, the Black Cuffs, leaving the garrison and another regiment, the Green Cuffs, replacing them and the effect it has on the local female population. I like it, not only because it has a curious haunting tune but I always have a faint private feeling it's half about the departure of winter and the coming of spring.

[Record: Louis Killen, 'Dollia']

A Newcastle street song by Louis Killen. You were born in Coventry weren't you?
That's right, yes.

Were you brought up in a house with a lot of books to explore?
I suppose I was. My father was not a literary man but he was a great collector of books and when I went up to Oxford I found that I had in fact been brought up with many more books than my contemporaries – you know, we had all Lawrence, we had all Hardy, we had all Huxley, we had all Somerset Maugham, Katherine Mansfield, Forster, and I had somehow absorbed these things, whereas my friends often were still grappling with them, but they were novels, they weren't poetry. I think perhaps I should make that point.

Now you read English at Oxford, with a view to what?
This was the War, 1940, I don't think one really had a view to anything in those days, one thought one would be called up after about four terms and after that it was all in the lap of the gods.

Had you started writing?
Oh yes, I suppose I began writing at the age when everyone does, not very well but prolifically, both poems and prose. I always thought I should be a novelist, that was what I wanted to be, but after a couple of novels, the third one never got finished, and I had to fall back on poems.

What was your first job?
My first job was the Librarian of the library of an urban district council in Shropshire, a very small one and one which I think is now much more flourishing as part of the county system. It was an ordinary public library where one lent books to old age pensioners and children and performed the various simple tasks like putting newspapers in the newsroom. I was the Librarian and the only Librarian. I stoked the boiler and opened the doors in the morning and closed them at night. I can really claim to have started at the bottom. The previous Librarian used to scrub the floors as well but I said I didn't want to do that.

And you also published your first book of poems at that time.
Yes, that was in 1945, and then the first novel *Jill* was 1946 and the second novel *A Girl in Winter* was 1947, and then a profound silence descended.

Now you've been a librarian ever since you started in Shropshire. You moved on to where – Leicester next?
To University College, Leicester, as it was in those days, now the University, that was in 1946, and in 1950 I went to Queen's University Belfast where I stayed till 1955, and then I was appointed Librarian of the University of Hull where I have been ever since.

How greatly has the Library increased in size in your twenty-one years?
I suppose bookwise there must have been about 120,000 books when I went and there must be just over half-a-million now. But this is only really due to the natural expansion of the University. This has been a tremendous boom period these twenty years, which has now alas finished.

Let's have your third record now, what's that to be?
Well, I should want something for Sundays which suggests Church music. There's an enormous amount to choose from, and

I think oddly enough Church music is a kind of music I like very much in the same way as jazz. I don't know why this should be so, unless agnostics are naturally romantic about religion, but I could pick any one of ten or twenty records but I think I would be very happy with Thomas Tallis's Forty-part Motet – *Spem in alium*, which is sung here by the Choir of King's College, Cambridge.

[Record: Tallis, Forty-part Motet – *Spem in alium*]

The closing passage of Thomas Tallis's Forty-part Motet – Spem in alium, *by the Choir of King's College, Cambridge. Now you're one of this country's best-known poets but your output has been remarkably small. A slim volume, really, every ten years.*
I suppose it depends whom you are comparing me with. I don't think it's too small compared with Housman, for instance. This has not been intentional, I write as much as I can and publish as much as I can. I think in the last ten years or so I have published almost everything I have written, there have been fewer false starts. Occasionally one publishes a poem and then decides it isn't worth collecting, there are perhaps half a dozen of those poems lying around, but I certainly haven't got a great mass of unpublished poems.

Do you write for yourself or to communicate a feeling to others?
I certainly write to be read, there would be very little point in writing something that nobody was going to read, but it is not quite communicating in the sense of writing a letter to the *Times* for instance. You try to create something in words that will reproduce in somebody else who has never met you and perhaps isn't even living in the same cultural society as yourself, that somebody else will read and so get the experience that you had and that forced you to write the poem. It's a kind of preservation by re-creation, if I can put it that way.

You are not in any way a 'difficult' or 'abstruse' poet, your poems are very simple and now this strikes me as being due to a great deal of effort to make them so.
I think that a poem should be understood at first reading line by line, but I don't think it should be exhausted at that first reading. I hope that what I write gives the reader something when they read it first, enough in fact to make them read it again and so on *ad infinitum.*

If just one of your poems was to survive which one would you like it to be?

That really is a most difficult question because one doesn't really think of one's poems as favourites or better or anything like that. I suppose I would choose 'The Whitsun Weddings' as being a fairly full expression of one particular theme that I wanted to deal with.

That was the title poem of the volume you published in 1964. You can never be persuaded to read your verse in public?

I've never much cared for the interpolation of any reader between the poem and the audience. It seems to me to be as likely to detract from the reader's appreciation as to add to it. Personally I don't think I am a very good reader, I haven't got a very dramatic voice, and balancing the times when I might make the audience understand the poem a little better I have to weigh the chance that I might just make them sound boring and unintentionally limit them in some way.

Although you have made one record of your poems which was very successful.

I've made three records actually, but in the spirit that I hope that this would not be the first time that people should meet the poems; I would hope that they would come to the records when they would know the poems and say, well, let's see what the author adds to this poem that we know already. I think that is a situation in which reading can be helpful.

I feel that I ought to be calling you of course, Doctor Larkin, you have a splendid number of Honorary Doctorates from, what is it, six or seven Universities?

I don't think it's quite as many as that but I have been very gratified by the offer of them.

And an impressive list of awards and prizes, the Queen's Gold Medal, Arts Council Awards and so on.

Yes, well they have to go to somebody, you know.

Record number four?

Well, record number four is in fact the last record that Bessie Smith, the blues singer, ever made, and this was in 1933. She didn't know it was her last record, in fact it proved to be so, she was killed in 1937 – it's called 'I'm Down in the Dumps', a more misleading title I can't imagine. She sounds full of life and, as she says, vitality, and for the first time she's playing with an accompanying group of Thirties' musicians – Jack Teagarden, Frankie Newton, even Benny Goodman is reputed to have been in the studio, and she obviously regarded it as the beginning of a new career and I think it could have been, if only the record companies had taken her up. I suspect that it is the first time that she ever recorded with a string bass, for instance, but it does show Bessie having successfully got into the Thirties and left the Twenties behind.

[Record: Bessie Smith, 'I'm Down in the Dumps']

Bessie Smith, 'I'm Down in the Dumps'. Now a few years ago you were offered a very daunting literary assignment.
You mean the job of selecting the *Oxford Book of Twentieth-Century English Verse*? Well, I didn't think of it as daunting when I accepted it, I thought it was a very great honour which it was. I thought it would be very lucrative, which it has been.

How long did it take you?
I undertook it in 1966, and I handed in the completed copy in 1971, so that would be about five years.

Yes, the last similar compilation was done by Yeats I do believe.
It was indeed, yes.

A massive job of reading. How did you set about planning it all?
It was quite easy for me as a Librarian to get and read the collected works of virtually every poet who flourished in this century.

How many roughly?
Oh heavens, I don't know, four or five hundred I suppose, but there came a point when I wanted to read the poets that I had never heard of and I thought the only way to do that was to go to a copyright library for a few months and prevail on them to let me go down into their stacks and literally handle every book they possessed, and I managed to do that through the kind offices of the Bodleian Library at Oxford. And that gave me a great many little finds that I was pleased to add and I thought might diversify the path of the reader along what was, unavoidably, a quite well-known highway. I mean you're not going to surprise anybody with Eliot or Yeats or Auden – but I was able to, I think,

rehabilitate Wilfrid Gibson for instance, a much underestimated poet, and occasionally one just stuck in a little poem one had found for the hell of it, that no one would ever have heard of.

Let's have record number five.
Well, I would like a record for Christmas. That argues that I would play it only once a year but I would probably play it more often than that, and it is the St George's Canzona's beautiful rendering of the 'Coventry Carol'. This suggests to me Christmas, not the Christmas of Dingly Dell, more the Christmas of the illuminated manuscripts and the books of hours with the red and blue robes and the gold crowns and the gold haloes and the snow, and so forth.

[Record: 'The Coventry Carol']

The sixteenth-century 'Coventry Carol' by the St George's Canzona. What's your next record?
I'm sure that there would be times when I should be home-sick for England, I should just want to lie back and think of England, and I can't imagine a better record to do it to than Elgar's Symphony No. 1 and in particular the third movement. This is a purely suggestive choice. I think of the Midlands, the South-West Midlands, the meadows, the rivers, the occasional church and cathedral.

[Record: Elgar, Symphony No. 1 in A flat]

The opening of the third movement of Elgar's First Symphony, Sir Adrian Boult conducting the London Philharmonic Orchestra. Have you done any fishing or anything useful like that?
I haven't, no. The only time I saw a fish caught I was so horrified that I could never try to do it myself.

Would you try to escape?
I should certainly consider the situation, it would depend how far off the mainland was and how many sharks there were in between.

Record number seven?
Record number seven is Billie Holiday's 'These Foolish Things'. I always thought that the words were a little pseudo-poetic but Billie here sings them with such a passionate conviction that I think they really become poetry. It also demonstrates a theory of

mine that you can't have a great jazz vocal without a great jazz accompaniment, and here you have Duke Ellington's marvellous altoist Johnny Hodges, and the pianist Teddy Wilson, making up a wonderful trio.

[Record: Billie Holiday, 'These Foolish Things']

Billie Holiday's 'These Foolish Things', recorded in 1936. Now we come to your last record, what's that to be?
Well, if I had a favourite composer, as I suppose everybody has, it would be Handel, and indeed I could have made up my entire choice from Handel but I couldn't not have one of his great roaring finales, you know, the musical equivalent of sunshine I think of them as, and one of the best is the final double chorus, 'Praise the Lord' from *Solomon*, which is here done by Sir Thomas Beecham and the Royal Philharmonic Orchestra.

[Record: Handel, *Solomon* – 'Praise the Lord']

Handel's roaring finale, 'Praise the Lord', from Solomon. *The Royal Philharmonic Orchestra, the Beecham Choral Society conducted by Sir Thomas Beecham. If you could take just one disc of the eight, which would it be?*
It would have to be one of the jazz records, I can't live without jazz. The Bessie Smith I think, it is so full of life and so invigorating.

And one luxury to take with you to the island?
Well, something to write on, something to write with. Could I have a typewriter and an unlimited supply of paper?

Yes indeed, what are you going to write?
Well, I might try to write another novel but if I fail to do that I could always write my life story, in the hope that the white ants would get it before I was rescued.

And one book, apart from the Bible, Shakespeare, and we put big encyclopaedias on the barred list.
I think I'd like the complete plays of Bernard Shaw. Shaw is such a sane and light-hearted writer and above all so free from self-pity. I think he'd be the ideal companion for a desert island.

The complete plays of Bernard Shaw and we'll give you the prefaces as well. And thank you, Philip Larkin, for letting us hear your desert island discs.

I look forward to being rescued.

Goodbye everyone.

BBC Radio Four, 17 July 1976

Meeting Philip Larkin

A. N. WILSON: *Are you writing poems at the moment?*
PHILIP LARKIN: Well, I haven't given poetry up, but I rather think poetry has given me up, which is a great sorrow to me. But not an enormous crushing sorrow. It's a bit like going bald. You know, you can't do anything about it. I suppose the last substantial poem I wrote was about 1977, since which I haven't really been impelled to write anything. And I would stress the word 'impelled'. I think you don't write poems because you want to or you try to, but because you have to. Something gets on your back and says – look here, you've got to do something about this. I haven't had that experience lately. This is, as I say, a sorrow to me, but I would sooner not write any poems than write bad poems, if you know what I mean.

And would you never think of sitting down and saying – well, look here, I haven't written for however many years it is; I'm just going to try to write a poem. That's not something you'd ever think of doing?
Well I did write a very little poem, which was the last one I published, about how you get a drink at a party, you know. And that sprang directly from listening to a poetry programme on the radio and thinking – my God, I could do better than this. But that's not quite what you mean, is it?

It's partly that, yes. I was wondering, for instance, why, instead of giving us a fractional autobiography in the form that you've done it in Required Writing, *you didn't write a sort of* Summoned by Bells *for us.*
I don't think the creative process works like that. I wouldn't have written a *Summoned by Bells*. I couldn't possibly have done. I suppose I might have written a prose autobiography, very glancing, very indirect – rather like Siegfried Sassoon. But you must remember that I work all day here, you know, and come home in the evening. What you're really asking is – what would it be like if I sat down after breakfast with my faculties fresh and so on. I often wonder that myself.

Required Writing *has been a great success commercially, I gather. And now you've won the W. H. Smith Prize, does that surprise you at all? The terrific success that it's achieved?*
It's hard to say. I think there could be several answers to that. I think one reason could have been the acumen of my publishers, who published it at £4.95 before Christmas, in paperback, instead of £12.95 after Christmas in hardback. But secondly, I like to think it is a readable book and an amusing book and an interesting book – for people who like literature.

Thirdly, I suppose – and rather reluctantly I suppose – it is a somewhat revealing book about myself. It's a kind of concealed autobiography. It's the kind of things I've had to do and the kind of things I've had to say in my life as a writer.

It contains a number of autobiographical essays, doesn't it? And also a couple of interviews. And I think many of the reviewers concentrated on those rather than the poetical passages in the book.
Yes, I think they did, to some extent. I don't blame them. It's much easier to write about that kind of thing. But of course, the real work in the book, I mean the parts I put the most effort into, were the critical essays in the second half of the book. I don't mind the interviews. They were very kind and they succeeded to some extent in removing this cycle-clip image that I feel I gathered in the early part of my career.

But then you've achieved rather a different and new image, haven't you?
I don't know. Have I? I like to think so. But of course, I really did put my effort into the reviews. I mean, when I review, I really take it very seriously. I really do read the whole book more than once when I write, and pages of notes and that kind of thing. It takes me an awful long time. And that is what I would really like to be judged by.

Obviously you're a very accomplished literary journalist. Did you ever consider devoting yourself full-time, as many people have done, to the writing life?
No, because, as I've just said, I don't write easily; I write very, very slowly and with great pains. And I think, to make a living by journalism, or by any other subsidiary literary activity, you have to be a quick reactor. I'm not a quick reactor; I'm a very slow reactor. Everything I do is done very slowly. At the same time, I must say I

should like to have made a living by writing – or at least have been paid for being a writer, put it that way. As I say somewhere, in one of the interviews, it's always been a source of mild surprise to me that what society has been prepared to pay me for is being a librarian. (There are many better librarians than me in the country.) And not for being a writer.

But you quite enjoy being a librarian, don't you? I mean would you be a librarian even if you didn't have to work?
That's a hypothetical question. I have always been a librarian and on the whole I have always enjoyed being a librarian. It's a very good job and I have tried to do it well. I was reading Evelyn Waugh's essays recently, and he gave an explanation of why he travelled. And it was simply to get out of the house. He said – if you have a job, you know, you leave the house at quarter to nine every morning and you thank God and you're back at a quarter to six in the evening. But if you haven't got a job, then how do you get out of the house? Well, the answer is you travel. I think being a writer depends very much on how long every day you can write. I've always found, myself, that you can't write poetry for more than say a couple of hours. After that, you're going round in circles. What do you do with the rest of the day?

Shopping, gardening.
Mm. But being in touch with other people, arguing with them, agreeing with them, discussing with them – that's what my job brings me, and that's the part of it I enjoy.

One of the things that's very striking in this book is your interest in fiction and novels, and in the interviews which are reprinted here, you talk about your career as a novelist. Why did that fizzle out, do you think, or why did you give up writing novels?
A very short career. I don't know, honestly. I suppose the short answer is that my novels really weren't novels; they were poems. Long, diffuse poems perhaps.

What does that mean? I mean . . . to an ordinary chap like me, they seem to be prose works which tell stories.
I say somewhere that poems are about yourself, whereas novels are about other people. I suppose I didn't really know enough about other people, or perhaps I wasn't really interested enough in other people to be a novelist. At the same time, I do think that the

novel, at its best, is a better picture of the human situation than the poem, because it has a broader impact; and the poem, or the lyric poem at any rate, is simply one emotion from one person; and OK, you do that and it's very piercing. But the novel is a kind of diffused impact of a great many emotions of a number of people, interacting and referring back to those circumstances and so on, which I think is much more difficult to do, but in the end much more impressive.

But you achieve it so triumphantly in both your novels, I should have thought – particularly in the second, A Girl in Winter, *of a whole world and the provincial town in which she lives and so on. I'm surprised that it wasn't something you wanted to carry on with.*
Well, I did want to carry on with it. *A Girl in Winter* I suppose was finished in about 1945, and between 1945 and 1950 I strove to write novels, many different novels, and they all failed. It had just gone. In the intervals, I scribbled down poems which were nothing to me, but they eventually began to form – you know – the basis of *The Less Deceived* in 1955.

Yes. You obviously have a great taste for crime novels. You never thought of writing a detective story?
Far too difficult. I do like detective stories, particularly the old-style detective story – the Dickson Carr closed-room one, or the Gladys Mitchell extraordinary legendary surreal novel. I did once begin to write a detective story called *The Mistletoe Murders*, which was predictably going to take place in a country house at Christmas, but I don't think it got any further than the first chapter.

Would you think that the reason you've won this prize is partly that you've written a very distinguished collection of journalism, but partly that you are also a very distinguished poet? And that really this prize is for your writings as a whole – not simply for this book?
Well, I should like to think that. I've looked at the previous prize-winners of what I can't help thinking as being the aristocracy of literary awards in England, and they all seem to me to be people whom I'm very honoured to be ranked along with. But I don't really feel that they've thought – oh, here's old Philip ... you know, we haven't done right by him. I would like to think that this book has struck the very distinguished judges as being good and they wanted to give it the prize.

Well, I'm sure, but it's also been a very popular book, as such books go, hasn't it?
So it seems.

And in a very surprising way, in many ways, considering the extremely private nature of your poetry, your poetry is also extremely popular, isn't it?
I hope so.

I mean it's widely read. And does that ever surprise you, that it seems to strike chords? I mean life is first boredom, then fear, seems a pretty devastating view of life, and yet everybody seems to want to rush out to the bookshops and buy it.
It does surprise me rather. You know, you write down things that you think are absolutely peculiar to yourself and nobody but you would be such a fool to invoke them or suffer them. Then you suddenly find people writing in from all over the place, saying – that's just what I felt, you know, man, that's it. And so on. I find this very, very gratifying indeed. And they're quite ordinary people; they're not people who write for the weeklies.

Now this is £4,000 tax free; have you decided how you're going to spend the money?
Well I think I shall buy a new suit. I need one and I gather they cost about that nowadays.

BBC Radio Four, 29 March 1984

III · FOREWORDS

Operation Manuscript

This is a small but peculiarly significant collection.

Looking at it, though, one is struck first by its casualness, its fugitiveness, even. Clearly writing a poem today doesn't call for a golden pen or a tablet whiter than a star: the poet uses a nine-penny ballpoint and the first paper that comes to hand – a sheet of typing paper (bank, not bond), or else ruled pages from a cheap exercise book. Sometimes he cannot manage even this: Ted Hughes slits open a large brown envelope and writes on the blank inner side, Edmund Blunden uses the back of an illustration from a Sotheby's catalogue. Others reach for paper showing where they are – Keith Douglas at the Middle East RAC Base Depot, or Edwin Muir at Battle Abbey College. Now and then we find the luxury of a notebook. Andrew Young has one; Roy Fuller's, red and wirebound, is marked 'Please return to Roy Fuller, 18 St John's Park, London, S.E.3' on the cover in ink; Auden's is labelled 'Simon Stationery, 890 – 3rd Avenue NYC '. Is there a distinction here, between the notebook men and the loose-sheeters? Oppositions recur: the sprawlers and the crabbed, when it comes to handwriting; even the legible and the illegible – it's odd to find Dylan Thomas's complexities expressed in the most regular of schoolroom characters, while Andrew Young, plain and straightforward on the printed page, employs when composing what amounts to private shorthand. Similarities are even more baffling. Why should two such dissimilar poets as Roy Fuller and Vernon Watkins have the same vivid, flourishing, romantic kind of script?

Such physical details – William Plomer's different-coloured inks; John Betjeman's sheet which arrived crumpled as if rescued from the waste-paper basket that morning – fascinating today, will be still more so in a century or so's time, but the significance of poetry manuscripts in general is far from being confined to *minutiae*. For

Introduction to *Poetry in the Making:* catalogue of an exhibition in the British Museum, April–June 1967

the scholar, concerned with finding out as much about an author and his work as possible, this is primary source material: this is what he wrote, how he wrote it, what he corrected, what he left. A manuscript will show how much trouble he took, how many drafts were necessary; a cancellation may clarify the meaning, for a writer will often put down the 'prose' word while groping for the 'poetic' one, or a cancelled expression may throw more light on what was in his mind, as in Charles Causley's sonnet about Shakespeare where 'a tree' was originally 'a mulberry tree'. But this contribution to our knowledge can be much greater. When Wordsworth published *The Prelude* in 1850, his edition gave no indication that this major and personal poem had been written as much as fifty years ago, and largely amended in retrospect. If Ernest de Selincourt had not been able to publish the 1805 manuscript in 1926, we should still presumably be unaware which passages had been excised and which changed – and in what direction. A similar instance is the original version, 340 lines long, of Coleridge's 'Dejection: an ode', first printed by de Selincourt in 1947, though the 1802 printed text was less than half this length. Shall we ever see *The Waste Land* as it was first submitted to Ezra Pound? At times, too, the printed text is not so much incomplete as misleading, presenting one poem as two as in the case of Swinburne's 'Duriesdyke', or Wilfred Owen's 'The Calls'. If a poet uses a notebook, of course, the whole chronology of composition may be preserved: Hardy's poems cry out for such rearrangement. And when a manuscript is the only source of material the poet has left completely unpublished its value is unparallelled.

None of these significances is the kind I think peculiar to this collection: that I shall come to. They have, however, led those concerned with literary scholarship to regard the acquisition and preservation of manuscripts as the prerequisite of their trade. Of course the interest is of recent growth: English studies itself is a comparative newcomer to the academic field. Until this century, the acquisition of literary manuscripts by libraries or museums was largely a matter of luck or goodwill, and then largely on the assumption that an author's papers would contain much that was unpublished. As little as thirty years ago there was scant interest in the manuscripts of published works, especially of twentieth century writers, except as a curiosity, and what interest there was came from private collectors.

Today the situation is indeed altered. Any two accounts of it, and how it came about, are bound to differ in emphasis. The importance of manuscripts to literary scholarship has already been demonstrated, and the rapid expansion during this century of such scholarship here and, even more, in America has created an enormous interest in them. They are sought after for the proper verification of texts and for the amplification of our knowledge of how a writer worked. Since this is the business of the scholar, the libraries to which such scholars look for material – the national and university libraries – have entered the field on behalf of the readers they serve.

There is no point in avoiding the fact that this scene is dominated today by the American dealer and the American library. As John Carter wrote in 1960, 'practically all authors' manuscripts end up in American institutional libraries'.[1] There are several reasons for this. It is tempting to say that American institutions have more money than British ones: this is, of course, true, and is aided by the fact that the American government allows income tax relief to patrons of libraries and museums, with the result that such a purchaser will pay less for an item than the saleroom price suggests. But there are other reasons. One is that American institutions take manuscripts more seriously than their British counterparts. It is not, I think, so much that they have grasped that the worksheets and manuscripts of the twentieth century will be the priceless heritage of the twenty-first century, as that they are prepared to regard living authors as proper subjects for research. (A well-known English novelist told me that there were 31 theses about him in America, 6 in Russia, 5 in Germany, 4 in other continental countries, and none in Britain.) British universities do not on the whole take this view, with the result that another reason for American superiority in the field is lack of competition. It is hardly surprising that a British librarian, secure in the knowledge that his university would not encourage purchases of contemporary manuscripts even if he had the money to make them, pays little attention to the large-scale acquisition policy – Operation Manuscript one might almost call it – mounted by certain American institutions. The magnitude of such policies may not even now be fully realised by those responsible for the

1 *Atlantic Monthly*, July 1960.

expenditure of the funds of British libraries. In May 1961, for instance, a sale at Sotheby's of 548 lots – not, we are assured, of undue rarity, comprising printed and manuscript material of the last 100 years – fetched £44,407. More than £27,000 of this was paid by a dealer working, it was assumed, on behalf of the University of Texas. To see how this circumstance is repeated over and over again one need only turn to the section on literary manuscripts in *American Book-Prices Current*. Already it can be said of the University of Texas, in the words of the late Mr Bertram Rota, himself a leading dealer in manuscripts, 'It is already hard to think where resources for the study of twentieth-century writing in English, from the conception of a book to its publication, could be found'.[1] Will this continue to be true of the twentieth century, and the twenty-first, and the twenty-second?

It is difficult to describe this situation without seeming to deprecate it. These papers, valuable as we all agree, are being assiduously bought up for preservation in the admirable libraries of the world's largest English-speaking country, our friend and ally. Here they will be cared for according to the best possible professional methods and studied devotedly by that country's scholars. Their original owners, either the authors themselves or their heirs, are being amply reimbursed. British institutions are thus being relieved of a task which by all accounts they were never keen on, and have in consequence one less call on their meagre funds. What is there to complain of?

Less, admittedly, than if such papers were disappearing into the libraries of private collectors, or being cut up for lampshades. What must be faced, however, is the increasing likelihood of a situation wherein the manuscripts of every considerable British writer since 1850 are in American hands. This means for British librarians the loss of the pleasure and privilege of keeping them here; for British writers the denial of the chance of knowing that their work has been so recognised by the major academic institutions of their country; and for British scholars the resignation to their American colleagues all tasks of scholarship necessitating the close consultation of relevant manuscripts. It means, in fact, that definitive editions of such British writers will in all probability be American – and if it seem merely chauvinistic to regret this, how

1 *Times Literary Supplement*, 14 July 1961.

acceptable would the reverse situation seem? No doubt many writers, at least, will think this an overstatement, and will assume that much of the difficulty may be mitigated by the cordial relations between the two countries and the existence of the medium of microform. Unfortunately this cannot always be taken for granted. Many British scholars will have had experience of a blank denial of access to, or photocopies of, material of this kind on the part of American libraries, even when the applicant has copyright permission or the material is out of copyright. Anyone wishing to test this statement might like to write to an American university library, requesting a microfilm of any unpublished literary manuscript known to be in their possession.

There is little evidence to show how all this is regarded by those currently responsible for English studies in our universities. I should reckon that their response would be a mixture of sheer unawareness and the contention that, however regrettable it may be, little can be done in the face of the financial resources commanded by American universities. How true this is depends on the three parties already named – the scholars, the librarians, and the writers. If the scholars continue to be indifferent to the virtual cessation of the acquisition of manuscripts by this country's libraries, they will clearly give their librarians no incentive, financial or otherwise, to adopt a more positive policy. Librarians, though far from indifferent to what is happening, will in that case be able to do little. But do both parties fully realise how their attitude is interpreted by the writers themselves? Some years ago I conducted a small-scale enquiry among authors into the migration of literary manuscripts, and in nearly every reply the same theme recurred: 'The whole point is that England is not really interested in the manuscripts of anyone not securely dead'; 'if almost any English university had asked me five years ago to give them my manuscript collection, which happens to be unusually complete, I should certainly have said yes'; 'I have never known [British libraries] take the slightest interest in such collecting'; 'I would have sold the same material to British sources, for less money, if anyone had asked me.'

I found this most interesting. Despite the unquestioned facts that writers as a class are underpaid, and that they have every right to sell their manuscripts to the highest bidder, I caught, or fancied I caught, a recurrent note of mingled regret and chagrin that it was not the libraries of their own country that were seeking to preserve their papers. I suspect that for some writers, at least when they are reasonably well established, it is not merely a question of the highest bidder; that to be approached on behalf of a national library or the library of one's school or university or home town regarding the sale of one's manuscripts can be a more heartening experience than cashing a large cheque from people one has never seen in the knowledge that one will never see one's manuscripts again either.

And how often, for that matter, is it a question of the highest bidder? The foundation of the worksheet collection in the Lockwood Memorial Library in the University of Buffalo was laid by solicited gift: the American librarian is now acquiring such material 'by private treaty, not through the auction mart' (David A. Randall, Librarian of the University of Indiana).[1] Many authors 'have had occasion to rejoice at the result of private negotiations' (Bertram Rota).[2] What happens a good deal of the time is that someone – a dealer, or a representative of an American university – approaches an author and makes him an offer. The author probably has little notion of the manuscript market – few people not actively engaged in it have – and accepts what he is offered. No doubt it is a fair price. But why should not the approach have been made by a British librarian, on behalf of the writer's own town, own school, own university? He is in a stronger position than his American colleague in every respect except that of money, and that, as I have tried to show, may not always prove the crucial one. There was an interesting example of this recently from France.[3] In 1962 the University of Texas approached the sole heir of Marcel Proust, Mme Gérard Mante-Proust, with a view to buying her complete collection of Proust's notebooks, manuscripts, typescripts, proofs and other relics, offering a sum said to be in the region of £110,000. Hearing of this, the Bibliothèque Nationale made an approach to the French government, and eventually acquired the collection for a reputed £80,000. The collection therefore remains in France, a circumstance which seems greatly to the credit of Mme Mante-Proust, the Bibliothèque

1 *Times Literary Supplement*, 11 August 1961.
2 *Times Literary Supplement*, 14 July 1961.
3 *The Times*, 8 August 1962.

Nationale, and, perhaps especially, the French government. One would like to think that in comparable circumstances the Treasury would behave with equal enthusiasm.

The significance I think peculiar to this collection will be now apparent. It represents a reaction, and a national reaction at that, to the situation set out above. The initiative of the Arts Council, the generosity of the Pilgrim Trust, and the willing cooperation of the British Museum have combined to found what has been boldly called The National Manuscript Collection of Contemporary Poets. This may seem a grandiose title for an assemblage of material which as yet occupies hardly two shelves of a library trolley, but it was chosen deliberately, to give honour to the writers represented in it, and as a public rebuttal of the belief that 'England is not interested in living writers' manuscripts'. England is. There are many more twentieth-century literary manuscripts in this country's libraries than is commonly supposed, and much more concern among librarians for their acquisition. But all the same the gesture needed to be made.

Properly regarded, however, it is more than a gesture, and more than a reaction: it can be seen as an example, first to writers themselves, that they and their work are valued by their country's principal repository of such material, and as an assurance that interest in further acquisition is certainly not lacking. It is an example, secondly, to librarians, library committees, boards of curators and trustees; to alert them to a situation and to show how with even the slenderest of means it may be combated by people on the spot. One hopes, too, that the example and its lessons will be marked by the Treasury and those concerned with the export of artistic monuments; it might lead them, for instance, to reconsider their ruling that manuscripts, documents and archives may be exported without a licence as long as they are less than 100 years old. This has proved tantamount to a direct encouragement to foreign libraries to concentrate on acquiring this kind of material, and its amendment would be the simplest way of correcting the whole situation.

Lastly, it must be thought of as a beginning. Despite the assiduity of those responsible for the Collection as it is shown here, and the many instances of cooperation and generosity which must be acknowledged, no one imagines that the two shelves of work-sheets it has been possible to acquire over four years represents a material stemming of the manuscript migration to America. The method it has demonstrated must now be applied on a broader and deeper scale. Means must be found to enlarge both the resources of the Collection and its scope – to put more money at its disposal, so that whole collections can be bought rather than single examples, and that these collections should represent the manuscripts, letters, notebooks and proofsheets of every kind of writer, novelist and playwright as well as poet. No one would wish to do less than this, if only it were possible. To examine all the ways of making it possible is the next task to which those concerned must address themselves.

1967

Adventures with the Irish Brigade by Colin Gunner

The key to this book appears on an early page. Colin Gunner, having decided to anticipate his call-up by volunteering, is duly sworn-in at the Recruiting Office and given a day's pay of five shillings. He stares at the two half-crowns with dissatisfaction. Where was the King's shilling? He protests, at first in vain, at length ('Quite right – the lad's entitled to one – get one at once, sergeant') with success: he leaves the room with two florins and the precious shilling. 'It hangs in my room still, unspent.'

This account of where that shilling led him contrasts vividly with other, more disillusioned narratives, for Colin Gunner's love affair with the Army never came to an end. Not that he had an easy war. In consequence of another gesture in the face of authority ('any infantry regiment of the line'), he, a Coventry boy of middle-class background, became attached to the kind of Irish regiment that, along with Scottish and Commonwealth troops, gets thrown into action whenever the going is tough. He seems (I cannot claim to have mastered completely the almost-illegible typescript he sent me) to have been posted from Catterick to North Africa and then to Italy, where he was to fight his way up to Monte Cassino and see the end of the war. Ice, mud, danger, dysentery, all came his way. Yet his enthusiasm did not dwindle. It is hard to analyse its source. Much is owed to the fellowship of comrade-in-arms, especially the Irish, who were new to him. Much arises from day-to-day humour of an elementary kind: the officer begging assistance to be catapulted into a cess-pit, the commandeered motor-cycle, the sad tale of the man who rented an apartment in Cairo. The fact that it was his war service that first awoke his interest in the Roman Catholic Church ('a twenty-one year old, non-church going, nominal Protestant') no doubt counts for much. At bottom, however, it is the glamour of that shilling that keeps him going; it is the historical tradition of the British Army, the drinking, the scrounging, the deserting, the endurance, the courage, all going back to the First World War, the campaigns of Edward and Victoria, to Waterloo and the Peninsular, all these seem to support him at the darkest moments. In the Second World War such sentiments were rare.

One might conclude from this that Gunner is a romantic, but this is not my recollection of him – for I must admit, and should perhaps have done so earlier, that we were schoolfellows. In fact he stays in my memory as quite the reverse: I remember him, on the day when, in common with all schoolchildren, we had been presented with a George VI coronation mug, shying his own into that squalid sewer the River Sowe (I have mine still). Perhaps he was a King's man, a supporter of Edward VIII; for me the action proclaimed him iconoclast and sceptic. We first met in the Junior School of King Henry VIII School, Coventry, in the early 1930s – or was it in the first form of the School itself? It was certainly before the traumatic influx of scholarship boys in the second form, and the start of Latin and French; he was sitting next to me when Jimmy Mattocks took us through *The Wind in the Willows* (missing out the chapter about Mole's old home, and Pan, and Rat's wish to emigrate), and he was there when we played cricket in white shorts (as opposed to white longs), and bowled fast. I remember him, and indeed school photographs bear this out, as a small, agile, tough boy, with a face like a nut, very much at home in the world of Bassett-Lowke, Warnford, and Rudge-Whitworth, and whose home background seemed, if not richer than mine, at least more sophisticated; his parents had a car.

At that time I was not happy at school. Admittedly it was an affair of being more frightened than hurt, but it was being hurt sometimes, and being frightened was not very pleasant. And in any case it was an affair of being more bored than either. The very words physics, geography, algebra, chemistry still conjure up in my mind a pantheon of tedium, and even if I had sought to master them I was badly handicapped by not being able to see the blackboard (I never said anything about this, and nobody noticed it). The one compensation was the discovery that Colin and I could make each other almost hysterical with laughter by weaving fantasies about the extraordinary characters that daily stood before us, roaring, scratching, gesturing, glowering – Knobby, Beaky, Squiffy, Pansy, Majack, Wooly Willy and the rest. The grotesque and memorable tapestry to which we added daily at break, or walking down Warwick Road after school, derived from a variety of sources: *The Magnet*, certainly, and *Tom Brown's Schooldays*, but also films such as *Dracula* and the more colourful aspects of the Hitler régime. I don't pretend that such inventions are uncommon, and I certainly have no intention of detailing ours in particular; all I say is that they made school bearable for me. Ironically, Colin was supposed to be a 'bad influence' in my school life; presumably my teachers thought that without him at my elbow I should have done better in class (my form position was always well down in the twenties). But in fact we were developing our imaginations independently of the School Certificate syllabus, and if anything were to be envied rather than reprimanded. Later on, we used to meet at the Central Library in the evenings, at the foot of the as-yet-unbombed cathedral, emerging (in my case) with literary biographies and argumentative books about religion, and (in Colin's) military and regimental history.

Colin had, as far as I know, no literary ambitions, but he was a natural writer, and I think this book shows as much. His English essays came back with 'Vigorous' written at the bottom, though an attempt to apply the same technique to physics questions ('Buzzz! When we hear the familiar summons of the electric bell, do we ever pause to reflect on the intricacies of the mechanism that ...' etc.) evoked caustic comment from the Mad Undergrad, as we called the physics master. On the basis of this talent, he planned to join the *Midland Daily Telegraph*, as it was then, but this intention was thwarted when he failed his School Certificate. This seems to me now, as it did then, a great injustice.

Such recollections make it difficult for me to introduce this book dispassionately, for so much of it is Colin in his habit as he lived – gay, rhetorical, courageous, sentimental, always ready with a quotation, never too subservient to the rules of punctuation or orthography. It reminds me of the creeping tedium of morning and afternoon school, the consultation of one's (usually new) watch, the grins exchanged across the classroom when the master in charge innocently made some remark that chimed with the Dickensian, or Rowlandsonian, life-style we had devised for him. But if I look at these pages with the eye of a stranger, I am still bound to acknowledge the helter-skelter of incident, the vivacity of detail, the always-present but never-laboured humour, and the equanimity with which their author encounters and relates a set of experiences which, even if, like the Clerk of the

Court in *The Wind in the Willows*, one believes only one-tenth of them, must have been more than usually shattering. The claims I would make for Colin's narrative refer more to temperament than to texture; here is someone meeting unpleasant events with insouciance and endurance, and above all a tactful modesty; and yet if the writing were not an extraordinary blend of unpretentiousness with complete confidence it would not be – as, in my view, it is – immensely readable.

1973

NOTE: Though Larkin sent this foreword to Gunner on 20 August 1973 (see *Selected Letters*), after protracted attempts to publish the book, it was in the end privately produced for Gunner in an edition of twenty-four copies delivered to the author on 14 August 1975 (see Bloomfield's *Bibliography*). One copy is in the Bodleian Library.

Fen Country: Twenty-Six Stories by Edmund Crispin

As an undergraduate, Bruce Montgomery habitually wore a suit and a handsome ring, both unusual among our contemporaries, and had the slightly-intimidating air of one who knew what he was going to do – or, if in those days none of us quite knew that, at least that he would settle with life only on his own terms. His genial sense of the absurd soon dispelled this impression, but on the whole it was not, in retrospect, an inaccurate one.

Leaving Oxford in 1943, he spent the rest of the war teaching at Shrewsbury School, where his pupils received a thorough grounding in detective fiction and M. R. James as well as more usual subjects. He had already written *The Case of the Gilded Fly; Holy Disorders* and *The Moving Toyshop* followed. As it happened, I was working near Shrewsbury myself at the time, and unwittingly provided the genesis of the last-named by reporting that when I left his lodgings to catch the midnight train there was always one particular shop with its awning left down, flapping eerily in the empty street. Bruce was fascinated. The runaway roundabout, later used by Alfred Hitchcock in *Strangers on a Train*, came from an evening we spent at a fair.

After the war he returned to Devon, where he lived for the rest of his life: first at home, then in a comfortable bungalow he built near Dartington (it reputedly had an atom-bomb-proof cellar). His vivacious inspiration (he published eight detective novels in eight years) sank, and he turned to the lucrative world of film music, becoming in consequence an even more overwhelmingly-generous companion than before. But it grew increasingly difficult to lure him away from Devon, where books, music and *The Times* crossword filled up intervals of working. He remained unmarried until late in life.

His views on detective stories, as on most other things, were traditional. John Dickson Carr was the master, and Bruce's account of 'the trickiest form of fiction humanity has so far devised' owed much to his work:

> For we have come to demand of it not only a mystery with a plausible solution, but over and above that a mystery with a surprise solution; and over and above *that*, a mystery with a surprise solution which by rights we ought not to have been surprised at at all.[1]

This was the kind of story he tried to write himself, but temperamentally he inclined more to the academic comedies of Michael Innes; 'Gervase Crispin' in *Hamlet, Revenge!* gave Bruce half his pseudonym (originally 'Rufus Crispin', from his own wavy red hair) and half the name of his detective, Gervase Fen, whose other name evoked his Oxford tutor, W. G. Moore, by way of 'Lead, Kindly Light' ('O'er moor and fen'). Fen reproduced much of Moore's appearance, and some of his mannerisms, but the caricature was an affectionate one: in the last year of his life Bruce wrote a tribute that was quoted at Moore's memorial service, for 'Fen' predeceased his creator by some nine months only in 1978.

Both Fen and Crispin are of necessity less exuberant in *Fen Country*, a collection of miniatures based on odd facts or notions no detective novelist can ignore, yet cannot always use in full-length pieces. No doubt Bruce would have revised them for republication, but their concise sobriety demonstrates a talent independent of his more colourful characteristics. Perhaps the savagely-autobiographical farce 'We Know You're Busy Writing' is an exception, but my favourite is 'Merry-Go-Round': it is just the kind of story that Bruce, with a fresh cigarette and another round of gins-and-tonic brought and lavishly tipped for, so much enjoyed telling in that ripely-modulated voice none of his friends will ever forget.

1979

1 From the introduction to *Best Detective Stories*, edited by Edmund Crispin (Faber and Faber, 1959).

The Arts Council Poetry Library Catalogue

I think if I lived in London I should often find myself in the Arts Council Poetry Library. It is just up the street from the offices of *Encounter* and round the corner from the Garrick Club (the only London club with a manuscript poem by a living author framed in its bar), and handy for the book and record shops in Charing Cross Road. Then again, it is so friendly and inviting (hardly like a library at all, you may say): newly furnished, brightly lit, and with knowledgeable staff who will help you if you want help, but otherwise just smile. At one end, under a wide window that catches the morning sun in Garrick Street, is a table where anthologists and American Ph.D students are working, because it is so much easier to find what you want here. Or you can sink into an armchair, and watch the visitors of the moment moving round the shelves – the office worker, the teacher, the androgynous creature dressed equally for the Western Desert or the Chelsea Arts Ball, the intent African and the person whose face you recognize, who seems to be checking his own books before turning, rather less willingly, to those of his contemporaries and juniors.

But it isn't easy to stay sitting down. No sooner have you found half a dozen titles that you remember being reviewed but have never seen than it occurs to you to wonder whether they have So-and-so's first, worst book, now unobtainable except at Sotheby's: you consult the catalogue (on pointlessly-large cards) and there it is, though prudently kept in the Librarian's office. And this brings you to the wall of magazines: not only the established household words, fat with subsidies, but all the tiny flickering poorly-printed outlets you have seen advertised in small type on the back pages of the weeklies, arranged alike on display racks with their back numbers neat in open boxes or sturdily reprinted and bound by Kraus of New York. Then on tables below are laid newly-compiled lists of poetry shops, poetry groups, poetry magazines (with names of their editors, so that you can begin your letter 'Dear

Mr So-and-so'), and notices of poetry competitions, poetry readings and poetry evening classes, today, tomorrow, next week. The idea of poetry, vague enough outside, is here immediate and busy, like a political campaign.

The Arts Council Poetry Library is one of the occasional pure flowerings of imagination for which the English are so seldom given credit: the creation of a public library devoted entirely to modern poetry. Nothing else: no criticism, no biography, simply books by well-known poets and unknown poets side by side in the democracy of alphabetical order. And there is something else unique about it: everyone knows that if you go to a library to consult a book, someone will have borrowed it, and if you go to borrow it, it will be marked for reference only. The Poetry Library solves this problem as far as it can be solved by having two copies of nearly everything, one for loan, one for reference.

It was opened in 1953, that Coronation year when England won the Ashes and climbed Everest. Among those who spoke were Norman Birkett, Herbert Read and T. S. Eliot. What they said is, maddeningly, not recorded, but no doubt it was echoed in the Library's first catalogue:

> Its purpose is the simple one of helping the reader of poetry, and particularly the younger reader, to get into easier and closer touch with the published verse of his poetic contemporaries; and literally in touch, so that, without obligation, he can handle their books at his pleasure and make use of them to his heart's content.

And this is what it is still doing. But after a quarter of a century it has, just by the passage of time, become a national resource in its chosen field. 'Having read in nearly a hundred of the most important European Libraries,' wrote a recent German visitor,

> I know of only two special collections containing the poetry of a national literature on a scale that could be compared with that of the Arts Council Poetry Library, namely in Uppsala and in Dortmund: but these are not open to the public, whereas the Arts Council Poetry Library offers access to anybody interested in poetry.

The present catalogue will show how wide its range is: British poets, American poets, translations of foreign poets into English, a multiple monument to a major art. And a growing monument, whose increasing use by every kind of reader is a constant tribute to the vision of those who conceived it, and to the knowledge and enthusiasm of those who continue it. Let us be thankful.

1981

A Rumoured City: New Poets from Hull, edited by Douglas Dunn

Poetry, like prose, happens anywhere. Hull got its clearance on this from Andrew Marvell many years ago; and if that singular Member of Parliament would have little in common with today's ancient and modern city lodged unexpectedly in the triangle of flat country between the Humber and the North Sea, it is still as good a place to write in as any.

Better, in fact, than some. For a place cannot produce poems: it can only not prevent them, and Hull is good at that. It neither impresses nor insists. When your train comes to rest in Paragon Station against a row of docile buffers, you alight with an end-of-the-line sense of freedom. Signs in foreign languages welcome you. Outside is a working city, yet one neither clenched in the blackened grip of the industrial revolution nor hiding behind a cathedral to pretend it is York or Canterbury. Unpretentious, recent, full of shops and special offers like a television commercial, it might be Australia or America, until you come upon Trinity House or the Dock Offices. For Hull has its own sudden elegancies.

People are slow to leave it, quick to return. And there are others who come, as they think, for a year or two, and stay a lifetime, sensing that they have found a city that is in the world, yet sufficiently on the edge of it to have a different resonance. Behind Hull is the plain of Holderness, lonelier and lonelier, and after that the birds and lights of Spurn Head, and then the sea. One can go ten years without seeing these things, yet they are always there, giving Hull the air of having its face half-turned towards distance and silence, and what lies beyond them.

These poems are not about Hull, yet it is unseen in all of them, the permission of a town that lets you write.

1982

An Unsuitable Attachment by Barbara Pym

'I sent my novel to Cape last week,' Barbara Pym wrote to me in February 1963. 'It is called (at present) *An Unsuitable Attachment.*' It was her seventh, 'which seems a significant number'. The significance was to prove greater than she could have ever imagined.

Barbara Pym was then in her fiftieth year. Her previous books had been well received by reviewers, and she had gained a following among library borrowers; it was time for a breakthrough that would establish her among the dozen or so novelists recognized as original voices and whose books automatically head the review lists. With this in mind, I had written to her in 1961 saying how much I liked her novels and suggesting I should do an article about them to coincide with the publication of her next, hinting that she should let me know when it was ready. She replied amiably, but was clearly in no hurry, and our correspondence lapsed; the letter I have quoted was the first for over a year.

She did not write again until May, and then, after a courteous page of generalities, it was to say that *An Unsuitable Attachment* had been rejected. Although she strove to maintain the innocent irony that characterized all her letters, for once it broke down: 'I write this calmly enough, but really I was and am very upset about it and think they have treated me very badly.'

> Of course it may be that this book is much *worse* than my others, though they didn't say so, giving their reason for rejecting it as their fear that with the present cost of book production etc etc they doubted whether they could sell enough copies to make a profit.

To have one's seventh book turned down by a publisher who has seemed perfectly happy with the previous six is a peculiarly wounding experience, and she felt it as such. It is also damaging: another publisher can be approached only from a position of weakness, weaker than if the novel were one's first. A second publisher sent it back saying 'Novels like *An Unsuitable Attach-*

ment, despite their qualities, are getting increasingly difficult to sell', while a third simply regretted it was not suitable for their list.

What was to be done? I wanted to try it on my own publisher, but Barbara demurred: she wanted to put it aside, to rewrite it, to write something else, and several years went by in which she did all these things, but to no avail. The new book, *The Sweet Dove Died*, was rejected as firmly as its predecessor, and the revised *Attachment* was unsuccessfully sent to a second round of publishers, including my own. I wish I had gone ahead and written my article; the honour of publishing the first independent appreciation of her work went instead to Robert Smith, whose 'How Pleasant to Know Miss Pym' appeared in *Ariel* in October 1971.

It was a strange and depressing time – strange, because (as Mr Smith's article indicates) her books retained their popularity. *No Fond Return of Love* was serialized by the BBC in 1965, while Portway Reprints, that infallible index of what people want to read instead of what they ought to want to read, reissued five others. Depressing, because the wall of indifference she had run up against seemed as immovable as it was inexplicable. For over ten years she had been a novelist: now, suddenly, she was not. The situation was galling. 'It ought to be enough for anybody to be the Assistant Editor of *Africa* [which is what she was], especially when the Editor is away lecturing for six months at Harvard,' she wrote, 'but I find it isn't quite.'

In 1971 she had a serious operation, and in 1973 retired to live with her sister near Oxford. There her disappointed silence might have ended, but for an extraordinary accident. 'In ten years' time, perhaps someone will be kind enough to discover *me*,' she had written at the end of 1967, and this was precisely what happened. In 1977 the *Times Literary Supplement* published a symposium on the most over- and underrated writers of the century, and two contributors named her as the second – the only living writer to be so distinguished. The rest is, as they say, history. Her next novel, *Quartet in Autumn*, was published before the year was out, followed by *The Sweet Dove Died*. Cape began to reissue her earlier books, Penguin and Granada planned a series of paperbacks. She was widely interviewed, and appeared on 'Desert Island Discs' and in a TV film called 'Tea With Miss Pym'. All this she sustained with unassuming pleasure, but the irony of the situation was not lost on her.

An Unsuitable Attachment, now that it is finally before us, clearly belongs to Barbara Pym's first and principal group of novels by reason of its undiminished high spirits. For although the technique and properties of her last books were much the same, there was a sombreness about them indicative of the changes that had come to her and her world in fifteen years' enforced silence. Here the old confidence is restored: 'Rock salmon – that had a noble sound about it,' reflects the vicar, Mark, at the fish and chip shop, buying supper for his wife Sophia and their cat Faustina, and the reader is back among self-service lunches and parish bazaars and the innumerable tiny absurdities to be found there. It is perhaps the most solidly 'churchy' of her books: Mark and Sophia in their North London vicarage are at its centre, and the Christian year – Harvest Thanksgiving, Advent, Christmas, Lent and Easter – provide both its frame and background. 'One never knew who might turn up in a church on Sunday,' Sophia thinks, and it is this kind of adventitious encounter that once again sets her narrative moving.

The book's chief failing is that the 'unsuitable attachment' between Ianthe Broome, the well-bred librarian with ladylike stockings and brown court shoes, and the younger John Challow, whose own shoes 'seemed to be a little too pointed – not quite what men one knew would wear', is not sufficiently central to the story and not fully 'done', as Henry James would say. Potentially the situation is full of interest: John's soppy, rather common, advances, coupled with his borrowing money from her, seemed faintly threatening ('John had been intended to be much worse,' Barbara wrote apologetically), and their relation at one time seems poised for disaster. When this does not happen, its 'unsuitability' becomes rather academic, something felt more by the other characters than Ianthe herself, who 'lets love sweep over her like a kind of illness' rather than agonize over differences of age and class.

Then again, it is a somewhat self-indulgent book, full of echoes. Sophia and her sister Penelope recall *Jane and Prudence*, or even Dulcie and Viola from *No Fond Return of Love*; Sister Dew resembles Sister Blatt from *Excellent Women*; but other parallels are more explicit. Barbara Pym was always given to reintroducing characters she had used before, and sometimes this is fully justified (the conversation between Wilmet and Rowena in *A Glass of Blessings* about Rocky Napier is only fully meaningful if we have met him in *Excellent Women*), but the concluding chapters of *An Unsuitable Attachment* are a real *omnium gatherum*: Esther Clovis and Digby Fox from *Less Than Angels*, Everard Bone from *Excellent Women*, Wilf Bason from *A Glass of Blessings*, and perhaps most extravagantly of all an older but otherwise unchanged Harriet Bede (complete with curate) from *Some Tame Gazelle*. It is all rather like the finale of a musical comedy.

Do these blemishes (if blemishes they are) mean that Cape's rejection of the book in 1963 was justified? Recently I wrote to their Chairman, who at that time had been their Literary Adviser and in his late twenties, asking whether Barbara Pym had been 'dropped', as she believed, simply because her books did not suit the spirit of the decade and would not make money. He replied readily:

> When *An Unsuitable Attachment* came in it received unfavourable reports. Indeed they must have been very unfavourable for us to decide to reject a new manuscript by an author for whom we had published several books. At that time we had two readers, both of whom had been here for many years: William Plomer and Daniel George. Neither then or at any time since has this company rejected a manuscript for commercial reasons 'notwithstanding the literary merit of a book'. Though of course the two must be relative to some extent.

The reports by Plomer and George were subsequently found and they confirmed that one was 'extremely negative' and the other 'fairly negative'.

The reader must make what he can of these two accounts. If her publishers are correct, it is surprising there was not someone at Cape prepared to invite Barbara Pym to lunch and say that while they had enjoyed publishing her books in the past and hoped to continue to do so in the future this particular one needed revision if it was to realize its potential value. It was the blank rejection, the implication that all she had previously written stood for nothing, that hurt.

But there is still much in *An Unsuitable Attachment* to cherish.

The increasingly hilarious appearances of Faustina, for instance, and the role she plays in Sophia's marriage ('she's all I've got'), are original and penetrating; at times, indeed, one wonders if the book's title would not be more applicable to this relation than to Ianthe and John. Nor does it lack the occasional plangent sentence of the kind that gives her books their special quality:

> Oh, this coming back to an empty house, Rupert thought, when he had seen her safely to her door. People – though perhaps it was only women – seemed to make so much of it. As if life itself were not as empty as the house one was coming back to.

Barbara Pym made no further move to publish this unlucky seventh novel during her lifetime, preferring to concentrate on new books, but now that there will be no more of these it is right that it should be issued. If its confidence, or over-confidence, was its own undoing, it is still richly redolent of her unique talent as it was before that confidence was so badly shaken. Her followers will need no further recommendation.

1982

The Condemned Playground
by Cyril Connolly

It was one of Cyril Connolly's cherished beliefs that he was a failure ('so repulsive in others, in oneself of course the only dignified thing'). The reasons he advanced were various. It was something to do with having been a success at Eton, something to do with being fat and lazy, something to do with not having enough money or having been born into the wrong age. But above all it was to do with reviewing. Reviewing was what you did if you were a failure; reviewing was what made you a failure:

> Reviewing is a whole-time job with a half-time salary, a job in which our best work is always submerged in the criticism of someone else's, where all triumphs are ephemeral and only the drudgery is permanent and where no future is secure except the certainty of turning into a hack.

Certainly he spent a large part of his working life writing about books. He wrote for the *New Statesman* in the 1920s and 1930s, for his own commandingly individual magazine *Horizon* in the 1940s, and for the remaining twenty years of his life for *The Sunday Times*. But he was very far from being a hack. Except for his early stint as a novel-reviewer, he chose what he wrote about, and chose it not only for the sympathy (or otherwise) he could bring to it, but for the chance it gave him to display his own talents. And these were different in kind from those of the MacCarthys and Mortimers of his day; perceptive, provocative and unpredictable, he was at his best when able to assimilate his subject into the scenario of his own temperament.

The Condemned Playground, spanning as it does his career as a literary journalist from his departure from Oxford up to the latter half of the second world war, contains some of his most exhilarating pieces, many of them contradicting his claim to have 'gone off the boil' during the 1930s. What strikes the reader most forcibly is his commitment to literature, to the notion that being a writer is the practice of a morality as well as an art. 'There are but two ways to be a great writer (and no other kind is worth the being),' as he says in *The Unquiet Grave*:

> One way is, like Homer, Shakespeare, or Goethe, to accept life completely, the other (Pascal's, Proust's, Leopardi's, Baudelaire's) is to refuse ever to lose sight of its horror. One must be Prospero or Caliban; in between lie vast dissipated areas of pleasure and weakness.

The dramatization is forthright, and perhaps not very convincing, but it demonstrates his conviction that only the best is worth bothering about: 'the true function of a writer is to produce a masterpiece', and this is likely to mean scorned delights and laborious days. Conversely, it postulates a contempt amounting to loathing for belles-lettres, for literature as a game or a commercial entertainment, for pandering and pot-boiling as a way of life.

This led him, as a young man, to fall upon the literature of his own time with farcical ferocity – on the one hand the Walpoles, Galsworthys and Linklaters and their middle-brow reputations, and on the other the multitude of professional time-killers ('Culbertson, Torquemada, Wodehouse, Dorothy Sayers, Duke Ellington') who proclaimed England a footler's paradise. In fact his fury spilled over onto England itself; the series of diary extracts 'England Not My England' (1927–9) purports to record the closing stages of his love affair with his native land ('Really, the most deplorable country, Americanized without America's vitality or variety of race'); the virulence of his distaste ('Women all dowdy, men undersized and weedy. Pathetic voices and gestures, newspaper-fed ignorance') recalls at times D. H. Lawrence: there is a study to be made of this literary hatred of England between the wars. Was it owing to the rise in the cost of living? The emergence of the working class? The strict sexual climate and laws against homosexuality? Whatever the reason, it meant a bunk for the boat-train and sunnier climes, with the leisure to reflect 'we have no paper for literary experiment in England, and literature is, after all, as technical a business as medicine or engineering'.

Perhaps inevitably, Connolly developed a thesis that in the last 100 years English literature had fallen away badly when compared with that of France. This view is developed more explicitly in the lecture 'French and English Cultural Relations' (1943):

> We stood aside from the conflict [between artistic values and bourgeois materialism], with the result that in the 20th century our art and literature became even more unreal: the fanciful pastime of well-to-do middle-aged children who had refused to grow up, and who could never hurt themselves because whenever they fell it was always on a thick green lawn.

If Connolly had extended these contentions to a full-length argument – a companion to *Enemies of Promise* – he might have found they required so many qualifications as to collapse of their own accord, but they matched the war-time enthusiasm for things Gallic that elevated writers such as Aragon, Cocteau, Malraux and Gide to an eminence they can hardly have expected. What is important is not whether what he says is true, but his passionate insistence on literary integrity: no compromise, no surrender, no children's books, no lecturing in America, no 'work for television' (and, presumably, no reviewing).

Some of Connolly's most damaging criticism, however, took the form of hilarious literary romping, for he was an extremely funny writer, as *The Rock Pool* had already shown. It is hard to read the first three paragraphs of 'More About the Modern Novel' without bursting out laughing (interestingly enough, they were written in 1935; the rest of the article dates from 1928); 'Told in Gath' transfixes middle-period Aldous Huxley with the cruelty of a one-time disciple; 'Where Engels Fears to Tread' resembles a speeded-up one-reel version of *The Condemned Playground* itself ('Barcelona' shows him grappling with the 'contemporary' issue of the Spanish war) based on the career of Brian Howard:

> Some of these young poets, I realized, had even attended my university! One quatrain in particular haunted me.
>
> M is for Marx
> and Movement of Masses
> and Massing of Arses
> and Clashing of Classes
>
> It was new. It was vigorous. It was real. It was chic!

So much for the pylon poets. So much, finally, for the whole business of reviewing:

> Never praise; praise dates you ... Remember that the object of the critic is to revenge himself on the creator, and his method

> must depend on whether the book is good or bad, whether he dare condemn it himself or must lie quiet and let it blow over ... He stands behind the ticket-queue of fame, banging his rivals on the head as they bend low before the guichet. When he has laid out enough he becomes an authority, which is more than they will.

With all its violent oscillation between defiant assertion and farcical derogation Connolly's literary method produces not so much criticism – he was never a critic in the fullest sense of the word – as self-portraiture, 'Narcissus with his pool before him,' as he ends his early and enlightening account of the later Joyce. The writers he deals with emerge exalted or damaged, the situations he analyses encourage or accuse, but always there is a faint whispering: 'I wish I were like that.' Or, conversely, 'That's why I came to nothing.' It is both his strength and his weakness.

The richness of *The Condemned Playground* resides not so much in its recognizable contentions as in its incidental satisfactions, the pleasure of meeting a well-read, widely-travelled mind in which the cushions of nostalgia alternate with the snap of inflationary epigram (the *Penguin Dictionary of Modern Quotations* has 55 entries for Connolly against 38 for Eliot). And how unexpectedly, in its last section, the book rises to its conclusion, the passages from wartime issues of *Horizon*. Here Connolly is no longer savouring the past, or savaging the present: he is looking to the future with a sober idealism that transcends the personality of the previous pages. The enemies are still there – 'poor bald old homopuritan Pinheads', 'the Publisher, with his Cold Feet', the not-so-young poet trying to reconcile 'communism with religion, pacifism with war, property with revolution, and homosexuality with marriage', and the culture-diffusionists of CEMA, ABCA, MoI and their latterday descendants – but they will be squashed if we remember that England, 'an ancient civilization that is not neurotic, where thought once more is correlated with action, and which fights for its beliefs ... should, in those invisible exports like poetry and fine writing, be in a position to lead the world':

> It will be a world in which the part played by the English will be of supreme importance. In fact, one might say that the whole of English history, tradition, and character will be judged in the future by how we rise to the occasion of the post-war years.

There were too many qualifications for this to be termed propaganda. In the narrow corner of the mid-war years, it was Connolly's commitment to the morality of art that surfaced again, a vision of something beyond the condemned playground in which his own talent had up till then alternately flamed and flickered.

1983

Earth Memories
by Llewelyn Powys

'I think Llewelyn,' wrote Somerset Maugham of the Powys brothers, 'by living so long cheek by jowl with death, alone of them learnt to be honest.' The comment was no doubt meant to be provocative, in the Thirties. But in a way it still is. For although we know Theodore Francis Powys, one of the few contemporary writers to be approved by *Scrutiny*, and John Cowper Powys, if 'know' is the word to use of that gigantic mythopoeic literary volcano whose works are still in process of assimilation by an industrious ant-army of critics, are we any nearer knowing Llewelyn?

And yet, of the three, Llewelyn is the easiest to know. To open nearly any of his books is to find him talking, in an extraordinary blend of modern English with Urquhart and Thomas Deloney, about his own life and convictions, his childhood at Montacute Vicarage in Somerset, his idle undergraduate days at Cambridge, his time as a farm manager in Africa and a freelance writer in America. Talking, moreover, not with the insistence of egotism, but as a way of sharing and celebrating experience with oddly-precise epithets and an occasional streak of rueful self-caricature, until suddenly his attention turns to man's predicament, to love and death; the whole architecture of the page changes, and the long sentences go sweeping on, clause after clause, at once impersonal and the apotheosis of personality, the embodiment of meaning rather than the assertion of it, the rhetoric that is Llewelyn Powys and nobody else.

To know Llewelyn is, inevitably, to know the other Powyses. The eighth of six sons and five daughters born to the Reverend Charles Francis Powys between 1872 and 1890, he was always passionately close to his family, and the devotion was returned: 'without doubt,' according to John Cowper Powys, 'Llewelyn was

Earth Memories by Llewelyn Powys was first published in 1934. This edition was published by Redcliffe Press, Bristol in 1983.

the best loved *of* all his brothers and sisters *by* all his brothers and sisters.' 'We're Powyses, you and me, Powyses, *Powyses*, don't you see?' was how a friend summarised the almost comic intensity of their family feeling. Time and again he describes the late Victorian life at the vicarage, the lamps, the long walks, the tennis parties, the elder sons reading the lesson in church. Theodore, in later life, would speak of 'your father' and 'your brother'; Llewelyn never sought to distance himself in this way from those he loved and the happy life they had shared.

To some extent he was influenced by them. He followed his brothers to Cambridge, where he did not distinguish himself, taking a pass degree. He spent the World War years in Africa with his brother Willie; after the war, he went to America, where John Cowper was earning a precarious and exhausting living as a lecturer. Llewelyn abandoned lecturing after one attempt – lacking John's histrionic power, he was an embarrassing failure – but remained there for several years, 'writing for the papers' as he deprecatingly called it, for the example of John and Theodore was always before him. Returning home, he finally found Theodore's way of living suited him best: with Alyse Gregory, his American wife, he settled in a remote cottage in Dorset, writing ever more deeply of his own memories and convictions. All these experiences were valuable to him, remote from his character though some of them seem in retrospect. His books about Africa, *Ebony and Ivory* and *Black Laughter*, gained him an accidental reputation in America as a sort of Conrad or R. B. Cunningham Graham. John Cowper has said that Llewelyn was famous in America, and Theodore in England, long before anyone had heard of him.

In one way, Llewelyn was a natural writer. His letters are vivid and personal, and often very funny. His first published work, part of *Confessions of Two Brothers* (1916) written with John Cowper, showed how easily he could dramatise his own experience, a talent he came to recognise as his principal gift (the family called it 'Lulu-ising'). Yet in another he found writing desperately hard. A remark by Theodore that 'there was always something wrong about writers who could not write about anything but themselves' depressed him deeply. Although he wrote one highly readable novel, *Apples Be Ripe* (1930), he could not think of plots. Literary journalism, in which 'new subjects' were all-important, was a strain for him.

What set Llewelyn apart from his brothers, and indeed shaped his whole life, was ill health. The first essay in this collection describes the onset of tuberculosis when he was twenty-five, and its subsequent visitations, and makes clear the extent to which it shocked him. For he had never been a weakling: as an American friend said, there was 'nothing of the invalid in his looks or manner'. Tall, with tightly-curled sandy-gold hair, he seemed to link his own exuberance to the native Powys toughness, nor for all his Epicurean convictions was he given to any sort of damaging excess. 'Not Lulu, not Lulu ill,' cried John Cowper when he heard. It was a kind of outrage.

The existing elements of his character were immediately and permanently polarised. No writer has been more constantly aware of the fact of death, of extinction, of joining 'that recumbent congregation of all nationalities that lie upon their shoulder-blades'. He could never forget that

> it was I, and I alone, who, when all my dramatisations and sensationalisms were over, would be spending cold nights, cold years, cold centuries, alone in a cold elmwood coffin.

It became the central plank of his philosophy. Who, with this certainty before him, could be concerned with social observance and advancement? Or regard religion's preposterous bait of immortality with anything but angry contempt? Or help striving daily, as he wrote to an American enquirer in 1932, 'to grow accustomed to the prospect of death with a serene mind'?

Yet it was not a negative reaction. The overwhelming importance of death was balanced by the overwhelming importance of living: 'love every moment of life,' he wrote on his death-bed, 'that you experience *without pain*.'

> Consider the glow, the glory of being alive, the incredible chance of it! How heart-piercing, how shocking, how supremely beautiful is this unexplained, wavering movement that troubles all that is, from the Milky Way to a common sting-nettle!

Endless variations on this theme can be found in books such as *Now That The Gods are Dead* and *Glory of Life*; in the present collection, the essays *Natural Happiness* and *Natural Worship* take it up again. At first sight his prose looks unfashionably 'grand', not entirely free of what he himself called 'flagrant clichés' and 'bloody banalities', together with the affectation of neo-Jacobethanisms such as 'both maid and yellow-hosed bachelor'. What saves it is his vehement and idiosyncratic vision; only he could write of slugs that 'with silent secret perspicacity, draw towards the undefended seedlings of their appetites', or

> Men and women, these bounding apes that must every day void dross, by a sweepstake chance have won divine thought, thought potent to destroy, potent to save.

The chief glory of life, inevitably, was sexual love and sexual enjoyment. 'It is the backbone of all life, the pliable, beautiful, spiked backbone upon which the fair grace of the flesh is built.'

> Lust is nature's free gift to us all, and the hours of its consummation are beyond all measure the most real and ecstatic hours of our lives.

After the mid-century revolution of our attitudes, such declarations may sound quaintly over-emphatic, but this is because they have been embraced rather than repudiated. Nor were they the hectic fancies of one deprived by upbringing and illness of direct sexual experience. The remarkable letters from Llewelyn to a young American poetess Gamel Woolsey, edited in 1973 by Malcolm Elwin as a footnote to his admirable biography, demonstrate that, where love was concerned, he spoke as he found. And so we are led to his last major book, the 'imaginary autobiography' *Love and Death* that arose from this strange relationship, in which the dying narrator recalls his passionate love for a girl who ultimately deserted him, reliving each episode to keep the thought of death at arm's length. In it Llewelyn's two great preoccupations are brought face to face, and the result is an audacious and poignant narrative richly summarising the desperate joyful brevity of life as he had known it.

In his later years of illness he grew a beard: the impulsive gold-haired young man with the 'woman's mouth' became a gaunt figure in a cloak and broad-brimmed hat, something of a sage. 'I'd forgotten how *wise* he became,' a friend said, reading his letters after his death, and it is true that Llewelyn Powys is one of the rare writers who teach endurance of life as well as its enjoyment. To love life and grow accustomed to the prospect of death is a simple enough message, yet in fulfilling it he learnt not only to be honest, as Maugham said, but to distil into literature the example of his own sensibility and courage.

> For at the end of all – what are we? A herd of dream cattle, images of breath, passing shadows that move swiftly across the world's pastures to a graveyard where, at a single clap, eternity is as a day and a day as eternity.

1983

IV · REVIEWS

Afternoon Men by Anthony Powell

Afternoon Men, 1931; *Venusberg*, 1932; *From a View to a Death*, 1933; *Agents and Patients*, 1936; *What's Become of Waring*, 1939; *A Question of Upbringing*, 1950; *A Buyer's Market*, 1952 – Anthony Powell is the only considerable English novelist I can think of whose career was genuinely interrupted by the war. And now that he has two post-war books behind him, we can congratulate ourselves doubly; that his talent has survived the enforced silence, and that his post-war success seems likely to bring about the reprinting of his earlier books, so long and so maddeningly unobtainable.

That they themselves were not popular successes, as I think may be fairly admitted, is probably because in the Thirties Powell was neglected in favour of a writer who, superficially at least, was producing the same kind of book – namely, Evelyn Waugh. Both excelled at comedy; both dealt with the London world of somewhat aggressively post-1918 manners; both wrote with exceptional literary acuteness and a quick eye for significant detail. Waugh, however, had got in first with *Decline and Fall* (1928), and in the novels that followed his fiercer, more satiric talent, with its preposterous ironies and extravagancies of character, quite outshone his quieter contemporary, whose recognition seems in fact only just at hand. But really they had not a great deal in common. 'The novels of Anthony Powell,' wrote Cyril Connolly in 1936, 'are unaffected monochromes of realism. Anything which might heighten the colouring is scrupulously omitted. They deal in nuances of boredom, seediness and squalor – "the artist is recognizable by the particular unpleasantness of his life" is his creed, and since he gaily accepts it his novels have a delightful quality, containing much of the purest comedy that is now being written.'

There is no better way of realizing the justice of this, and at the same time seeing how far apart Waugh and Powell were even in those days, than by reading *Afternoon Men*, published when Powell was 26, and now the second of his books to achieve post-war re-issue. (For those who are interested, *From a View to a Death* was reprinted in 1948.) Its plot is simple. Atwater, the unimpressive young hero, works in a London museum, and in his spare time goes to parties. At one of these, which he attends with his painter friends Barlow and Pringle, he notices a girl called Susan, and at another he asks her out to dinner. The dinner is unfortunately not too successful, for several people join them unasked, including a man named Verelst who is obviously taken with Susan also. A second date Susan breaks by telephone, and their relationship is virtually terminated during a fragmentary conversation at a boxing match. Atwater goes to stay with Pringle in the country, and Pringle tries to drown himself when he discovers his fiancée Harriet making love with Barlow. Atwater then returns to London to learn that Susan and Verelst have gone to America together. He is very unhappy, and the book ends with his accepting an invitation to another party.

The pattern (boy meets girl, boy loses girl, *da capo*) is a familiar one, but the book is distinguished firstly by Powell's dry and unmistakable way with words, and secondly by his talent for making out of a sequence of day-to-day banalities a dance-figure at once absurd and solemn. The style itself is a dead-pan, damped-down colloquialism, trembling perpetually on the edge of mannerism, at times faintly like a kind of anglicized early Hemingway, afflicting the reader with a metaphysical desire to scratch. Its chief effect, however, is cumulative and comic. This is hard to catch in short quotation, but here is Pringle quarrelling with Barlow:

> Pringle said: 'You've been a bad influence on me ever since I met you. I've even felt my painting getting worse and worse.'
> 'In what way?'
> 'In every way.'
> 'I'm sure you're wrong.'
> 'I know I'm right.'
> Barlow said: 'How you put the paint on or the subjects you choose?' Really interested, he had stopped lighting his pipe.
> 'I always disliked you,' said Pringle. His voice had become so high that he was nearly screaming. Barlow struck another match.

And this is Nosworth, Atwater's colleague at the Museum:

> He was approaching fifty, and very tall and yellow. He was a good archaeologist, so they said, and he wore a hard, turned-down collar a size or more too large for him. His face stood out yellow against the buff distemper. He stood there without moving or speaking, with several heavy books under his arm, as if petrified, or like something out of the Chamber of Horrors.

It may be guessed from these passages how this style functions in collaboration with a remarkably selective eye; scenes of apparent irrelevance or triviality are at once raised to distinction. Drab, curiously authentic little incidents they are for the most part: Mrs Race playing a record of *Belgium put the kybosh on the Kaiser*, Lola's friend Gwen breaking a sherry cork while trying to pull it, Verelst in his well-made shoes recommending a hotel to Atwater for its cuisine. Nor does Powell neglect the long-term effect: the bottle of medicine Pringle is praising to Atwater on page 1 and sampling on page 87 is accidentally broken by Harriet on page 189 when Pringle is supposed to be dead, and when he returns it is almost the first thing he misses. But this methodical plainness is most striking when Atwater and Harriet, lying on a cliff, see far below them Pringle walk down the beach and begin to undress. Harriet remarks lazily that he has forgotten his towel:

> Pringle stood there scratching himself. He did this for some time and then walked towards the sea. He stepped gingerly as the stones evidently hurt the soles of his feet, and when he reached the sea he stopped and looked back in the direction of the house.
>
> Harriet said: 'He's just remembered his towel.'

But Pringle, as the reader guesses, is bent on suicide.

The fascination of this book is watching the amount of comedy that can be achieved by a writer who makes so little call on comedy's conventional properties. It proves extraordinarily large. And it is equally extraordinary how little has dated or gone dead. In short, my advice is: buy *Afternoon Men*, buy *From a View to a Death*, and keep a sharp look out for the others.

Q, 7, Michaelmas 1952

Not Literary Enough

When I read Mr Heath-Stubbs as an undergraduate in 1940 I was doubly crestfallen: at his serene individuality, practised scholarship and extensive and peculiar vocabulary, and at my failure to appreciate him. It was not that I thought his poems bad: I just could not see why they had been written. My attention, hovering over them like a mine-detector, reported no tension, no emotional pressure, and moved elsewhere.

I say this because although I have read *A Charm Against the Toothache* in the hope of revising this opinion, I find I have not done much more than confirm it. Of course, Mr Heath-Stubbs's poetry has not changed all that much; his strongest card is still his dramatic/historical imagination, here displayed in 'Donna Elvira' and 'Dionysius the Areopagite', a form in which his formidable vocabulary and ability to spin a succession of precise and brilliant images come dazzlingly into their own. Then there are one or two charming topographical/historical pieces ('Memories of Paul Verlaine', 'Dr William Turner', 'Obstinate in Non-Attendance') – charming, but hardly more than fourth leaders; and some experiments in humour I beseech Mr Heath-Stubbs not to repeat. Then – and this *is* novel – there is a group of personal poems, wry or distressed, that speak of himself and his life and its dissatisfactions. It is these, with their refusal to be self-important or self-righteous, that win the reader's goodwill, and, despite metrical hints that Captain Carpenter is sleeping there below, I should pick 'Epitaph' as the most effective poem in the collection.

But for all that I cannot ignore lines like the following, each of which concludes a poem and must therefore be taken as important:

> Except the unlimited, treacherous ocean of love.
>
> In the heart of a poem's crystal alone can the Spring come true.
>
> The city of mud and pearls has broken another poet.

Review of John Heath-Stubbs, *A Charm Against the Toothache* (Methuen, 1954)

These are postures so familiar to have lost all emotional force or even flavour, and I am astonished that Mr Heath-Stubbs does not see their effect on the poems they conclude. But then, I find whole poems ('Song for All Fools' Day', 'Prayer to St Lucy', 'Elegiac Stanzas') written apparently in the belief that traditional poetic stances can be carried off with no more support than good poetic manners, and I am forced to complain that too much of Mr Heath-Stubbs's poetry assumes that attitudes and properties successful in the past are thereby guaranteed successful indefinitely, and allow him to dispense with original and re-creating emotion. No doubt this is what people mean by calling him 'too literary'. But it is precisely Mr Heath-Stubbs's literary sense I think defective. I think it should prevent him from speaking of 'the Muse' or 'that Irish sorcerer' (W. B. Yeats), from rewriting the 137th Psalm to the tune of *The Shandon Bells*, from writing lines such as I quote above, or (another ending):

> The sun will not haver in its course for the lack of you,
> Nor the flowers fail in colour, nor the bird stint in its song.
> Only the heart that wanted somehow to have opened up
> Finds the frost in the day's air, and the nights which appear too long.

In fact, for a writer born with an equipment and individuality such as few achieve throughout their career, I should say Mr Heath-Stubbs is not literary enough – a conclusion having, I hope, at least the charm of novelty.

Poetry and Audience, 21 June 1954

Beyond a Joke

Reading Mr Betjeman's latest book of poems, I am left with the feeling that in some astonishing unacknowledged way he has crept up with the leaders. What do we ask of poetry: emotion, technique, humour? Betjeman has all of these. Yet the *cognoscenti* do not take him seriously: his poems are classed with, say, Osbert Lancaster's cartoons – *rentier* satire, 'amusing' *pastiche* – or condemned as something rather infantile and ingrown, not to be mentioned in the same breath as Mr W. R. Rodgers or Mr Norman Nicholson. This is the penalty he pays for twenty-odd years passionate celebration in poem, essay and lecture of a great many things we were brought up to think uninteresting, regrettable, or downright hideous: nineteenth-century ecclesiastical and domestic architecture, for instance; seaside bungalows, sports girls, the Church of England, verse novels, gas lighting, branch railways. These and their like form his poetic subject-matter, and in the early days, when every austere six-bobsworth of Auden, Spender and MacNeice was *de rigueur* for the good citizen, Betjeman's delighted gurglings at thorough-paced awfulness were dismissed as, at best, a cod; at worst, bourgeois taste at its most corrupt. It is only fair to say that the get-up of his early books pandered to such dismissals; anyone who has seen them will remember the photographs, rubrications, and other playfulness, and how on the title-page of *Continual Dew* was drawn a section, to scale, of a dripping kitchen tap.

This did not last. The lay-out of *Old Lights in New Chancels* (1940) and *New Bats in Old Belfries* (1945) was as chaste as the poetry was aesthetically serious, and by the time Mr John Sparrow compiled the *Selected Poems* in 1948 it was possible for him to treat of his author as a 'remarkable and original artist'. Rightly he laid chief emphasis on Mr Betjeman's development from a connoisseur of architectural freakishness to a master of a new kind of topogra-

Review of John Betjeman, *A Few Late Chrysanthemums* (Murray, 1954)

phical verse, ardent instead of reflective, in which the place was evoked as much for the kind of life lived there as for its own character:

Bells are booming down the bohreens,
White the mist along the grass.
Now the Julias, Maeves and Maureens
Move between the fields to Mass.
Twisted trees of small green apple
Guard the decent white-washed chapel,
Gilded gates and doorways grained,
Pointed windows richly stained
With many-coloured Munich glass.
('Sunday in Ireland')

Fling wide the curtains! – there's a Surrey sunset!
Low down the line sings the Addiscombe train,
Leaded are the windows lozenging the crimson,
Drained dark the pines on resin-scented rain ...
('Love in a Valley')

Till the tram went over thirty, sighting terminus again,
Past municipal lawn tennis and the bobble-hanging plane;
Soft the light suburban evening caught our ashlar-speckled spire,
Eighteen-sixty Early English, as the mighty elms retire
Either side of Brookfield Mansions flashing fine French-window fire.
('Parliament Hill Fields')

The feeling in these lines is equalled only by their precision: compare them, for instance, with *Dover* by the myopic Auden. And sometimes into the foreground will heave one of Mr Betjeman's formidable heroines:

Miss J. Hunter Dunn, Miss J. Hunter Dunn,
Furnish'd and burnish'd by Aldershot sun,
What strenuous singles we played after tea,
We in the tournament – you against me!

Love-thirty, love-forty, oh! weakness of joy,
The speed of a swallow, the grace of a boy,
With carefullest carelessness, gaily you won,
I am weak from your loveliness, Joan Hunter Dunn.
('A Subaltern's Love Song')

These quotations will have shown, too, how the excitement is heightened by an unusual yet quite unaffected use of verse forms so intricate, various and compelling that the reader has a poem half by heart before he realizes it. Victorian in their emphasis – and sometimes quite frankly in their origin – they raise the question whether Mr Betjeman has not in fact been accidentally shut out of the nineteenth century, and is trying all he knows to get back. His love of English landscape, for instance – how out of date in these days of Mediterranean-or-bust! And famous Pam ('Pam, I adore you, Pam, you great big mountainous sports girl') – surely behind her lurks the shade of Ada Mencken, the bouncing circus lady who captivated Swinburne? His talent for detail, again, his concern with the rich surface of things, recalls the marvellous minor Ruskinians like John Brett, whose paintings to-day seem so little regarded:

> So on this after-storm-lit evening
> To him the raindrops in the tamarisk,
> The fuchsia bells, the sodden matchbox lid
> That checked a tiny torrent in the lane
> Were magnified and shining clear with life . . .
> ('North Coast Recollections')

And now and then he will produce an effect comparable to a Pre-Raphaelite 'literary' picture, in which figures and setting are eloquent of a deducible emotional crisis:

> Pale green of the *English Hymnal*! Yattendon hymns
> Played on the *hautbois* by a lady dressed in blue,
> Her white-haired father accompanying her thereto
> On tenor or bass-recorder. Daylight swims
> On sectional bookcase, delicate cup and plate
> And William de Morgan tiles around the grate
> And many the silver birches the pearly light shines through.
> ('The Old Liberals')

But despite such indications, we cannot really class Mr Betjeman as a strayed Victorian: he is much too good at our present day for that, even if he does not like it, and when he speaks of it only a moderately sharp ear is needed to catch the fascination it has for him:

> Well-cut Windsmoor flapping lightly,
> Jacqmar scarf of mauve and green
> Hiding hair which, Friday nightly,
> Delicately drowns in Drene;
> Fair Elaine the bobby-soxer,
> Fresh-complexioned with Innoxa,
> Gains the garden – Father's hobby –
> Hangs her Windsmoor in the lobby,
> Settles down to sandwich supper and the television screen.
> ('Middlesex')

The reader may at this point be wondering what the quotations I have made add up to: whether they are any more than a series of brilliant *vignettes*, and whether a poet should not be able to do more than hit off a place or period. I can only reply that what I have quoted are Betjeman poems in miniature: he really does devote his best efforts to catching the interplay of time and place, so that his poems in one light seem authentic social history, in another to demonstrate acutely the passage of time, in a third to show the inherent dignified sadness of life. For though he can be funnier than any other poet to-day, Mr Betjeman's most characteristic reference is to the melancholy of Tennyson and the sadness of Hardy. Perhaps this is due in part to the fact that, for him, the modern poetic revolution has just not happened; there has been no symbolism, no Ezra Pound, no objective correlative, no rediscovery of myth, no *Seven Types* or *Some Versions*, no works of criticism with titles like *Communication as Discipline* or *Implicit and Explicit Image-Obliquity in Sir Lewis Morris* – his poems are written in the strong unregenerate belief that poetry is a simple matter of trying to construct a verbal device that will preserve and reproduce any given feeling or set of feelings indefinitely, and that nothing is to be gained by *questioning* an emotion once it has been experienced. Probably it is this extraordinary unselfconscious loyalty to the subjects that move him that makes Mr Betjeman seem so un-contemporary. Yeats may make poetry by quarrelling with himself; that is not Betjeman's way. His subjects are unusual, unfashionable, suspect, comical and eccentric, but he stuck to them. How has it paid-off, poetically?

On the evidence of *A Few Late Chrysanthemums*, excitingly well; I could instance some six poems that seem to me to capture a tone deeper and in some cases more complex than he has done before – the figures in the foreground, the business girls, the mother of five, the clergyman's widow, are chosen by a sensitive compassion rare in poetry to-day. And there are other hints that hitherto-separate aspects of his talents are linking up. Take one of the best poems in the collection, 'The Metropolitan Railway'. Here the railway is treated affectionately as an antique, in the old style ('Early Electric! With what radiant hope/Men formed this many-branched electrolier'), but because it was once a symbol of progress into a happy future he connects it with the young married couples who used it when it was new, and who are now as quaint and out-dated as Baker Street Station Buffet:

> Cancer has killed him. Heart is killing her.
> The trees are down. An Odeon flashes fire
> Where stood their villa by the murmuring fir ...

At the end the reader is left with a blend of emotion unusually full for a poem, or at least for a modern poem: the six stanzas have been more like a novel. Indeed, I think one of the strengths of Mr Betjeman's poetry is that he has refused to relinquish emotions and situations that other poets have let slip into the film and the novel and other mass-media: it can lead to sentimentality, but on the other hand it can lead to works such as Hardy's *Satires of Circumstance*. And since I have mentioned Hardy, I should like to end by quoting a sentence he copied into his diary from Leslie Stephen: 'The ultimate aim of a poet should be to touch our hearts by showing his own, and not to exhibit his learning, or his fine taste, or his skill in mimicking the notes of his predecessors.' I think this is even more relevant now than it was then, and one reason why I regard Mr Betjeman's poetry as important is that it bears it out so well.

Q, 11, Hilary 1955

Abstract Vision

For nearly twenty years Miss Kathleen Raine has sought to express in her poetry abstract themes fundamental to man and his position in the universe – the unity of creation, the conflict of spirit and selfhood – and the publication of her *Collected Poems* demonstrates how far the height and intensity of this purpose set her apart from her contemporaries. I can think of few recent poems as free from jargon, vulgarity and smartness as those in this book. Her work lacks every quality traditionally associated with the title 'poetess': there is no domesticity, no cosiness, and 'love poems of a personal nature', the introduction tells us, 'have also gone'. What remains is the vatic and universal. The visible world exists, but only as

> Upheld by being that I cannot know
> In other form than stars and stones and trees.

And everything she considers is pressed into its place in the eternal pattern:

> The sweet-eyed unregarding beasts
> Waking and sleeping wear the natural grace.
> The innocent order of the stars and tides
> An impulse in the bloodstream circulates

There is no doubt that the quality of these preoccupations and the pure underivative language in which they are expressed have resulted in some very fine poems ('Shells', 'The Invisible Spectrum', 'Air') which prove Miss Raine to be one of the most serious living English poets – serious, that is, in the sense of utter devotion to her vision. But I think it is arguable that she has not so far written the poems she will be known by. Perhaps the poetry of abstract vision carries a high failure-rate simply because the reader can come so little of the way to meet it: certainly I find Miss Raine's impact greatest when she writes most simply (as in the haunting group of 'spells', whose rhythms recall old Celtic folk-poetry), and

Review of Kathleen Raine, *Collected Poems* (Hamish Hamilton, 1956)

it may be that the way forward for a talent of this order lies paradoxically in a cruder, more strongly marked mode of expression. But this collection makes it clear that the distance Miss Raine has already travelled is sufficient to earn the honour and gratitude of her age.

Manchester Guardian, 17 April 1956

Shem the Penman

The study of James Joyce is still at the stage of elucidation. Mr Kenner, a Canadian critic already well known for his resourceful and intelligent writing on modern literature, takes as his thesis that Dublin – lyrical, epical, and dramatic – lies at the heart of Joyce's concentric works, and conducts the reader through them with a staggering wealth of allusion and cross-reference. In fact, the thesis seems often mislaid as Mr Kenner repeatedly slices through his vast subject-matter from different angles. In addition to reminding us of such matters as the schematization of *Ulysses* and the aesthetic of Aquinas, Mr Kenner offers a diverting comparison of Stephen Bloom with Holmes-Watson, an assessment of the effect reading Carroll had on Joyce's notions for *Finnegans Wake*, and a dazzling flow of exegetical comment of the sort that can be neither proved nor disproved. 'Only once Christ as Bread of Life appears darkly, behind Bloom's gift of Banbury cake to the seagulls . . .' Nearly all of it is intensely interesting, yet it leaves one wishing that Mr Kenner had passed at some point from elucidation to evaluation.

Why, for instance, does the two-page shorthand transcript of the reminiscences of Joyce *père* ('We all went in and by God Almighty such a drinking of champagne I never saw in my life. We could not wait to draw the corks, we slapped them against the marble-topped counter . . .') make one momentarily so impatient with the contrivances of Joyce *fils*? Surely, now we know more of Joyce's method and aims, critical opinion should be forming about the success of the first and the vitality and depth of the second, as with any other writer. Mr Kenner does not attempt this. 'One can imagine what Dr Johnson would have said,' he writes at one point. The next task for Joyce critics is to prove that Dr Johnson would have been wrong.

Manchester Guardian, 3 July 1956

Review of Hugh Kenner, *Dublin's Joyce* (Chatto and Windus, 1956)

No More Fever

There is nothing in this collection to make anyone alter his view of the latter-day Auden. Whether you believe his last book of any interest was *Another Time* (1940), or whether you find his American output subtler, more mature and of deeper import than anything he produced before the war, the poems offered here will confirm you in your view. They carry straight on from *Nones*, and two poems from that volume are included among them. *The Shield of Achilles* is made up of fourteen unrelated pieces, flanked on one side by a sequence of seven poems on natural phenomena ('Mountains', 'Lakes', 'Water' and so on – each of them 'for' someone), and on the other by seven more entitled *Horae Canonicae* ('Prime', 'Terce', 'Sext' and the rest), a group suggesting loosely that the 'hours' in question are of the day of the Crucifixion.

The astute reader will suspect from this outline alone that the pressure of poetic energy in the book is low, and he will be right. Although in theory a set of seven poems entitled 'Mountains', 'Lakes', 'Water', and so on (each of them 'for' someone) has as good a chance of success as any seven poems conceived and executed separately, in fact it is more likely to mean that the poet was outside the compulsion necessary for poetic success and was free to choose a smart frame for some poems he thought it might be rather nice to write. At any rate, that is what I feel has happened here. The *Bucolics*, as this group is called, bear all the marks of having been written in despite of something more important. They are garrulous, ingenious, playful-sentimental, and get nowhere. In addition, they are phrased in the kind of no-style that was a feature of *Nones*:

> Romance? Not in this weather. Ovid's charmer
>   Who leads the quadrilles in Arcady, boy-lord
> Of hearts who can call their Yes and No their own,
>   Would, madcap that he is, soon die of cold or sunstroke:

Review of W. H. Auden, *The Shield of Achilles* (Faber and Faber, 1955)

These lives are in firmer hands; that old grim She
Who makes the blind dates for the hatless genera
Creates their country matters. (Woe to the childbed,
Woe to the strawberries if She's in Her moods!)

What chance has this wilful jumble of modes of any aesthetic coherence or effect? It would not be so irritating if the characteristics so jumbled were admirable in themselves. But they are not. Far too noticeable is a kind of lisping archness that sets the teeth on edge:

Five minutes on even the nicest mountain
Is awfully long.
('Mountains')

And:

Moraine, pot, oxbow, glint, sink, crater, piedmont, dimple...?
Just reeling off their names is ever so comfy.
('Lakes')

And what has happened to the 'light manner', the legacy of Byron and Praed, by which Auden once set such store? The lightness nowadays is of wastepaper rather than light metal:

How fascinating is that class
Whose only member is Me!
Sappho, Tiberius and I
Hold forth beside the sea.
('Islands')

These faults are less apparent in the second set, the *Horae*, but there is no gain in precise incontrovertibility: the tone never rises above a well-bred neo- (and sub-) Eliotese:

We shall always now be aware
Of the deep into which they lead, under
The mock chase and mock capture,
The racing and tussling and splashing,
The panting and the laughter,
Be listening for the cry and stillness
To follow after: wherever
The sun shines, brooks run, books are written,
There will also be this death.
('Nones')

Much of this section is very good reading, as an essay might be very good reading (in particular, 'Sext'); some, even, moderately amusing (in particular, 'Vespers'), but when a poet, calling himself a Christian, elects to write on such a theme I think we have a right to expect a more significant conclusion than the pious coronal of hopefulness put forward in terms so conventional as to be meaningless:

> ... That we, too, may come to the picnic
> With nothing to hide, join the dance
> As it moves in perichoresis,
> Turns about the abiding tree.

There is not much comfort to be taken from the middle group of individual poems which, according to my theory, might have been expected to redeem the mediocrity which surrounds them. 'The Willow-Wren and the Stare' is a promising idea, but again the no-style – a kind of mixture of Age-of-Plastic nursery-rhyme, ballet folk-lore, and Hollywood Lemprière – prevents its complete realization. 'The Truest Poetry is the Most Feigning' is a joking guide to the writing of good poetry:

> Be subtle, various, ornamental, clever,
> And do not listen to those critics ever
> Whose crude provincial gullets crave in books
> Plain cooking made still plainer by plain cooks ...

and reiterates Auden's often-expressed belief that poetry is 'the luck of verbal playing', which is I suppose the opposite taste. 'Ode to Gaea' starts finely, with a hint of the old Auden sweeping range:

> Leaves by the mile hide tons of
> Pied pebbles that will soon be birds ...

and would be impressive if this level was sustained, but all too soon it declines to the non-serious status of 'But who on Cupid's coming would care to bet?', a poetry written it seems by someone no longer capable of strong feeling, or of conveying strong feeling in poetry, or of thinking that it matters whether it is conveyed or not, since poetry is all luck anyway.

Since Auden has apparently settled into this mode for good, I think it is unlikely that he will produce anything more of interest. It is a sad occasion when this is said of any writer, and especially so in the case of one who meant so much to his younger contemporaries, and was instrumental in bringing so many of them to the practice of reading and writing poetry: but then so has the deterioration been sad, from the powerfully-suggestive, elliptic originality of 1930 to the silly verbose stew of the present day. It leads one to wonder whether one's evaluation of Auden in the old days was at fault, and looking back one does indeed feel that he was not all that was claimed for him, even in the Thirties: his talents were for mimicry and synthesis, creating only the appearance of intelligence and knowledge; his ideas of good and evil were crude and immature; in fact, his continual recourse in image and metaphor to the life of childhood suggested that his poetic personality had been arrested. Most of all, his work lacked, and still lacks, unsentimental unsmart charity.

On the other hand, the obscurity of his earlier poems does not in retrospect seem wilful or self-important mystification. The lines have an oblique potency, a strength drawn from the very fact that their meaning or relevance must not be made plain, like the utterances of the Saga heroes who so haunted Auden's youthful imagination:

> Go home, now, stranger, proud of your young stock,
> Stranger, turn back again, frustrate and vexed:
> This land, cut off, will not communicate,
> Be no accessory content to one
> Aimless for faces rather there than here.
> Beams from your car may cross a bedroom wall,
> They wake no sleeper ...

Auden's prime gift was his tremendous power to convince. He had the talent for finding images, rhythms and phrases that completely won the reader's confidence, no matter how little was otherwise conceded; he had the knack of writing lines that seemed to embody the precisest expression of the most important matter, however unsusceptible to paraphrase:

> Then lightly, my darling, leave me and slip away
> Playfully, betraying him nothing, allaying suspicion:
> His eye is on all these people about us, leading
> Their quite horrified lives,
> But if we can trust we are free.
> Though alone among those
> Who within earshot of the ungovernable sea
> Grow set in their ways.

It was a talent which enabled him to produce passages of mesmeric beauty, as if he were simply transcribing a seamless vision:

The Summer holds: upon its glittering lake
Lie Europe and the islands; many rivers
Wrinkling its surface like a ploughman's palm.
Under the bellies of the grazing horses
On the far side of posts and bridges
The vigorous shadows dwindle; nothing wavers.
Calm at this moment the Dutch sea so shallow
That sunk St Pauls would ever show its golden cross
And still the deep water that divides us still from Norway

and it is for such lines, rather than the more vigorous doctrinaire myth-making, that we most regret his decline.

The reasons for this decline will no doubt be discussed for a long time yet, and we shall need to know much more about the nature of the poetic impulse before we can make a final judgment. The coincidence of its onset, however, with Auden's departure for America simply cannot be ignored, even if we do not go as far as saying that nobody writes well away from home. I think, myself, that if I were analysing Auden's poetry with a view to diagnosing its latter failure – and I do no more than throw this out as a hint – I should start from the fact that if one were to mark all the passages in his work that might be called *typical* Auden one would find that a surprisingly high proportion of them consist of direct or indirect expression of emotions connected with dread, guilt, disaster or disease. I need mention only a few instances:

Holders of one position, wrong for years.

In sanatoriums they laugh less and less,
Less certain of cure; and the loud madman
Sinks now into a more terrible calm.

Hearing of harvests rotting in the valleys ...

From gradual ruin spreading like a stain ...

It does seem to me, therefore, that a great deal of Auden's 'inspiration' – and this applies equally to Christopher Isherwood, another regrettably-similar case – depended on continual contact with the atmosphere of pre-1939 Europe where these emotions were so prevalent, and I fancy that his decline as a poet dates from the time when he cut himself off not from England as such but from the insecurity that England represented. It is not for me to say in what sense America meant security to him, even if I knew the answer, but I do think that much of the low-pressure non-serious element in his present work is directly traceable to his change of country. In the best Auden, the pre-1939 Auden, we find, as he found in Spain, 'our fever's menacing shapes are precise and alive'. It may be, of course, that there is no more fever today in England, America, or anywhere else. In that case the decline was inevitable.

Listen, Summer 1956

Chosen and Recommended

Mr W. S. Merwin is already well enough known to us for it to be a surprise to learn that this is his first volume to be published here. As *Kenyon Review* Poetry Fellow for 1954 (when most of these poems were written) he might be called a 'professional' poet, and indeed a professional air rises undeniably from his work. His subjects – animal, vegetable, and biblical – are treated pleasantly, skilfully, yet a little conventionally; his not-quite-unusual language, his not-quite-conversational rhythms, his conjunctions (147 'ands' in 233 lines) buttonhole the reader with impeccable charm, but rarely do more. His best poems – 'Burning the Cat' or 'Thorn Leaves in March' – are sensitive meditations that rise artlessly to a diffused climax, and he is always master of a fanciful precision:

> They carry the ends of our hungers out to drop them
> To wait swaying in a dark place we could never have chosen.
> By motions we have never learned they feed us
> We lay wreaths on the sea when it has drowned them

Mr Merwin may soon outstrip his good manners; in the meantime they certainly throw Miss Kathleen Nott's volume into glaring relief. Her struggling, confused, often over-written poems seem to be seeking to express apprehensions and ideas (the north, love, nature) for which she can find inadequate symbols only; aiming higher than Mr Merwin, she falls lower. Obscurity is inevitable (for which I blame her); the ridiculous hovers perilously near ('this faceless love whose bowels had eaten reason'); one longs in vain for a simple condensed effect. Yet when Miss Nott does succeed ('the nameless cemeteries on secret maps like sewers') she is both original and strong; in 'Storm', for instance:

Review of *Green with Beasts* by W. S. Merwin (Hart-Davis, 1956) and *Poems from the North* by Kathleen Nott (Hand and Flower Press, 1956)

And even the locked firs
All once mad dip for the storm, and there is huge sky
over their leaning light-sleeved, many-dark wristed

Or 'New Elegy in a Country Churchyard':

And we still tend
the dead as if they were strange plants with an uncertain promise in them ...

Or 'The Moment of Snow':

All this whiteness might
be only fear of leagues and even clots of snow
claw on the black and numb declivities of the fir-boughs
like polar cubs in flight from their own natures

In such passages Miss Nott shows a talent very different from the ordinary, that one wants to see more consistently harnessed. If it were, one would not be forced to agree with the Poetry Book Society, which makes Miss Nott its recommendation, but Mr Merwin its choice.

Manchester Guardian, 14 October 1956

Separate Ways

It is a pleasure to recommend these three books, not only individually but collectively, as showing how three different – even antagonistic – methods can each be justified. The work of Mr Kingsley Amis, for example, is labelled like a trunk with misapprehensions ('Anti-Wet Scum'), and this selection of 45 poems may help to peel some of them off. The broad farce ('A Dream of Fair Women'), the literary politics ('Against Romanticism'), the deliberate anticlimaxes ('Going well so far, eh?') fall into place as different ways of discrediting the insensitive, the flatulent, and the dishonest: they also blend into a style which (as in 'To Eros') is utterly unmistakable:

> If only we could throw you away,
> Garotte you, weight you, sink you in the bay,
> We could start living, we say.
> Our girls would all relapse
> Back into girls – not all that bright perhaps,
> But ever such decent chaps . . .

a style that will exasperate only those who cannot see when a poem is being funny and serious simultaneously. This manner is his principal achievement; without it he seems dragged down by his own literal-mindedness, and, although he has two very untypical successes ('The Real Earth', 'The Small Room'), one quickly sees where his considerable strength lies. *A Case of Samples* shows what scrupulous skill is guiding that strength.

A volume of *Selected Poems* is an honourable stage in a poet's career, and any reader previously unacquainted with Mr Durrell's work should be grateful that he has reached it. His great talent has always been to find the unexpected and entirely right epithet:

Review of Kingsley Amis, *A Case of Samples* (Gollancz, 1956); Lawrence Durrell, *Selected Poems* (Faber and Faber, 1956); and Siegfried Sassoon, *Sequences* (Faber and Faber, 1956)

The Ocean's peculiar spelling
Haunts here, cuddled by syllables
In caves perpendicular, a blue recitation
Of water washing the dead
On the pediments of the statues

and his poems have a brightness, colour, a sudden staggering clarity ('punish the blue with statues') that seem to identify them with their Mediterranean subjects. Beyond this, however, praise must be qualified. Mr Durrell commands a good flourish of rhetoric:

And then turning where the last pale
Lighthouse, like a Samson blinded, stands
And turns its huge charred orbit on the sands
I think of you ...

but apart from topography and literary re-creation his themes are slight and not very interesting and two essays in the comic are dire. Only a Mediterranean addict would find Mr Durrell a poet of first importance, but anyone not responding instantly to his use of words should not be reading poetry at all.

Mr Siegfried Sassoon's poetry has always seemed less sophisticated than his prose, those early, artless, almost Isherwoodian exploitations of personality such as *The Weald of Youth*, and at any rate latterly has registered more misses than hits. But he remains one of the few living English poets whose poems are sustained by the depth of feeling in them, and for this he deserves praise and allegiance. The sixty-odd poems in *Sequences* provide a fresh conspectus of his talent – at its best with the immediate and colloquial, less successful with Eternity, Armageddon and the Universal. Some half-dozen poems, such as 'Cleaning the Candelabrum' and 'October Trees', are of his best, and all are imbued with his own peculiarly casual modesty that covers a passionate responsiveness:

Aged self, disposed to lose his hold on life,
Looks down, at winter's ending, and perceives
Continuance in some crinkled primrose leaves,
A noise of nesting rooks in tangled trees.
  Stillness – inbreathed, expectant.
    Shadows that bring
Cloud-castled thoughts from downland distances.
  Eyes, ears are old. But not the sense of spring.

These lines could be an epigraph for the whole of this intensely appealing collection.

Manchester Guardian, 30 November 1956

You Do Something First

'For a very long time everybody refuses,' wrote Gertrude Stein of experiment in the arts, 'and then almost without a pause everybody accepts.' Has she herself been so accepted? The splendid Yale edition of the 'Unpublished Writings' would argue almost classic status, but surely few people to-day are prepared to tackle her specially maddening kind of obscurity in which the very shape of a sentence plays at being its own meaning and whole passages are rendered unendurable by the repetition of particular sounds ('I have tried earnestly to express, Just what I guess will not distress Nor even oppress or yet caress,' and so on). *Stanzas in Meditation and Other Poems, 1929–1933*, which according to Mr Donald Sutherland's preface constitutes 'the climax of her heroic experimentation with the essentials of writing', contains 164 stanzas, shaped like poetry, but which so far from sounding climactic read like a series of casual reflections, incomprehensible for the most part, but relieved by occasional doodles ('I refuse ever to number ducks') and dark simplicities ('I could join if I change'). Mr Sutherland tries hard to encourage the beginner, but it must in all honesty be said that only the larger libraries need feel responsible about Miss Stein's poetry.

Miss Elizabeth Sprigge's biography *Gertrude Stein: Her Life and Work* induces a more charitable frame of mind. It is hard not to be fascinated first of all by the far-off pre-1914 climate of innovation, when all the arts blew up together and secondly by her slow, good-humoured, imperturbable subject. After reading Miss Sprigge one feels that whatever else Gertrude Stein was she was not a phony, and indeed that the mainspring of her style was a laborious and not over-intelligent effort to speak the truth as she conceived it. 'You think that I'm a fool and that I write nonsense,'

Review of Gertrude Stein, *Stanzas in Meditation and Other Poems* 1929–1933 (Oxford University Press for Yale University Press, 1956) and Elizabeth Sprigge, *Gertrude Stein: Her Life and Work* (Hamish Hamilton, 1956)

she said to Mamoulian. 'I assure you that if I wrote nonsense you wouldn't have heard of me,' which seems unanswerable enough, but, like James Joyce (whom she had no use for), Gertrude had an unconvinced brother, in whose opinion she and Picasso were 'turning out the most Godalmighty rubbish that is to be found'. Which is the truth? Miss Sprigge's artfully chosen quotations are eloquent for Gertrude's humour and horse-sense, but she does not include Picasso's remark that Gertrude preserved: 'You do something first and then somebody else comes along and does it pretty', which goes a long way towards summarizing her literary position. Miss Sprigge leaves her readers anxious to judge for themselves, which is one of the surest signs that her book is a success.

Manchester Guardian, 29 January 1957

Mrs Ridler and Miss Millay

The shadow of Canterbury must hang inhibitingly over all verse plays about English martyrs, recalling the dictum that one function of a masterpiece is to make future use of the genre impossible. However, Mrs Ridler was commissioned to mark the four hundredth anniversary of the death of Thomas Cranmer by a play to be performed in St Mary's, Oxford, in 1956, and has wisely refused to make a theoretical study of sanctity. Nor is her Cranmer the shady figure of the successive recantations, but simply a man who does not know what to do for the best. In his own words:

> My soul is in a storm.
> I cannot hear God for the howling of argument

and Mrs Ridler has not omitted to indicate the parallel between his martyrdom and more modern instances of enforced spiritual conformity. At the same time, there is nothing strained or hysterical about her presentation: Ridley, Cranmer, and Latimer are stolid, level-headed men, joking to keep their courage up, as free from opinionation as from rhetoric. The verse, too, is quiet and straightforward, seeming to rely for colour upon situation and delivery, yet relaxing at times to suggest that outside this one terrible time and place the world is still sane and beautiful:

> On one side the fields and the pale green spires
> Of beginning spring, rising over the red earth
> As flames above a bed of fire: then the fall
> Of the yellow fiery willow. On the other side, the city:
> O Oxford, how piously you lie there, pointing
> Your fingers heavenward as though your thoughts
> Were all fixed above.

Review of Anne Ridler, *The Trial of Thomas Cranmer* (Faber and Faber, 1956); *Collected Poems of Edna St Vincent Millay*, edited by Norma Millay (Hamish Hamilton, 1956); and Ezra Pound: *Section: Rock Drill 85–95 de los cantares* (Faber and Faber, 1956)

Mrs Ridler's remarkably objective tone contrasts sharply with the work of the American poet Edna St Vincent Millay, whose *Collected Poems* proves an irritatingly inadequate monument to its author. Dateless and with no preface, it seems to represent a selection by its editor, Miss Norma Millay, from her sister's books, along with some previously unpublished poems, and a final salvo of 178 sonnets that cannot be all one sequence. In spite of these handicaps, the book is fascinating. A 'modern' sensibility with only the fag-end of the nineteenth-century tradition to rely on, Miss Millay wrote her unstable, unhappy poems directly from experience; she seems to throw out what she has to say in the old romantic fashion, with no anaesthetics:

I am not resigned to the shutting away of loving hearts in the hard ground
So it is, and so it will be, for so it has been, time out of mind:
Into the darkness they go, the wise and the lovely Crowned
With lilies and laurel they go but I am not resigned

Notwithstanding the frequently second-hand epithets and some remarkable flaws in taste, this large collection has a poignancy (rare in these days) that springs from sincere and bitter grief at death and pain and loneliness: those who know only the facetious 'I burn my candle at both ends' will be surprised how much Miss Millay achieves with the single asset of emotion.

Mr Pound's latest eleven 'Cantos' seem similar in method and perhaps material to what has gone before: a tesselation of languages and civilizations and periods streaked by a kind of Josh Billings humour and a preoccupation with international finance. Comprehension and appreciation will depend on the reader's knowledge and liking of what Mr Pound is doing in this long twentieth-century poetic curiosity, the ultimate (and immediate) value of which I personally think very small. However, the numerous splinters of rhetoric, the sardonic asides and the evocative images of this historical kaleidoscope are sufficiently fascinating to suggest that those who think otherwise may well be right.

Manchester Guardian, 26 March 1957

Poetry at Present

Mr Bayley's enjoyable book propounds a simple thesis: the early romantics set out to rescue poetry from its status as polite social accomplishment and make it a medium wherein the imagination could realize its unified apprehensions. As the century progressed, however, the increasing contradictions of the Victorian age proved too much for most poets, and this task of imaginative apprehension passed to the less self-conscious novelist, leaving 'romantic poetry', as we now remember it, private, escapist, and devitalised. To-day the balance has been restored; Yeats, Auden, and Dylan Thomas, by reasserting the romantic principle of total acceptance and responsibility, have effected a poetic rehabilitation which Mr Bayley sees as essentially a survival of the original romantic inspiration.

Realizing that concepts such as romanticism are difficult to nail down, Mr Bayley tends to define what he is talking about by describing the different dilemmas that typify it, so that the reader is hurried from viewpoint to viewpoint without being at all clear what has been decided or whether he agrees with it. One chapter – a welcome defence of natural taste against the analytics of the new criticism – seems virtually irrelevant. Sometimes one's confidence in Mr Bayley's judgement slackens momentarily, as when he tells us, for instance, that *The Age of Anxiety* is Auden's best book. But one's chief criticism is that his analysis of Yeats and Auden make his verdict on them come as a complete surprise. 'Crudely speaking,' he writes, 'the criterion of romantic success is to imagine a world different from anyone else's,' and he points out that in fact both Yeats and Auden created 'a universe of essentially the same kind, insulated, unique, and founded on the same original rejection by the Symbolists of the nineteenth-century material world in favour of a mind-created structure'. To do so, however, Yeats was

Review of John Bayley, *The Romantic Survival* (Constable, 1956) and Babette Deutsch, *Poetry in Our Time* (Oxford University Press, 1956)

forced to make a principle of artificiality, while Auden frankly admits that poetry is one thing and real life another. All this seems quite true, but instead of adding that this is just why both poets seem inferior to, for instance, Hardy, Hopkins, and Owen, Mr Bayley inexplicably forgoes his advantage, and his subjects leave the ring gaily rosetted as lineal descendants of Wordsworth and Keats, who, whatever their drawbacks, would never have imagined that their poems referred to anything but 'the very world, which is the world of all of us'. It would be unfair, however, to do nothing but argue with this book, though that is the price it pays for stimulating the intellect: the essay on Auden is by far the most illuminating I have so far read, and although he fails to get a proper purchase on the work of Dylan Thomas, Mr Bayley does very rightly insist that all estimates must begin at the chief characteristic of Thomas's poems, the sensation 'that we are being assaulted by some means other than words'.

Miss Babette Deutsch, whose *This Modern Poetry* put many of us in the picture nearly twenty years ago, is much less exciting than Mr Bayley: her long straightforward book tours the gallery of twentieth-century poetry pointing out (with quotations) the different groups of exhibits and labelling them The Earthly and the Definite (Imagists, Lawrence, Ernest Walsh, Elizabeth Bishop, William Carlos Williams, and e. e. cummings) or Science and Poetry (Auden, Karl Shapiro, William Carlos Williams, and Hugh MacDiarmid). In fact, this is probably all one can safely do with the poetry of one's own day, and Miss Deutsch certainly draws attention to many lesser-known American writers, but her judgements are so insipid (whose 'most memorable poems divide their beauties between praise of nature and praise of poetry that is nature's luminous mirror'? Dylan Thomas's), and a book of this type needs a bibliography so badly that it can be recommended only to those readers who are new to the field it covers and will have time to correct their perspectives later.

Manchester Guardian, 7 May 1957

Recent Verse – Some Near Misses

Each of these books represents a writer who is out of his apprenticeship and knows what he wants to do; two of them – *The Minute* and *Visitations* – are choices of the Poetry Book Society. Yet in spite of this maturity, it would be hard to call any of them wholly successful: too often the reader is asked to concede that a particular effect has been gained simply because it has been striven for. This is typical of the modern writer-reader relationship.

Mr Holloway, already well known for his work in literary criticism and philosophy, presents something of a puzzle as a poet. His sizeable collection, published by the enterprising Marvell Press, leaves no doubt of his variety of manner and independence of current affectations; his command of word and image is impressive; his rhythms are forceful and unstudied:

> This is the grave season of the sun's transit.
> The coast is mistlost under frost. All day
> A squab red foghorn, lonely by the bay
> Tromps out a rough music; and is never answered
> Except in echo whined from the wide seaboard
> Where bobbing gulls miraculously sleep.

Why, then, should these admirable properties not cohere more frequently to engage the reader's emotions? Partly, perhaps, because many of his poems try to mean one thing by saying another ('A Game of Cards', 'In the Dark'), while others work out an abstract situation ('Elegy for an Estrangement') and mislay its emotional content in the process. Yet Mr Holloway certainly has his emotional territory, and exploits it capably in 'Poem for Deep Winter', 'Warning to a Guest', and 'A Voice for Winter' – the time

Review of John Holloway, *The Minute, and Longer Poems* (Marvell Press, 1956); Charles Causley, *Union Street* (Hart-Davis, 1957); Richard Wilbur, *Poems 1943–56* (Faber and Faber, 1957); and Louis MacNeice, *Visitations* (Faber and Faber, 1957)

of the year beyond the autumn solstice, cold, the fog, sea. In this vein his bleak, uncomfortable tone is most effective:

> On the rock tower the wind-gauge twirling
> The geese arrive. The sun grows scanter.
> Wire-fine mercuried column dying.
> Night's chasm always deepening. Winter.

These poems, together with 'The She', 'The Confluence', and 'Afternoon Tea', display a talent as difficult to classify as to ignore.

Mr Charles Causley's collection is sponsored by Dame Edith Sitwell (Introduction) and the late Mr Roy Campbell (blurb) – writing, one nevertheless suspects, at different times in his poetic career. *Union Street* is a progress from reportage in the manner of the early MacNeice or Alan Ross to a kind of latter-day balladry. The earlier poems are not only often brilliant ('past mountains deep and green as Victorian postcards') but very funny ('Chief Petty Officer', *passim*), and make Mr Causley's more recent work seem unduly literary and even mechanical. A verse from 'Recruiting Drive' shows both the strength and weakness of his later manner:

> You must take off your clothes for the doctor,
> And stand as straight as a pin,
> His hand of stone on your white breast-bone
> Where the bullets all go in.
> They'll dress you in lawn and linen
> And fill you with Plymouth gin,
> O the devil may wear a rose in his hair
> I'll wear my fine doe-skin.

If you like this kind of thing, as the American tourist said of the Acropolis, then this is the kind of thing you'll like: it certainly is nearer the popular conception of poetry than the three other books reviewed here.

Mr Richard Wilbur, a leading young American poet, is known in this country chiefly by his poem 'The Death of a Toad', which seemed to promise at last a talent with a central sap of unliterary feeling:

> A toad the power motor caught
> Chewed and clipped of a leg, with a hobbling hop has got
> To the garden verge, and sanctuaried him
> Under the cineraria leaves...
> The rare original heartsblood goes,

Spends on the earthen hide, in the folds and wizenings, flows
In the gutters of the banked and staring eyes.

This large selection from his first three books, however, reveals Mr Wilbur as rather more conventional than one hoped; his material rarely outstrips the literature and foreign travel and teased ideas ('A Problem from Milton', 'Lamarck Elaborated') common to his English counterparts, and his most striking moments are acute pieces of description rather than newness of feeling:

Imminent towns whose weatherbeaten walls
Looked like the finest cheese
Bowled us enormous melons from their
Tolling towers.

Mr Wilbur is an expert and enjoyable poet, but his level is not that suggested by 'The Death of a Toad'.

Those who prefer seriousness to solemnity, and like poetry with a recognizable relation to life as they know it, have always favoured the work of Mr Louis MacNeice, even when his verse lost its characteristic night-club romanticism and snapshot imagery. Change in writers is, of course, permissible, even inevitable, but Mr MacNeice's subjects are still Ireland, the ancient world, the British Museum, character-sketches, and metaphysics, and the lack of impact of *Visitations* can only be ascribed to a lessening of power. 'Wessex Guidebook' shows the familiar skill in selecting detail:

Thou shalt! Thou shalt not! In the yellow abbey
Inscribed beneath the crossing the Ten Commandments
Are tinted red by a Fifteenth Century fire:
On one round hill the yews still furnish bows
For Agincourt while, equally persistent,
Beneath another, in green-grassed repose,
Arthur still waits . . .

There are also one or two agreeably waspish remarks, but otherwise this collection is, as they say in another milieu, strictly for the fans.

Manchester Guardian, 4 June 1957

Ideas about Poetry

Both these books are concerned with reinterpretation – that is, with throwing fresh light rather than presenting fresh material. Mr Kermode's study is of the concept developed by the Symbolists that poetry is not another mode of rational expression but an epiphany of the creative imagination, where form is meaning and meaning is form and whose archetype is the Image. After dealing with aspects of Symbolist theory such as the isolation of the artist, the dancer, and the tree (largely with reference to the work of Yeats), Mr Kermode turns to the twentieth century, and maintains that, contrary to general belief, this view of poetry is still current and in fact forms the backbone of much recent theory. (A hurried X-ray of the writings of T. E. Hulme, Pound, Eliot, Lewis, and Langer supports this contention.) His conclusion is that we should free ourselves from its domination, if only to enable us to regain enjoyment of 'some of the poetry of the past which has been excluded by early Symbolist assumptions' – imprimis Milton.

Romantic Image is a curious book. Mr Kermode devotes more than half of his space to an exposition of notions already familiar to readers of Yeats and anatomists of romanticism like Praz, and it cannot be said that he makes the rigmarole of Salome and masks and dead faces any less dreary than his predecessors have done. Where he really catches our attention is in the latter part of the book, where he labels Hulme as a romantic, knocks on the head 'the dissociation of sensibility' as a convenient fantasy of literary historians, and comes out (though feebly and too late) with 'an admission that art was always made *for* men who habitually move in space and time, whose language is propelled onwards by verbs, who cannot always be asked to respect the new enclosure laws of poetry, or such forbidding notices as "No road through to action."' One wishes he had constructed the book around this

Review of Frank Kermode, *Romantic Image* (Routledge and Kegan Paul, 1957) and Robert Langbaum, *The Poetry of Experience* (Chatto and Windus, 1957)

section, for it is the best part, and with a greater attention to stylistic persuasiveness might have started a critical landslide. It is time some critical missiles were guided into this area of literature, and Mr Kermode clearly could have done so if he had kept his conclusions firmly in view throughout.

The thesis of the American critic, Mr Langbaum, covers a wider period. His attitude to the dissociation of sensibility is orthodox, and he sets it after 'Newton, Locke, and the Enlightenment'. Romanticism – in the historical sense of the word – was 'in large measure literature's answer to science ... essentially a doctrine of experience, an attempt to salvage on science's own empiric grounds the validity of the individual perception against scientific abstractions'. This being so, primary poetic form was the dramatic monologue (now the norm of poetry, according to Mr Randall Jarrell), and the greater part of Mr Langbaum's book is devoted to a study of the genre. His approach is more varied and subtle than the customary summary on the basis of 'a handful of poems by Browning and Tennyson', and not all readers will still be there for the conclusion that post-Enlightenment poetry must be 'understood as the instrument of an age which must venture a literature without objectively verifiable meaning – a literature which returns upon itself ... manifestations of a life which as life is self-justifying'. None the less, Mr Langbaum has certainly a point to make, and those whose business this kind of speculation is should not ignore it.

Manchester Guardian, 23 July 1957

Thomas Hardy and the Cosmic Mind by J. O. Bailey (1957)

Dr Bailey's study of *The Dynasts* directs our attention to a remark attributed to Hardy by William Archer in his *Real Conversations* (1901): 'Do you know Hartmann's Philosophy of the Unconscious? It suggested to me ... that there may be a consciousness, infinitely far-off, at the other end of the chain of phenomena, always striving to express itself, and always baffled and blundering....' Though Hardy was here speaking of psychic phenomena, Dr Bailey has taken the hint, and argues that it is the concepts of the once-renowned *Die Philosophie des Unbewußten* (published in English in 1884) that underlie *The Dynasts*, rather than those of Schopenhauer or Haeckel. For Hartmann, the 'Immanent Will' was not the blind automatism of the determinists, but something more dynamic, akin to the unconscious of the psychologists, that may in time and in part be perceived and therefore understood by the conscious mind by a process analogous to instinct or extra-sensory perception. The result of this will be a closer approximation of the course of human affairs to the conditions of human happiness, and represents a kind of philosophical version of evolutionary theory known as meliorism. Hardy did not, however, follow Hartmann to his depressing conclusion that a fully conscious Will would realize that its only true happiness lay in self-annihilation. Rather, he adapted Hartmann's 'scientific' apparatus to support a characteristic modification of his own: consciousness will refine the Will, whose aims in consequence will no longer be inseparable from pain: 'Consciousness the Will informing, till It fashion all things fair!'

Dr Bailey contends that these notions governed Hardy in his selection and handling of material, and his publishers suggest that *The Dynasts* is 'the contribution of a poet-philosopher to a hopeful and even religious view of the world'. This runs counter to Hardy's own explicit statement that 'the views in [my works] are *seemings*, provisional impressions only, used for artistic purposes', but Dr Bailey rather surprisingly puts this aside, insisting that 'these statements do not say – Hardy never said – that he did not seriously mean the doctrines of *The Dynasts*'. He proceeds therefore to a detailed examination of the supernatural apparatus in the drama, showing how it looks back to Hartmann and forward to Professor Rhine, and how the more general references to the Will and its part in human affairs agree with Hartmann's description of the Unconscious and how it works. This is well enough, but if these concepts are put forward as anything more than literary machinery Dr Bailey surely owes his readers an examination of them in their philosophical context, and even a reminder that Lange, for instance, dismissed *The Philosophy of the Unconscious* as unworthy of close consideration. The literary reader, however, may simply object that while Hardy may have tricked out his dramatic sense of destiny with current German theories the core of *The Dynasts*, as of *The Trumpet Major*, is Napoleonic history. The imaginative unimportance of the philosophic underpinning is made plain by the singularly dismal quality of the verse that expresses it, a point that Dr Bailey might well have examined. As it is, his work reads more like an attempt to regiment Hardy on the side of the hopeful and religious angels than a piece of literary criticism.

Modern Language Review, January 1958

Reports on Experience

As Maugham-award deportee, Miss Jennings would clearly be more at ease than at least one of her predecessors, and indeed 'in Italy', her publishers say, 'Miss Jennings finds an outward world which enriches and extends her inward world.' Miss Jennings herself lends support to this by quoting on her title-page Traherne's 'It becometh you to retain a glorious sense of the world.' If for a moment Charles Ryder and the hothouse at Tring seem to threaten, the moment is soon past: the steady, calm, precise voice is unchanged:

> I visited the place where we last met.
> Nothing was changed, the gardens were well-tended.
> The fountains sprayed their usual steady jet;
> There was no sign that anything had ended
> And nothing to instruct me to forget ...

and the characteristic low-toned texture is preserved by ringing the changes on half a dozen colourless words such as 'shadows', 'light', and 'darkness' (I counted 52 uses of the word 'shadow' and its derivatives in 50 poems – a frequency equal to that of 'lad' in 'A Shropshire Lad'). What I think Miss Jennings and her publishers mean is that in *A Sense of the World* she has given up the 'mythological' or 'symbolic' poem she so inexplicably favoured at one time, and also to some extent poems anatomizing mental or emotional concepts, and begun to work more from things seen and felt.

> After the griefs of night,
> Over the doors of day,
> Here by this window-sill
> I watch the climbing light
> As early footsteps steal
> Enormous shadows away ...

Review of Elizabeth Jennings, *A Sense of the World* (André Deutsch, 1958); Alan Ross, *To Whom It May Concern* (Hamish Hamilton, 1958); and R. S. Thomas, *Poetry for Supper* (Hart-Davis, 1958)

This is much to be encouraged, especially when it is clear that her skill at marrying metre to natural word-order is undiminished, but Miss Jennings is still an explainer rather than a describer, and still loves to invent preposterous explanations for simple happenings, as in 'The Bird Catchers'. What does seem new about this collection is the group of religious poems at the end. These, though not pictorial, are mostly studies of particular events and people ('The Annunciation', 'Gift of Tongues', 'Augustine') made with the dispassionate devotion of the Old Masters. Peguy and Claudel may be the signposts to the road Miss Jennings is taking next.

Mr Alan Ross, on the other hand, has always been a describer and is intermittently aware of the fact:

> At this moment I want no more
> Than that I could transmit a likeness
> On to paper, taking this pencil
> Into my confidence....

This gives his work a foundation in common sense and ensures a readable surface:

> Now the arthritic gulls,
> Seedy with displeasure, crotchet on railings,
> Falling with a flat splash on wet bread....

Indeed, there is such a confusion of properties in *To Whom It May Concern* – Baudelaire, Stanley Matthews (a poem from him about Mr Ross would be interesting), the Mediterranean, heterosexual love, horse-racing – that Mr Ross's poetic personality might expect to be unique: his character-sketches, such as 'Beachcomber', are serious and admirably written, his poems about love verge sadly on the acute, his landscapes are at once comic and three-dimensional. Occasionally he touches our feelings:

> Beneath the ice-floes sleeping,
> Embalmed in salt,
> The sewn-up bodies slipping
> Into silent vaults ...
> On that long Watch that encompasses
> The Dogs, the Middle, the Forenoon ...

But except in certain sporting pieces, where success depends largely on the reader feeling as Mr Ross does about, say, Barnes and Rhodes, this new collection never quite emerges from the tutelary shadow of Mr MacNeice.

I missed Mr R. S. Thomas's first collection (though not the applause it earned), but I am afraid I do not think *Poetry for Supper* shows him as all he was cracked up to be. As is well known, Mr Thomas's poems derive from his life as a Welsh country minister, and are in consequence mainly about poverty, hard work, natural sights and sounds, and the dissolution of Welsh peasant culture. It is a grim world, yet, as he says, not all hate and dirt and ugliness:

> Among the fields
> Sometimes the spirit enchained
> So long there by the gross flesh, raised
> Suddenly there its wild note of praise.

Nor is it without humour, as shown in the sketch of the chapel deacon, and there are some considerations of the poetic craft as conscious as any that ever came out of Langham Place. Occasionally, too, appear such lines as:

> Slowly the cloud bruises
> Are healed by sunlight.

There is no doubt that Mr Thomas is the kind of poet one would like to be good, because he avoids a great many ways of being bad, but I find in this collection little sense of the inner organization that gives a poem cohesion, and his images and metaphors are too often repetitive and second-rate ('black ink of the heart's well', 'the easier rhythms of the heart', 'the mind's darkness', 'the mind's acid'). Mr Thomas's admirers seem to me to be mistaking sympathetic subject matter and good intentions for evidence of real poetic talent.

Manchester Guardian, 5 September 1958

No Fun Any More

This book opens promisingly with an account of Mr Spender's walk-out from a Foyles' literary luncheon because Lord Samuel was illustrating modern poetic obscurity by quoting some Dylan Thomas (a source unrecognized by the principal guest, Mr Betjeman). Mr Press sees this incident as representative of the lack of relation between poetry and the general reader to-day, and asks is 'obscurity' really the cause, as Lord Samuel was claiming? Rather than answer this directly, he prefers to make a general survey of what is and has been meant when a poem is termed obscure. This is unfortunate, for it commits him to rehearsing a number of points that are really no more than platitudes outside the sixth-form room. Few readers will need to be told that when vocabulary and reference grow obsolete they constitute obscurity, and they will be familiar with other suggested factors such as the supposed superior quickness of the poetic mind, the complexity of the modern world, and the bafflingness of private jokes and allusions. It is also unfortunate because it spares Mr Press from facing what he all but admits on page 4: 'I think it must be allowed ... that contemporary verse at least appears to be more obscure than the bulk of older poetry.' This sounds as if Mr Press and Lord Samuel are on the same side, which is what the reader wants to know, but instead Mr Press conducts him through poetic opacities of every description, as if

> If I do prove her haggard
> Though that her jesses were my dear heart-strings,
> I'd whistle her off and let her down the wind
> To prey at Fortune

were equally 'obscure' as

> And when we were children, staying at the arch-duke's,
> My cousin's, he took me out on a sled,
> And I was frightened.

Review of John Press, *The Chequer'd Shade* (Oxford University Press, 1958)

In the last chapter, again, the fact that the genesis and operation of poetry is at least partly subconscious is adduced to prove that 'there will always remain an element of obscurity in poetry', as if this sort is what Mr Press has been talking about all along. By the end the reader suspects there are 77 types of obscurity, and feels himself quite unable to tell whether a poet is 'raising language to its highest power' or whether he is just guilty of a 'combination of insolence and incompetence which so many poets are not ashamed to exhibit.'

This muddled, readable, and extremely well-documented book seems designed to persuade us that modern poetry is not obscure if we 'recognize sympathetically the principles upon which it is composed', and that any residual puzzlement is no different from that common to the poetry of other ages. To say so is to ignore the inexplicable fact that forty or fifty years ago obscurity suddenly became fun in a way it never had been before, and which none of Mr Press's reasons seems to throw any light on. Now it is fun no more. Deserted by the tide of taste, the modern movement awaits combing like some cryptic sea-wrack; obscurity, as the general reader has always known, is its definitive characteristic, an obscurity unlike previous types in being deliberate and unnecessary. Mr Press comes near to acknowledging this episode in Europe's psychic history in his penultimate chapter, which is an account of the switch from poetic statement-by-logic to statement-by-images, but he makes little attempt to explain it. Nor does he make any final comment on the part played by obscurity in alienating poetry's former public. Mr Press makes merry with those who say that they don't read modern poetry for this reason, but surely they are right: like any consumer, they have stopped buying a product that no longer pleases them. Sales of *Georgian Poetry* went regularly into five figures: what about the sales of *New Verse*, or *New Lines*? And whose fault is it? Mr Press's gentle exposition for the lower levels of English teaching says so little about the wider implications of its subject that one is almost grateful: it is still open for full treatment.

Manchester Guardian, 18 November 1958

Graves Superior

To make a thirty-shilling book by collecting fugitive and not-so-fugitive pieces would be dangerous for any writer less gifted than Mr Graves. His forceful colloquial talent and magpie interests are peculiarly suited to miscellany form. Here is Graves the Majorcan, arguing with priests about a bicycle; Graves the visiting lecturer, corrupting the faithful in American universities; Graves the reviewer, so charming the reader that the original book is forgotten; Graves the essayist, displaying that slightly horrifying expertise equally about Judaism, ancient history and mushrooms, and momentarily persuading the reader to share his absorptions and, of course, Graves the poet:

> Love, the sole Goddess fit for swearing by,
> Concedes us graciously the little lie:
> The white lie, the half-lie, the lie corrective
> Without which love's exchange might prove defective.
> Confirming hazardous relationships
> By kindly *maquillage* of Truth's pale lips . . .

Mr Graves descants upon the judgement of a young critic who told him – I must say he rates ten out of ten for temerity – that while his poetry is *good* it is not *great*. Much as one sympathizes with Mr Graves's feelings (especially as his critic went on to cite as the right stuff something by Ezra Pound), one is forced to admit that one does want to draw this distinction, even if these terms are not the happiest. It is ironic that Graves, whose view of poetry causes him to speak of 'a poem which is moon-magical enough to walk off the page – if you know what I mean – and to keep on walking, and to get under people's skins and into their eyes and throats and heart and marrows . . .' should appear incapable of writing that kind of poem himself. (This is, I think, amply demonstrated by his inability to leave a poem alone when he has finished it.) In the present collection of twenty-two (one at least

Review of Robert Graves, *Steps* (Cassell, 1958)

a revision), three or four strike me as good in Mr Graves's deflationary neo-ballad-maker's way, principally 'The Twin of Sleep', 'Read Me, Please!' and the engaging 'A Slice of Wedding Cake'.

> Why have such scores of lovely, gifted girls
> Married impossible men?
> Simple self-sacrifice may be ruled out,
> And missionary endeavour, nine times out of ten.
> Repeat 'impossible men': not merely rustic,
> Foul-tempered or depraved...

The talks are even more enjoyable, in a casual bladder-banging style that seems tacitly to acknowledge the many interlocking rackets necessary to bring speaker and audience together, yet equally sets out things one has always believed but never before seen in print: 'If a poet, called upon to read his poems, chants or croons or declaims, something is wrong. A true poem is best spoken in a level, natural voice: slowly or solemnly, and with suppressed emotion, but in a natural voice ... not the one in which we try to curry favour with children at a party, or with an election crowd, or with a traffic cop...' Neither respectful nor vulgar, unlettered nor pedantic, unbalanced nor entirely sane, Mr Graves is as good a poetic mentor as the young are likely to get. His advantage as a scatterer of other people's nonsense resides chiefly in the intimidating quality of his own: his talk to the New York Y. M. H. A. Centre identifies itself in its opening words: 'I shall tell you frankly how the White Goddess affair started for me, how it continued, and –' It is the soft-footed compulsive accent of the ghost story, and sure enough it takes us to the ragged Tree of Death, and ends with a man hanging. Very suitable for Christmas.

Manchester Guardian, 2 December 1958

MR ROBERT GRAVES

In a review of Mr Robert Graves's *Steps*, which appeared in the *Manchester Guardian* on December 2, this sentence appeared: 'Neither respectful nor vulgar, unlettered nor pedantic, unbalanced nor entirely sane, Mr Graves is as good a poetic mentor as the young are likely to get.' Mr Graves asks us to make clear that no reflection on his mental health was intended and that we have every reason to believe his mental health to be as excellent as ever. We gladly do that and we are sorry if anyone has read into the phrase any such reflection.

Manchester Guardian, 30 December 1958

Poetry Beyond a Joke

Charmingly bound in blind-tooled ivory cloth, with gold Baskerville on the spine and a rose top-edge, this collection finally puts to flight the notion that Betjeman is no more than a dealer in a few preciosities such as Anglicanism or ghastly good taste. No doubt the photographs and rubrications of his early books helped to foster this view of his work as 'amusing' yet infantile pastiche: since 1940, however, a succession of more chastely designed volumes has ousted the element of undergraduate hoax, of Osbert Lancaster and Arthur Marshall, and after *A Few Late Chrysanthemums* we have had to accept that what poets are supposed to do Betjeman does – not, perhaps, in ways we think proper or ways sanctified by recent example, but which henceforward must be marked – or re-marked – on the map.

Yet it would be wrong to claim that the later poems represent any radical alteration of poetic method. The first poem in the book, published in 1930, might have been written yesterday:

> She died in the upstairs bedroom
>   By the light of the ev'ning star
> That shone through the plate glass window
>   From over Leamington Spa.

Only mediocrities develop, Wilde said, and if Betjeman could hit the target so unerringly at 25 he had clearly no need to change. What he did was enlarge his range of subjects. Little in the earlier books presages the discoveries of the Forties:

> The gas was on in the Institute,
>   The flare was up in the gym,
> A man was running a mineral line.
>   A lass was singing a hymn.

> On the floor of her bedroom lie blazer and shorts
> And the cream-coloured walls are betrophied with sports.

Review of *John Betjeman's Collected Poems*, compiled, with an introduction, by Lord Birkenhead (John Murray, 1958)

And westering, questioning, settles the sun
On your low-leaded window, Miss Joan Hunter Dunn.

Rumbling under blackened girders, Midland, bound for Cricklewood,
Puffed its sulphur to the sunset where that Land of Laundries stood.
Rumble under, thunder over, train and tram alternate go,
Shake the floor and smudge the ledger, Charrington, Sells, Dale and Co.,
Nuts and nuggets in the window...

To love and topography the Fifties added a deeper sense of time and mortality and a charitableness towards ordinary people that in no way blunted his feelings about the Age of the Common Man. And now, so far from being the laureate of a few private fads, Betjeman goes further than anyone else towards summarizing 'Dear old, bloody old England. Of telegraph poles and tin' simply because no one else has his breadth of poetic reception. Betjeman picks it all up: the decay of surviving nineteenth-century institutions, the decline of the Church, the altered countryside and ways of living, subtopia and socialism, and all the tiny vivid little manifestations of sadness and snobbery and silliness, and with his simple loving enthusiasm transmutes it to poetry. He is a subtle poet, but not a sophisticated one. Poetry for him is not a moral or sociological gymnastic, but a spontaneous overflow of natural feeling which directs his choice of words and informs them when found:

Cancer has killed him. Heart is killing her.
The trees are down. An Odeon flashes fire
Where stood their villa by the murmuring fir ...

Those who 25 years ago tried to dismiss Betjeman as 'bourgeois taste at its most corrupt' now call him a remarkable minor poet it would be a disservice to over-estimate. This seems to me to ignore his particular worth at this time. Almost alone among living poets, Betjeman has knocked down the 'No Road Through To Action' sign; he is in the best sense a committed writer, whose poems spring from what he really feels about real life, and as a result he brings back to poetry a sense of dramatic urgency and a jumble of properties it had all but lost. In the 36 lines of 'Felixstowe, or The Last of Her Order', for instance, or 'Eunice', there is a whole life it took delicacy to perceive and subtlety to express, and its impact has the fullness of a novel. Similarly, the quality in his poetry loosely called 'nostalgia' is really that never-sleeping alertness to note the patina of time on things past which is the hall-mark of the mature writer:

> And from Greenford scent of mayfields
> Most enticingly was blown
> Over market gardens tidy,
> Taverns for the bona fide,
> Cockney anglers, cockney shooters,
> Murray Poshes, Lupin Pooters
> Long in Kensal Green and Highgate silent under soot and stone.

For this reason it is my considered opinion that it would do no harm to over-estimate Betjeman's poetry for a bit. Some people have been puzzled by Edmund Wilson's remark last May that Auden, Thomas, and Betjeman were the best post-Eliot English poets; to me it seems eminently sensible, and my only regret is that he did not add that, of the three, Betjeman is the only one who is still a positive poetic force.

Manchester Guardian, 19 December 1958

West Britons and True Gaels

The choice of this collection might have occasioned a display of political or other narrowness that would have been at variance with the status of the Oxford series. Mr Donagh MacDonagh, however, lays down in his introduction to *The Oxford Book of Irish Verse* that he and his fellow-editor, the late Lennox Robinson, have allowed a poet to be Irish 'by birth, by descent, by adoption,' and this tolerance ensures justice of representation across the whole field of Anglo-Irish poetry. In some ways the tolerance seems overdone, for it is hard to feel that the term 'Irish poetry' rightly means anything except either poetry in Gaelic or verse born of the nineteenth-century literary movement based on the 'matter of Ireland' and fired by political nationalism. Fitzgerald's 'Rubaiyat' or Goldsmith's 'The Deserted Village' seem out of place. The essentially nineteenth-century poetry the national movement produced avoided the more typical blemishes of its contemporary equivalent in England, either deliberately or because the revolutionary spirit drove out sentimentality, vulgarity, and facetiousness. Nor did Ireland's agricultural background provoke flights into medievalism or classical antiquity as the quickest way out of Manchester. The most distinctive contribution of these poets is a hesitant freshness of metre found in translated Gaelic:

> Ringleted youth of my love,
>   With thy locks bound loosely behind thee,
> You passed by the road above,
>   But you never came in to find me;
> Where were the harm for you
>   If you came for a little to see me,
> Your kiss is a waking dew
>   Were I ever so ill or so dreamy.

Review of *The Oxford Book of Irish Verse*, edited by Donagh MacDonagh and Lennox Robinson (Oxford University Press, 1959)

With Yeats, the course of Irish poetry curved back to rejoin the Anglo-American mainstream, and with the gaining of independence the ruling passion of nationalism died. The divergence had produced no major talents – except, of course, Yeats – but its many minor voices are always pleasant to listen to:

> This is just the weather, a wet May and blowing
> All the shining, shimmering leaves tossing low and high.
> When my father used to say: ''Twill be the great mowing!
> God's weather's a good weather, be it wet or dry.'

Among those absent from these pages are Aubrey de Vere, Charles Gavan Duffy, both Standish O'Gradys, Lionel Johnson, John Hewitt, and anyone under thirty, which prevents the book from being entirely representative. Of those included, however, Seamus O'Sullivan, Gogarty, and Synge make a familiar and formidable turn-of-the-century trio; more recent times show the more cosmopolitan talents of Graves, MacNeice, and W. R. Rodgers succeeded by Valentin Iremonger, Roy McFadden, and Thomas Kinsella, as if Irish writers are staying at home again once more. Amusingly enough, the last named – the youngest contributor in the book – chooses to show us that the ancient Triads of Ireland can still be far from irrelevant in their sentiments: 'Three scarcities that are better than abundance: a scarcity of fancy talk, a scarcity of cows in a small pasture, a scarcity of friends around the beer!'

Manchester Guardian, 20 February 1959

The Industrial Muse by Jeremy Warburg

Mr Jeremy Warburg's intention in his anthology *The Industrial Muse* is to show the assimilation of industrial imagery and subject-matter by nineteenth- and twentieth-century poets, and to this end he has collected a variety of poems and extracts of different degrees of familiarity. The result leaves the reader wondering whether Mr Warburg has used his material in the most effective way. Certainly nineteenth-century poets made an effort to grapple with the changing scene, but they were most vivid when rejecting, not assimilating – Blake speaking of 'Eternal Death with Mills and Ovens and Cauldrons', Tennyson claiming that as a result of Progress 'crime and hunger cast our maidens by the thousand on the street', and Morris exhorting his readers to 'dream of London, small and white and clean'. Such examples could be multiplied, and apart from denunciation there is little in the last century but mock-heroics and facetiousness. Nearer our own time Mr Warburg might have looked for examples of what the machine meant to Wyndham Lewis ('Engine Fight-Talk', for instance), and noted its importance to the pylon poets in showing that they were politically fitted to play their part in bringing about the public ownership of the means of production. However, this is not an over-serious book, as its typography and rather tiresome pseudo-vignettes demonstrate, and can be read simply for the occasional unexpected felicity. It does suggest, none the less, that an investigation of the time required to render some new factor acceptable to the poetic imagination would be interesting, and the lighter poem 'Underground' by May Kendall hints at an easier assimilation at the level of the broadsheet and music-hall song.

Modern Language Review, April 1959

Betjeman En Bloc

What exactly *is* Betjeman? Surely one of the rare figures on whom the aesthetic appetites of an age pivot and swing round to face an entirely new direction. It is hard to tell whether such figures govern or are governed by the tendencies they focus so sharply; individually they may not rank as major talents – Morris, Langley – but for a time they have the curious power to alter people's ideas of what is beautiful. Throughout the work of the writer, broadcaster, propagandist and poet John Betjeman can be traced the same insistent pattern, a rejection of modernism. If the spirit of the first third of our century was onwards, upwards and outwards, the spirit of Betjeman was backwards, downwards and inwards. If the architecture of the age was Nuremburg, its heroes the working class, its concrete by-passes lit with sodium, Betjeman exalted Comper interiors, clergymen's widows and gaslight. This opposition was not confined to aesthetics. If the age had no religious beliefs and thought everyone was a socialist nowadays, Betjeman professed Christianity and proclaimed a benevolent class system the best of all possible worlds. In a time of global concepts, Betjeman insisted on the little, the forgotten, the obscure: the privately-printed book of poems, the chapel behind the Corn Exchange, the local landscapes in the Museum (open weekdays 2 p.m. – 4 p.m.), and slowly our tastes have begun to turn his way. We have stopped laughing at the Victorians. Local history is a recognized syllabus subject in schools and universities. The glamour of left-wing politics has unaccountably dulled.

His *Collected Poems*, whose astonishing success (over 30,000 in two months) by now need not be underlined, show clearly that his position in literature is analogous. He is against the kind of poetry this century has made its own. He has written and created a taste of comprehensible poems in regular metre, and his themes have earned him every vituperative adjective in criticism – cosy,

Review of John Betjeman, *Collected Poems* (John Murray, 1958)

nostalgic, bogus, adolescent, snobbish, corrupt. This has not hindered the growth of his reputation. The three most noteworthy talents in post-Eliot English poetry, said Edmund Wilson last year, are Auden, Dylan Thomas and John Betjeman, and though an American is not likely to be the best judge of Betjeman's quality, at least Mr Wilson cannot be associated with the Princess Margaret/Top People/U- and Non-U *blague* that hangs obscuringly round Betjeman's name. Auden dedicated *The Age of Anxiety* to him. And he must have the largest public of any living poet. 'There has been nothing like it since *Don Juan*,' said his publishers, who of course also published *Don Juan*.

The chief significance of Betjeman as a poet is that he is a writer of talent and intelligence for whom the modern poetic revolution has simply not taken place. For him there has been no symbolism, no objective correlative, no T. S. Eliot or Ezra Pound, no rediscovery of myth or language as gesture, no *Seven Types* or *Some Versions*, no works of criticism with titles like *Communication as Discipline* or *Implicit and Explicit Image-Obliquity in Sir Lewis Morris*. He has been carried through by properties and techniques common to all but his immediate predecessors: a belief that poetry is an emotional business, rather than an intellectual or moral one, a belief in metre and rhyme as a means of enhancing emotion, a belief that a poem's meaning should be communicated directly and not by symbol. These were characteristics of poetry in the days when it was deemed a kind of supernatural possession. (How much today requires the hypothesis of divine inspiration?) And the result is that Betjeman's poems, however trivial or light-hearted their subject, always carry a kind of primitive vivacity that sets them apart from those of his contemporaries, and captures the reader's attention without his intellectual consent:

> In among the silver birches winding ways of tarmac wander
> And the signs to Bussock Bottom, Tussock Wood and Windy Brake,
> Gabled lodges, tile-hung churches, catch the lights of our Lagonda
> As we drive to Wendy's party, lemon curd and Christmas cake.
> Rich the makes of motor whirring,
> Past the pine-plantation purring ...

There is in Betjeman someone who weeps at Victorian ballads ('My heart finds rest, my heart finds rest in Thee') and roars out Edwardian comic songs ('There's something about a 'varsity man that distinguishes him from a cad'), someone to whom every

Betjeman poem seems to *matter* in a rare refreshing way. For Betjeman's poetry is nothing if not personal: it is exclusively about things that impress, amuse, excite, anger or attract him, and – and this is most important – once a subject has established its claim on his attention, he never questions the legitimacy of his interest. Energy most modern poets spend on screening their impulses for security Betjeman puts into the poem. If this had not been so, he would never have been able to celebrate Pont Street and the doctor's intellectual wife in the decade of the Left Book Club, Miss Joan Hunter Dunn during the blitz, or 'Sunday Afternoon Service' in the year of Labour's post-war victory:

> Even the villas have a Sunday look.
> The Ransom mower's locked into the shed.
> 'I have a splitting headache from the sun,'
> And bedroom windows flutter cheerful chintz
> Where, double-aspirined, a mother sleeps;
> While father in the loggia reads a book,
> Large, desultory, birthday-present size ...

The public has been a long time taking him seriously partly because of this, but a much larger reason is of course that many of his poems are funny. Readers find it exceedingly difficult to combine the notions of being serious and being funny. Yet Betjeman is a particularly good example of this ambiguity, because the things that oftenest make him giggle – sex and class – clearly matter to him tremendously, and indeed they do to most of us. It may be that some of Betjeman's appeal springs from his preparedness to release feelings we are not entirely unashamed of, and are therefore inclined to make fun of. Certainly the attraction of some of his verses is complex enough for any sophomore:

> Gaily into Ruislip Gardens
>   Runs the red electric train,
> With a thousand Ta's and Pardon's
>   Daintily alights Elaine;
> Hurries down the concrete station
> With a frown of concentration,
> Out into the outskirt's edges
> Where a few surviving hedges
> Keep alive our lost Elysium – rural Middlesex again.
>
> Well-cut Windsmoor flapping lightly,
>   Jacqmar scarf of mauve and green
> Hiding hair which, Friday nightly,

Delicately drowns in Drene;
Fair Elaine the bobby-soxer,
Fresh-complexioned with Innoxa
Gains the garden – father's hobby,
Hangs her Windsmoor in the lobby
Settles down to sandwich supper and the television screen.

This kind of writing has earned Betjeman the reputation of a right-wing satirist. But only obtuse reading could take this as a hostile portrait. Elaine, the mindless consumer of branded products, has declined from the Tennysonian standard her name recalls just as rural Middlesex is no longer the paradise of Betjeman's boyhood, but her frown of concentration and her Friday ritual are too endearing to suggest that Betjeman wants to do away with her. There is a half suggestion that the unquestioning simplicity of her life might be enviable. Again:

When shall I see the Thames again?
The prow-promoted gems again,
As beefy ATS
Without their hats
Come shooting through the bridge?
And 'cheerioh' and 'cheeribye'
Across the waste of waters die,
And low the mists of evening lie
And lightly skims the midge.

Only Betjeman would use the ATS and their valedictions as part of a topographical evocation, instead of as a contrast to it. And when he writes of the death of a working-class mother:[1]

But her place is empty in the queue at the International,
The greengrocer's queue lacks one,
So does the crowd at Macfisheries. There's no one to go to Freeman's
To ask if the shoes are done.

The element of satire is entirely missing, and we are bound to concede that, comic or serious or serio-comic or whatever we please, Betjeman is an accepter, not a rejecter, of the life of his time and the people who live it. The idea that he is a precious aesthete whose sensibilities are alternately quivering before Victoriana and shuddering at words like 'serviette' is wholly wrong. On the contrary, he is a robust and responsive writer, registering 'Dear

1 This poem, 'Variations on a Theme by T. W. Rolleston', is unaccountably missing from the volume under review.

old, bloody old England' with vivacious precision and affectionate alliteration quite beyond most avowed social realists. His gusto embraces it all – the mouldy remnants of the nineteenth century, the appalling monoliths of the twentieth, the dead Church, the dying peasantry, the conurbation and candy-floss and King's College, Cambridge, all the sadness and silliness and snobbery is potential Betjeman material. Satire in Betjeman either dissolves in laughter and affection before it reaches its target, or else it never quite comes to life:

> The children have a motor-bus instead,
> And in a town eleven miles away
> We train them to be 'Citizens of today'.
> And many a cultivated hour they pass
> In a fine school with walls of vita-glass.
> Civics, eurhythmics, economics, Marx,
> How-to-respect-wild-life-in-National Parks;
> Plastics, gymnastics – thus they learn to scorn
> The old thatch'd cottages where they were born.
> The girls, ambitious to begin their lives
> Serving in Woolworth's, rather than as wives;
> The boys, who cannot yet escape the land,
> At driving tractors lend a clumsy hand.
> An eight-hour day for all, and more than three
> Of these are occupied with making tea
> And talking over what we all agree –
> Though 'Music while you work' is now our wont,
> It's not so nice as 'Music while you don't'.

This Peter-simplified view of England, perhaps not more unjust than views from the opposite side from 'Wystan, Rex, all of you who have not fled' in the Thirties, shows the political colour of Betjeman's adherences. But broad political generalization of any shade robs Betjeman of one of his style's chief weapons – the precise name, the unique instance ('Oh! Fuller's angel-cake, Robertson's marmalade' etc.), and this lack of particularity lessens his power to convince. His villainous Town Clerk is just a bogy, his Welfare State education a very distant prospect. The real explanation may be that Betjeman is too much of his age – he is after all a TV star, not a hermit – to attack it convincingly.

Beside this informed relish of the present stands Betjeman's enormous sense of the past – or, to be more exact, of the last century:

... The still-new stucco on the London clay,
Hot summer silence over Holloway.

Dissenting chapels, tea-bowers, lovers' lairs,
Neat new-built villas, ample Grecian squares,
Remaining orchards ripening Windsor pears.

Hot silence where the older mansions hide
On Highgate Hill's thick elm-encrusted side,
And Pancras, Hornsey, Islington divide ...

... From various black Victorian towers
The Sunday evening bells
Came pealing over dales and hills
And tanneries and silent mills
And lowly streets where country stops
And little shuttered corner shops ...

In these startlingly-vivid evocations of the Victorian town that Betjeman has done so much to reinstate in public taste there is much of Morris's exhortation to dream of London small and white and clean. But in Betjeman there is a much deeper emotional involvement. It is almost as if it were a Paradise and he were irrevocably shut out of it by being born at all. Betjeman has an acute response to the doctrine of the Fall – 'Not my vegetarian dinner, nor my lime-juice minus gin,/ Quite can drown a faint conviction that we may be born in sin'; 'How did the Devil come? When first attack?/ These Norfolk lanes recall lost innocence' – and his passionate celebration of Edwardian and Victorian times is less a sign of conventional Freudian 'regression' than of a yearning for a world, as it were, unburdened by himself:

These were the houses they knew; and I, by descent, belong
To these tall neglected houses divided into flats.
Only the church remains, where carriages used to throng
And my mother stepped out in flounces and my father stepped out in spats
To shadowy stained-glass matins or gas-lit evensong
And back in a country quiet with doffing of chimney hats.

He is sensitive too to the passing of time and its sad dispersals:

There in pinnacled protection
One extinguished family waits
A Church of Ireland resurrection
By the broken, rusty gates.

Sheepswool, straw, and droppings cover
Graves of spinster, rake and lover,
Whose fantastic mausoleum
Sings its own seablown Te Deum,
In and out the slipping slates.

It is only a short step from this awareness to the dread of death that has appeared more and more frequently in the last fifteen years. This has not produced his best poems, nor would one expect it to. Fear of death is too much of a screaming close-up to allow the poetic faculty to function properly, but demands expression by reason of its very frightfulness. None the less it benefits his poetry, making the colours brighter and the beauties more transiently poignant by contrast, giving a seasoning of honesty and a grim sense of proportion that 'reconciled' writers all too often lack. It is typical of Betjeman's sincerity that he is prepared to acknowledge that his religious beliefs cannot banish the disquiet inseparable from ideas of oblivion. In a way, it is typical of his religion, too, which is far from the dramatic 'conversional' kind frequently favoured by literary men. Betjeman came to the Church of England by admiring its architecture, and his beliefs seem dependent not only on actual churches and their furniture but on England itself and its everyday life:

And London shops on Christmas Eve
Are strung with silver bells and flowers
As hurrying clerks the City leave
To pigeon-haunted classic towers,
And marbled clouds go scudding by
The many-steepled London sky.

And girls in slacks remember Dad,
And oafish louts remember Mum ...

Some readers find Betjeman's religion has an appearance of affectation for this reason, as if it would not exist outside the familiar Betjeman scene. Religious feeling should be more free of the accidents of time and place if it is to sound natural: it should not seem to require Tortoise stoves and box pews, nor be distracted by the wiring of a public address system. But the whole strength of Betjeman's poetry is that it is written from his feelings and no one else's: his kind of religion has a right to be accepted in the same way as his kind of girl. Betjeman resembles the old gentleman who deleted from his prayer book all expressions praising God, in the belief that they would be distasteful to that well-bred Person. We cannot call beliefs insincere just because they cannot be divorced from character.

But some critics of Betjeman's ethos go further, claiming that any sincere religious feeling should make his open interest in class distinction impossible, and deploring what they call his readiness to side with the richer governing class in order to laugh at those with different class habits. I think this criticism is based on a misunderstanding. Betjeman is undeniably fascinated by class habits, but rather as Professor Higgins was fascinated by speech habits. Just as Higgins could place Eliza in Lisson Grove by her vowels, so Betjeman can place Elaine in Ruislip Gardens by her Windsmoor and Jacqmar scarf. It is a kind of social expertise peculiar to certain writers – Mary McCarthy is another – to hit off character and situation by such means, by always insisting on the brand and the name and the make and the actual expression and the details of clothes and furniture:

> And plants for indoors are the fashion –
>   Or so the *News Chronicle* said –
> So I've ventured some housekeeping cash on
>   A cactus which seems to be dead.
> An artist with whom we're acquainted
>   Has stippled the dining-room stove
> And the walls are alternately painted
>   Off-yellow and festival mauve.

I cannot see why Betjeman should be crimed for bringing off the subtle class-suggestiveness of the fifth line of that verse, for instance. It is just what people like that would say, and as admirable a stroke as the cheerioh and cheeribye of the ATS. Again, many readers have complained about 'How To Get On in Society', a poem made up almost entirely of solecism and false gentility, and originally set as a competition in *Time and Tide*, presumably to see who could spot the greatest number of *gaffes*. Here again I think readers have misunderstood Betjeman's intention. The poem satirizes a woman who is trying to 'get on in society' by assuming a 'superior' manner of talk and behaviour. It is not laughing at natural class-habits, like dropped h's, but at 'superior' unnatural ones going off half-cock ('Are the requisites all in the toilet?'). This seems to me legitimate.

Betjeman is a kind of distorting mirror in which all the catch-phrases of modern criticism appear in gross unacceptable parody. He is *committed*, *ambiguous*, and *ironic*; he is *conscious of literary tradition*, but does not quote the right authors. He is a *satirist*, but his satire, directed against liberal atheists, hums disconcertingly round our own ears. He has his own *White Goddess*, in blazer and shorts. And he has *forged a personal utterance, created a private myth, brought a new language and new properties to poetry*, and even, since the publication of his *Collected Poems*, *given poetry back to the general reader*, all these equally undeniably, yet none of them quite in the way we meant. No wonder our keen critical tools twitch fretfully at his approach.

If we are to take Betjeman seriously, what kind of seriousness does he exemplify? As I said before, his chief claim on our attention is that he has changed our idea of what is beautiful. This is not simply a matter of creating a new fashion in architectural appreciation, or putting into currency a new set of aesthetic attitudes. For his feeling for the present is at least as his feeling for the past, and the paradox of his work is that it has for the first time brought into poetic focus Elaine and the concrete platform at Ruislip Gardens, the very things that have displaced the lost Elysium of rural Middlesex.

Boys and girls
Weed in the sterile garden, mostly sand
And dead tomato-plants and chicken-runs.
Today they cleaned the dulled Benares ware
(Dulled by the sea-mist), early made the beds
And Phoebe twirled the icing round the cake
And Gordon tinkered with the gramophone
While into an immense enamel jug
Norman poured 'Eiffel Tower' for lemonade.

The 'funniness' of Betjeman's poetry is on the wane, and instead of taking the poems with it, as many expected, there is left a confident apprehension of the look and sound of present-day England and its inhabitants, and an unhesitating demonstration of the kind of poetry that can be made of them:

From the geyser ventilators
  Autumn winds are blowing down
On a thousand business women
  Having baths in Camden Town ...

Deep down the drive go the cushioned rhododendrons,
  Deep down, sand deep, drives the heather root,
Deep the spliced timber barked around the summer-house,
  Light lies the tennis-court, plantain underfoot.
What a winter welcome to what a Surrey homestead!
  Oh! the metal lantern and white enamelled door!
Oh! the spread of orange from the gas-fire on the carpet!
  Oh! the tiny patter, sandalled footsteps on the floor! ...

Keys with Mr Groombridge, but nobody will take them
  To her lonely cottage by the lonely oak
Potatoes in the garden, but nobody to bake them
  Fungus in the living room and water in the coke ...

Of the poetry Betjeman has made of the past there is no need to speak. If today a railway lamp, a Norman Shaw house or a Victorian interior seems beautiful or affecting, this is largely his doing. But again this is not a question of starting a new fad in taste, but of making us see in what way these things represent vanished societies made up of such people as ourselves, who will in turn vanish as they did. Behind Elaine and Ruislip Gardens Betjeman can see Middlesex as it was, not in the spirit of someone looking for anti-planning, anti-red-tape-and-concrete propaganda, but in an evocation, seemingly as effortless as it is exquisite, of England before 1914, and its shadowy perspectives that reach back into the previous century:

Parish of enormous hayfields
  Perivale stood all alone
And from Greenford scent of mayfields
  Most enticingly was blown
Over market gardens tidy,
Taverns for the *bona fide*,
Cockney anglers, cockney shooters,
Murray Poshes, Lupin Pooters
Long in Kensal Green and Highgate silent under soot and stone.

The meeting and conflict of present and past is one of Betjeman's most fruitful situations for poetry, as it was for Hardy, and lies behind many of his best climaxes:

Cancer has killed him. Heart is killing her.
  The trees are down. An Odeon flashes fire
Where stood their villa by the murmuring fir ...

But the strongest and most enduring thread that runs through the contradictions of impulse in this puzzling dazzling body of work is a quite unfeigned and uninflated fascination by human beings. From the Wykehamist, the Death in Leamington, and the 'Varsity Students right through to Eunice, the lady who reads the *News Chronicle*, and the Little Sister of the Hanging Pyx, Betjeman has always written about people, sometimes mockingly, sometimes angrily, but never unfeelingly. Human lives, and human lives in time, are his central themes; neither the screens he throws up of absurdity and satire, nor the amount of exploring he does down alleys of minor interests, should prevent the recognition of his poetry's lasting quality as well as its novelty.

As for this book, you will of course buy it; it is in print again now with some of the more obvious misprints removed, but 'Chirst' on page 123 surprisingly remains, and 'I know that I wanted to ask you' on page 143 should surely be '*what* I wanted'. I hereby offer to correct the proofs of Betjeman's next book of poems for nothing, if that is the only way to protect them from such blemishes. The printing and binding are charming. The Earl of Birkenhead's *Introduction* is not as good as Warden Sparrow's in 1945, nor the author's own in 1948. The selection – all that the Earl of Birkenhead wishes to preserve – is, with the exception already noted, not bad.

Listen, Spring 1959

Keeping Up with the Graveses

This fourth version of Robert Graves's *Collected Poems* bears a frontispiece portrait of the author as male maenad which can conveniently be checked against his own self-description on page 301:

> Crookedly broken nose – low tackling caused it;
> Cheeks, furrowed; coarse grey hair, flying frenetic;
> Forehead, wrinkled and high:
> Jowls, prominent; ears, large; jaw, pugilistic;
> Teeth, few; lips, full and ruddy; mouth, ascetic.
>
> I pause with razor poised, scowling derision
> At the mirrored man whose beard needs my attention,
> And once more ask him why
> He still stands ready, with a boy's presumption,
> To court the queen in her high silk pavilion.

This note of self-questioning, this 'boy's presumption', has long been a characteristic of Mr Graves's poems. Even in the 41 pieces in the two sections that have been added to his last collected volume (1947) there is sometimes, along with the stylistic assurance and practised reaching after epithet, the same unsureness about what subjects are really worth a poem, the same inability to be finally, overwhelmingly memorable. It is this illusion of novitiate hesitance – as if his every poem were his first – that makes Graves's work so free of the vices common to poetic middle-age – clichés of vision, hastily inflated philosophy, the plain loss of interest – and it is kept fresh by his continual readiness to try for new effects:

> You, love, and I
> (He whispers) you and I.
> And if no more than only you and I
> What care you and I?

Review of Robert Graves, *Collected Poems* (Cassell, 1959); Robert Lowell, *Life Studies* (Faber and Faber, 1959); John Berryman, *Homage to Mistress Bradstreet* (Faber and Faber, 1959); Christopher Logue, *Songs* (Hutchinson, 1959); and Rex Taylor, *Poems* (Hutchinson, 1959)

Counting the beats,
Counting the slow heart beats,
The bleeding to death of time in slow heart beats,
Wakeful they lie.

Mr Graves's constant revisions and regroupings and discardings (which he once more mentions with an odd complacency, as if they do him credit) support this view that there is uncertainty as well as certainty at the heart of his talent, in addition to other long-recognized pairs of contradictions – flippancy and devotion, level-headedness and poetic fury, contemporary vernacular and the trappings of romanticism. That he is still capable of adding to his canon poems as good as anything he has ever written this latest collection demonstrates even more unquestionably.

Of the two American poets whose books are noticed here, English readers are more likely to feel at home with Mr Robert Lowell, whose work is liberally informed with European properties such as Italy and Ford Madox Ford. In *Life Studies*, however, his historical sense comes into its own with a series of autobiographical poems dealing with his American childhood and later life as a writer. These are curious, hurried, offhand vignettes, seeming too personal to be practised, yet none the less accurate and original:

I borrowed Grandfather's cane
Carved with the names and altitudes
Of Norwegian mountains he had scaled –
More a weapon than a crutch.
I lanced it in the fauve ooze for newts.
In a tobacco tin after capture, the amber yellow mature newts
Lost their leopard spots,
Lay grounded as numb
As scrolls of candied grapefruit peel.

Elsewhere the brevity is manifestly under the pressure of distress:

Father's death was abrupt and unprotesting.
His vision was still twenty-twenty.
After a morning of anxious repetitive smiling,
His last words to Mother were:
'I feel awful.'

In spite of their tension, these poems have a lightness and almost flippant humour not common in Mr Lowell's previous work, matched with a quicker attention to feeling which personally I welcome. If these qualities are products of the stresses recorded in the final few poems of this book, Mr Lowell will not have endured in vain.

The title-poem of John Berryman's *Homage to Mistress Bradstreet* is buttressed by both early and late poems to form an introduction to his work for English readers: a seemingly uncharacteristic dramatic monologue in the person of a seventeenth-century settler in the New World, it is a tight-knit, elliptical piece (with notes) which, apart from isolated lines ('Headstones stagger under great draughts of time'), yields on first reading less than Mr Edmund Wilson's judgement ('the most distinguished long poem by an American since "The Waste Land"') leads one to expect. In other poems Mr Berryman occasionally shows himself capable of powerful imaginative coherences:

> Slumped under the impressive genitals
> Of the bronze charger, protected by bronze,
> By darkness from patrols, by sleep from what
> Assailed him earlier and left him here,
> The man lies. Clothing and organs.
> These were once
> Shoes. Faint in the orange light
> Flooding the portico above the whole
> Front of the State House. On a February night.

In the main, however, this is difficult, coldly rhetorical poetry with insufficient literary distinction to atone for a lack of communicated feeling.

The publishers of *Songs*, by Christopher Logue, claim that at a time when all other poets are like 'bald men fighting over a comb' he scoops the pool by being both committed and lyrical. I am afraid that with the best will in the world his work in the former role strikes me as banal and hysterical, and in the latter as afflicted with the *faiblesse* that nowadays inevitably attends words like King, Queen, Tom o' Bedlam, Adam, Eve, Lady, Philosopher, Gardener and so on. His more successful versions of, or poems after, Homer and Pablo Neruda suggest that he is unable to organize a strong effect without another writer in the background. Admirers of Mr Logue's recent poetry-and-jazz recital 'A Red Bird Dancing on Ivory' will find the text here.

Mr Rex Taylor presents in *Poems* a curious group of pieces bearing (as his publishers admit) the stamp of the influence of

Edward Thomas – curious, in that they hit off precisely Thomas's meditative, fitful wandering line without seeming mere copies:

> Lying like so much snow upon the land,
> Unknown of wind, yet drifted there
> In hedgerow and coppice, the hawthorn's bloom
> Makes me suddenly aware
> How near to winter this month of May is
> In all that nature takes or gives –
> When thinking of a sudden flush of snow
> That marked March's end, and which still outlives
> The heat of the sun; lying among
> Dead leaves and stems of briar, where,
> As its head, each hedgerow has the same drift of white:
> And all the sweet of spring is in the air.

This collection is well worth reading. Mr Taylor's next book may be even more so.

Manchester Guardian, 15 May 1959

Look, No Kangaroos

There is one sense in which an English reviewer is almost certain to be prejudiced about Australian poetry: he expects it to be different from its English equivalent. This is not to say that he automatically expects it to be worse. Since the distant and the unknown is always inclined to exercise a romantic fascination, he is more likely to assume it will be better. But since its authors have grown up about as far away from him as they possibly could, in an environment he knows nothing about, he is confident that they will produce a poetry which in subject-matter and style will be refreshingly new. Good or bad, what they write will be *different*.

I am afraid that for this reason Mr Randolph Stow will disappoint him, for there is nothing in *Act One* to indicate conclusively that he spent his childhood under the Southern Cross rather than within sound of A40. Mr Stow has chosen to adopt a manner that may be new in Australia but which falls on English ears with depressing familiarity: the literary manner. His very title is literary; his sub-titles – *Scene One, Interlude for Voices, Scene Two* – complete this preliminary removal of what he has to say into the vitiated realm of paper and ink. A prefatory poem is called 'An Apology for his Making', while later on there is a 'Complaint' and a 'Fancy'; he is always ready to call a poem a tale or a parable or a dream, and within them we soon encounter some of poetry's most veteran walkers-on – Icarus, Adam, Endymion, Tithonus, *et al.* – well supported by a faceless cast of maids, shepherdesses, farmers' boys, and children. It may be objected that one cannot derogate literature by calling it literary, but alas, one can. To be literary means to receive one's strongest impressions – one's subject matter – secondhand from literature instead of first-hand from experience, and to set it down in terms and styles that have already lost their freshness by being used by someone else instead

Review of Randolph Stow, *Act One* (Macdonald, 1957) and Geoffrey Dutton, *Antipodes in Shoes* (Edwards and Shaw, 1958)

of thinking up your own. Here, as examples, are the openings of five of Mr Stow's poems:

> Once in this angry land, they say, a boy,
> Fervid with springtime, came upon a maid
> Brown as a harrowed field. It was a day
> Bright with new birth, and he, being green and high
> Of blood, smiled hotly at her ...

> She has put on a silver gown and gone,
> Crook-backed and crooked-minded to berate
> The sky in paddocks slow with afternoon ...

> Here once she lay, the wanton-minded maid,
> Letting her sun-bright lids delight in dreams
> Of ripe gold thighs. Her tendrilled hair lay spread
> Dark on the capeweed flowers, and her head
> Drowned in the sky's blue pasture ...

> A mad-eyed house
> A mad-eyed house
> In a valley among the sandhills, miles alone;
> A crazed old man, watching with eyes of stone ...

> Tithonus, speak; come, you old locust, you
> In the dry ruins, you, creeping and crying
> Over the broken ruins. Come, you knew
> Things as they were, now tell ...

Each of these typifies to me this wan convention, where what the poem has to say is either an insipid literary notion or else has been stylized long past the point where the reader loses interest; equally, it may be said that anyone reading this review who actually wants to know how any of these five poems continues is a natural customer for Mr Stow, and should act accordingly.

Do they fairly represent the whole collection? Yes and no. Not a single poem, to me, carries with it the solid impact of experience. But Mr Stow has the virtues of literariness as well as its vices. He is deft, neat, and charming, especially about childhood:

> My childhood was seashells and sandalwood, windmills
> And yachts in the southerly, ploughshares and keels,
> Fostered by suns and by waves on the break-water,
> Sunflowers and ant-orchids, surfboards and wheels,
> Gulls and green parakeets, sandhills and haystacks, and
> Brief subtle things that a child does not realise,
> Horses and porpoises, aloes and clematis –
> Do I idealize?
> Then – I idealize.

'As I Lay Dying' is a trick poem that springs its trap effectively, and 'The Conventional Young Man, At Springtime' deserves a less deprecatory title. Mr Stow's literariness is proper in 'The Language of Flowers':

> I sent my love clematis. She walking white
> In her garden, reading Rossetti, veiled her sight
> Under blue eyelids, blushingly comprehended
> Her mental beauty thereby was commended

and a very different poem, 'Country Children', though not a success, makes the strongest impression of a worthwhile subject. But the rest do no more than demonstrate that Mr Stow is a sensitive writer on faint and conventional themes. Having shown that he can assume this style – could it be a reaction from a depressingly boisterous literary environment? – perhaps he will drop it in favour of something more effective – and, incidentally, his publishers do him no service by insisting that one of the poems gained second prize at a Cheltenham Festival. For an English reader it sums the book up too acutely.

Mr Geoffrey Dutton's talent is nothing if not many-sided. His collection, *Antipodes in Shoes*, shows that he can turn a poem about a renowned place ('Salonika', 'Attica'), produce a pastiche ('Now winter days constrict The sun's unheated hours') or a translation ('Delie CXLVIII'), play with 'the metaphysical' ('Love's Compass') and 'the Movement' ('You must admit that poets can talk sense'), and for good measure throw in some epigrams and a piece or two of comedy/satire. His world is not Mr Stow's: it is the real world of travel and military service and love affairs and the seediness of postwar societies. On the other hand his talent is less devoted: writing poems, he seems to say, whether about one's friend's houses or one's country's defects or one's girls, is a facility natural to an educated man, and such topics are suitable exercise for it. The very diversity of modes suggests the lack of any central idiosyncratic vision. One could not imagine Mr Dutton making poetry the sole business of his life.

His best manner is a rather heavy masculine-sounding description:

> The tug thuds, and breaks across its bow
> The bank-wide onrush of the yellow Rhone.
> Behind, the barges, black, enormous, plough
> Like sullen oxen this elusive soil

Which slides by the poplars at their ease, alone
While these are roped together to their toil.
Firmly as France lies underneath my feet
The paddles cut their chunks of water out....

As a style, it is inclined to stodginess, which Mr Dutton tries to remedy with some tricks of alliteration that unite him to W. H. Auden rather than William Langland:

A rock is regained, sheer with sheoak,
Choice of my childhood, a cliff-high open chimney
To which I heaved huge boulders
And sent them bouncing, in great bites of grass ...

But when it serves him well in sharp-eyed, passionless descriptions such as his poem about a deserted French aerodrome:

Aircraft, drawn up in wingless rows, squat
Blunt-nosed like bees along the grass ...
A rudder waves in the wind, control-wires slap,
Fabric like a windsock flaps in the dust.
Bolts shine like bones
At the shoulders amputated of their wings.
The shattered instruments measure the speed of rust.

Mr Dutton devotes a number of pages to poems of a humorous or satiric flavour. Some of these are, frankly, awful:

No owls or cheetahs
Could drive my car.
Who the hell
Do you think you are?

but on the whole one welcome the sound of real kicks on real bottoms, as in his set of Skeltonics entitled 'The State of England Nowadays, 1949':

So many who abhor
But what an encore
Saw I never;
So many manuals
The recent war
On how to be Daniels
When surrounded by spaniels
Saw I never ...

His satire is the thirty-ish kind, against regimentation and repression and all that, expressed in language at times reminiscent of the early Day Lewis:

Through solid niceness let
A shudder of unreason run.
Stick up the bank-clerk brain
With the body's gun . . .

Of course, there were worse periods than the Thirties. But one cannot read far in Mr Dutton without the image recurring to one's mind of a kind of Australian Anthony Knebworth – young, passionate, slightly Byronic, yet at the same time full of good-humour, fun, decency, energy, and so on. It is an admirable type and I should be the last to denigrate it. But it is not, basically, a poetic one.

Australian Letters, 2:1, June 1959

Texts and Symbols

The themes of Mr Vernon Watkins's poems, as by now is well known, are of the widest: birth, death, creation, renewal, the cycle of the seasons, life outside time. The visible world is to him both text and symbol, and his prevailing mood is present ecstatic. Hence when in his latest collection, *Cypress and Acacia*, he does his subject-matter justice, the result is an effortless mesmeric kind of writing of an instantly recognizable tone:

> Over sea, gold distance hung in a fiery crucible.
> No fingers, however cunning, could shift the grains
> Of hurrying sand. Mathematical, yet inscrutable,
> Each rose with the rising wave, then slipped through the hourglass.
> No shore could set a term to the curlew's call.
> The voice returned to itself round the sevenfold world
> And perched on mystery. Night, like a working goldsmith,
> Heard waves beat on the indestructible core.

Mr Watkins's romanticism remains serious and sincere: he is an alert and conscious artist, never (or very rarely) sprawling, never trigger-happy, never self-indulgent. Nor does he go around boxed in a portable private pasteboard 'universe': his eye reports sanely on creation:

> The mare lies down in the grass where the nest of the skylark is hidden.
> Her eyes drink the delicate horizon moving behind the song.
> Deep sink the skies, a well of voices. Her sleep is the vessel of summer.
> That climbing music requires the hidden music at rest.

Nevertheless, it must be admitted that if poets were divided into those who never get off the ground and those who never come down to earth Mr Watkins would be in the latter class. He remarks the visible world only to transcend it, and this sometimes confers an inhumanity and ultimately a slight boringness on his work.

Review of Vernon Watkins, *Cypress and Acacia* (Faber and Faber, 1959);
Anne Ridler, *A Matter of Life and Death* (Faber and Faber, 1959);
and Andrew Young, *Quiet as Moss* (Hart-Davis, 1959)

Comparing him to Dylan Thomas is like comparing 'A. E.' to Yeats: one misses the verbal force and the sudden direct outcroppings of humour and realism that made exalted mannerisms more tolerable. I also find Mr Watkins in some places mightily obscure:

> And men may find beneath the sun,
> Dashed into pieces by old wrong,
> A relic, lost to nature, one
> Whose passion stops the mouth of song.

Reading Mr Watkins, I realize that, like the dwarf in Grimm, 'something human is dearer to me than all the world'. But some of this poetry is not to be ignored, for though Mr Watkins will never capture either the realist or romantic publics, he has his own vision and voice:

> Calm is the landscape when the storm has passed,
> Brighter the fields, and fresh with fallen rain.
> Where gales beat out new colour from the hills
> Rivers fly faster, and upon their banks
> Birds preen their wings, and irises revive....

I am sorry to say that in comparison Anne Ridler's latest collection, *A Matter of Life and Death*, seems to me tuneless and stodgy. Mrs Ridler also sees human and divine love in a relation that sends strong steady ripples from one to the other ('Love is our argument of joy'), but her verse seems to take no strength or inner organization from it, even when using a stanza form:

> Quitted but in your arms I lie:
> Give and take are equal joy.
> Is it to live like God, to want
> And have at once? To have what's spent,
> To nourish need because fulfilment
> Cannot fail; postpone its coming,
> Then with this voluntary need
> Turn to will a world of good.

It is as if she has wilfully rejected the old ways of being poetic without having found a new way. Nor do I find her statements more than mildly convincing:

> Yes, on the face of the new born,
> Before the soul has taken full possession,
> There pass, as over a screen, in succession
> The images of other beings:
> Face after face looks out, and then is gone.

> Nothing is lost, for all in love survive.
> I lay my cheek against his sleeping limbs
> To feel if he is warm, and touch in him
> Those children whom no shawl could warm,
> No arms, no grief, no longing could revive.

The reader may judge from these quotations whether or not he shares my deafness. The volume includes 'Evenlode', a pleasant piece for broadcasting about river-mortals and immortals.

In *Quiet as Moss* Andrew Young once again shows his talent for remarking the small and vivid details of natural scenes which he renders in economical and unaffected verse. It is harder than it looks to write a stanza such as

> The stable-boys thud by
> Their horses slinging divots at the sky
> And with bright hooves
> Printing the sodden turf with lucky grooves.
> ('Wiltshire Downs')

and the same poem ends with an almost-Hardyesque image:

> And one tree-crowned long barrow
> Stretched like a sow that has brought forth her farrow
> Hides a king's bones
> Lying like broken sticks among the stones.

These poems abound in precise and felicitous descriptions ('And bracken lifts up slender arms and wrists And stretches them, unfolding sleepy fists') and have an occasional agreeable turn of humour, such as the one about the absent housewife who had pegged out a line of windblown washing ('I thought, She little knows That ghosts are trying on her children's clothes'). But they read like the work of a man who, while possessed of intelligence and deep feeling, knows he cannot make his poetry a vehicle for more than the things he notices on his walks. Such self-knowledge would be rare, but it may account for the reader's continual subdued sense of disappointment. Miss Joan Hassall contributes twelve charming wood-engravings (the one repeated on the dust-jacket benefits by enlargement), and either these or the poems are chosen by Leonard Clark.

Manchester Guardian, 27 November 1959

Down among the Dead Men

It is hard for anyone brought up to regard Georgian poetry as an outgrown shallow pastoral playfulness (that is, for anyone under forty) to realize that it represented a robust zestful upsurge of realism – a movement into which the young D. H. Lawrence, for instance, fitted quite naturally. Nevertheless, this is so. 'There can seldom have been so flat a period of writing,' Mr Alan Pryce-Jones says in a long and careful introduction to his choice from these poets, 'as that through which the poets were stumbling when … Rupert Brooke's early verses and Masefield's *The Everlasting Mercy* enlarged the scope of poetic imagination by suggesting a fresh selection of possible themes for poetry.' And yet in barely half a decade it was all over. 'Very few literary fashions have endured so short a time as that for Georgian writing. Within five or six years it had become a term, first of ridicule, then of abuse.' The venom that greeted Mr Eliot was in part the venom of those who in their own opinion had been elbowed away from the praise-trough unduly early.

Pre-Eliot poetry, like pre-1914 England, is beginning to have a certain period fascination. More, it is becoming harder to avoid recognizing that whatever we think of the Georgians, poetry in our day is more remote from the concerns of its readers than it was in theirs. We may expect, therefore, if not a revival, a quickening of interest in these poets, and a renewed speculation about what would have happened to the course of English poetry if Owen, Thomas, Rosenberg, Brooke and the rest had not been killed. No doubt poetry, like every other branch of art, was bound to go through a period of *Modernismus*, and certainly there could have been much worse exemplars than Mr Eliot, but it would have been interesting to observe the continental impact refracted through

Review of *Georgian Poets*, selected by Alan Pryce-Jones (Hulton, 1959); *The Collected Poems of Sir John Squire* (Macmillan, 1959); and Ralph Hodgson, *The Skylark and Other Poems* (Macmillan, 1959)

stronger native talents than for the most part survived. Did the Great War itself make poets more serious? The trouble with the Georgians, Mr Pryce-Jones implies, was not so much lack of talent as limitation of sympathy: 'It is hard not to be struck by the extent to which their preoccupations fall short of what is now expected of a poet.' Well, perhaps it is; but such preoccupations do not in themselves make poetry.

This latest addition to Hulton's Pocket Poets, a series as attractive as it is cheap, makes an interesting hour's reading. Ready as I was to see the Georgians rehabilitated, though, Mr Pryce-Jones pulls nothing out of the bag to stop me groaning at the very names of Lascelles Abercrombie, AE, Gordon Bottomley, Frank Kendon, Francis Ledwidge, *et al.*, and perhaps in an effort to avoid anthology pieces he does other writers – Sassoon, for instance – less than justice. On the other hand, he hits off the early Lawrence perfectly with a plummy bit of erotico-mysticism, *Trespasser* period. For me the star pieces are Harold Monro's 'Midnight Lamentation' and J. C. Squire's 'Winter Nightfall', but they shine only fitfully. It is well worth half a crown, anyway, to find out if this period awakens a response in you.

To lift up the flagstone inscribed *The Collected Poems of Sir John Squire* is a hazardous experience for one trained to think of this author as the epitome of all that the Heroes of the Revolution delivered us from. What was Squire really like? Mr John Betjeman, whose short preface demonstrates his familiar skill at making things sound attractive without actually lying, says that Squire's chief gifts were descriptive. Perhaps; but one's principal impression is of an introspective, sombre-minded man, with little originality and no power to concentrate an effect, but with a welcome freedom from pretence and complacency. His speculations are never far from darker topics:

> Beneath my skull-bone and my hair,
> Covered like a poisonous well,
> There is a land . . .

He cannot escape his preoccupations: they depart only if they choose, and if they do not

> Yes, I know, I know;
> One's mind should not think of death or the dead overmuch, but
> one's mind's made so

That at certain times the roads of thought all lead to death.
And false reasoning clouds one's soul as a window with breath
Is clouded in winter's air,
And all the faith one may have
Lies useless and dead as a body in the grave.

It is this sense of the terrible underlying the normal that makes 'The Stockyard' Squire's most powerful poem. 'You have come to see the filthiest thing in the world,' he tells himself as he starts on a conducted tour of the Chicago slaughterhouses, and after he has described what he was shown we are ready to agree with him, not so much out of horror at the ceaseless suffering as from outrage at the organization of so gigantic a piece of insentience. He departs, but the memory pursues him; again, he cannot escape it:

But at night in the Opera ...
It stole to me, chilling my spirit,
The inveterate miasma of death,
A presence drifting as only I knew
Over all that gaiety, sensibility,
Refinement, innocent playing with toys.
And I thought no longer of only Chicago ...

No poet after Passchendaele could have thought of only Chicago. I cannot pretend I think very highly of Squire as a poet, but in future we shall have to throw stones at someone else.

Curiously enough, animal suffering is the keynote of another poet in Mr Pryce-Jones's collection, who has published his first book of poems since 1917. Free association with the name of Ralph Hodgson is certain to produce 'I hear a sudden cry of pain' or "Twould ring the bells of Heaven', and it is not surprising therefore that the most striking piece in his collection *The Skylark and Other Poems* is 'Hymn to Moloch', published during the campaign for the Plumage Act in 1921. In it, a kind of malevolent Mr Glum prays for help in his trade in ornamental feathers:

With best lines in Paradies
Equal to what
Is fetchin a pony
A time in the at,
An ospreys an ummins
An other choice goods
Wastefully oppin
About in the woods....

We thank thee most earty
For mercies to date,
The Olesales is pickin
Nice profits per crate,
Reports from the Retails
Is pleasin to read;
We certainly thank thee
Most earty indeed.

It is therefore a disappointment that the rest of this collection, made up of poems written over the last forty years, is characterized by wan ellipsis and facetiousness on subjects which, with exceptions ('Silver Wedding', for instance), do not catch the attention.

Spectator, 18 December 1959

Imaginary Museum Piece

It is rather surprising that in an age when poetry is run by whey-faced juiceless creatures in universities Donald Davie should be the only one whose work is complemented even faintly with a published poetry theory. Forcibly nominated as a foundation member of the Movement he has had to spend a lot of time fighting his way out of the fly-papers of anti-wet scum (remember Mr Maugham's Christmas message?), toughness, *terza rima*, and so on.

He has done this the more decisively by recently espousing and expounding a critical doctrine enjoining on the writer an eclecticism comparable to that exercised, for instance, by the modern painter: the English poet must make himself at home among the styles, subjects, and languages of the ages, and be free to incorporate in his own work such features as appeal to him. (Clearly the amount of 'culture' this entails sets him for ever apart from the movement plug-uglies.) It is hard not to see some connection between this theory and Donald Davie's latest book of poetry, *The Forests of Lithuania*. This, instead of being a collection of lyrics concerned with the life of the author in the Fifties, is a long poem in six parts 'adapted' (we are not told whether this means translation or what) from the celebrated Polish poem 'Pan Tadeusz' (1834) by Mickiewicz, which is a narrative set in Lithuania during the Napoleonic Wars.

I do not mean to imply that Davie has produced this unusual poem to avoid his own charges of narrowness and provincialism. Obviously he enjoys taking a holiday among past works of literature, and this enjoyment is the reverse side of his 'imaginary-museum' theorizing. Is the theorizing justified thereby? Personally I am always sorry when poets desert their private agonies to rehash others' literature. Nor can I make much of the poem itself: in spite of the fact that the original was a narrative – a kind of

Review of Donald Davie, *The Forests of Lithuania* (Marvell Press, 1959) and P. J. Kavanagh, *One and One* (Heinemann, 1959)

novel in verse – the story-line of *The Forests of Lithuania* eludes me. Nor can I attempt to estimate how much credit in a case like this should be given to Davie for images, adjectives, and so on. All I can say is that he has devised a most telling metre – a varying two or three stress unrhymed line – in which to set out his descriptive passages and episodes:

> Can this be the place? a piano,
> Sheet-music upon it, books . . .
> And see, across a chair
> The white gown freshly shaken.
> Cross to the window. A brook
> That ran through nettles once
> Borders a garden plot
> Of grass and mint. Those beds
> Were lately rained upon:
> The watering-pot that stands
> Half-full has felt
> Just now her hand, the gate
> Swings from her touch. . . .

Lines such as these should be enough to demonstrate that this poem is far from the customary stale upholsteries of translation and has a firm articulate sensitive voice of its own. Its dry civilized tone and fastidious choice of epithets renders the poem a pleasure to read in spite of continued bewilderment as to what it is about and why it was written.

Mr P. J. Kavanagh's book, *One and One*, is his first, and a bright collection it is, too, each poem founded on a forceful and for the most part comprehensible idea. But the brightness is a little reminiscent of the poems of Aldous Huxley, and his typographical and stylistic affiliations are at times twentyish:

> she is death's antithesis
> time itself shall cherish her
> knowing better than to try
> the granite bloom of innocence.

These characteristics may indicate early work, for other poems have a greater firmness and maturity of manner:

> The rain is the same.
> Some of the trees original.
> Certainly the stream
> Is the one that woke you, lulled you,
> The tiny bridge identical.

And what has happened since you climbed the stair
Would neither have surprised nor killed you …
('Yeats's Tower')

Maturity of subject-matter, too, is only just round the corner, and will presumably eliminate further poems about the Muse and the ubiquitous flippancies. In the meantime Mr Kavanagh at least makes us read on: no small feat in these no-fun days.

Guardian, 1 January 1960

Lies, Fleas, and Gullible Mayflies

'I never read your *Guardian* reviews,' a friend told me recently, 'they're too full of lies.' Suppressing retorts both Shakespearean ('Go shake your ears!') and Shavian ('What else but lying makes our life on this earth tolerable? What is religion? Lies. What is patriotism? Lies. What is our hope for the future, our faith in ourselves, our love of our neighbour? Lies, lies, lies, I tell you, Ramsden,' &c.), I pressed for clarification. 'All this oily reviewers' patter,' I was told. 'Interesting, significant, valuable. Why not be honest and say there's no difference between a louse and a flea?'

I suppose there is a lot of fun to be had from reading the quotations on any dust-jacket more than five years old, simply because of reviewers' besetting vice, that of taking, or appearing to take, their contemporaries too seriously. Indeed, if one goes back to the advertisements at the end of, say, an Edwardian novel, one can find names spoken of as imperishable that have not only faded but, as Lawrence might have said, 'collapsed into utter non-being'. Can reviewers be dismissed therefore as a crowd of gullible mayflies or venal time-servers? I am not so sure. It is no use remonstrating with a reviewer for speaking of the latest Poetry Book Club choice in terms that leave no adjectives for, say, Hardy, Tennyson, and Pope. If he tries to keep the same critical standard for the lot he will find himself unable to say, not only anything favourable, but anything *at all* about the month's poetry, simply because critical perspective means that if the classics are in focus then ephemera are not even visible, and vice versa. He cannot send his editor a sentence saying that by any real standards Mr A, Mr B, and Miss C do not exist. The only way out is to get the eye up against the stuff to the exclusion of all else. There is an enormous difference between a louse and a flea if you can stand getting near enough.

Review of Vernon Scannell, *The Masks of Love* (Putnam, 1960) and
Peter Redgrove, *The Collector and Other Poems*
(Routledge and Kegan Paul, 1960)

Mr Vernon Scannell's poems *The Masks of Love* seem to derive from Auden in their loose good-humoured mixture of psychological insight and social realism, but they lack the master's intercontinental sweep and geologist's precision, offering instead the cosy, careful conventionalities of his Common Man. This character, under the name of Simon Frailman, is in fact the subject of a rather arch sonnet-sequence in this collection ('"It's not too late," the glass says to his lips; / "It's not too late," the whisper in the bowel'), and he also reappears, with literary affiliations, in 'Biographical Note': he

> Does not complain and manages to laugh
> And seems, in fact, to love his family.
> But what amazes most, he works away
> At wretched stints to earn their bread and broth,
> Tending his small gift, fragile as petal or moth.

Most of these poems, in fact, exhibit one aspect or another of his life: his children, his jealous wife, his silver wedding, his muddled search for happiness, and their motto might be the couplet

> His life has never been, and is not now,
> As cosy as these dead-pan facts allow.

Mr Scannell's sunless domesticities give his work an authentic ring and a certain obstinate truthfulness that compensates for any unoriginality of epithet or rhythm. A likeable collection.

Mr Peter Redgrove is very much more idiosyncratic than Mr Scannell, but in *The Collector and Other Poems* he too has much to say about a rather younger kind of domesticity, the first house, the first pregnancy, the first child, all recorded in a style at once eager, extravagant, obsessively detailed, and a little mad. He spends so long describing an ordinary thing that in the end it becomes interesting, like something magnified or slowed down to an extreme degree. A woman washing with her eyes shut, for instance:

> Sluices her bunched face with close hands, finds natural grease,
> With clinking nails scrabbles for the body of the sprawling soap,
> Rubs up the fine jumping lather that grips like a mask, floods it off,
> Solving the dingy tallow.
> Bloods and plumps her cheeks in the springy towel, a rolling variable
> darkness
> Dimpling the feminine fat-pockets under the deep coombs of bone
> And the firm sheathed jellies above that make silent lightning in their bulbs.

Allied with some bizarre subjects ('To a Murderer Who Dismembers', for instance, and finding a dead baby when mushrooming), this style suggests a talent at present spending itself excitedly on all sorts of sensations and ideas, some of them acceptable but too many trivial or disagreeable. Mr Redgrove is most immediately appealing when writing of worms, birds, and insects, for which he displays real feeling:

> Fine-grained eyes, hemispherical and dull,
> From lakes of sewage bordered by dusty hills
> You infect my meal with your self-interest
> Steadfast in the light with dabbing trunks ...

Guardian, 5 February 1960

Collected Poems by Roy Campbell

The third and presumably final volume of the late Roy Campbell's *Collected Poems* [Bodley Head, 1960] comprises a selection of the many translations he made throughout his life, notably from Baudelaire, Lorca, St John of the Cross, and other Romance writers. Translations always perplex me. I frankly confess I cannot judge whether such lines as

> Blurring with flowers the eyes of human leopards,
> I've whirled Floridas none yet set eyes on

produce in me the emotion awoken in a French reader by

> J'ai heurté, savez-vous, d'incroyables Florides
> Mêlant aux fleurs des yeux de panthères à peaux
> D'hommes!

Almost all translations seem to me condemned to be poetic zombies, assemblages of properties walking around with no informing intelligence or soul, unless the original poem can be digested in the imagination of its translator and used to produce a new poem. This Campbell sometimes did, in his particular romantic way, and his easy and almost insolent skill in rhyming go to make his versions convincing. There is a hitherto unpublished version of Horace's 'Ars Poetica'. The volume has a preface by Dr Edith Sitwell.

Guardian, 25 March 1960

Gleanings from a Poor Year for Poetry

The appearance of the *Guinness Book of Poetry 1958–59* – the third issue – establishes it alongside the P.E.N. Club's *New Poems* as an annual feature of the local poetic scene. Comparison of the two is interesting. Both volumes change their trio of editors every year. *New Poems*, the elder by about seven years, appeals publicly for contributions (which must not have appeared in *book* form); then, after its editors emerge from the subsequent deluge of rubbish, a direct solicitation of well-known names begins, and the book is made up almost entirely in this way. (It is a point of honour with poets never to send poems unasked.) Payment is at the rate of a guinea or two per poem; there used to be a sherry party, but this seems to have lapsed. The Guinness method is more discreet and lavish. The editors make up their selection solely from poems *published for the first time* during the year under consideration, approaching each author on harp-stamped paper with an offer of five guineas for permission to reprint (some tough customers may bargain for more). In addition, each poem so chosen stands a chance of winning one of the *handsome cash prizes* given to those the editors consider first, second, and third best (all sums running into three figures). Finally, there is a party where these prize poems are read aloud, with (one hopes) plenty of the company's incomparable product to soothe the feelings of the unsuccessful.

One might expect, therefore, the Guinness volumes to be better for two reasons: first, they pay more, and secondly, by limiting their consideration to poems already published they should automatically secure a higher class of entrant. And yet there is not much in it. More potent factors are the rottenness of poetry in any year and the ability of a given team of editors to do their job conscientiously and intelligently in securing the half-dozen good

Review of the *Guinness Book of Poetry 1958–59* (Putnam, 1960); Edwin Muir, *Collected Poems* (Faber and Faber, 1960); and Peter Levi, *The Gravel Ponds* (André Deutsch, 1960)

poems that is the most they can hope for. In the present volume the editors (John Lehmann, John Press, Donagh MacDonagh) 'felt it impossible' to choose between poems by Auden, Edith Sitwell, Robert Lowell, and Edwin Muir, so they divvied up four ways, with something under the plate for Mr William Plomer. Personally I think one of the poems by K. W. Gransden, Richard Murphy, Matthew Mitchell, and D. J. Enright might have been included, but it was clearly a thin year, unless there were more fish in the Liffey than ever came out of it. It will be interesting to see what the P.E.N. Club team produces.

This is not the occasion to say why I found Edwin Muir unreadable, but I must be honest and admit that I have never read him and do not mean to start now. It is clear from the reception accorded to his latest *Collected Poems* that he has many distinguished admirers, and that he was much loved as a man during his lifetime; this volume was made up first by Muir himself, who added 27 poems to the earlier collection made in 1951 by Mr J. C. Hall, and secondly after his death by Mr Hall and Muir's widow, Mrs Willa Muir. It includes all unpublished poems found among his papers, some of which would in course of time have been published in Muir's next book.

During a long poetic career Edwin Muir was at once guided and inspired by themes and images springing from the non-rational unconscious, and by the memory of his own Scotch heritage and upbringing. His fidelity to these sources was eloquent of a devotion to poetry both simple and passionate, and he was always aware of

> Heaven-sent perplexity –
> If thought should thieve
> One word of the mystery
> All would be wrong.
> Most faithful fantasy
> That can believe
> Its immortality
> And make a song.

He was not to my mind an individual poet, but he was an independent one, and his spirit was admirably far from the contentions of poetic fashions.

Mr Peter Levi's first book, *The Gravel Ponds*, shows him to be a deft and slightly precious writer with nothing particular to say. He can write gracefully:

What if the world were a horrible mad fit,
Human reason sand, and God a mere unknown,
And no philosophies could temper it
To shivering flesh and nerve, breakable bone,
But the mind's vigour alone?

I would not choose to be masked in any defence
Beyond the fight and heat of an animal,
And heart's power against heart's pretence;
Some wild thing's ways, not copied or learnt at all,
Some quiet of innocence.

But he does not leave the reader feeling that there is the slightest danger of the world's being a horrible mad fit; and while he shows us time and again that he sees and thinks things which might reasonably be supposed to have a place in a poem, the characterlessness of his approach renders them insipid. The collection is a choice of the Poetry Book Society.

Guardian, 29 April 1960

Exhumation

It is typical of Mr Day Lewis that he should have gained an exhibition at Wadham College on the strength of his English essay and 'an entirely spurious reputation as a Rugby footballer'. These joint recommendations foreshadow later dualities: the poet and Nicholas Blake, the pyloneer and the Georgian, the Communist and the cricketer. There has always been this suggestion of adaptability about him, whether one calls it seeking a personality or running with the hare and hunting with the hounds, and its result has been to vitiate each character in turn as it is put forward.

On picking up Mr Day Lewis's autobiography our unspoken request is no doubt the same as that of the Cambridge undergraduate's on page 208: 'Tell us about the Thirties.' (Mine would, strictly, be tell us about Auden, as the most interesting part of the Thirties.) Mr Day Lewis does his best to explain how it was natural in those days for one's feelings about love and justice and delight in existence to become confused with Marxism, tractor films, and the CPGB: he protests that he and his friends were not 'a lot of starry-eyed suckers leaping down into the political arena', but well-intentioned men who saw their own intelligence and sensitivity simply as additional reasons why they should try to help society through a hard period to a new age. But it clearly seems an awfully long way off, and in this book Day Lewis the Georgian is in command. It takes him sixty-four pages to get to school at all, and 156 to get to Oxford; not until page 181 does he step beyond the enormous bat-shadow of education, and the remaining 26 per cent of the book deals almost scrappily with his adult life, petering out about 1940 with no suggestion that the tale will be taken up again in a later volume. This is the Forrest-Reid-Walter-de-la-Mare view of life: nothing quite equals being a kid. Somewhere, no doubt, there was all the time a buried Day Lewis writing poetry, having affairs, being sarcastic, worrying himself sick, but he never

Review of C. Day Lewis, *The Buried Day* (Chatto and Windus, 1960)

gets hold of the pen, despite the author's bland preparedness for him to do so ('let him say what he will, then, this awkward young customer'). After a while the reader regrets this.

The Buried Day, to be fair, is a product of Mr Day Lewis's sense of his own past and of what he owes to the dead, not of any emotional exhibitionism or desire to explain that he was right all along. Its meditative tone, unsensational matter and mildly amusing anecdotes are therefore appropriate, and anyone undertaking to read it from interest in its subject will find it easy enough going. But it is a dull and somewhat arch book, much nearer, as writing, to Richard Church than W. H. Auden, and unlikely to send anyone in search of Mr Day Lewis's other books.

Spectator, 20 May 1960

Last-but-one Round-up

The shower of *Collected Poems* we are going through at present underlines to what an extent this kind of volume has become a recognized milestone in a writer's life. It would be interesting to find out when the practice began. Certainly it was not always so: when Heminge and Condell performed their act of simple piety ('do not envie his Friends, the office of their care, and paine, to haue collected & publish'd them') Shakespeare had been dead seven years. Later it became a kind of positive last appearance, like Dame Melba in Brisbane, a guarantee that the author really was going to shut up, and its compilation was recognized as suitable occupation for his dotage. But to-day it happens much earlier: when a poet has published half a dozen slim volumes, and is in consequence one of the first 57 names that spring to any mind contemplating the poetic scene, his publisher, who has let them all drop out of his list surreptitiously as a cat lets something unchewable fall on the carpet, sees it would be profitable to issue the material for his seventh s.v., not one of its own for 10s 6d but bound up with the pick of all the other books for 30s. This he therefore does. The author relishes this assurance that he has 'arrived', and spends a happy few weeks 'revising', i.e. monkeying about with, the text of 'all he wishes to preserve'. The weeklies have a sitter for their literary leaders. Is everybody happy? as Ted Lewis used to say. That's the idea!

My objection to the genre is quite simply that they are not collections but selections. If one is interested in a poet one wants all his poems in the order they were published, not a selection according to his own idea of himself reshuffled to conceal how bad he was when he started, the whole with lots of alterations to suit the latest fashion in adjectives. Above all one does not want it tied up with new material. If I have the first six volumes, then to compel me to buy the bulk of them all over again in order to get

Review of William Plomer, *Collected Poems* (Jonathan Cape, 1960)

the seventh is something for which, as Jack Tanner said, I know no polite name. Indeed, one suspects that even the author, once the hectic glow of being collected has died down, would really prefer all his books in print and selling separately.

It is only fair, however, to make clear that Mr William Plomer's *Collected Poems*, at least, contains a negligible amount of previously unpublished work, and is only 18s (published by Cape). It is welcome also because it provides a conspectus of a talent one has probably known previously in one mood only. For his most celebrated poems are, of course, the historical-satirical ballads (A or even X certificate) in which a person or period is 'hit off,' in the sense both of being preserved and hit for six; or else something inexplicable and macabre, a thigh in a cupboard, forms the disturbing centre of a tale which is clearly cautionary if only one knew what one was being cautioned against:

> 'Your Flecker is foxed, you old fool, and I'm through!'
> Then out of the door in a tantrum she flew,
> Leaving poor Jukes, in the black-out, in bed
> With his past, and the book, and a bruise on his head.

Moral (presumably): don't try to flog books to tarts, especially if they know anything about them. Whether it was worth drawing is a question that rises in the mind more than once, for though these poems are often satisfying savage and acute, the sorts of things Mr Plomer finds funny or telling can seem distressingly childish. So far from being original, too, they suggest Auden, without the clinical callousness and Betjeman without the energy and warmth. It is much more agreeable to turn to pieces that make clear what a pictorial poet Mr Plomer is:

> A white-hot midday in the Snake Park.
> Lethargy lay here and there in coils,
> And here and there a neat obsidian head
> Lay dreaming on a plaited pillow of its own
> Loops like a pretzel or a true-love-knot.
> ('In the Snake Park')

> A mouth like old silk soft with use,
> The weak chin of a dying race,
> Eyes that remember far too much ...
> ('A Levantine')

It may also surprise some to come upon the alert tenderness of 'A Young Jackdaw', 'The Caledonian Market', and 'September

Evening: 1938', a tenderness that seems inconsistent with the spirit of the ballads, but perhaps no more inconsistent than that Mr Plomer, lover of Greece and Japan, should have written (in 'The Bungalows') the most successful of Welfare State poems:

> . . . Begrudging vulgar fantasy
> To cheap and ordinary homes,
> Discrimination might deplore
> That concrete frog, those whimsy gnomes,
>
> Nor see them as blind tribute to
> The rule of dreams, or as a last
> Concession to the irrational,
> The old, wild, superstitious past.
>
> The commonplace needs no defence,
> Dullness is in the critic's eyes,
> Without a licence life evolves
> From some dim phase its own surprise;
>
> Under these yellow-twinkling elms,
> Behind these hedges trimly shorn,
> As in a stable once, so here
> It may be born, it may be born.

After this one sees nothing unusual when he parodies Hardy. While not all Mr Plomer's poems will find admirers, all his readers will find something in his poems to admire.

Guardian, 10 June 1960

Open Your Betjemans

A penalty of being one of the poets people really enjoy reading is that your work is liable to be anthologised in collections slanted towards particular occasions, purposes or audiences – *Shakespeare at War* (on paper like rationed bread), *Daily Thoughts from Rudyard Kipling, The Gardener's Tennyson*. Though this kind of publication seems less frequent nowadays (now I wonder why that could be?), examples still turn up occasionally, and the latest is John Betjeman: nine stretches of *Summoned by Bells*, and thirty-nine poems (none previously unpublished) arranged under titles like 'Poems of People', 'Poems of Places', 'Discovering Architecture', and so on, supplied with stock drawings by Edward Ardizzone and about twenty pages of notes by the editor, Miss Irene Slade.

This claim that Betjeman, so far from being the preserve of fiftyish church-tasters, can communicate with those born since D-Day immediately raises the question, Who are 'the young'? According to Miss Slade's notes, they are those who don't know the meanings of words like *choleric, Haslemere, dissenting minister, lichen, oyster-catcher, début, Strauss, pagan*. Fair enough, but what in that case will they make of:

> On a secluded corner of the beach
> A game of rounders has been organised
> By Mr Pedder, schoolmaster and friend
> Of boys and girls – particularly girls.
> And here it was the tragedy began,
> The life-long tragedy of Jennifer
> Which ate into her soul and made her take
> To secretarial work in later life
> In a department of the Board of Trade.
> See boys and girls assembled for the game.
> Reflected in the rock-pools, freckled legs

Review of *A Ring of Bells*: Poems of John Betjeman introduced and selected for the young by Irene Slade (John Murray, 1962)

> Hop, skip and jump in coltish ecstasy.
> Ah! parted lips and little pearly teeth,
> Wide eyes, snub noses, shorts, divided skirts! &c.

'This reference to Jennifer's work with the Board of Trade in later life,' Miss Slade assures us, 'means that she didn't marry and have children of her own. She was so upset by Mr Pedder's snub to her that she never got over it, and was suspicious of all young men from then on.' With the best will in the world, I can't see 'the young' getting much out of this malicious, slightly gamy portrait of a non-alcoholic child-fancier, and Miss Slade's solemn note completely misses the ironic overtones of the passage, aimed at people who think that childhood snubs lead to the Board of Trade, and at the world of adolescent self-pity generally. In fact, Miss Slade, apart from her thorough Verity's Milton type of annotation of proper names, is not always reliable: her note on the Cambridge 'wind/To blow the lamps out every time they're lit' is quite off the point ('the traditional rivalry between the two universities'), and in my view her interpretation of 'Group Life: Letchworth' (here printed, wrongly, in stanzas), particularly the note on 'ex-Serviceman', is open to question. She also persists in using the genteelism 'wealthy', a practice doubly out of place in this context.

Naturally all lovers of poetry (as distinct from desiccated PhD-fodder) must hope that this curious book will distend many stockings on December 25. The claims Miss Slade makes for her author, the aspects of his work she chooses to emphasize, are on the whole just: she underlines the enthusiasm and accuracy of his response to our own day as well as to the reigns of Edward and Victoria, the directness of his approach, his capacity for original observation. I do not agree that his style is 'uncomplicated', nor that he writes about 'familiar objects and experiences' ('Green is a light which that sublime Burne-Jones/ White-hot and wondering from the glass-kiln drew'), but I can see what she means. And her more-than-faint suggestion that Betjeman has not in some senses grown up ('his loves, hates, fears, weaknesses and strengths are much the same now as they were then') could indeed be supported by Betjeman's own pronouncements. Nevertheless, though I love Betjeman and believe he will conquer in any shape or form, I should not like to see him distorted into a kind of Sunday-Pic poet for the young in heart, as might happen if this book were taken up by schools. Far better give the kid the new five-bob *Collected Poems*, and let him find his own level. And save, of course, ten bob.

Spectator, 9 November 1962

Groupings

How many exported lecturers, still half-stunned by last night's *saké* or local whisky, have not reached for the appropriate olive-green British Council specific against all those bland attentive faces in an hour's time? Very few: nor can their trust often have been misplaced. For the stay-at-home, however, there is mild fun to be had from studying the list of titles: nine for the sixteenth century and earlier, twenty-one for the seventeenth, twenty-three for the eighteenth, forty-one for the nineteenth, and no fewer than *fifty-nine* for the twentieth: clearly, one realizes, *literature is getting better*. What two names appear both as subjects and authors (you'll never get them both)? Why, when the Powys brothers (not to mention the Brontë sisters) have to huddle between the same covers, should two members of the Sitwell family have a pamphlet each?

Such editorial decisions should, of course, not be interpreted as critical statements, yet I had a pang of regret at seeing the Powyses once more bundled together, so encouraging the party-smarty to go on saying he can't tell them apart. Mr Churchill does his best in a sympathetic thirty pages to emphasize the unlikeness of T. F. Powys from John Cowper and Llewelyn, giving him two of his five sections, but although he accords pride of place to John Cowper he does little to explain the dynamic of his work. And in my view he is less than just to Llewelyn, who, as Somerset Maugham said, 'by living so long cheek by jowl with death alone of them learnt to be honest'. Thirty pages are really not long enough to describe this astonishing trio.

Regret at *The Powys Brothers* was followed by stupefaction at *Ronald Firbank and John Betjeman*: who *is* responsible for these pairings? If their claims to separate treatment are really weaker

Review of R. C. Churchill, *The Powys Brothers* (Longmans, for the British Council, 1962) and Jocelyn Brooke, *Ronald Firbank and John Betjeman* (Longmans, for the British Council, 1962)

than, say, Christopher Fry's or Sir Herbert Read's, they might have doubled up respectively with Saki and Sir Max Beerbohm (to name two writers at present excluded) with more appropriateness, though curiously enough the name one thinks of first in connection with both is the same: Evelyn Waugh. Mr Brooke is a Firbank fan, and tries his best to make him sound attractive, but in the end has to admit you either like him or you don't. With Betjeman, he says all the usual things (and one unusual one, too, likening him to both Huysmans and Kipling), but fails to equal the perception of Sir Kenneth Clark, who is quoted on the inside cover as speaking of Betjeman's 'sensitive response to everything which expresses human needs and affections'. This is really the first thing to grasp about Betjeman, and it is hoped that all those Japanese, Sudanese, Lebanese, etc., students will take the point.

Spectator, 15 February 1963

Christina Rossetti

The principal contention of Mrs Packer's substantial life of Christina Rossetti is that the major part of her love poetry concerned not James Collinson, the Pre-Raphaelite painter with whom she broke in 1850, nor Charles Bagot Cayley, whose courtship 'did not begin until 1862 or thereabouts', but the Edinburgh painter and poet, William Bell Scott, whom she met in 1847 and continued to meet until his death in 1890. The reason that William Michael Rossetti did not admit this in his celebrated memoir was a potent one: all the time she knew him, William Bell Scott was married.

Mrs Packer has based her study on a considerable amount of material previously unconsulted: the Rossetti papers in the Bodleian, for instance, and other letters and manuscripts both in libraries and in private hands. Unless I have misread her text, however, she does not claim that her hypothesis is directly substantiated in any of these new sources. It takes its origin in a conviction that the force and feeling of Christina's poems of the eighteen-fifties, for instance, is quite unaccounted for by her life as we have known it, and that the particular character of these poems – the hopelessness and sense of guilt – can be explained only by the inadmissible nature of the attachment that is now claimed to have inspired them. Unfortunately there is little, if any, objective evidence: William Michael's description of Scott as 'a man whom Christina viewed with great predilection', the unpublished version of the poem 'Parting After Parting', 'Written in the train from Newcastle' after leaving the Scotts (who lived there):

Parting after parting
All one's life long:
It's a bitter pang, parting
While life and love are strong

Review of Lona Mosk Packer, *Christina Rossetti* (Cambridge University Press, 1962) and *The Rossetti-Macmillan Letters*, edited by Lona Mosk Packer (Cambridge University Press, 1962)

– these, and a number of more shadowy correspondences between the datings of poems and Scott's movements and behaviour, make up the bulk of Mrs Packer's case. 'In advancing my hypothesis', she writes, 'I have supported it by a detailed and carefully constructed edifice of indirect evidence in the hope that when the small pieces of the puzzle are all fitted together, the total design ... will be revealed.'

This sounds cautious enough. By page 72, however, Mrs Packer is writing 'To be deprived of the beloved's presence after enjoying it is a grief well known to lovers ... but added to the burden in Christina's case would have been the humiliating torment of acknowledging a love that could flourish only in darkness and secrecy', and we settle to a routine of 'we might surmise', 'she must have known', and 'What were her thoughts, as in company with Scott's wife, she journeyed northward into Ayrshire and Alice's territory?' which does little but arouse our impatience.

The portrait here drawn suffers by being both indistinct and incomplete. Her insistence on interpreting Christina Rossetti's attitudes ('With her realistic appraisal of human relationships, tinged as it was by pessimism, she understood that her ability to retain masculine interest had with this disadvantage shrunk to an alarming margin') clouds and blurs the actual image; a much plainer echo of her speaking voice is found in *The Rossetti-Macmillan Letters*, sixty-eight of which show Christina writing to her publisher about her 'dear Copyright' and other matters in a gently firm – and sometimes quite extraordinarily adroit – tone. It is to be hoped that all British publishers will regard their correspondence files as potentially valuable archives to be preserved for scholars.

Again, Mrs Packer lays her chief emphasis on the lack of fulfilment Christina's life brought her: we must not, she says, think of her as 'a sex-starved spinster', but this is really very much how she is presented. While this is useful in pointing out the recurrent ripe fruit–guilt association (forbidden fruit), and promoting a Freudian interpretation of that extremely curious poem 'Goblin Market', it tends to limit understanding of her character. Mrs Packer makes little of the Christina Rossetti of whom Sir Maurice Bowra wrote 'In the end she is a great religious poet, because religion called out in her all that was essentially and most truly herself.' Her account of Christina's rejection of

Collinson because of his reconversion to Roman Catholicism suggests she is unable to envisage such a renunciation for such a reason: she must have been tired of him anyway. True, she fainted on meeting him subsequently in Regent's Park, but 'in the nineteenth century ... fainting was fashionable'. One wonders what Mrs Packer would have said if Christina had fainted on meeting William Bell Scott.

And yet Mrs Packer is surely right: something must have provoked the desolation of those early poems, and the figure of Collinson hardly seems fitted to sustain the role. For that of the later poems there is ample cause. Once turned forty, she suffered Graves' disease: 'her hair was falling out, so that she had to wear a cap. Her skin had turned a dry, rusty brown. Her eyes protruded wildly. Her features had become sharply thin in sunken cheeks ...'.

> Youth gone, and beauty gone if ever there
> Dwelt beauty in so poor a face as this.

In 1876 she set up house with her mother and two elderly aunts in Torrington Square, and in the same year her sister Maria died. Gabriel died in 1882, her mother in 1886, her aunts in 1890 and 1893. By this time 'the mischief', as she called her own affliction of cancer, had recurred after an operation two years earlier, and the close of her life was extremely painful. Mrs Packer has unearthed a scarcely believable letter from the next-door neighbour in Torrington Square:

> I have come to town for three winters for my literary work, and have chosen this place because of its QUIETNESS. But since my return on the 17th September I have been perfectly unable to work, from the distressing screams that sound clear from her Drawing-room to mine, *especially* at the hours I have hitherto devoted to writing ... I have a strong suspicion that her screams occur when she is left alone.

The neighbour had to wait until 29 December before her devotion to literature could be resumed. On that day in 1894 a life ended which had produced a body of work unequalled not only for its objective expression of happiness denied, but also for a certain unfamiliar steely – and in the last analysis cryptic – stoicism.

Listener, 26 March 1964

Bond's Last Case

These two stories, according to the blurb, were written in 1961 and 1962 respectively, and would have formed part of a similar collection to *For Your Eyes Only* if the late Ian Fleming had lived to add others to them. As it is, they presumably represent the last hard-cover splutterings of his remarkable talent. I am not surprised that Fleming preferred to write novels. James Bond, unlike Sherlock Holmes, does not fit snugly into the short-story length: there is something grandiose and intercontinental about his adventures that requires elbow-room, and such Bond examples of the form as we have tend to be eccentric or muted.

These are no exception. It would be difficult to deduce from them the staggeringly gigantic reputation, amounting almost to folk-myth, that has grown out of the novels. Indeed, it would be difficult nowadays to deduce it from the novels. No sooner were we told that the Bond novels represented a vulgarization and brutalization of Western values than the Bond films came along to vulgarize and brutalize – and, in a way, sterilize – the Bond novels. With our minds full of Sean Connery in Technicolor, or whatever it's called now, this study of a retired Secret Service major drinking himself towards his final coronary, and its cover-mate, an assignment for 007 in Berlin to out-snipe a sniper, seem sensitive, civilized, full of shading and nuance.

How easy, for instance, to see in the career of Major Smythe an allegory of the life of Fleming himself! The two Reichsbank gold bars that the major smuggles out of the army on his discharge from the Miscellaneous Objectives Bureau are Fleming's wartime knowledge and expertise; he emigrates to Jamaica and lives on them – selling a slice every so often through the brothers Foo (presumably his publishers), and securing everything his heart desires: Bentleys, caviare, Henry Cotton golf clubs. For a time all is

Review of Ian Fleming, *Octopussy* and *The Living Daylights* (Jonathan Cape, 1966)

well. Then he has a heart attack; his wife takes an overdose; he has another attack, finding himself unwilling or unable to follow the regimen his doctor specifies:

> He was still a fine figure of a man, and it was a mystery to his friends and neighbours why, in defiance of the two ounces of whisky and ten cigarettes a day to which his doctor had rationed him, he persisted in smoking like a chimney and going to bed drunk, if amiably drunk, every night.
>
> The truth of the matter was that Dexter Smythe had arrived at the frontier of the death-wish ...

However inappropriate to Fleming's life the details may be, this evocation of a fifty-ish ex-service émigré, whose only interest now is tropical fish, going steadily to pieces has a genuine plangency. Bond figures in the story only as a shadowy emissary from 'Government House', come to dig up the nasty business of how he got the gold bars in the first place.

By contrast, the second story shows Bond as a kind of Buchan hero. Lying for three evenings on a bed covering the windows at the back of the Haus den Ministerien, Bond romances about a blonde cellist in a girls' orchestra that regularly enters the building, presumably to rehearse. When finally the British agent makes a dash for the frontier, and the sniper appears at the window, it turns out to be – as if you didn't know – the cellist. Bond's reaction is interesting. Instead of shooting the sniper before the sniper can shoot the agent, he deliberately alters aim (the agent escapes only by luck) so as to miss her, except perhaps her left hand. The Secret Service No. 2, who is with him, is understandably annoyed:

> 'You had clear orders to exterminate ... You should have killed that sniper whoever it was.'

But Bond is unmoved:

> 'That girl won't do any more sniping. Probably lost her left hand. Certainly broke her nerve for that kind of work. Scared the living daylights out of her. In my book, that was enough.'

This is the moralist Bond, who toys with resigning in *Casino Royale* and is quite incompatible with the strip-cartoon superman of the film versions or of popular belief, but who fits well with Kingsley Amis's suggestion, in his amusing and pertinent *The*

James Bond Dossier, that Bond is a re-hash of the Byronic hero. Perhaps. But it would support equally well the *Sunday Times*'s simpler and more devastating diagnosis quoted on the paperback editions: 'James Bond is what every man would like to be, and what every woman would like between her sheets.' Or are these still just two ways of saying the same thing?

Spectator, 8 July 1966

Poets in a Fine Frenzy and Otherwise

'He neither evaded nor substituted, preferring, for example, Wordsworth to Byron ... Nature and natural language to seraglio and seraglio talk, or faeries and faery talk, or mists, or infinity; preferring objectivity to autotoxication or autoblabbery, *here and now to somewhere else and then* –' This is Grigson on Landor, but it might well be said of the editor of *New Verse*, the teaser of Dylan Thomas, the scourge of the Sitwells. He, too, has won something of a Cobbett-like reputation in criticism, and the names on his contents page – Wordsworth, Crabbe, Barnes – suggest open-air English virtues: observation, realism, beauty, resolution, and independence.

Readers of this collection of reprinted pieces will soon find, however, that in it Mr Grigson inclines to a stance suspiciously close to Mr Alvarez and the Necessary Nervous Breakdown. Two of the longer essays here are on Christopher Smart and John Clare; fair enough, but Mr Grigson is always ready to remind us of 'De Quincey ... pierced by minarets; of Hölderlin, mad in his tower above the still Neckar; of Collins howling in Chichester Cathedral; of Blake observing angels or the ghost of a flea ...'; we grow accustomed to the discreet nudge that 'under the stories ... is the Crabbe who suffered (and recorded) visions under opium'. 'In his end Wordsworth became melancholy, if not mad' ('his sister,' Mr Grigson adds as if in consolation, 'became altogether mad'); 'Clare's asylum foretells our need for an asylum ...' – oh, come off it, one feels inclined to retort, what about Shakespeare, Chaucer, Keats, Hardy, Milton? Doesn't their absence of need for an asylum foretell the converse? One would have thought Mr Grigson would have been the last man to encourage the look-at-me-I'm-round-the-bend school.

However, not all the book is about madness: it consists of eighteen pieces written at different times for various audiences

Review of Geoffrey Grigson, *Poems and Poets* (Macmillan, 1969)

at various levels, and provides an admirable conspectus of Mr Grigson's perspicuity in the knock-about world of literary journalism. An essay I am particularly glad to see reprinted is the introduction to the volume of selected poems by William Barnes in the Routledge and Kegan Paul Muses' Library: this did much to introduce to the general reader a writer who was not only one of the best minor poets of the nineteenth century but who was a forerunner of Thomas Hardy, the most considerable English writer since Shakespeare before D. H. Lawrence. Another pair of estimations I find particularly effective are the pieces on Hopkins and Whitman: Mr Grigson picks up Hopkins's own statement that Whitman's mind was peculiarly congenial to his own (but could this be because they were both homosexually inclined?) and depicts Hopkins as a kind of Whitman of inscape.

Occasionally an essay is blemished by a 'contemporary' allusion (Herrick looked like a retired major out of *Mrs Dale's Diary*; 'Resolution and Independence', though an inspiring poem, isn't likely to be taken like a Purple Heart), but in the main Mr Grigson's writing is clear and perceptive. Just at the end, while proclaiming himself 'A Man of the Thirties', he takes a heartening swipe at 'the Sixties of the twisted mouths and snot-like surfaces of Francis Bacon, [and] the awkward mumble from the confessional box where Robert Lowell kneels behind his curtain'. But by then the breadth of his sympathy has been so amply demonstrated that such self-limitation does not really wash.

Guardian, 13 February 1969

Hardy's Mind and Heart

Hardy studies are still shuddering from the impact of the speculations put forward in the 1960s by Miss Lois Deacon, notably in *Providence and Mr Hardy*. 'What has Providence done to Mr Hardy,' wrote Edmund Gosse, 'that he should rise up in the arable land of Wessex and shake his fist at his Creator?'

Miss Deacon claimed to have stumbled on the answer: a love affair with Tryphena Sparks in his late twenties that not only ended unhappily, but produced a son. And not only this, but that the unhappy lovers were not cousins, as they thought, but uncle and niece.

The tale could be set aside on two counts. First, it is, for the most part, speculation, unsupported by conclusive documentary evidence. Secondly, even if it were proved up to the hilt, it would not alter a syllable of Hardy's work or its value. At the same time, it is undeniably fascinating. There is just enough circumstantial evidence to lure the reader's credulity on from page to page, until he is in danger of swallowing the entire contention.

Prof. F. R. Southerington's *Hardy's Vision of Man* is inscribed 'in recognition of Lois Deacon', an indication from the outset that he is of her party. It is in three main sections, The Man, The Novels, and The Dynasts, and is founded on much painstaking research, especially into original letters and documents on both sides of the Atlantic.

The author admits in his introduction that the book, which began as a study of Hardy's thought, became increasingly concerned with strong elements of autobiography he found the novels to contain – or, as one might irreverently put it, Tryphena-hunting. To find her in Sue Bridehead is no surprise (though I have never thought the tribute to Tryphena 'she was the only woman in

Review of F. R. Southerington, *Hardy's Vision of Man* (Chatto and Windus, 1971) and Michael Millgate, *Thomas Hardy: his Career as a Novelist* (Bodley Head, 1971)

Topsham who never lost her temper' fitted Sue at all convincingly), Prof. Southerington also sees her traces in Fancy Day, Elfride in *A Pair of Blue Eyes*, and in less likely figures such as Tess and Arabella.

He does not, however, pursue her into *The Dynasts*. There is a study of the thought behind this curious failed masterpiece, and more particularly of the concept of Will. In all, despite many interesting moments, the book does not give a unified impression, perhaps because of a divided purpose.

Prof. Michael Millgate will have none of her, or very little: 'It seems regrettable that recent attempts to establish Tryphena Sparks as a major influence on Hardy's life and work have compromised their potential usefulness by indulgence in irresponsible speculations of an almost entirely unsupported kind.' His book, *Thomas Hardy: his Career as a Novelist*, is a detailed account of the novels, setting them solidly in their social and intellectual background, not neglecting the little-known essay 'The Dorsetshire Labourer', and giving many striking examples of Hardy's researches into local history for his own imaginative purposes.

The praise of *Under the Greenwood Tree* ('it is essential not to undervalue its immense page-by-page vitality and toughness of texture') is especially welcome, but is far from being an isolated example of the author's perception. This is a more readable work than that by Prof. Southerington, and has something of the warmth and humanity of its subject.

Daily Telegraph, 3 June 1971

Stevie, Good-bye

Two of my favourite quotations are 'The business of a poet is to move the reader's heart by showing his own' and 'Only mediocrities develop.' Both applied to Stevie Smith's poems, and this posthumous collection shows it was so to the end.

Poetry today being what it is, she had long ceased to seem eccentric or freakish. Her method was to take a pot-shot at anything that, poetically, took her fancy, and the subjects she held up triumphantly forced us time and time again to admit there had been something there after all. They are an extraordinary collection: cats, Excalibur, childhood, Racine, Cranmer, Fafnir and the Occasional Yarrow are jumbled with strange refinements of feeling and situation – almost, as in 'Autumn', capsule novels: –

> He told his life story to Mrs Courtly
> Who was a widow. 'Let us get married shortly,
> He said. 'I am no longer passionate,
> But we can have some conversation before it is too late.'

She showed her heart by blurting things out, artlessly, in a *faux-naïf* style that enabled her to slide from Daisy Ashford/Lorelei Lee mannerisms at one end of the scale to a strong and sternly pure rhetoric at the other, a reminiscence of Lawrence and Blake: –

> But they cried: Could not England, once the world's best,
> Put off her governing garment and be better dressed
> In a shroud, a shroud? O history turn thy pages fast!

Did she move her readers? On occasion, certainly: a handful of poems – 'Not Waving But Drowning', 'The Singing Cat', and 'I Remember' are three – will draw away from the rest as her reputation settles down. Many others start well and then peter out (in this, at any rate, she resembles Emily Dickinson, to whom the introduction compares her, not altogether convincingly). A

Review of Stevie Smith, *Scorpion and Other Poems*, with an introduction by Patric Dickinson (Longman, 1972)

more serious drawback was her quaintness, frivolity, fantasy, call it what you will: all too often one found oneself rejecting poems ('Nourish me on an egg, Nanny') as facetious bosh. And sometimes the sense of bosh seeped into other poems, so that one could never forget when reading one that this was a *Stevie Smith* poem. Worse, it tended to devalue her seriousness: for some readers, she was simply not to be taken seriously at all.

They are the losers. She was for all this a writer of individuality and integrity, who had perfected a way of writing that could deal with any subject, and a tone of voice that could not be copied. Did she, truly, not develop? Unless one has all the books, it's hard to be specific (a *Collected Poems* as soon as possible, please): in her later poems she became a little sadder and more ominous, and if this is development then to this extent she developed. But there was little or no change in style: *Scorpion* renews her engagement with several familiar subjects: cats ('Oh I am a cat that likes to/ Gallop about doing good'), love ('Francesca in Winter') and general reflections on the human condition ('The Word'); there is a story ('Angel Boley') that might have been written by T. F. Powys, and another ('The House of Over-Dews') that has little point. Her long poem commissioned by the *Guardian* on 'a subject suitable for Whitsun', as it was put to her, deals with the Holy Spirit, and has one of her firmest endings: –

> I do not think we shall be able to bear much longer the dishonesty
> Of clinging for comfort to beliefs we do not believe in,
> For comfort, and to be comfortably free of the fear
> Of diminishing good, as if truth were a convenience.
> I think if we do not learn quickly, and learn to teach children,
> To be good without enchantment, without the help
> Of beautiful painted fairy stories pretending to be true,
> Then I think it will be too much for us, the dishonesty,
> And, armed as we are now, we shall kill everybody,
> It will be too much for us, we shall kill everybody.

'I aspire to be broken up,' she ends another poem, a note sounded, not surprisingly, throughout this last collection. 'Scorpion so wishes to be gone,' ends a third. 'Farewell' is, inexplicably, reprinted from *Not Waving But Drowning*, but 'Oblivion' gathers this subject up again and expresses it a little disconsolately but with a moving conviction. In the end, though, it is 'Grave by a Holm-oak' that one would pick as a valediction from this honest and arresting talent, if only because it is a better embodiment of her wintry cadences: –

You lie there, Anna,
In your grave now,
Under a snow-sky,
You lie there now.

Where have the dead gone?
Where do they live now?
Not in the grave, they say,
Then where now?

Tell me, tell me,
Is it where I may go?
Ask not, says the holm-oak,
Weep, says snow.

Observer, 23 January 1972

Archibald MacLeish

When Archibald MacLeish was appointed ninth Librarian of Congress by President Roosevelt in 1939, 1,400 members of the American Library Association signed a letter to the Chief Executive beginning 'We think that the confirmation of Mr Archibald MacLeish as librarian of Congress would be a calamity.' He was, they admitted, one of the four great living American poets, but as librarian of Congress – well, as soon (their President, Milton J. Ferguson, snorted) make a man Secretary of Agriculture because he likes flowers on his dinner table.

Perhaps they were forgetting – or perhaps they were remembering – the case of 'my old friend John Russell Young', whom President McKinley made librarian in 1897 because his wife's health had unexpectedly stopped his taking up a job in China. Their professional pride was offended by the appointment of this outsider. They need not, however, have worried. By 1944 MacLeish had gone – 'a rolling stone gathers no mausoleum', as he said – but long before this, the Association had given him a standing ovation at its conference at Milwaukee in June 1942, for, remarkably enough, he had been a success. This ex-Yale, ex-Harvard lawyer, this lecturer, this *Fortune* editor, this Curator of the Nieman Foundation of Contemporary Journalism, this *poet*, had taken the Library of Congress, beaten the dust out of it, shaken it into a new pattern, and made it newsworthy (there were more references to the Library in the *New York Times* during MacLeish's term than in all the previous thirteen years). When he went on his way, the staff he left behind felt they had had a brush with a comet.

Even if one reads nothing else in this book, the well-known essay 'The reorganization of the Library of Congress, 1939–44'

Review of Archibald MacLeish, *Champion of a Cause*. Compiled with an introduction by Eva M. Goldschmidt (American Library Association, 1971) deserves an hour of any librarian's time. MacLeish appears to have compressed into five years – three of them war years at that – reforms that, if possible at all, might be expected to take half a century. He denies that he intended to change anything: on his first day, he was asked to sign the day's ration of papers. Since he could not vouch for their accuracy, he tried to route them to someone who could. Within a month he had a committee to report on 'the whole question of acquisitions'. Within a few more, he had a committee of outsiders 'to examine the Library'. Their report led to changes too intricate to detail here. Suffice to say that a honeycomb of watertight and even hostile departments, with differing procedures and responsibilities that either overlapped or failed to meet, was tidied into five major divisions: Administrative, Reference, Processing, Law Library, and Copyright.

Outsider or not, MacLeish emerges as very much the twentieth-century librarian. He believed in 'government by discussion', instituting the daily meeting between division heads. He laid down canons of selection and canons of service. He was in full reaction from the European tradition of 'custody':

> At the beginning of our discussion two views were advanced . . . one, that a library is a kind of machine to drop a book into a reader's hand, the machine having no further responsibility, or, indeed, interest – except to get the book back; the other, that a library is a group of human beings who accept a responsibility to make any part of the printed record available to society, by whatever means is most intelligible and most effective, the responsibility ending not with the mechanical delivery of the book but with the identification and production of the text or information needed.

There is, of course, much more in the book than this one treatise. MacLeish was a war-time librarian, and there is plenty of rhetoric about flying the flag of truth and reason higher than our enemies can cut it down: the Nazis, typically, were book-burners. After the Nazis came MacCarthyism, and the case of one Dr Albert Sprague Coolidge, who was passed over by a later Librarian of Congress from serving on the advisory committee to his own family's Coolidge Foundation because he lacked 'objectivity': 'The gelded librarian is a sacrifice which only MacCarthyism demands and MacCarthyism in decay need not now be handed its dearest victim.' And there were the endless skirmishes with Mencken's booboisie, always ready to hound some small-town librarian whose tastes were too advanced: 'If you could take *Lolita* off the shelves by mob action in the Congress or out of it, you could take Marx off the shelves, and ... Thoreau could follow.'

MacLeish did not cease to defend libraries and librarianship when he left Congress (the last address is dated 1967), but he never posed as anything but a writer. Indeed, 'I knew what a library was: it was the last place a writer ought to be found until he was stone cold.' Paradoxically, the overall effect of his book is to suggest that a librarian is a good thing to be. In another of his typical almost seventeenth-century arguments-by-alternatives, he says we are keepers of books, but in what sense? The mere physical book, the paper and board, so that we are no more than check boys in the parcel room of culture? Or the intellectual book, the construction of the spirit, that is preserved not by warehousing but by our own ceaseless and passionate advocacy? If so, our role is the greatest cause of our time. Well, such flights may owe a little to the Nieman Foundation of Contemporary Journalism, but they are heartening, and there is not so much well-written and forthright praise of our profession about that we can afford to disregard them.

Journal of Documentation, XXVIII:1, March 1972

The Hidden Hardy

Today is the 132nd anniversary of Hardy's birth. The coincident appearance of this book demonstrates that current interest in him is high – higher, perhaps, than ever before. For these letters are no new discovery: they were bequeathed by their recipient, Florence Henniker, to her friend the second Mrs Thomas Hardy, who after Hardy's death in 1928 showed them to Barrie and asked if she should publish them. He was mildly encouraging, but the furore occasioned by the Shaw–Terry correspondence prevented her taking the idea further. Since her own death in 1937 they have apparently lain in Dorset County Museum without attracting any particular attention. They contain no startling revelations. In both manner and matter they look rather dull.

But in recent years we have awoken to the fact that Hardy's life, and for that matter his letters, may not be entirely what they seem. For a quarter of a century after his death 'the good little Thomas Hardy', to use Henry James's patronizing phrase, tended to be taken at his face value, a bourgeois countryman who, apart from being a genius, exemplified pedestrian provincialism. Few perceived that, even in its surface quietness, his life was really rather remarkable. Despite modest birth, he entered and moved freely in Society: he first met Major Henniker, Florence's husband, at the Guards' Mess, St James's, and Mrs Henniker at the Vice-Regal Lodge in Dublin. His first marriage was admittedly unhappy, but the surviving anecdotes of it bring him no discredit. Although his books are instinct with passion, with natures thwarted by mischances both social and inherited, no gossip tells of Hardy in the grip of anger, love or sorrow. His days pursued their orderly way to international fame, the Order of Merit, a visit from the Prince of Wales. His death revealed an estate of £90,000, but little else.

The fact is that much of what we know of Hardy is simply what

Review of *One Rare Fair Woman: Thomas Hardy's Letters to Florence Henniker 1893–1922*, edited by Evelyn Hardy and F. B. Pinion (Macmillan, 1972)

he chose we should know. His protracted old age gave him plenty of time to decide what evidence of himself he should leave behind. 'Examine and destroy useless old mss,' a celebrated jotting runs, 'entries in notebooks, and marks in printed books'; as day succeeded drab day at Max Gate, round which the trees planted to please his first wife had grown to dispirit his second ('This place is too depressing for words in winter'), the meticulous obliterating work went on. Photographs were burnt ('The flame crept up the portrait line by line'), old poems rewritten and the originals scrapped. After his death his widow finished the job. Basketsful of papers, letters and documents were fed onto a bonfire, and she herself raked the ashes. Whatever survives is unlikely to have done so by chance.

What caused all this? It seems to have begun as a necessary concomitant of writing his autobiography – necessary, because for Hardy one suspects that autobiography was not, as with other men, simply a personal version of his life – a kind of speech for the defence – but an attempt to give such a version the status of truth. Posthumous publication under his wife's name may have sprung from modesty, but it also lent the authority of impersonality. And once it was completed, the records had to be destroyed in order to replace actuality by fiction, an account shaped by himself and illustrated by incidents of his own choosing. Thereby what he wished to be remembered would be remembered; what he wished forgotten would be forgotten.

This was less a falsification than a shifting of emphasis, but these letters show very well how it worked. There are only eight references to Mrs Henniker in the whole of the *Life*: he met her in 1893 ('a charming *intuitive* woman apparently') by invitation at her brother's, the Lord Lieutenant of Ireland. A letter to her in the same year is quoted, and by Christmas they had, seemingly, collaborated in a story called 'The Spectre of the Real'. The next mention is not till 1911, when 'the Hardys' friend, Mrs Arthur Henniker', came to see a performance of some of his dramatized stories in Dorchester. In 1919 he writes to her again, after his 79th birthday, and the following year, in the company of his second wife, he shows her areas of Dorset, where she 'had ideas of buying a house'. Another visit is mentioned in 1922, and then in 1923 he notes her death: 'After a friendship of 30 years!'

The exclamation mark was Hardy's single concession in the *Life* to the degree to which his emotions had been involved. Not that such involvement is explicit in the letters: 'I know, of course, that there is nothing in my epistles which it matters in the least all the world knowing,' he wrote even in 1893, that first seven months of their acquaintance from which 24 letters survive, but even so one can trace, in addition to a certain skittishness, hints that his feelings were being deliberately disciplined. 'I *have* entered on my scheme – the plan I spoke of – little pleasure it has given me ...' (29 June); 'I adhere desperately to my plan, with poor results; but time may help it ... I sleep hardly at all, and seem not to require any' (2 July); 'You may be thankful to hear that the *one-sidedness* I used to remind you of is disappearing from the situation...' (10 September). What plan? What one-sidedness? Professor Pinion suggests that Hardy was purposely using social distractions to blunt his feelings, but the one-sidedness remains a puzzle: class differences? marital unhappiness? love itself?

> As for one rare fair woman, I am now but a thought of hers,
> I enter her mind and another thought succeeds me that she prefers;
> Yet my love for her in its fullness she herself even did not know;
> Well, time cures hearts of togetherness, and now I can let her go.
>
> 'Wessex Heights' (1896)

The second Mrs Hardy, whom Mrs Henniker introduced to him in 1904, indicated fairly plainly that this referred to her friend, adding that she was, on the contrary, 'sincere and affectionate'; two other poems ('A Broken Appointment' and 'A Thunderstorm in Town') are on the same authority to be similarly associated. Others, like so much else, are a matter for conjecture. The signature of the letters graduates from 'Ever sincerely' through 'Ever yours' to 'Ever affectionately', and throughout he never ceases to urge a meeting: 'I wish you would come down to Salisbury' (1898); 'Why don't you get a sea-side home near here' (1899); 'I wish you could come down to the sea-side near here' (1906); 'Meanwhile cannot you come for a week-end or a week-middle' (1914); 'I wonder if you will ever come again' (1918). Early on he trails a more deliberate invitation:

> I have been thinking that the sort of friend one wants most is a friend with whom mutual confessions can be made ... Do you want such an one for yourself? – I wonder if I shall ever find one.

They had met at a critical time in his life: his marriage, then about twenty years old, had become a source of pain, and he was writing *Jude*. His letters are those of an unhappy man asking for sympathy, and making the best of friendship when he found this was all he could get. 'Seriously,' he wrote in 1896, 'I don't see any possible scheme for the union of the sexes that w[oul]d be satisfactory.' And so the relation stabilized and the correspondence (to judge from the book) settled into some half-dozen letters a year, perhaps less. Occasionally there is a sentence that rings the inimitable note (as on the death of his mother at the age of 91):

> Owing to her deafness, and, of late years, inability to go out except in a Bath Chair, she has been for some time out of sight of the world, but to myself and my sisters she did not seem old.

But for the most part they are day-to-day jottings: weather, ailments ('a front tooth came out'), literature ('he [Bridges] hands on the torch no further than the rest of them'), bicycling, public affairs ('The Irish temperament, I fear, will not be satisfied for long with *any* rule'). He was always ready to discuss her work (Mrs Henniker was a prolific writer of novels and stories), and they shared a concern for animal welfare: one forgets how, in the horse age, the streets were nightmares of brutality ('I met an electric omnibus, and it seemed a joyful presage of the future'). By a strange coincidence, both his first wife and her husband died in 1912, but there was no hint of a closer relation in consequence, even though Hardy was to marry again in 1914.

Why did he play down the friendship in the *Life* – because there was nothing in it, or because there was? Mrs Henniker's replies (of which Dorset County Museum holds about 40) apparently add nothing to our knowledge, and in the end one wonders whether it is not the secretiveness that is the whole point, and not anything it might have hidden. Why only eight mentions of 'the Hardys' friend, Mrs Arthur Henniker'? The countryman's natural reserve? A wish to demolish the scaffolding once the poem is finished? Or the consequence of a character that was neither simple nor outwardly emotional, but self-possessed, cool, aloof? 'Hardy, how is it that you do not like us to touch you?' he reports a schoolfellow as saying, and that is it: the notion of strangers handling the materials of his life was wormwood to him. Indeed, it informed one of his most beautiful passages:

> 'And all her shining keys will be took from her, and her cupboards opened: and little things a' didn't wish seen, anybody will see; and her wishes and ways will all be as nothing!'

So, day after day, the smoke billowed across the garden at the back of Max Gate in January 1928, destroying – what? Recollections of the Jungfrau in 1897, or comments on Justin McCarthy's *Reminiscences*? Or evidence, plain and staggering, of what lay behind the anguish of both novels and poems? We do not know: probably we shall never know. Hardy preferred that we should not.

New Statesman, 2 June 1972

Articulate Devotion

I wonder if I am alone in finding the notion of conventional love poetry a little dated at present. After all, it's the orgasm we are interested in now; and if the nuclear family is under fire as socially undesirable, what about the nuclear couple? Almost élitist, wouldn't you say? As for fidelity, a leading sociologist suggested recently that people were nowadays having three marriages, for youth, maturity and old age respectively, a pattern long foreshadowed by Connolly's 'the woman who shares your early struggles is very different from the one you would choose to share your later successes'. Personally, I doubt whether the average meed of sexual satisfaction per head varies perceptibly from century to century. But ideas on how to get it may, and these in turn render the love poetry of one age meaningless or even antipathetic to the next.

Of these two anthologists, the elder (as might be expected) sees this more clearly. 'If our own time, for various reasons,' Mr Grigson writes in his introduction, 'is stingy with love poems or poems about love, stingy in fact with the cadences of poetry, the taste cannot have vanished', but all the same it's something of a survival, and this tends to be how he treats it. Of his 126 poets, just 63 were born before 1700, and The Bible and Anon tip the stylistic balance towards the archaic; dead names (Corydon, Cynthia, Queen of Paphos) and outworn attitudes ('a gown of gray my body shall attire'), dispersed as they are through the book, set the scene well in the shadow of *amour courtois*.

Shakespeare and Donne overtop it. Herrick and Rochester elude it, but there are many others, and it is something of a puzzle that later selections as a whole fail to make vigorous contrast. There are individual exceptions, of course: a sequence of four of D. H. Lawrence's German-idyll poems, Hardy's 'After a Journey',

Review of *The Faber Book of Love Poems*, edited by Geoffrey Grigson (Faber, 1973) and *The Penguin Book of Love Poetry*, edited by Jon Stallworthy (Allen Lane, 1973)

Barnes's 'In the Spring', Dowson's 'Non Sum Qualis Eram' and Eliot's 'La Figlia Che Piange' all assert their celebrated quality, and there is plenty of Patmore, Tennyson and Christina Rossetti, but Victorian romanticism was something of a harking-back, and heavy representation of the marmoreal Landor and the chilly Clare scores few points for any more realistic tradition.

Nor is much attempt made to carry the selection up to our own time – Graves has six solid entries, and there are four each by E. J. Scovell and Grigson himself, but no Betjeman, Auden, Dylan Thomas, Lowell or anyone later except Adrian Mitchell. Popular love poetry is explicitly rejected, as is 'the unmeasured, thin-rolled short crust of translation (Chinese, Japanese, Polish, Russian, and so on), useful, but now so easily accepted in itself as verse', a sentiment Grigson judges fit for repetition even in the small space of his introduction: such self-imposed limitations make either for purity or narrowness, according to taste, and that is the principal impression the volume makes.

Mr Stallworthy, on the other hand, aims for heterogeneity: 'The evidence of the poets is as conflicting as it is voluminous,' he writes; 'there are almost as many definitions of love as there are poets.' Therefore let us have conflict – of definition, of mood, of period, of style, of nationality; among the witnesses called are Martial, Neruda, Lady Heguri, Meleager, Anna Akhmatova and Yehuda Amichai, their short crust of translation balanced by the vernacular of, among others, e.e. cummings, Alun Lewis, John Heath-Stubbs, Roethke and Stephen Spender, not to mention Grigson's omissions listed *supra*. Stallworthy has more of a taste for the obviously popular: 'So, we'll go no more a-roving' and 'Cold in the earth, and the deep snow piled above thee' are both in his book, but not in Grigson's. He is readier to admit the dimension of humour, as in Berryman's

> Fainting with interest, I hungered back
> and only the fact of her husband & four other people
> kept me from springing on her

and also the dimension of obscenity: there are six poems by Rochester in each anthology, but it is Stallworthy who gives him his head:

> Nor shall our love-fits, Chloris, be forgot,
> When each the well-looked link-boy strove t'enjoy,

> And the best kiss was the deciding lot
> Whether the boy fucked you, or I the boy.

Donne, Graves, Yeats and Hardy are his best-represented poets, and he ends with a stirring *omnium gatherum* entitled 'Reverberations', in which Crazy Jane and the Bishop, 'The Disabled Debauchee', 'Surprised by joy' and 'Judging Distances' all rub shoulders, on what principle it's hard to establish.

Both anthologies have none the less much in common: both divide into subject-sections, 'Absences, Doubts, Division' being largest in Grigson and 'Celebrations' in Stallworthy, as might be expected. Both have in many cases made an identical choice, from 'I am the rose of Sharon' to 'She Tells Her Love While Half Asleep'. (It is a sign of the times to see Rupert Brooke ignored, and I should have expected Stallworthy, at least, to find room for Kingsley Amis and David Holbrook.) All the same, the two books are fated to be contrasted, and in the event it must be said that while Grigson's is more homogeneous, even more dignified, Stallworthy's contains enough Grigson-type choices alongside his own more eclectic selections to make it the more interesting, and even the truer portrait of love as we see it. Each has its *trouvailles*: I don't think Stallworthy has anything to equal Lord De Tabley's 'The Churchyard on the Sands', unless it is Lady Catherine Dyer's epitaph on her husband's monument, ending

> Mine eyes wax heavy, and the days grow cold.
> Draw, draw the closed curtains: and make room:
> My dear, my dearest dust; I come, I come.

At such moments both books can humble the attention by epiphanising the degree of articulate devotion of which our species was once uniquely capable.

Observer, 21 October 1973

The Puddletown Martyr

These are hazardous times for Hardy biographers. The bonfires are still burning at the bottom of Max Gate garden, letters, diaries, photographs, notebooks ('he, she, all of them – aye'), and the ascending smoke assumes lurid shapes, like gargoyles, or foetuses in bottles. The little old gentleman with the light waistcoat and auctioneer's hat puts away his bicycle and trots in for luncheon with the Prince of Wales, but behind him innumerable dark trees thresh and ply, moaning of concealment, of betrayal, of domestic Sophoclean atrocities. 'What has Providence done to Mr Hardy,' demanded Edmund Gosse as long ago as 1896, 'that he should rise up in the arable land of Wessex and shake his fist at his Creator?' The last ten years have brought grim guesses in reply: births unregistered, parentages unacknowledged, speechless agonies in the eweleaze under the pitiless sun. The Life (for 'Speaking generally, there is more autobiography in a hundred lines of Mr Hardy's poetry than in all the novels') has been invaded by the Works.

Faced with the long and blameless senescence, the scrupulous destruction of private papers, the Chinese wall of the pretended biography, the Hardy biographer can take one of two courses: he can either treat the row of serene volumes as an explosive enigma, a kind of large-scale *Sonnets* from which a human anecdote must be construed, or he can turn investigator, a tracer of unpublished letters, a searcher of the records of long-closed schools and hospitals, a visitor of museums and registries. Dr Gittings elects the second: 'The only true method is to start from the facts of the life itself.' Only then can sober consideration begin.

Eschewing sensationalism, Dr Gittings opens on the theme of class – less on its obvious manifestations in *Tess* and *Jude* than with an interesting account of how Hardy stealthily withdrew from his family background. In the *Life* he either upgrades the status of his

Review of Robert Gittings, *Young Thomas Hardy* (Heinemann, 1975)

relatives or omits them altogether; in a genealogical table he constructed in his old age his own branch of the family ('Hardy had about thirty first cousins') was left virtually blank. At his first wedding his wife's family was represented but his was not: afterwards, her relations came to stay but his did not. Gittings does not bother to explode the legend of a reluctant Hardy dragged into Society by his wife (indeed, this belongs several decades later than 1876, when the present volume ends), but his case that Hardy was determined to get away from 'the people who toiled and suffered' might have been strengthened by doing so. (It is salutary to remember that Hardy first met Mrs Henniker at the Vice-regal Lodge in Dublin in 1893, and dined with her husband the Major in the Guards' Mess, St James's, in the following year.) Gittings thinks that by *The Hand of Ethelberta* 'the note of social protest, which had begun with *The Poor Man and the Lady*, is virtually dropped'. To this deracination he ascribes some of the stress and turmoil of the later novels, not altogether convincingly: most English writers have been only too glad to get out of the working class, if they have had the misfortune to be born in it. But it is amusing that someone who wrote 'all things merge in one another – good into evil, generosity into justice [etc.]' should have been so keen to avoid merging with his awful Puddletown relatives.

Gittings deals fairly with the first marriage, and with Emma. He rejects the notion, entertained by Hardy and disseminated by his second wife, that there was madness in Emma's family: her eldest brother certainly died in an asylum, but of Bright's disease. With her life-long energy and high spirits she was, according to Gittings, a perpetual adolescent. He also points out, shrewdly, that both parties were deceived in each other: Hardy thought Emma was an intelligent and well-read woman, which she wasn't, and Emma took Hardy for a successful London professional man, which he wasn't either. It is hard to know who got the worst of it. Emma's eccentricities and overbearing manner must have been gall to Hardy, but she had to endure his poems to other women and to discover 'that this obsessive, complicated, brooding mind could be unconsciously insensitive and accidentally cruel'.

Gittings also accords a central position to Horace Moule, the first of Hardy's two mentors (the second was Leslie Stephen). Moule, who had attended both Oxford and Cambridge, was Hardy's university, telling him what to read and how to write; indeed, if Gittings offers a reply to Gosse's question, it is Moule's alcoholism, illegitimate child, and suicide that he names:

> The certainty is that, from the time of the death of Moule, Hardy never portrayed a man who was not, in some way, maimed by fate ... we can date the emergence of Hardy as a fully tragic artist, an expounder of life's true miseries, from the suicide of his friend, and the appalling revealed ironies of that personal history.

The existence of the illegitimate child apparently rests on the authority of the second Mrs Hardy, who told R. L. Purdy about it in 1933. One wonders if it is more firmly founded in fact than Emma's inheritance of madness. Gittings also brings forward Moule's successor in Hardy's life, Leslie Stephen, who acted as American-style editor to *Far From the Madding Crowd* ('Muttering to himself in the manner pilloried by his talented daughter in *To the Lighthouse*, he would go through the manuscript scribbling in its margins and sometimes all over it'). It was Stephen who gave Hardy his poetic credo in a sentence that is really all anyone needs to know about writing poetry:

> The ultimate aim of the poet should be to touch our hearts by showing his own, and not to exhibit his learning, or his fine taste, or his skill in mimicking the notes of his predecessors.

One is grateful to Dr Gittings for his meticulous research (who would have dreamed that Hardy had 'a walk-on part in *The Forty Thieves* at Covent Garden'?) and for his considered judgements, but at the same time a certain disappointment must be registered. The picture of Hardy that he draws – a prosaic, undecided, somewhat devious young man concerned to rise in Society – hardly squares with the poignant perception of even his earliest work. One asks sometimes whether he really *likes* Hardy: his first chapter repeats the view that the crypto-autobiography is dull. Since the greater part of it is a fascinating jumble of anecdotes, vignettes and observations taken from Hardy's diaries before their destruction, it is in fact supremely readable, especially precious for its aphorisms on poetry ('the emotion of all the ages and the thought of its own'). Then we are invited to smile at Hardy's 'grand assault on poetry' in 1865: on the evidence of the 1866 poems alone, this is like deriding Jack Johnson for learning to box. His contention that what makes Hardy 'consistently our most moving lyric poet' is that his 'Words ... were never solely literary; they were almost always linked to a remembered and familiar tune, undivided' omits the element of *meaning*: almost always, too, Hardy is saying something original. Dr Gittings makes a foray into the question of Hardy's sexual development, or lack of it: 'speculation about almost every woman he meets' may be a sign of 'delayed or imperfect physical development', but it might equally be the opposite. There is no mention of his strange comment on the servant-girl's baby: 'Yet never a sign of one is there for us' – strange, in that it seems too intimate a reflection for one of Hardy's temperament to publish (it is in the *Life*), unless it is a deliberately planted false clue. And in that case what are we to make of the last will (14 August 1922), providing for 'the first child of mine who shall attain the age of twenty one years'? Nor is Dr Gittings entirely guiltless of unjustified assertion: his claim that in 1871 Hardy sent valentines to both Emma Gifford and Tryphena Sparks is made on entirely circumstantial evidence. There is no proof that Hardy ever sent a valentine to anyone.

Dr Gittings reserves the heretical *Providence and Mr Hardy* (1966) for an appendix. Few of his readers will be unaware of its contention that Hardy was, at the time he met Emma Gifford, engaged to his cousin Tryphena; that he had an illegitimate son by her; and that she turned out to be not his cousin, but his niece. Taking these assertions in order, Gittings concedes that the first may well be mostly true: the second Mrs Hardy (that source again!) used to say that Tryphena sent back Hardy's ring, which he then bestowed on Miss Gifford. The second he shoots down in flames: it rests on the unsupported statement of Mrs Bromell, an 85-year-old sufferer from cerebral atherosclerosis; no birth, death, marriage, census, school, apprenticeship, or employment records support the existence of such a son, and the 'long, hot autumn of 1867', when he was supposedly conceived had in fact an above-average rainfall. And there is not only no factual support for the third, 'it is based on a denial of all personal and documentary evidence'.

If Dr Gittings is frankly severe about this book, it is because it has had an influence entirely out of proportion to its merits: it 'seems to have exercised some sort of hypnotic effect on many people's critical faculties'. On the other hand, Dr Gittings does not deal with what for some readers was the strongest part of its appeal: that it provided a hypothetical explanation for some of Hardy's most puzzling poems. The last stanza of 'On a Heath', for instance, is crucial to the Lois Deacon-Terry Coleman argument:

> There was another looming
>   Whose life we did not see;
> There was one stilly blooming
>   Full nigh to where walked we;
> There was a shade entombing
>   All that was bright of me.

If this is not an unborn child, one wants to ask, what is it? In 1920 Vere Collins put the question to Hardy himself:

> C. Who or what is that referred to in the last stanza?
> H. There is a third person.
> C. 'Another looming', 'one stilly blooming', 'a shade entombing' – are not there three different things?
> H. No, only one.

The same speculations apply to 'The Place on the Map': 'And the thing we found we had to face before the next year's prime ...' Well, of course, we have Hardy's often-repeated assertion that 'those lyrics penned in the first person ... are to be regarded, in the main, as dramatic monologues by different characters': the little old gentleman shuts the front door firmly in our faces. But the poems remain, and Gosse's question remains. The Deacon-Coleman solution may have been wildly and ludicrously wrong, but it *felt* true. Even though it is put to flight, its place is unlikely to be taken by the unfortunate Mr Moule.

New Statesman, 18 April 1975

Shelving the Issue

The existence of public libraries was kept from me as long as possible (the knowledge would, it was thought, interfere with my studies), but when the secret broke at last I rapidly became what in those days was an especially irritating kind of borrower, who brought back in the evening the books he had borrowed in the morning and read in the afternoon. This was the old Coventry Central Library, nestling at the foot of the unbombed Cathedral, filled with tall antiquated bookcases loaded with rows of drab quarter-leather library bindings (blind-stamped 'Coventry City Libraries' after the fashion of the time), with my ex-schoolfellow Ginger Thompson (now Guildhall's Librarian) at the counter to stamp the books you chose, and the Golden Cross nearby where (in sixth-form days at least) they could be examined at leisure.

Such was my first experience of the addictive excitement a large open-access public library generates: the sense of imminent discovery, the impulse to start on twenty books at once, the decades-old marginal addenda ('Surely the problem of free will . . .'), not to mention their several atmospheres: the silence of wet artisan-haunted winter nights, the holiday-fattened shelves of summer afternoons. Is it a peculiarly Anglo-Saxon addiction? D. H. Lawrence, years after going to Eastwood Mechanics' Institute every Thursday night to choose books for the whole family, was writing of Australia:

> Mondays, Wednesdays and Saturdays were the library nights. When you had crossed the iron footbridge over the railway, you came to a big wooden building with a corrugated-iron roof . . .

Old habits die hard: his alter ego, Richard Lovat Somers, went off with 'a Mary E. Mann and a George A. Birmingham'.

England, at any rate, still leads the world in public library

Review of Thomas and Edith Kelly, *Books for the People: An Illustrated History of the British Public Library* (André Deutsch, 1977)

provision, and this year marks the centenary of the foundation of the Library Association. The present volume may be published in consequence of this: it is hard, really, to think of any other reason. Professor Kelly's *History of Public Libraries in Great Britain, 1845–1965* (1973) tells the tale at greater length, with fuller detail and some of the same illustrations: as far as I know it is still in print at much the same price. Unless one postulates a hostess who would use it for her coffee-table, the intended function of this new version seems obscure. However, Professor Kelly (I am assuming the text to be chiefly his) tells the tale of successive Acts and Reports expertly enough: the urban centres, the county system, the major impulse towards larger authorities brought about by the Local Government Act of 1972, and now the Dainton Report (1969) and the British Library Act (1972) which have

> created for the first time a comprehensive and rationally organised system of reference and lending libraries at the national level, serving as libraries of last resort not only for the public library system ... but also for the libraries of all kinds of other organisations which have in the past participated in regional and national cooperative schemes.

It is in many respects a noble story, and is here diversified with copious illustrations from a wealth of sources – *Punch* cartoons to the currently-fashionable archaic photograph that in fact constitutes the book's chief appeal. I particularly liked 'Staff of York City Library, 1895' (even the youngest wears a watch-chain), and on the same page 'Miss Kate Lewtas, Librarian of Blackpool 1891–1902' looks out at us with an eerily immediate beauty.

One doesn't expect controversy in a work of this format, but since Professor Kelly makes the point that 'the old notion of the public library as mainly a working-class institution is now quite dead' the opportunity might have been taken to inquire whether today people should use public libraries for nothing any more than they should use public baths for nothing. 'The free library principle is still sacred,' intones Professor Kelly at the conclusion of his other book. But is it? Anyone counting the recently-registered family saloons outside public libraries on Saturday mornings will be more inclined to judge it completely anachronistic.

This relates, of course, to Professor Kelly's other great omission, the campaign for payments to authors under a Public Lending

Right, and supplies the answer to the question of how such payments are to be funded. It is difficult for an author not to regard the whole public library system as based on the exploitation of author and publisher alike, and to find this as shocking as the revelation would be that the Church of England was financed from red-light rents. Although the view is not unanimously accepted (what do the Performing Rights people say, incidentally, about libraries lending gramophone records?), it deserves stating in this context: Professor Kelly's failure to do so unavoidably confers on his book a faint yet pervasive obsolescence.

New Statesman, 10 June 1977

In the Seventies

Hardy's burial fifty years ago in Westminster Abbey, with the Prime Minister, the Leader of the Opposition, representatives of the universities of Oxford and Cambridge and six of the most famous writers of the day acting as pallbearers, was an occasion that would seem to admit little chance of a subsequent increase in reputation. Yet, half a century later, there has certainly been no decline. If Hardy's fame has grown no higher, it has become deeper, broader, more luxuriant; no doubt the present volume, the first of a complete and informatively edited collection of his letters, was timed to appear this year, but it needs no anniversary to justify it. Hardy's stature now is such that its publication was inevitable.

At the same time, any reviewer of this first instalment would do well to follow the example of its editors and be frank. We know already that Hardy was not a natural correspondent: as Professor Pottle said, he husbanded his genius and never intentionally spilled any of it into this form. We have what he wrote to his first wife (*Dearest Emmie*, 1963) and to Florence Henniker (*One Rare Fair Woman*, 1973), and its drab discretion ('Will you caution the servants about turning on and off the gas') suggests that, even if other substantial collections were still unpublished, they would in all probability be equally unremarkable. And there is nothing here to contradict this, even though the first may be the least interesting volume of the seven that are promised. Although it reputedly contains less than a seventh of the total collection, it covers well over half his life – up to, in fact, the great watershed of his reputation, *Tess of the d'Urbervilles* in 1892 (there are more letters here from that year than any other). People do not seem to have kept Hardy's letters at this time: apart from those to Emma Lavinia Hardy and Edmund Gosse, these that we now have are mostly to

Review of *The Collected Letters of Thomas Hardy: Volume I, 1840–1892*, edited by Richard Little Purdy and Michael Millgate (Oxford University Press, 1978)

editors, publishers and occasional correspondents. They have, of course, the value of scarcity. But they have little of the expansiveness that the editors promise for later volumes, when Hardy, secure in a comfortable and world-famous old age, became 'less – rather than more – cautious'.

This is much to be regretted, for the first half of any man's life is usually more significant than the second. Ambition, philosophy, love and marriage are likelier there, and Hardy was no exception:

> In the seventies I was bearing in my breast,
>   Penned tight,
> Certain starry thoughts that threw a magic light
> On the worktimes and the soundless hours of rest
> In the seventies . . .

It was the decade of his courtship and wedding of Emma Gifford, and their subsequent two years' idyll at Sturminster Newton ('their happiest days'); of *Under the Greenwood Tree, Far from the Madding Crowd* and *The Return of the Native*; of his abandonment of one profession, and success in another. Had Hardy possessed a different temperament, what letters we could have had! But he didn't: the starry thoughts remained penned tight, at least as far as personal expression went.

This is not to say that the present collection is without interest. One cannot read six or seven hundred letters by even as reticent a man as Hardy without learning something about him. Possibly the first thing one registers is the rapidity with which he was accepted as a successful novelist by smart circles. It is something for 'an obscure young architect with few professional prospects, somewhat countrified manners, an unprepossessing appearance, and a not especially striking personality' to be elected a member of the Savile Club seven years after publishing a first novel at his own expense; yet in another three or four years Hardy was lunching with Lord Houghton, regretting his inability to dine 'to meet Turgenev', sending ferns from 'Mellstock' to Lady Pollock, and touching Irving personally for two seats for his *Romeo and Juliet*. Plainly Hardy loved it, and when Emma Lavinia could not accompany him he let her know what she was missing:

> Lady Winifred's divine blue looking decidedly crumpled about the neck – the stick-up ruff I mean – not so well as when we saw it in all its new glory. Lady Margaret was in black lace . . .

We have become used to the idea that Hardy's character had unexpected facets; in 1875, for instance, when he joined the Copyright Association (a prudent step: the saddest letter in the book dates from 1872 and reads: 'Dear Mr Tinsley, I offer you the copyright of *Under the Greenwood Tree* for the sum of £30 to be paid one month after publication'), as little as two months afterwards he was a member of a delegation that called on Disraeli to request an inquiry into the copyright laws. Clearly the new member must have possessed a more than averagely forceful and cogent personality, to be pressed into such service so soon. Then in 1879 he was a foundation member of the Rabelais Club, a body dedicated to 'virility in literature' (hard to imagine what eponym would be chosen today: Henry Miller?); the invitation came to him as 'the author of the most original, the most virile and most humorous of all modern novels' (in fact, *The Return of the Native*). Remarking drily that the name of Rabelais would be 'misleading to many', Hardy accepted: 'I like the principles of the club immensely.' The notion of hearty literary trenchermen jesting about the way of a man with a maid is somewhat depressing today, but there is no doubt that Hardy won a reputation for outspokenness almost as soon as he began to publish.

Club life must have suited him: he was fortunate to be elected to the Athenaeum in the spring of 1891 – fortunate, because *Tess* appeared later that year, and would certainly not have been to episcopal tastes. This club proved a refuge when *Tess* was attacked: 'it is odd that nearly every adverse criticism is written by a fellow-Savilean'. His evident 'clubbability' must have resulted in part from his own modesty and readiness to please (sometimes evincing an almost Heep-like humility, as when he speaks of Max Gate to Curzon as 'a little place I have for writing in'). He sent his books to well-known people with agreeable notes: *The Woodlanders* to Swinburne, *Far from the Madding Crowd* to Frederick Locker ('when I consider the perfect taste that is shown in all your writings'), *A Group of Noble Dames* to Alfred Austin ('what a master of expression you are') and Lord Lytton ('the number of people who buy [your] books must be enormous'). People sent him books in return: 'when, alas,' he acknowledges to Edmund Gosse, 'did I ever write anything to rival

> His eye that darts above his pipe
> Keen as the flashing of a snipe
> Through beds of windless rushes'

– when, indeed? No doubt this was all part of the life of a professional author of the time, as was writing to Edmund Yates:

> I wish you would say in one line in next week's *World* (if you feel like it) that you think it rather ungenerous of the *Globe* to find fault with my verses spoken by Miss Rehan at the Lyceum Theatre . . .

or again, some years later:

> I do not consider it an undue advertising of oneself to send you for the *World* (if you think it of any interest) the enclosed information which I derive from numerous unexpected letters

– presumably in praise of *Tess*; they were not used, which is just as well if their authors had not envisaged publication. The tone of Hardy's letters is uniformly mild and courteous: one searches in vain for a single angry sentence, though it never does to underrate his irony:

> The other day I read a story entitled 'The Wages of Sin' by Lucas Malet, expecting to find something of the sort therein [that is, plain speaking in sexual matters]. But the wages are that the young man falls over a cliff, & the young woman dies of consumption – not very consequent, as I told the authoress.

Nor was he likely to upset people about politics ('I . . . have always been compelled to forego all participation in active politics') or similar controversies ('I have not as yet been converted to a belief in the desirability of [women's suffrage]'). Yet his opinions, however innocently expressed, always ran directly counter to what was accepted:

> I have sometimes had a dream that the church, instead of being disendowed, would be made to modulate by degrees (say as the present incumbents die out) into an undogmatic, non-theological establishment for the promotion of that virtuous living on which all honest men are agreed . . .

It was thus that Hardy, so to speak, backed into controversy over *Tess*: one thinks of Leslie Stephen's exasperated comment: 'You have no more consciousness of these things than a child.' He may have been hurt by the hostile reviews, but more often he sounds either bored or irritated ('The review in the Quarterly is, after all, a mere manufacture, to suit the prejudices of its fossilized subscribers & keep the review alive upon their money'). Other remarks, however ('They are reprinting frantically'), make it clear there were commercial compensations ('I wonder if you think well of the City of London Electric Lighting Co. as an investment?'). But there is not, at this crisis in his life, any more than there was in the preceding twenty years, a single passage that can be cited to prove that its author was not only a man of genius, but of a genius that might be thought peculiarly suited to letter-writing: what more natural for a man who used to notice such things to jot them down in a letter? Here is no darkling thrush, no abandoned sunshade, no satire of circumstances noted from these years when observation was at its sharpest and sensibility at its keenest. As the editors write:

> Hardy's profound reserve – rooted in his personality, his upbringing, his class-consciousness, his sense of his professional decorum – made him, and makes him still, one of the most elusive of literary figures ... the central enigma of his long career is that a man who took such risks and issued such challenges as a novelist and poet should in his own life have been so discreet, so unsure, so self-defensive.

Only one letter indicates Hardy's native temperament to any degree; in April 1889, as the *Early Life* records, he received 'a long and interesting letter from J. Addington Symonds at Davos Platz concerning *The Return of the Native*', and here is his reply:

> The tragical conditions of life imperfectly denoted in The Return of the Native & some other stories of mine I am less & less able to keep out of my work. I often begin a story with the intention of making it brighter & gayer than usual; but the question of conscience soon comes in: & it does not seem right even in novels to wilfully belie one's own views. All comedy, is tragedy, if you only look deep enough into it.

'Tragedy is true guise, Comedy lies', was the form the aphorism had taken by the time of *Winter Words*; characteristic, but not quite what was hoped for from this volume.

In the seventies those who met me did not know
Of the vision
That immuned me from the chillings of misprision
And the damps that choked my goings to and fro
In the seventies ...

It is a pity that these letters give no plainer delineation of that vision. Instead, we have Hardy dealing with life deftly and discreetly, promptly and pertinently, coolly and courteously, wishing merely to be considered 'a good hand at a serial'. It is a thought-provoking and at times impressive sight, but not, finally, a compelling one.

New Statesman, 27 January 1978

Amis and Auden

Oxford anthologies are traditionally authoritative, and this creates problems for their compilers. In the first place, they have to include not only poems they like themselves, but poems other people like, or at any rate expect to find there. Secondly, they have to endure the equally traditional abuse of reviewers who object not so much to their choice as to seeing it elevated to a canon. And thirdly, if their anthology has been done before, there is the whole question of their relation to their predecessors.

Predictably enough, Kingsley Amis has run into the second of these, chiefly on the charge of failing to solve the first, but I am inclined to think that his principal difficulty has lain in the third. Amis is good at seeing where Auden was wrong (incidentally, has anyone congratulated the Press on its courage and acumen on picking Auden for 1938, Amis for 1978? So much for the play-safe image of Oxbridge publishing), but Auden was partly right too, and this Amis seems to overlook. The page and a half of his introduction he spends in getting Auden out of the way does not mention what seems to me his most significant passage:

> Light verse can be serious. It has only come to mean vers de société, triolets, smoke-room limericks, because, under the social conditions that produced the Romantic Revival, and which have persisted, more or less, ever since, it has only been in trivial matters that poets have felt in sufficient intimacy with their audience to be able to forget themselves and their singing-robes.

A poetic situation made up of singing-robes on the one hand and A. A. Milne on the other (I don't, by the way, agree with Amis that Auden's reference in *Letters from Iceland* to 'Milne and persons of that kind' was necessarily sympathetic) was plainly intolerable

Review of *The New Oxford Book of Light Verse*, chosen by Kingsley Amis (Oxford University Press, 1978)

to him, and the original *Oxford Book of Light Verse* set out to undermine such a stultifying dichotomy once for all. Since anthologies tend to portray their compilers, it bore a strong resemblance to the extraordinary sounding-board that was Auden's literary sensibility in the Thirties, and so carries something of the same excitement. Its doctrinaire preface was soon forgotten: what it did was help put an end to various oppositions such as high and low verse and vernacular and poetic diction that were still lingering on between the wars. Poetry, as Auden wrote in that preliminary bombardment 'The Poet's Tongue' (1935), was about birth and death and the beatific vision, but it was also about 'everything we remember no matter how trivial; the mark on the wall, the joke at luncheon, word games ...' The object of Auden's Oxford anthology was to bring this about: light verse was either promoted to poetry, or done away with altogether (and, *mutatis mutandis*, the same with singing-robes).

As one might expect, Amis is opposed to Auden's populist theory. He sees, too, that concentration on tone and language to the exclusion of subject-matter led to perversities such as claiming 'Danny Deever' as light verse (and he might have mentioned Housman's 'The stars have not dealt me the worst they could do'). Despite 'the joke at luncheon', Auden's collection is not particularly amusing (I don't recall any suggestion in his introduction that light verse can be funny), and Amis is naturally determined to put that right; it is the same with technical proficiency, which Amis sees as one of its essential characteristics. But what Amis doesn't seem to see, or perhaps he simply doesn't agree, is that Auden's anthology put an end to the light verse tradition as he found it: the facetious Victorian waggery that continued up to 1939 *Punch*, the whimsical *Elia* stuff about your old pipe and your old college and 'the ladies', the mock-heroic odes to collar-studs and versified Pooterisms about the 'funny side' of life. There may have been anthologies of stature published after 1938 with 'light verse' in their titles, but I don't remember them. Different, and significantly different, terms were used.

In producing a 'reactionary' anthology to counter Auden's 'revolutionary' one, Amis is seeking to correct Auden's misapprehensions. The difficulty is that doing so he condemns himself to opposing his apprehensions also: to resurrecting, in fact, something of the tradition of 'vers de société, triolets, smoke-room limericks' (there may not be many triolets in his selection, but the other two terms cover a fair amount of it), and since Amis's taste is reasonably healthy, it suffers a degree of internal conflict in the process. Not surprisingly, he finds light verse hard to define. 'Light verse is not one thing but many,' he says, offering instead a series of suggestions ('Genial, memorable, enlivening and funny'; 'To raise a good-natured smile'; 'The graceful surmounting of self-imposed obstacles'). This lends his introduction a hesitant air, of alternating aggression and self-defence: he advances an elegant passage on the genre by A. A. Milne ('it observes the most exact laws of rhythm as if by happy accident, and in a sort of nonchalant spirit of mockery at the real poets who do it on purpose'), but has to admit that Milne wrote nothing in it worth reprinting. He rehearses the various antitheses of light/heavy, light/high, high/low, finding in each an element to add to the composite description he is constructing; then, as if appalled at his own impartiality, gives the bum's rush to Chaucer, Dunbar, Skelton, a good deal of Anon, Dryden, Pope and the Anti-Jacobin. It is as if he is unable to swallow whole the tradition he is bent on reviving: parodies, limericks, vers de société and comic songs are in, epigrams, unconscious humour, satire and nonsense are out. Several inoffensive morsels are savaged on the way.

Identifying light verse with the nineteenth and twentieth centuries (a policy Milne advocates, and which Amis supports with the contention that it was essentially a reaction to Augustan 'correctness') means that the book is rather short; the pre-1800 selection is an almost-cursory fifty pages, with Rochester and Swift on the credit side and Samuel Butler and Samuel Wesley to balance them. Representation of the nineteenth century is, of course, much more expansive, though perhaps not quite so much as might be expected: Byron and Praed are, so to speak, the opening bats, and really no one else comes near them. Calverley (except for the sequence 'Dover to Munich') is prolix and piffling; Carroll and Gilbert are good, but over-familiar; the supporting cast includes Hood, Tennyson, Browning and Hardy, some of whom might have been represented more fully. 'Youth and Art' and 'The Pied Piper of Hamelin' could have backed up 'The Spanish Cloister'; some of Tennyson's dialect poems, such as 'The Spinster's Sweet-Arts', are not too incomprehensible; and is Hardy's 'The Ruined Maid' really light verse, by any definition?

'The Curate's Kindness' would have been less ambiguously so. Some Clough would have been welcome, and perhaps another example of Locker-Lampson.

But even Amis cannot reconcile me to the Victorian habit of doing a joke to death, as in Hood's 'Faithless Nelly Gray' (puns), 'Mr and Mrs Vite's Journey' (obsolete Cockney trick of pronouncing w as v), and 'Hans Breitmann's Barty' (Dutchmen talking funny). Then there are Thackeray's excruciating 'Little Billee', Stevenson's pointless 'Not I', and other painful reminders of what we have long outgrown. Perhaps for historical reasons they have to be in, but it is really altogether too late in the day to be asked to find them amusing.

The book cheers up about the date of its charming jacket (Gregory's 'Boulter's Lock'); that is, at the turn of the century, and from, say, Housman to Amis himself there is a good deal of fun to be had. Amis's big find is the pseudonymous Victor Gray/Ted Pauker, reputedly a Janus equally virtuosic with limerick and broadsheet; his 'A Grouchy Goodnight to the Academic Year' converts Praed's stanza to a hatchet:

> Then alas for the next generation,
> For the pots fairly crackle with thorn.
> Where psychology meets education
> A terrible bullshit is born.

Gray/Pauker should be collected at once, *in toto*, and with some editorial attention: I fancy Amis is wrong in printing 'Charlotte Brontë said, Wow, sister! *What* a man!' The surname rather spoils the rhythm, and quite spoils the joke. It is Betjeman rather than Auden who demonstrates the reunification of light verse and poetry that Auden preached, and many of the minor *trouvailles* (Wynford Vaughan-Thomas, Alan Bennett) bear his imprint; here as elsewhere he is the presiding genius of the second half of the century. Amis's selection of his own work leans heavily on *The Evans Country*, which is all right: if one is to have Evans, one must have a lot, but it keeps out equally worthy things. It is a particular delight to have 'The Helbatrawss': the subheading might have been retained, which as I remember was 'Ah' er Charley Bordilair's Froggy', and a note given that it was a dig at the Fifties fashion of translating from French into Lallans (it is, I believe, a perfectly good translation in itself). The inclusion of Wodehouse and Coward pleases me at any rate, but I should have liked a lot more Gavin Ewart, and the one-poem ration of Kipling is astonishing, especially from Amis. 'The Sergeant's Wedding' is only one of several qualifiers.

Amis's determined opposition to Auden's Baez-Guthrie Sisam-Coghill Group Theatre-Young Communist League aberrations is both reasonable and successful. But in undertaking to put together again what Auden had disintegrated he set himself a task incompatible with taste and intelligence (as one reviewer said, he sounds ill at ease), one that would compel him either to reprint too many trivialities or only to half-represent what in any case now survives mainly as a historical concept. We must be grateful to him for adhering to the second alternative, and for collecting so many genuinely funny pieces that would otherwise be difficult to come by. Perhaps the Cataloguing in Publication Data on the title-page verso ('Humorous poetry, English') sums it up best after all. And concerning minutiae, why 'Chosen and edited by' on the cover, and 'Chosen by' on the title-page recto? And why is it thought better to leave great gaps at the bottom, of, e.g., pages 139, 225 and 236 rather than set the reader the really-not-so-very-arduous task of following a verse from one page to the next?

The New Review, 5:2, Autumn 1978

The Ascent of WHA

'The blessed will not care what angle they are regarded from/ Having nothing to hide,' Auden wrote, and again: 'The proper subject for gossip, as for all art, is the behaviour of mankind.' Such sentiments must fortify any biographer facing not only one of the century's major poets but one of its most complex characters.

But, given that he can now tell the truth about Auden, is he able to show us what that truth was? To what archetype did those successive intimidating personae relate: the Thirties loud-speaker, relaying indiscriminate quackery and loveliness, the great American windbag, the Mediterranean interfoliation of the Oxford English Dictionary with the Opera Directory?

Charles Osborne abides such questions with smiling and practised efficiency. If this is not an 'authorized biography', as he disclaims, it is still a skilful and dependable amalgam of printed sources (many of them beyond the reach of the average reader), unpublished letters and personal reminiscence, all presented with evident though not uncritical affection.

Every biography, even that of a writer, has to balance active with passive, what the subject did against what happened to him. We see the tow-haired undergraduate attain by easy stages to the carpet-slippered wedding-cake-left-out-in-the-rain, the early challenge 'You don't understand: I'm going to be a great poet' shrink to the soodling thread of 'In the end, art is small beer.'

Auden's life – like most lives perhaps – reads as a studied avoidance of the threateningly unpleasant in favour of the available pleasant. His pre-war travels (with the exception of his two months in Spain) were mostly subsidized by publishers. His emigration to America was precipitated by the imminence of European hostilities (in spite of Osborne's sympathetic defence, it still reads that way). College teaching was succeeded by the

Review of Charles Osborne, *W. H. Auden: The Life of a Poet* (Eyre Methuen, 1980).

more impersonal lecture circuit, with summers in Europe. Finally, Christ Church received its honoured guest, and all was forgiven.

As a life it is enviable rather than admirable, and bears out Stephen Spender's early summary:

> His aims were to fulfil his potentialities, obtain satisfaction for his desires, and maintain his attitudes, without prejudice and without accepting any authority outside his own judgment. At the same time he avoided coming into unnecessary conflict with the interests and views of those around him ...

Osborne's occasional failing as a biographer (apart from minor matters such as quoting a revised version of 'Dover' as the original – and wasn't it Freddie Bartholomew in *The Devil Takes Count*?) is that he takes for granted episodes the reader would like unravelled. How oddly unlike Spender's summary, for example, was Auden's spell as house-mother of a Brooklyn menage including Salvador Dali, Benjamin Britten and Gypsy Rose Lee:

> Auden's management of the house is remembered by survivors [the word is typical Osborne humour: 'not unsqualid' is another instance] as having been exemplary. He devised menus, hired and fired servants and dealt with difficult tenants as to the manner born.

Nor is it easy to reconcile his habitual sniping at 'heters' with his mid-Forties affair with Rhoda Jaffe, which got as far as apologies for not marrying her.

How, after spending the entire war in America, had he the pachydermatous cheek to return to England in May 1945 in the uniform of an American major and tell his friends that London hadn't really been bombed?

In consequence the unaided reader has some difficulty getting him into focus. After the amazing early brilliance (it is hard to realize that the catastrophic *New Year Letter* was published when he was only 34) he became more discursive, less immediate. Dirty and dogmatic, he seems to fit into the Johnsonian tradition, but this cannot be sustained.

Auden had no central morality: he was continually trying on opinions for size and discarding them as quickly. He had no typifying emotional resonance: opera, with its simplified and exaggerated attitudes, came to suit him perfectly. Even his aesthetic touch, to judge from an early willingness to scrap lines friends didn't like and his later suppression of some of his best poems, seems to have been oddly uncertain.

At the same time, he was all his life tough and unbudgeable. His homosexuality brought no inner conflict (he saw, as Osborne says, no reason to pretend or proclaim), and he was prepared to withstand his emotional vicissitudes, which at times sound even worse than their heterosexual equivalents:

> The triple situation of being sexually jealous like a wife, anxious like a nanny, and competitive like a brother is not easy for my kind of temperament. Still, it is my bed and I must lie on it.

His nomadic life, which must have meant constant discomfort by conventional standards, appears to have suited him.

Lastly, people liked him, even loved him. This is perhaps the biggest taking-for-granted in Osborne's account: Auden is presented as a character, a comic, a collector's piece, but rarely shown as meriting the kind of affection displayed in Spender's *W. H. Auden: A Tribute* or possessing the latterday wisdom of the closing *obiter dicta* ('The really serious things in life are earning one's living so as not to be a parasite and loving one's neighbour').

It is hard for someone who did not know Auden to estimate the injustice of this. Perhaps it is the kind of treatment he would have preferred. It cannot be said to detract unduly from Osborne's commodious base camp, from which future assaults on his subject's craggy eminence are certain to be made.

Guardian, 6 March 1980

'A decent minor poet'

In one sense, Day-Lewis (he hated the name Cecil) was the most successful of the 1930s poets. It was he who picked up the honours that Auden had fled from: Arts Council chairmanships, British Council tours, the Royal Society of Literature, the Laureateship, lectureships and fellowships galore.

At the same time he won the least critical acclaim. Privately he marked his talent beta double-plus: others were even less generous. As collection succeeded collection he was written off as derivative, a describer of easy emotion in undistinguished diction.

This is ironic, for this authoritative life by his eldest son demonstrates how central poetry was in his existence. 'Poetry was the point of my life,' he said a few weeks before his death. It is also unfair: his poems came from his own experience, and could be both adroit and moving.

'I only began really enjoying life at the age of fifty-five,' he said in his mid-sixties, an odd remark that on the evidence sounds insincere. It is true that his childhood was a lonely one (he was an only child, and his mother died when he was 4), and he was not at ease with his clergyman father. His temperament was subject to fits of depression, and his eight years' schoolmastering were no doubt dreary enough.

However, as one of the *New Signatures* writers he was soon famous (T. E. Lawrence told Winston Churchill that England had at least one great man), and his country dwellings with his growing family sound enviable. By 1935 he was able to live by writing, chiefly owing to his Nicholas Blake detective stories.

What stopped him 'enjoying life' was, chiefly, his divided emotional loyalties. Sean Day-Lewis has the family's agreement to speak frankly about his father's infidelities, and he does so without rancour or sensationalism. Cecil, handsome and young-

Review of Sean Day-Lewis, *C. Day-Lewis: An English Literary Life* (Weidenfeld and Nicolson, 1980)

looking (at 34 he was mistaken for an undergraduate by Oxford proctors), was attractive to women and attracted by them.

His first marriage was prolonged until 1950 'for the sake of the children'; when he left his wife, it was not for Rosamond Lehmann, who had shared his life during the war, but for the 25-year-old Jill Balcon, whom he married in 1951. There was much suffering all round, from which Day-Lewis was not exempt: as one of his characters says, 'my senses do not run on a separate circuit from my conscience.' Inevitably, the reader's sympathies go to his first wife Mary: 'she still loves me, whereas I have not loved her for a long time.'

As a Communist, Day-Lewis undoubtedly saw more of 'the flat ephemeral pamphlet and the boring meeting' than the author of that famous line, though as father of a young family he was careful not to let them imperil his livelihood. Stephen Spender, whose comments are unfailingly perceptive, said later:

> For Day-Lewis, communism meant the village pub ... I did have one conversation with him in which I did manage to persuade him that he ought not to look at those nice chaps ... but at what the leaders were talking about and doing.

He spent the war in the Ministry of Information, after Home Guard service in Devon.

In the post-war decades as a 'public' writer he was hard-working, graceful and sensible, and deserved his rewards. The Laureateship delighted him, and he saw that the Queen's Gold Medal for Poetry went to those who should have had it years before: Graves, Spender, Fuller, Stevie Smith. But the last years of his life were ravaged by illness: blood pressure, a heart attack, glandular fever, finally cancer. He met them with resilience, courage and humour, working until almost the end.

Sean Day-Lewis devotes three pages to a dispassionate summary of his father's poetic reputation, and seems inclined to settle for Samuel Hynes's description 'a decent minor poet'. It is not a bad epitaph, particularly when the emphasis falls, as it must in this case, on the first adjective. But not a dull minor poet: Day-Lewis was the reverse of dull, as this book amply and enjoyably demonstrates.

Guardian, 20 March 1980

Chatterbox without Charity

It is impossible to imagine getting a letter from Evelyn Waugh, unless it were of the 'Mr Waugh deeply regrets that he is unable to do what is so kindly proposed' sort. In the first place, one would have to have a nursery nickname and be a member of White's, a Roman Catholic, a high-born lady or an Old Etonian novelist; but even if that difficulty were overcome one would need to know about two hundred similar persons who were continually chucking or being chucked by their life partners, going bankrupt or mad, and becoming incapacitated for days by heavy eating or drinking, and having a consuming interest in their goings-on. For Waugh was an avid gossip: 'please tell me any English gossip you hear,' he implores Nancy Mitford in Paris; and to Cyril Connolly in London, 'do dictate a page of social gossip. I have no idea what my friends or enemies are doing.' Connolly's high-minded refusal ('I don't find other people's misfortunes uproariously funny') was prudent:

> After the first course Boots ['Smarty Boots', i.e. Connolly] had a seizure, fell off his chair frothing and gasping, was carried straight to a waiting van and whisked off to Tring where he spent the first fortnight of married life in a padded cell.

The degree to which these letters are readable depends on how far Waugh can convert the gossip into his own kind of black comedy. His patient and thorough editor cautions us against assuming anything Waugh writes to be 'true': when he says of a dinner acquaintance 'Her new daughter is a negress', the footnote stolidly comments 'Not a negress.' 'Quennell had a seizure brought on by sexual excess,' Waugh writes; the footnote says 'Hangover.' Comparable conventions abound, particularly to his letters to Nancy Mitford, such as his horribleness to his second

Review of *The Letters of Evelyn Waugh*, edited by Mark Amory (Weidenfeld and Nicolson, 1980)

wife ('The only servant in the house is my pre-war valet. Laura makes his bed and cooks his meals'). But what of his assurance to her, written from the Hyde Park Hotel, that he is 'looking eagerly' in the *Times* each day for news of the arrival of their next child, before going on to say 'The Court Ball was wholly delightful'?

A writer's letters stand midway between literature and biography. Since Waugh's biographer Christopher Sykes has already used much of this material, it is not likely to tell us much about Waugh we did not know already, but they remind us what a self-contradictory man he was. His constant travelling before the War (between his marriages he never had a home of his own) seems unaccompanied by an interest in or liking for the countries he visited, but even after 1945, when he was settled in Gloucestershire, he continued to regard such trips as part of a writer's life.

He was a brave man who joined the Army with alacrity in 1939, only to be told in 1943 that he was 'so unpopular as to be unemployable'. He was a major writer, but his mentions of literature are sparse and terse: 'the worst book in the world' (*Dombey and Son*); 'nothing any character thinks or says or does has any relation to human nature as I know it' (*La Chartreuse de Parme*); 'Well, the chap was plain barmy' (Proust). At the same time his own artistic commitment remained absolute: 'while I have any vestige of imagination left, I must write novels'.

None of this caused him any heart-searching: his nature was impenetrably invisible. There are no letters about his conversion to Roman Catholicism (and nothing in the *Diaries* either) yet it was fundamental to his life. The most remarkable letters in the book are those urging John Betjeman (whose wife was turning to the Catholic Church) to undergo instruction likewise. Waugh writes urgently in black-and-white terms ('[1] We may both we wrong; [2] We can't both be right,' etc.) that typifies the unsentimental nature of his devotion remembered by Father d'Arcy.

Betjeman, though distressed, stood firm ('it is not so much a matter of which church, as of loving God') and Waugh later apologized for being 'a bully and a scold'. Later, however, he was writing to Edith Sitwell, 'Is it exorbitant to hope that your example and prayers may bring Osbert to the Faith?'

His piety, that divided the world into 'Papists and heathens', did little for his charity. There is a shocking sentence to the Marchioness of Bath saying that 'Mr Masaryk defenestrating himself would make a good subject for a picture', and there is a constant barrage of remarks such as 'Alfred Duggan kicked the bucket', 'Two [dance] bands, one of niggers and one of buggers' and 'There are 2 jews in this club.' This may be part of Waugh's epistolary irony, and understood as such by his correspondents, but they support Claire Luce's quick judgement that he had 'no heart'. Yet against them can be set his letters to his wife and family, nearly always affectionate, sometimes charming, as if a totally different person had held the pen.

'Beware of writing to me,' his last letter begins. 'I always answer.' Even so, the collection hardly sustains its editor's claim that Waugh was the last of the great letter-writers. The world his gossip evokes has none of the appeal of Horace Walpole's, for instance; it is curt, cheap, brutal. Its humour lacks the rich lunacy of the novels; its observations, despite their impeccable language, have no charity. Towards the end, when his infirmities ('carrying too much weight ... no teeth') seemed an outward expression of his inner *accidie*, some sentences take on a greater resonance: 'He takes away all zest in human affairs to give us the chance of seeing our immortal destiny.' None has quite the poignance of Pinfold's 'Why does everyone except me find it so easy to be nice?'

Guardian, 4 September 1980

Castigations

Satire is the ridicule of vice and folly, which means it must be funny. As Mr Grigson says in his preface, 'Without the joke everything goes; and we may be left only with complaint, invective, or denunciation.' Equally, however, it must by definition condemn what it ridicules, which means it must be moral, and morality has its ups and downs.

Most people today, if asked to name the worst of the vices, would pick Cruelty, and yet it was never one of the Seven Deadly Sins. In fact it is remarkable how the Deadly Seven have been assimilated into our society: Pride and Anger, true, are still regarded as suitable cases for treatment, but only in terms of psychopathology; Lust and Gluttony are flourishing industries, while the rest have achieved political amalgamation and on occasion the responsibility of government.

Mr Grigson is less keen on the moral side. 'To have narrowed my choice by too severe a definition would have been wrong, I think; and one thing I have done is to include, as well as the classics of satire, much that I would call satire of a milder levity.' This allows us to profit from his wide reading, but it also admits poems that are not condemnatory, such as Max Beerbohm's 'A Luncheon' and others that are not funny, such as those by Edgar Lee Masters.

The book is inevitably a little unbalanced, in that its first 200 pages represent the full blast of the Age of Satire: splenetic outbursts against tobacco, Tunbridge Wells, Scotchmen, the Church, government, mankind itself, as well as individuals such as Dryden's celebrated portrait of Shadwell and Arbuthnot's epitaph on Colonel Chartres ('HERE continueth to rot . . .'). The relentless misanthropic moralizing suggests that poetry had to take a high line to avoid charges of frivolous indecency (such as

Review of *The Oxford Book of Satirical Verse*, chosen by Geoffrey Grigson (Oxford University Press, 1980)

the novel laboured under for years); Swift's lines to an intending poet

> Whether your interest most inclines
> To satire, praise, or hum'rous lines

imply that what we think of as poetry – the personal lyric – had no standing. Satire pretty well *was* poetry, just as the poet was a wit rather than an aesthete, and as such someone to be reckoned with. It would never have occurred to Pope that 'poetry makes nothing happen':

> Yes, I am proud; I must be proud to see
> Men not afraid of God, afraid of me.
> Safe from the Bar, the Pulpit, and the Throne,
> Yet touched and shamed by ridicule alone:

The only question was whether satire should be general or personal:

> Who starved a sister, who foreswore a debt,
> I never named – the town's enquiring yet.
> The pois'ning dame –
> *Friend*. You mean –
> *Pope*. I don't.
> *Friend*. You do.
> *Pope*. See! Now I keep the secret, and not you.

Sometimes the satire is unintentional:

> 'Mongst all these stirs of discontented strife,
> O let me lead an academic life,
> To know much, and to think we nothing know,
> Nothing to have, yet think we have enough ...

would hardly convince the Association of University Teachers.

In the nineteenth century satire seems to lose its authority, as if it is no longer the voice of a small integrated establishment. Mr Grigson gives Byron over forty pages, backed up by Shelley and Thomas Moore (some original finds here), but their drubbing of George III, Castlereagh, Wellington, Southey and other villains of the age is very much attacking from the outside, and the lapidary classical note is replaced by the snook-cocking of the broadsheet. It is odd to find Byron arraigning the waltz ('And wakes to wantonness the willing limbs') on the grounds of the Hanoverian connections. Wasn't it Viennese? But any stick would do to beat

George III with. Mr Grigson might have included some poems from the *Anti-Jacobin* to balance matters.

One theme common to both centuries was poetry itself; or, more specifically, other poets. Whether it is Henry Carey on Ambrose Philips ('Now he pumps his little wits, Shitting writes, and writing shits') or Byron on Wordsworth ('Could not the blockhead ask for a balloon?'), it's clear that other people's writing is both vice and folly. Swift's lines:

> In poetry the height we know;
> 'Tis only infinite below . . .

could be paralleled in any age, although in our own the form is more likely to be a review in a little magazine – perhaps sponsored by the Arts Council, so that it may be the voice of the Establishment after all.

Twentieth-century satire has been the novel's prerogative (*Brave New World*, *Animal Farm*): certainly Mr Grigson's pages report isolated successes rather than a constant barrage. Kipling's 'The Gods of the Copybook Headings' seems more frightening every time one reads it, but is balanced by excellent Woddis-like Belloc (where is Woddis, by the way?). Increasingly we find it hard to be funny about our hates: Betjeman is the master here, and might have been represented by some additional conservationist pieces such as 'Slough' and 'Harvest Hymn'. Roy Campbell is given plenty of space, but without his pro-Franco anti-Macspaunday savagery, and some of Gavin Ewart's unique sexual charades surely earn a place. Towards the end of the book satire seems to be rising above the occasional and personal again; Adrian Mitchell's ghastly 'Fifteen Million Plastic Bags' and Kingsley Amis's 'The Last War' are both about the coming nuclear holocaust, and Clive James sums it up on the book's last page, calling Paris

> A single finger's tremble from disaster.
> But then, who isn't?

One closes the book with a faint sense of disappointment. Is this all our poets could do to castigate vice and folly? Perhaps, after all, poetry indeed makes nothing happen, and the business of satire has passed from Pope to Mrs Partington.

Observer, 7 September 1980

Four Legs Good

It was the late Edmund Crispin who recommended Dick Francis to me. 'If you can stand the horse parts', he said, 'the mystery parts are quite good.' I found this an understatement in reverse. The horse parts, as everyone knows by now, are brilliant vignettes of a tiny portion of English life: the world of steeplechase racing. Novel by novel we meet the jockeys, the trainers, the owners (usually being taken for a ride in another sense), the bookmakers, the bloodstock agents, the sporting journalists. We learn what it is like to be a stable-boy at a skinflint North Country trainer's, to ride in freezing February fog (the first sentence of the first novel is 'The mingled smell of hot horse and cold river mist filled my nostrils'), to be Clerk of a run-down course that wrongdoers are determined to close. But the mystery parts, if inevitably less realistic, arise naturally from the greed, corruption and violence that lie behind the champagne, big cars and titled Stewards; they concern horse pulling and betting frauds, and lead to wads of used notes in anonymous envelopes, whispered warnings by telephone, and sudden hideous confrontations with big men in stocking masks.

These two elements are welded into adult reading by the Francis hero. Francis has no recurrent central character, no Bond or Marlowe; his heroes are jockeys, trainers, an owner who manufactures children's toys, a journalist, a Civil Service screener. But they tell the story in the first person, and they tend to sound alike; they are bachelors, or widowers, or separated: very twice-shy men, living in caravans or undistinguished flats. Sometimes they are handicapped, psychologically (*Blood Sport*), physically (Sid Halley in *Odds Against* has a crippled hand) or circumstantially, in *Forfeit* living with a paralysed wife, in *Knock Down* with an alcoholic brother. Their narratives are laconically gripping, and graphic in a way that eschews Chandler's baroque images and Fleming's

Review of Dick Francis, *Reflex* (Michael Joseph, 1980)

colour-supplement brand names. They combine unfailing toughness with infinite compassion.

There is a lot of pain in Francis novels, which puts some people off. Their heroes are beaten up thoroughly and in detail, taking days to recover; we are regularly reminded that steeplechase jockeys are used to breaking their bones and rapid recoveries. There can be pain for horses, as in *For Kicks* or *Flying Finish*, and pain between men and women, as when the hero in *Forfeit* has to perform the nightly routine of attending to his paralysed wife's physical needs when she has just learnt of his unfaithfulness to her. But there can be liberating happiness also: the loner heroes often find warm-hearted unselfish women (Francis's women are usually as nice as his men, with the exception of a few fiendish bitches), and the love scenes, usually long deferred, are unpretentiously honest. *Bonecrack*, which I suppose I should under pressure nominate as my favourite, is a moving, original and exhilarating study of parallel escapes from parental domination.

It would perhaps be pushing it a little to say that each Francis novel is a different story enclosing the same story, but it seems like this at times, as if the whole sequence were an allegory of the suffering individual inside endless inimical environments. Francis gives colour to this by his perversely-uninformative titles. One can just remember that *Nerve* is about a jockey losing, or not losing, his nerve; *In the Frame* is about sporting pictures; *Flying Finish* is about horse transport by air. But what is *Rat Race? For Kicks? Risk?* They seem designed to throw the station-bookstall reader into an agony of indecision as he struggles to remember whether he has read them before. He needn't worry: they are all worth reading.

The theme of the latest, *Reflex*, is, I suppose, photography. Philip Nore, a thirtyish National Hunt jockey, is an amateur photographer who comes into possession of some puzzling negatives left by a malicious lensman who has died in mysterious circumstances. Persons unknown are violently anxious to locate these, and their efforts to do so, and Nore's efforts to solve the technical problems of developing them, are the book's centre. Coincident with this, a hostile dying grandmother offers him a hundred thousand pounds to find out what happened to a younger sister he never knew he had, which would involve learning what happened to his mother and who his father was.

Nore is a true Francis hero: photography 'keeps you a step away from the world ... Gives you an excuse not to feel', and he suffers grievous bodily harm in Chapter 16. His problems are resolved with varying degrees of thoroughness: he finds a nice girl, and after cracking the negatives puzzle decides to become a photographer rather than to go on riding. He believes he discovers his sister; his grandmother more or less tells him who his father was, and leaves him half her money.

One hesitates to criticize a Francis novel, but *Reflex* displays in a less extreme form a defect of its predecessor *Whip Hand*, in which three themes proved in the end to have nothing to do with each other. Francis usually observes Chekhov's dictum that if there is a pistol hanging on the wall, sooner or later someone in the story must fire it, but in fact the sister search is irrelevant to the photography problem, and when she is found in unhappy circumstances the hero does nothing to rescue her. Although this outcome is supposed to change Philip Nore's attitude to life ('I had roots') his final resolution (one can't give the game away) is not altogether convincing. I have a feeling that Francis is tending to put too many themes into his books at present to compensate for the lack of real dominance of any one, and is failing to relate them satisfactorily: this, coupled with a certain blandness in the writing, suggests there may be a limit to the number of imaginative thrillers to be derived from the steeplechase scene. One can't exactly complain about this: Francis has written a dozen superb novels in less than twenty years, but there have been occasions since 1972 when the vein has shown signs of being worked out. This is one of them.

Times Literary Supplement, 10 October 1980

The Life under the Laurels

The reaction against Tennyson seems to have set in at his funeral. 'A lovely day,' wrote Henry James, 'the Abbey looked beautiful, everyone was there, but something – I don't know what – of real impressiveness – was wanting.' Burne-Jones was more explicit: 'O but yesterday was so flat and flattening. I'll never forgive the Queen for not coming up to it, and I wish Gladstone had.' True, among the bearers were one duke, two marquises, two earls, a baron and the American minister, but as Robert Bernard Martin points out in this biography of Tennyson 'there was not a poet among them'. One thinks of Hardy, borne by the Prime Minister, the Leader of the Opposition, Barrie, Galsworthy, Gosse, Housman, Kipling, Shaw, and the heads of the two Oxford and Cambridge colleges of which he was an honorary fellow.

But perhaps the reaction had always been incipient. There was a curious hostility to Tennyson among his contemporaries, in contrast to – even because of – his staggering popularity. Carlyle said *The Princess* had 'everything but common sense'. Patmore would not change one of his own poems for fifty *Mauds*. Mrs Browning said the *Idylls* left her cold. 'The real truth is,' wrote Matthew Arnold, 'that Tennyson, with all his temperament and artistic skill, is deficient in intellectual power.' And Gosse pronounced, in no less conspicuous a place than the eleventh edition of the *Encyclopaedia Britannica* in 1911, that 'among all the English poets it is Tennyson who presents the least percentage of entirely unattractive poetry', a meiosis worthy of the early Amis; while for Samuel Butler

> Blake was no good because he learnt Italian at 60 in order to study Dante, and Dante was no good because he was so fond of Virgil, and Virgil was no good because Tennyson ran him, and as for Tennyson – well, Tennyson goes without saying.

Review of Robert Bernard Martin, *Tennyson: The Unquiet Heart* (Clarendon Press/Faber and Faber, 1980)

Not for Professor Martin he doesn't. In the preface to this substantial volume, the first major biography of its subject since Sir Charles Tennyson's account in 1949, he justifies its production by saying that it needs no justification: 'almost no one seriously interested in the subject could fail to recognize that Tennyson is among the great English poets'.

> If our own age has not learned much else, it has at least come to a belated recognition of the greatness of the age of Victoria. To-day the condescension of W. H. Auden and Harold Nicholson [sic] to Tennyson seems at least as outmoded as Tennyson seemed to them.

But does it? We should remember that Nicolson at least was trying to *rehabilitate* Tennyson, to raise him from the fallen pantheon of nineteenth-century Nobodaddies by showing him to be an absurd and suffering human being much like ourselves. His Tennyson was a wild and rather silly young man of stormy ancestry who, after a youth of amatory and financial troubles, sailed into the haven of the most Victorian of marriages and the most Victorian of laureateships, fossilizing (to use Auden's word) into a picturesque and still rather silly old man who was, underneath, the same frightened and love-needing personality that had fled to the established virtues for protection against hostile circumstances. However, we take the point: Tennyson is to be turned right way up again, even though Professor Martin warns us that 'to ignore the imperfections of a man is to patronise him, as if the whole truth of his character was not to be faced'.

The portrait takes some time to emerge: Professor Martin is no impressionist, still less a cartoonist. His narrative inches forwards, sometimes by as little as two years to a chapter, with a wide-angled approach that while focused on Tennyson by no means ignores his family and friends. He handles a wealth of detail (much of which, inevitably, is familiar ground) with an easy unaffected style that occasionally rises to epigram ('the facility for happiness, like a good French accent, is usually learned early in life or not at all'). The myriad brush-strokes of his research are applied with well-documented deliberation, and the canvas is a large one – too large to be done justice by a short review. But when the picture is finished, it seems at first glance an assemblage of features: features that do not altogether coincide with the artist's original intention, and which show an obstinate tendency to remain features rather than a coherent portrait.

Perhaps the most prominent is that of heredity. Professor Martin's opening paragraph gives Tennyson's rejoinder ('not long before his death') to the Bishop of Ripon: 'But there is heredity; it counts for so much.' Heredity was the epileptic fits of his father, coupled with alcoholic excess and laudanum, that produced periods of frenzy ('he kept a large knife and a loaded gun in his room') alternating with protracted and expensive 'cures'; heredity was his elder brother Frederick quarrelling with their father to the point of threatened murder; it was his brother Charles becoming an opium addict, his brother Arthur an alcoholic, his brother Septimus frequenting institutions devoted to nervous diseases, his brother Edward's confinement to a lunatic asylum when nineteen, to stay there the rest of his life. In comparison, Tennyson's incessant smoking and bottles of port seem emblems of stability. But for the first twenty years of his adult life his family hung over him like an unpaid bill; his mother had to be visited, but he could no more live alone with her than he could set up a house and family of his own, leading instead an almost nomadic existence in lodgings and rooms or at the houses of his friends.

Heredity in particular was a fear that he had inherited his father's epileptic tendency and that it would be transferred to any children he might beget. This is one of Professor Martin's original contentions: in 1836 Tennyson had met Emily Selwood, a bridesmaid at his brother Charles's wedding, and although the attraction does not seem to have been passionate on either side they were soon unofficially engaged. Tradition has it that a real engagement was 'cruelly delayed and thwarted because of his lack of a profession' (*Chambers' Encyclopaedia*, 1973); Sir Charles Tennyson says that Emily's father grew increasingly unhappy at Tennyson's absence of steady employment and income, and in 1840 he forbade their continued correspondence, whereupon Emily saw and heard nothing of Tennyson for nearly ten years. The story is an odd one. Whatever Mr Selwood's role in the matter, there is a valedictory letter from Tennyson on January, 1840, in which he says 'I fly thee for my good, perhaps for thine.... If thou knewest why I fly thee there is nothing thou would'st more wish for than that I should fly thee.' Such dark hints, as Professor Martin claims, must refer to something more than poverty, or not having a job.

His own theory is that Tennyson about this time experienced a number of symptoms that might have pointed to epilepsy, and spent much of the 1840s attempting to cure himself. He draws attention to the passages inserted into the third edition of *The Princess* (1847) in which the Prince suffers from cataleptic or epileptic seizures inherited from his family; the hero of *Maud* is a prey to insane ravings and fits as his father was before him; while *In Memoriam* 'is in large part concerned with the meaning of trances, whether they are malign in nature or whether they are genuine pathways to suprasensory knowledge'. 'It can hardly be coincidental', he goes on,

> that these major poems, all three of which were begun in the 1830s or 1840s, are so saturated with references to the fear of fits and trances, followed by either recovery from them or the discovery that they are not malign in their effect.

Professor Martin is interesting on hydropaths; in 1845 voluntary commitment to mental hospitals became illegal, and 'water establishments' sprang up to cater for the large class of sufferers from 'hypochondria' and other semi-psychosomatic ailments who still wanted treatment. The 'water cure', based on the teaching of an Austrian layman named Preissnitz, involved the incessant application of water, both internally and externally, to purge the system of impurities, and to this Tennyson submitted himself a number of times in the middle 1840s. 'The water cure would do him good if he gave it fair chances,' wrote FitzGerald, 'but he smokes, and drinks a bottle of wine a day. He looks however twice as well as he did a year ago.' This was in early 1845.

Tennyson's last cure was at Dr Gully's at Malvern in 1848, after which he seems to have regarded himself as fully restored. 'Dr Gully had no doubt made it clear ... that his illness was not inherited epilepsy' but gout, the treatment for which was total abstinence. Gout however was much less dreadful than epilepsy, and in 1849 he renewed his suit to Miss Selwood. Not unnaturally, she was slow to entertain it a second time (opinions again differ why), but they were married in 1850 on 15 June, *In Memoriam* having been published on the first of that month.

This theory, and it is only a theory, combats the long-held assumption that Tennyson did not marry because he could not afford it, but the Tennyson of 1849, however clean a bill of health he had received, was still a much better marital prospect than his counterpart of 1840, financially at any rate. Professor Martin devotes many passages to showing that Tennyson was always better off than he thought he was. In 1845 Peel offered him a pension of £200, which Tennyson accepted, thereby provoking Bulwer Lytton's vicious lines about 'School-Miss Alfred', and Martin comments:

> In no serious way could Tennyson have thought he was poor once he had received the pension. If, as seems probable, he was no longer receiving any money from FitzGerald, he still had some £500–£700 annually, if one takes into account the income from his capital, earnings from his poetry, the pension, and £100 from his aunt Russell. It was equal to the benefices of only the most luxuriously provided clergymen of the day, and well beyond the dreams of most professional men.

This is no doubt true, but Tennyson had grown up in an atmosphere of financial insecurity: he had lost some of his own money and that of his family in the wood-working scheme of the madhouse-keeper Allen, and there was always the possibility that he would have to support his incapacitated brothers as well as his unmarried sisters (one of whom, Mary, was described as 'something like what Alfred would be if he were a woman, and washed'). Given a timorous nature streaked with provincial hard-headedness, imagined poverty might account for reluctance to marry as effectively as the real thing.

These are Professor Martin's two principal contributions to Tennysonian biography. He has no revelations to offer on the sexual front: 'There is not the slightest evidence that Tennyson ever had any sexual experience with another person until his marriage at the age of forty-one', a phenomenon he explains by the moral climate of the age and the poet's own lack of sexual drive. His dismissal of the homosexual element in Tennyson's feelings for Arthur Hallam is sensible enough, though he does not mention, as Christopher Ricks did, both Tennyson's and Hallam's love of Shakespeare's sonnets, and the 'sort of sympathy with Hellenism' it expressed, at least according to their contemporary Jowett. In fact the character he draws is of someone demanding much from others, and not giving a great deal in return: Edward Lear, for instance, was amazed at the invalid Emily Tennyson's constant attention to her husband: 'What labour for him! – and how little he seems to regard it!' As Professor Martin says:

> There can be few poets in the language who more consistently and successfully wrote about friendship, and there were probably equally few with whom it was more difficult to maintain untroubled relations over a long period. As a friend he was a born sprinter rather than a long-distance runner.

FitzGerald was a case in point. A Cambridge friend, his affection for Tennyson and his admiration for his poems were strong and deep; for some years, according to this account, he contributed £300 a year to Tennyson's income. But he grew increasingly out of sympathy with Tennyson's work, and impatient with his love of high society in fine houses, while Tennyson for his part became careless about answering FitzGerald's letters. 'I sometimes wonder if People used to be so indifferent about seeing one another as all of us, so old friends, seem to be!' FitzGerald remarked. At last in 1876 Tennyson and his son Hallam called on him unexpectedly, 'and all the affection he had suppressed over the years when he had received no letters from Alfred now came to life in a joyous burst'. They spent two days together in an ecstasy of reminiscence, and FitzGerald gave him his treasured portrait of Tennyson by Samuel Laurence for Emily Tennyson, but the reunion was not sustained. 'Alfred himself never writes, nor indeed cares a halfpenny about one', was the lonely FitzGerald's final conclusion. It is one of the saddest stories in the book.

Such themes emerge only intermittently from a wealth of more familiar material – the growth of Tennyson's reputation, his houses, his relations with the Queen, his various publishers (Payne, Moxon's successor, fastened a pair of ass's ears to the portrait of Tennyson hanging in his office) – but they seem the most definite characteristics of the portrait Professor Martin draws. If Nicolson's Tennyson was endearingly silly, Martin's is cold and somewhat remote. He fails to bring out the gruff mingling of integrity and absurdity of so many of the anecdotes: the famous retort to Jowett ('If it comes to that, Master, the sherry you gave us at luncheon was beastly') is bisected with 'answered Tennyson coldly'. True, we do not know how Tennyson answered. But he is unlikely to have exhibited that repose which stamps the caste of Vere de Vere. The effect is rather like an edition of the poet's works with none of the dialect poems.

Professor Martin has tried to be fair to Tennyson, neither making fun of him nor seeing him, as his age did, as a figure out of Homer or even the Bible. The result is not a Great Victorian, but a personality at once dependent on others and inclined to neglect them, moody and sometimes panicky, close-fisted financially and emotionally and in every other way – except, of course, for the poems. In sum, there is a dimension lacking. It would be tempting to call this the life of a poet without his poems, if Professor Martin did not explicitly deny this in his preface. Nevertheless, it is the life of a poet without something, and perhaps poetry is the most convenient shorthand for it.

Times Literary Supplement, 7 November 1980

Words for Music Perhaps

Collaboration in the arts is always interesting. And when the collaborators are major figures of their time, it is doubly so: what they produce should be the sum of its distinguished parts. Or if this is too much to hope, then at least it should realize aspects of their talents that would otherwise have lain hidden.

The combination of Auden and Britten was especially promising, for superficially at least they had much in common. Each was a virtuoso: Britten actually *liked* composing to order, however difficult the circumstances ('we have to record separately – me, having to conduct from an improvised visual metronome'); while Isherwood's conviction that Auden could write anything, even a double ballade on a brand of toothpaste ('and it would be good'), is well known. They came from the same background, even the same school, and were both homosexual in what sound like different ways; Auden was six years older, but he loved music and was an enthusiastic amateur pianist. Above all, their artistic roles were running parallel: in the heady political Thirties, Auden was the progressives' poet, Britten their composer. They should have got on like a house on fire.

Their association was at any rate fruitful, starting with *Coal Face* and *Night Mail* for the GPO Film Unit, developing with settings of Auden's poems and cabaret songs, and expiring with the opera *Paul Bunyan* they wrote in America during the war. As an artistic partnership it covered a longer span of productive years than the more celebrated Auden-Isherwood duo. Whether it represented in any sense a marriage of minds is more questionable. Britten was deeply impressed by Auden, and admired his work, but the older poet was a dominating, even a domineering character, and one gets the impression that Britten was sometimes an unhappy and even an unwilling follower. This seems to have been specially

Review of Donald Mitchell, *Britten and Auden in the Thirties: The Year 1936* (Faber and Faber, 1981)

true when they both went to America, which Britten found he disliked, and lived in the celebrated Middagh Street household in New York that Auden directed and Britten eventually retreated from.

Such at least is the picture Donald Mitchell presents, and he supports it with a fascinating hitherto-unpublished letter from Auden to Britten from the Berg Collection in New York Public Library, in which Britten is taken to task (affectionately, but taken to task none the less) for 'playing the lovable talented little boy' and being bourgeois, and so denying the 'demands of disorder' that are so essential a part of an artist's life and were doubtless well satisfied at Middagh Street. It is the kind of letter Auden's friends must have been used to, and one would like to see Britten's reply. Dr Mitchell does not rebut the charge – indeed, he claims that this conflict of order and chaos was a principal theme of Britten's later creative life – but he rightly implies that it is no more than a symptom of the fact that Auden and Britten were developing into very different personalities.

But his book is not really, or not exclusively, about this. As a musicologist, and as Britten's official biographer, Donald Mitchell is chiefly concerned with the music the association produced, and the sides of Britten's character it exemplified. He uses Britten's diaries of the pre-war years (the book's mystifying sub-title is not adhered to) to demonstrate his political awareness, though this hardly seems sophisticated – 'I like Fridays because apart from the daily paper there is the *Radio Times* (occasionally *World Radio* too) & *New Statesman*.' In the fashion of the time, Britten was prepared to lend his talent to propagandist causes, writing music for Rotha's 'Peace Film' and composing a 'Pacifist March' with words by Ronald Duncan ('Corr-u-ga-ted iron for our roof'). But the picture he draws of Britten in general is of a tremendously hard, inventive and reliable worker, who would have given 'the demands of disorder' very short shrift if he had ever noticed them. In fact the book is about Britten, not Auden, and reads a little like a draft of a chapter from the forthcoming biography (it is, of course, based on Dr Mitchell's four Eliot Memorial Lectures at the University of Kent in 1979).

What his thesis turns on is not so much the nature of the collaboration as the quality of the music it produced. At the very end he rather indignantly takes up Clive James's contention that

'Auden never met his Kurt Weill. He met Britten, but the results were meagre.' Dr Mitchell replies:

> If we added together all the Auden-Britten collaborations . . . we should find that we have amassed a very large body of work which made a decisive contribution to the making of the Thirties. The joint work of composer and poet constitutes part of the very sight and sound of the Thirties.

This is supported by numerous musical quotations and their analysis. It is an area of debate a purely literary reviewer finds it hard to enter. I know one Brecht-Weill piece, 'Mac the Knife', because I have a record of Louis Armstrong playing it; but Armstrong did not record 'Out on the lawn I lie in bed' or even one of the cabaret songs, by which I mean that whatever the musical worth of these pieces they cannot be said to have penetrated the popular mind, and I take leave to doubt whether they do in fact constitute the very sight and sound of the decade. The few recordings I have been able to borrow for the purpose of this review strike me (to quote Dr Mitchell from a different context) as 'too clever, too sophisticated, too eclectic, too polished, too heartless even'. But this is no doubt my fault.

In the last analysis, Donald Mitchell ascribes the breakdown of the partnership to Auden's increasing unsettability:

> I am not sure that Auden ever wholly comprehended that while words are words, words written for transformation into and by music – for consumption by music – are something entirely different.

I think this is very likely true: American Auden, as distinct from the Auden of *Look, Stranger!*, was a ponderous windbag. On the other hand, real poems are not meant to be set to music: they are not meant to be made into posters, or read at 'happenings', or to be diluted or distracted by anything that is not themselves. They are self-sufficient as eggs. Therefore if successful setting requires 'something entirely different' from the poem as poem, the parting of the ways between poet and composer is not hard to forecast. Henceforth Britten was happier with Montagu Slater, Eric Crozier and the rest.

Times Literary Supplement, 27 February 1981

Horn of Plenty

The most remarkable phenomenon in the English poetic scene during the last ten years has been the advent, or perhaps I should say the irruption, of Gavin Ewart. Since 1971 he has published six collections, plus a 400-page *Collected Poems*, and now here comes another, over a hundred pieces that would make three slim volumes from a more parsimonious talent. Add to this the fact that he published his first poems in 1933 at the age of seventeen, and that twenty-five years separated his first book and his second, and the phenomenon grows even more prodigious.

It is not only that he writes so many poems: what he writes is so extraordinarily varied. The Gavin Ewart Show, as one of his collections was aptly titled, is clever, farcical, literate, fantastic, indecent, and above all very funny. It is also rueful, affectionate, self-parodying, introspective. And, finally, it is sombre, unerringly realistic ('the fox's teeth are in the bunny/ and nothing can remove them, honey'), evoking rather than exploring illness, old age, loss, death. A sonnet on Shakespeare's universality ends:

> It's better for a writer, in most cases, to get out and about.
> If he gets stuck in his own psyche for too long
> He bores everybody – and that includes himself.

There is not much danger of Ewart doing this. The back streets of Fulham, Yorkshiremen in pub gardens, a laboratory rabbit, office friendships, a cutting, a quotation – anything can start him off, and when he brings us back from the outing we are usually either shaken or stirred, and sometimes both, reflecting that there is really nothing, however surreal, extravagant, improper or mundane, that Ewart could not write a poem about.

The New Ewart does nothing to alter this view. Once more the cornucopia is upended: 'Bring out number, weight and measure/ in a year of dearth', as the (unascribed) epigraph puts it, and

Review of Gavin Ewart, *The New Ewart* (Hutchinson, 1982)

Vesuvius, women, Montale, animals, dying, drink, dolls, tumble round our feet. The first lines ('I wake the wifehag in the marriagebed') are as ever unpredictable or outrageous ('It certainly is the smell of her cunt/That makes you fall on your knees and grunt'); the topics (the letter F, the death of W. S. Gilbert) as randomly right. There are funny nightmares about dreadful poetry editors, and the familiar erotic speculations ('Me in my dirty mac, ho ho!') and sometimes a sharp vision as in 'Afrokill', lions eating a zebra ('The striped horse/is red inside'):

> Lastly come the hopping
> horrors
> with big wings,
> clean wavebreak
> on shipwreck ribs.

But as always in Ewart compassion is lurking: a mother has grown old, and died; likewise a cat. The poems about them aren't grouped together but strung out at intervals, so that the reader keeps coming back to them, first one ('To her/I am a coloured blur/A just-heard voice') then the other:

> I do not hope to see my cat again
> Or look upon that friendly furry face
> In some imagined, altered, other place . . .

Finally a sonnet unites them: 'Both of these, to see, were equally pathetic.' It is a defence of the unity of suffering.

The Collected Ewart, then, was not a line drawn beneath a poetic career; *The New Ewart*, one is tempted to say, is but old Ewart writ more or less the same size, and cheerfully prepared to go on while the machine is to him. What are we to say of this astonishing unstoppable talent? To look at a series of Ewart worksheets is revealing: there are all the poems, written out neatly in a level and legible hand, with virtually no corrections – perhaps an 'a' for a 'the', or a 'yet' for an 'and', but all seemingly written straight off, without agonising or second thoughts. Automatic writing? They have none of its characteristics. They rhyme and scan and have shape; each has an individual point and makes it, and is different from the others. It is the work of someone possessed of a copious, varied and inventive talent who gives it full rein and is not unduly worried about the impression it makes; as with Betjeman, the energy other poets spend on screening their impulses for security

Ewart puts into the poem. Let 'em all come, he seems to be saying; what I have written, I have written. This is brought out strongly in the *Collected* volume, in which what the author 'wishes to preserve' (there is a squib about this phrase in the present book) is, quite simply, everything he has ever published.

> This is not because I consider them all equally good but because I have aimed at completeness. I have also borne in mind the fact that a poem that has ceased to have much merit for me may have hidden admirers who would be disappointed not to find it.

Such a policy of inclusiveness, in writing as well as republishing, has consequential risks. I sometimes counter, when the virtues of this or that poet are being urged on me, with the challenge 'Recite some', a ploy I think I picked up from Vernon Watkins. As a criterion it has some merit, but the few lines of Ewart that stay in my mind are largely irrelevant (no one, surely, can go to a party without remembering 'Hands that wiped arses/Are holding glasses'). This may be because he has written so much, but more probably results from writing easily; his dégagé manner eschews almost on principle the consciously memorable. There is no Ewart poem by which he stands or falls, nor would he wish there to be; in this he is something like Enright. Yet it is the poets whose lines stick to us like burrs that we value most; time alone can tell whether Ewart's will do this, but at present I doubt it.

Again, to write whatever comes into one's head means that some of it will seem to others trivial or indecent. Ewart is well aware of this: 'They'll say (if I'm lucky):/He wrote some silly poems, and some of them were funny' are the last lines in *The Collected Ewart*. In fact they will say a lot more than this, but his tireless willingness to experiment, to parody, to follow a random phrase through to its conclusion ('A Good Mouse Needs No Preparation'), can exasperate those who believe poetry springs from hiding-places ten years deep and from nowhere else. In this he is something like Stevie Smith: both of them see something move, take a pot-shot at it, and what they hold up, we are bound to admit, is not unlike a poem, although another part of us is muttering impatiently. In the present collection, 'For the Ghost of Nancy Mitford' is Left-Book-Club imperceptive; 'For Patience Strong' suggests her pieces do not scan, which of course they do, impeccably; while 'Dialogue Between the Alcoholic and his Better Self', though a good idea, isn't in the end quite funny enough. But three flops out of 106 is an enviable record.

As for the indecency, or frankness, or erotic farce or whatever one likes to call it, there is less of it in *The New Ewart*; the male fantasies that start at five and grow fierce at fifty, as he said, may be cooling off. All the same, although one can say pretty well anything these days, Ewart has a reputation for such preoccupations ('sex-mad Ewart' was *Private Eye*'s recent unfair label): they flourish most luxuriantly in *Pleasures of the Flesh* (1966), which W. H. Smith reputedly refused on moral grounds to stock (a rare distinction for a poet today), and which featured Eight Awful Creatures such as The Masturbon, The Fux, The Stuffalo and so on (suggested, I believe, by much more respectable concepts in a book for children by Ted Hughes). Of course a lot of it is very funny: 'Office Primitive' ('Me likum girlum, Hatum work./Smokum. Drinkum. Strokum pussy./Go bus every day. Lovum stockings') is another of my irrelevant memories, and when the thick monograph on Ewart and Sex is written (probably in German) it will certainly have to acknowledge that much of Ewart's 'shockingness' (if it is shocking) is disinfected by laughter. His own admissions suggest that he is trying to be truthful about sex in general and in his own case in particular ('Once, Eliot, I was shy as you/and impotent as you (I guess)'), and his condemnations are reserved for those who want to stop him or make him feel bad about it:

> But if you use the words, describe the actions, they go up in flames.
> Somehow they are not easy (we are not easy)
> about being sexual creatures.

'To the Puritans who are the Gods of This World' denounces the lay figures of Masturbating Mildred and Would-Be-Fornicating Fred at length, and this is all very liberal and reasonable, though hardly original. If the reader has any reservation, it is that the sex Ewart is defending, or claiming the right to express, so often seems not a lawless passion or a sensual tenderness, but the familiar fetishes of tits, knickers, pubic hair and so on. It may be argued that for most men this is what sex means much of the time, but it is hard to feel high-minded about it.

But to be occasionally trivial or gamey is, as I said, the price of

Ewart's wide-angled virtuosity that often goes just as far in other directions. There is the *Hiawatha*-humour of 'The Meeting':

> Everything was twice repeated,
> sometimes more than twice repeated,
> as they worked through the agenda
> (it seemed elastic, that agenda,
> becoming longer, never shorter),
> their utterances grew long, not shorter,
> it was just like spreading butter ...

and then the unique echoing lyricism of 'The Dying Animals', achieved by a formal limitation that, as so often, allows an expansion of feeling:

> The animals that look at us like children
> in innocence, in perfect innocence!
> The innocence that looks at us! Like children
> the animals, the simple animals,
> have no idea why legs no longer work.
>
> The food that is refused, the love of sleeping –
> in innocence, in childhood innocence
> there is a parallel of love. Of sleeping
> they're never tired, the dying animals;
> sick children too, whose play to them is work.
>
> The animals are little children dying,
> brash tigers, household pets – all innocence,
> the flames that lit their eyes are also dying,
> the animals, the simple animals,
> die easily; but hard for us, like work!

Not a typical Ewart poem, you may say. But is there such a thing? The more he writes, the less likely it becomes. And this is what underlies his claim on our attention, this ability from time to time to pull out of the bag a new Ewart.

Quarto, May 1982

A Late Bonus

You must understand the title if you are not to be disappointed. 24 of the 29 poems here presented were shipped to Canada along with a great turn-out of papers when the poet left his Cloth Fair flat in 1971 (doesn't anyone think of British libraries on such occasions?), and were subsequently disinterred by their present compiler, Bevis Hillier, the Laureate's official biographer. Sir John, with the aid of the ever-helpful John Sparrow, brushed them up and added some more from the magazines, so that we have, in his publisher's words, 'a rich unexpected harvest'.

This, at a time when Betjeman might reasonably be allowed to have shut up shop, is certainly something to be grateful for. Any poem by him is worth reading, even if it fails, because it will contain something of his own original voice and vision, and here there are many felicities: beautiful lines, moving lines, funny lines, lines that stay with us almost against our will:

> I haven't hope, I haven't faith.
> I live two lives and sometimes three.
> The lives I live make life a death
> For those who have to live with me.

And again:

> The Advent wind begins to stir
> With sea-like sounds in our Scotch fir,
> It's dark at breakfast, dark at tea,
> And in between we only see
> Clouds hurrying across the sky
> And rain-wet roads the wind blows dry

And even:

> Will members please Note that next Sunday in the Free Trade Hall
> The Peascod Players will do *Everyman*.
> The play lasts seven hours ...

Review of John Betjeman, *Uncollected Poems* (John Murray, 1982)

When Betjeman speaks, the notion that poetry is something you must learn to enjoy fades like the classroom cant it is.

But good lines do not make good poems, and here I must disagree with the implication that these are a bunch of wonderful pieces that their author, in his lovable, absent-minded way, somehow forgot about. Betjeman is sharper than that. *Uncollected Poems* means poems that at the time did not seem worth collecting, or in most cases even publishing.

This is not to say that they are bad (though there is not much to be said for 'Dumbleton Hall' or 'The Lift Man'). Some are inconclusive: the powerful 'Guilt', from which my first quotation comes, tails off incomprehensibly. 'Civilised Woman', unusually for Betjeman, strikes a socially uncertain note. But for the most part these are themes that he has handled elsewhere, and sometimes better; the three religious essays in octosyllabics ('Advent 1955', 'The Parochial Church Council' and 'The Conversion of St Paul'), effective though they are, might have been dropped from *Poems in the Porch*; the touching 'The Retired Postal Clerk' recalls (apart from 'Woak Hill') 'The Cockney Amorist' and 'A Wembley Lad'; 'Advertising Pays' is not as corrosive as 'Executive', and although 'Thoughts on a Train' ('No doubt she is somebody's mistress') is different from 'Lenten Thoughts of a High Anglican', it inevitably suggests it, and so on.

While for the most part the poems are not dated, they appear to be in chronological order from 1940 to 1977, and so provide a fresh conspectus of Sir John's preoccupations, and a fresh reminder of their unpredictable richness. This in turn justifies Mr Hillier's fourteen-page foreword. It is odd that when there are so many poets whose work badly needs explanation or apology, this should be at least the fifth account of the one who is doing very nicely without them, but that's literature for you.

Mr Hillier, a fugitive from the art world (he was once editor of *The Connoisseur*), tells a good story or two (thank heaven the IRA read Betjeman before it could manage to shoot him), but mostly summarizes the views of his predecessors with his own enthusiastic amplifications. One wonders what his biography will be like (and even if it will materialize: the life of Hopkins, confidently announced in 1971, didn't); such a task requires a breadth of knowledge and sensibility equal to those of its subject, but this may come more easily to an Art Deco expert than to his structuralist equivalent. At any rate, one looks forward to it.

And despite the reservations made earlier, it has to be admitted that Betjeman rejects are better than other people's export models, or at any rate so instinct with his own vitality that they will survive their inadequacies. 'The Old Land Dog' is hilarious pseudo-Newbolt; 'An Ecumenical Invitation' a demonstration of anti-Catholic karate; 'To the Crazy Gang' a roaring piece of nostalgia; and they are balanced by that other voice that is like none of them:

> What is conversion? Not at all
> For me the experience of St Paul.
> No blinding light, a fitful glow
> Is all the light of faith I know
> Which sometimes goes completely out
> And leaves me plunging round in doubt
> Until I will myself to go
> And worship in God's house below –
> My parish church – and even there
> I find distractions everywhere.

What Betjeman achieves is done simply by saying what he thinks and feels, without minding whether he is laughed at. And the further he gets from his fellow-poets, the nearer he gets to his readers.

Observer, 3 October 1982

A Slackening of the Reins

From *Banker* I learn that merchant bankers are always looking for people to lend money to, since they live off the interest, and that these people can be as diverse as stud-farmers and strip-cartoonists. Also that Captain and Amphoteric kill skin fungi, and potassium is as essential to animals as it is to plants.

Of course there is more to it than this. The narrator, Tim Ekaterin, is a young merchant banker who is taken to Ascot, where one of the party, a horse-healer, is nearly knifed. Through promotion he learns more about banking (and so do we), and helps a stud-farmer buy a stallion who won an Ascot race. More information: did you know a stallion covers an average of forty mares a year?

Tim is in love with his sick chief's wife; there are outings and visits, but no action. Only in part three does the pace suddenly quicken; the stallion's foals are born deformed, and Tim, seeing his firm's investment going bust, investigates, encountering the usual hideous ordeal Francis arranges for his heroes. A leisurely conclusion ties up the ends; the chief dies, presumably leaving the way open for Tim (up till now another of Francis's self-contained efficient bachelors) and the widow to come together.

This is a much slower-moving book than most Francises, almost as if he is coming to enjoy describing situations without tightening them into reader-garrotting tension. There are one or two blind alleys too: the knifer is discovered (Tim just meets him socially), but let go without contributing anything really vital to the plot. Leakage of information at the office is similarly cleared up; the story would have been the same without it. And womenfolk, normally one of Francis's strongest points, are less striking than usual, the bouncing schoolgirl something of a stereotype, the fascination of the chief's wife stated but not shown.

Two years ago I said that *Reflex* and its predecessor *Whip Hand*

Review of Dick Francis, *Banker* (Michael Joseph, 1982)

suggested that there may be a limit to the number of thrillers to be derived from the racing scene. Their successors, *Twice Shy* and now *Banker*, have not altered this view. The former broke down by having two heroes, the switch coming half-way through; *Banker* suffers from lack of action and what in 1980 I called 'a certain blandness in the writing'. Francis can only be judged by his own high standards. The absolute sureness of his settings, the freshness of his characters, the terrifying climaxes of violence, the literate jauntiness of style, the unfailing intelligent compassion – all these make him one of the few writers who can be mentioned in the same breath as Fleming. But if they flag, or are not bound together in a logic of action, to say otherwise is to devalue the superb series up to *Bonecrack* (1971), and the isolated successes since then of *Knock Down*, *Risk* and *Trial Run* (which simultaneously removed any need to go to Russia along with any desire to).

The temptation, already hinted at, for Francis to become 'a real novelist' must be very strong. Let us hope he resists it; he is always twenty times more readable than the average Booker entry. His place is at Hedley Humber's starveling stables, or with the boiler at Seabury racecourse, or facing the madness of Mrs Roxford.

Observer, 17 October 1982

Under a Common Flag

There cannot help being a new generation of poets every twenty years, so equally there should be anthologies to announce them. There hasn't been a serious anthology of British poetry since A. Alvarez's *The New Poetry* in 1962, so it is time for another. And here it is.

Such is the basic contention of Blake Morrison and Andrew Motion, compilers of the present volume, and immediately small quibbles rise. Shouldn't poets announce themselves rather than be presented as part of a typified group, and haven't they in fact always done so? And what about Edward Lucie-Smith, and Michael Horovitz, and the *Penguin Modern Poets* series? But never mind. The compilers are explicit. 'This anthology is intended to be didactic as well as representative' runs their first sentence.

More quibbles: can it be both didactic and representative? Robert Conquest's *New Lines* (1956) presented nine poets with only twelve years between their ages who constituted a recognizable (though unintentional) spearhead of style and feeling; this was didactic. *The New Poetry*, though ostensibly didactic, was much more representative, with twenty poets spanning 27 years, and was in fact divided against itself, using half its contributors to shame or buck up the other half, and in any case being much more tentative than the passage quoted above ('... a good deal of poetic talent exists in England at the moment. But whether or not it will come to anything –').

Alvarez weighs heavily on Morrison and Motion, as they admit. They follow his pattern of twenty poets, fully represented (perhaps this is all they meant by representative), and clearly hope their anthology will be as influential as his. But where is the message? If Conquest was for common sense, and Alvarez anti-genteel, what are Morrison/Motion advocating? Hard to say:

Review of *The Penguin Book of Contemporary British Poetry*, edited by Blake Morrison and Andrew Motion (Penguin, 1982)

> They have developed a degree of ludic and literary self-consciousness reminiscent of the modernists ... It manifests, in other words, a preoccupation with relativism ... The new poetry is often open-ended, reluctant to point the moral of, or conclude too neatly, what it chooses to transcribe.

Not easy to make a slogan out of that, even though its authors tailor their definition to the talents they have assembled. Can it be that to have two compilers, instead of a single Conquest or Alvarez, inevitably inclines to compromise, a lack of cutting edge? Or is it the poets themselves?

Crudely, and no doubt unfairly, they can be grouped: the Martians (led by Craig Raine), the Ulstermen (Seamus Heaney with Faber and non-Faber colleagues). There are Fleur Adcock, Carol Rumens, Penelope Shuttle, Anne Stevenson and Medbh McGuckian, who is Ulster, female, and something of a Martian into the bargain. And lastly there are what would be the English except for Douglas Dunn. Without doubt, the Martians are most striking:

> Clothes queue up in the wardrobe,
> an echo to the eye, or a jangle of Euclid.
> The wall-phone wears a pince-nez
> even in the dark – the flex
> is Jewish orthodox.

The compilers emphasize how influential Raine and Reid have become in a short time. But wasn't Norman MacCaig doing something like this years ago?

The Ulstermen, linked to some extent by ancestry, temperament and what might be called the Matter of Ireland, are nevertheless individual voices. Heaney's dense and burnished rurality is already famous, and is echoed with more directness by Michael Longley, but Paul Muldoon's hilarious 'Immram' soon outsoars Donegall Place:

> He was covered in bedsores.
> He raised one talon.
> 'I forgive you,' he croaked, 'And I forget.'
> On your way out, you tell that bastard
> To bring me a dish of ice-cream.
> I want Baskin-Robbins banana-nut ice-cream.

On the troubles of the Province they are oblique, using them more as a background than a foreground to the dourness of personal life. Tom Paulin comes closest to their awfulness:

> The city is built on mud and wrath.
> Its weather is predicted; its streetlamps
> Light up in the glowering, crowded evenings.
> Time-switches, ripped from them, are clasped
> To sticks of sweet, sweating explosives.

Fleur Adcock's 'The Soho Hospital for Women' brings us even nearer to what we like to think of as reality, and is amusingly counterbalanced by Anne Stevenson's 'A Daughter's Difficulties,' a letter from a young American bride in 1840 (though sounding more like 1940) which is certainly narrative, though not perhaps the kind the compilers find their contributors concerned with.

Tony Harrison seems a fugitive from a more vernacular and confessional tradition:

> Though my mother was already two years dead
> Dad kept her slippers warming by the gas,
> put hot water bottles her side of the bed
> and still went to renew her transport pass.
>
> You couldn't just drop in. You had to phone.
> He'd put you off an hour to give him time
> to clear away her things and look alone
> as though his still raw love were such a crime.

To call his 'Long Distance' the most moving poem in the book is no doubt a sign of unregenerate taste, like being unable to banish the idea of Heaney as a left-footing John Hewitt, or preferring Douglas Dunn's 'Terry Street' to his later Alexandrianism, and raises the question of how far the unreformed reader will spend his time picking out bits that remind him of earlier modes rather than enjoying the new manner the compilers are anxious to celebrate. Despite James Fenton, and the enigmatic coloured prints of Andrew Motion, his praise is likely to be faint; these writers are (for the most part) serious, non-extravagant, carefully and even ingeniously observant, responsive to the real or imagined situation, but in the last analysis this is only to say that they are not very interesting. Many of them have achieved success as individuals: are they more impressive under a common flag? I think not.

Given the compilers' terms of reference, one would not expect to find Brian Patten and Roger McGough in their pages, or James Simmons and Peter Reading, but it might have livened things up a little. It would also have gone some way towards justifying the title. To call this an overstatement is one's last, and perhaps one's largest, quibble.

Observer, 14 November 1982

Brief for Betjeman

The current television series, 'Time With Betjeman', allows us to study his face. Like most old faces, it has collapsed somewhat, but is still watchful, the eyes moving from speaker to speaker, faintly apprehensive.

When he himself says something, there is a hint of the old nostril-lifting irony, the corners of the mouth turning down crookedly; then suddenly comes the uproarious back-of-the-pit horse-laugh wide open, all teeth and creases. And above it the extraordinary powerful skull, like a Roman bust, or a phrenologist's model waiting to be marked into 33 sections and labelled with Superior Sentiments and Reflective Faculties. Impossible to characterize such features: the top half is authoritative, perhaps a famous headmaster, but lower down is the schoolboy; furtive, volatile, ready to burst out laughing, never entirely at ease.

Betjeman himself is equally hard to place, even though it is 25 years since the publication of his *Collected Poems*, that amazing literary landslide which once again demonstrated that the English are prepared to buy poetry if they like it. By now we have just about come to terms with the paradox of his personality. What remains is the paradox of his popularity. Previous comparable phenomena – *Omar Khayyam*, *Barrack-Room Ballads*, *A Shropshire Lad* – were sharply defined appeals to narrow but powerful areas of feeling. Betjeman is nothing like that. His widely heterogeneous world of farce and fury, where sports girls and old nuns jostle with town clerks and impoverished Irish peers, is as remote from the common reader as remorse and religion, architecture and Archibald and the rest of his favourite subjects. Yet the common reader, and his children after him, have lapped it up. What is the secret? Must we alter our whole concept of poetry to admit this Eighth Type of Ambiguity?

Review of Patrick Taylor-Martin, *John Betjeman: His Life and Work* (Allen Lane, 1983)

This, basically, is the question Patrick Taylor-Martin sets out to answer, and he meets it squarely. Betjeman is not a *régisseur* of the outrageous but a poet of common emotion, strongly felt and strongly expressed:

> He is a poet whose response to experience, both visual and emotional, is direct and spontaneous. He says what he feels without self-consciousness. He is frightened of death and says so; he feels guilty about neglecting his parents and says so; he does not want his son to die and says so ... Although he runs the risk of sentimentality and self-pity in accepting the emotions of the moment as valid, Betjeman only rarely falls into these traps. In earlier poems he avoids them by the use of irony and subtle self-mockery ... In later poems, they are avoided not by a device but simply by the patent sincerity of what he is saying and the genuine passion with which he says it.

This is very much the Plain Man's Guide to Betjeman. Mr Taylor-Martin was not one of the leisured set in Canterbury quad but a history graduate of Hull. Nor is he a Betjeman addict: the subject was, he says, suggested to him, and he claims no personal knowledge of the man he is writing on. In fact his account leans a good deal on what other people have said about Betjeman, and what Betjeman has said about himself. 'He is an accepter rather than a rejecter of life,' Mr Taylor-Martin announces on the jacket, a sentiment I seem to remember publishing in 1959, and most writers on Betjeman will find themselves liberally quoted (there is no index). Not always accurately: I did not say that Betjeman was the equal of Eliot. Mr Taylor-Martin has missed my qualification 'leaving aside the question of their respective poetic statures'.

It is a thorough and painstaking book. Once the life is out of the way (and I was delighted to learn that Betjeman abandoned English at Oxford in favour of Welsh, causing a don to be imported from Aberystwyth twice a week), the reader is conducted steadily through the early, middle and late collections (under titles such as 'Laurels and Gaslight' and 'Clay and Spirit'), *Summoned by Bells*, and the miscellaneous prose. Individual poems are elucidated and paraphrased (though for the most part quotations speak for themselves), and praise and blame thoughtfully apportioned; when Mr Taylor-Martin finds a poem wanting (such as the elegy on the Marquess of Dufferin and Ava) he clobbers it ('plangent banality'), but is properly appreciative of 'Middlesex' and 'The Metropolitan Railway'. Incidental sidelights abound: Betjeman was the only contemporary in Auden's *Oxford Book of Light Verse*. At Oxford he went out with an eton-cropped waitress called Olive Sparks.

Unfortunately the commentary adds little to our understanding of the poems themselves; the level is sixth-form, first year, adult education. I have been waiting for years for someone to explain 'The Irish Unionist's Farewell to Greta Hellstrom in 1922'; Mr Taylor-Martin calls it baffling. Nor is his tone impeccable: he can refer to 'such gurus of the modern movement as Eliot, Yeats and Lawrence' or call 'Pam' 'a harridan' ('haggard or ill-tempered old woman,' says my dictionary). He makes exceptionally heavy weather of *Summoned by Bells*, saying it can only be appreciated if we accept 'that the provision of pleasure is a legitimate goal for a writer'. Cor pierrez les corbeaux.

But however one quarrels with Mr Taylor-Martin's judgement on specific poems (and his touch is less sure in the later books, where he has fewer other critics to quote from), his unswerving devotion wins our sympathy. He is like a good barrister; without any personal commitment to his client, he is determined to do his best for him, making every legitimate point, turning each charge aside deftly. Is Betjeman out of step with the twentieth century? Then who is in step – Eliot, Pound? And who today is in step with them? Does Betjeman hate mass democracy because it threatens his pals in the aristocracy? No, because it destroys individuality. And so on. His final speech for the defence ('The Limits of What's Human') is instinct with warm and generous advocacy.

The trouble with the Plain Man's evaluation of Betjeman, putting one's money on the 'serious' poems and trying to forget the rest ('bad poems by his own standards, and not even very good light verse'), is that it misses the primitive, farcical, even Dionysian element in his work that expresses an essential side of his personality that may even power the rest. Mr Taylor-Martin's struggle with Captain Webb ('the nonconformist industrial setting is fondly described') ignores the sheer thumping silliness ('The *gas* was on in the Institute, the *flare* was up in the *gym*') that is the whole intoxicating point.

Admittedly it is on the serious poems that an admirer's case must ultimately rest. But to class 'Hunter Trials' among 'jolly children's poems', or say that 'petulance rather than indignation' is the keynote of 'Group Life: Letchworth', suggests a dead spot in Mr Taylor-Martin's appreciation that allows him to call 'Lenten Thoughts of a High Anglican' 'exquisitely lyrical'. It makes him concentrate too exclusively on the top of Sir John's head. He is forgetting the horse-laugh.

Observer, 13 March 1983

The Powys Pantomime

There were six Powys brothers. Three of them – a schoolmaster, an architect and a farmer in Africa – were unexceptional sons of their clergyman father. The other three made up the most extraordinary family in English literature.

Different from the rest of mankind, they were also different from one another. Who would relate the haggard and hawk-faced John Cowper, barnstorming through an America of derby hats, cheap hotels and burlesque shows, with the reclusive Theodore (T. F.) in remote Dorset, pondering on God and darning his own stockings? They could also be different from themselves: compare Llewelyn the Ugandan sheep-farmer with Llewelyn the frail patient in a Swiss tuberculosis sanitarium. Yet their family feeling was intense to the point of absurdity.

They were, as the saying goes, gentlemen: somewhere in their ancestry was Sir Thomas Powys of Lilford, the poet William Cowper, even the family of John Donne. But they had no inclination to the gentlemanly professions, the Church, the Army, the Bar ('liars, murderers and thieves,' commented Theodore tranquilly). Forced to supplement their father's necessarily modest allowance (and the Reverend Charles Francis Powys sounds the most sympathetic of men), John Cowper lectured in girls' schools, Theodore tried to become a farmer, Llewelyn dabbled unhappily in temporary schoolmastering and private coaching.

Slowly, almost tortuously, they wound their ways towards writing. Theodore made his name in 1923 with *Black Bryony* and *The Left Leg*: he was 48. Llewelyn, who had followed John Cowper to America, produced *Ebony and Ivory* that year and *Black Laughter* the next: he was 39. By the time John Cowper began to publish his own gigantic novels at the end of the Twenties he was nearing 60, and overshadowed by Llewelyn in America and Theodore in England.

Review of Richard Perceval Graves, *The Brothers Powys*
(Routledge and Kegan Paul, 1983)

They were never successful writers, financially; on his death in 1923 (a crucial year for their fortunes) their father left them £3,000 each (a handsome sum in those days), but the rented apartment, the earth-closet cottage and the tiny village house remained their natural habitats. Were they good writers? Opinion fluctuated wildly. Theodore was taken up to some extent by *Scrutiny* in the Thirties, but commands little attention today; Llewelyn is traditionally thought of as the weakest of the three; John Cowper's reputation has risen steadily since his death in 1963, borne up by a forest of theses. To my mind Llewelyn is the most readable, Theodore the most moving; John Cowper, apart from his *Autobiography* and letters, I cannot get on with at all.

But the interlocking private worlds of their personalities, of which their books are so direct an expression, have persisted – have become, indeed, a formidable cult. Llewelyn was first responsible for this. His talent for self-dramatization ('Luluising,' the family called it) produced vivid pictures of the childhood they had shared, and of their contrasting characters, but his 'Skin for Skin' ('it is the *stuff*, no mistake,' wrote Arnold Bennett) was followed by John Cowper's *Autobiography* in 1934, and in 1936 Louis Wilkinson published an account of the whole family, leaning largely on their letters to him, called *Welsh Ambassadors*. The frankness of this annoyed the non-writing brothers, and Littleton countered with *The Joy of It*, but this simply served to ensure that their idiosyncrasies were firmly fixed in the public mind – more firmly, perhaps, than their books.

Mr Graves has devoted himself to assembling a coherent triple biography from the now-numerous printed sources, backed up by information gained from surviving friends and relatives, and a remarkable piece of craftsmanship it is. His account brings their natures into sharp relief: John Cowper, who could cope with life only by mythologizing it, yet lived to be 91; the eager sun-loving Llewelyn, from his middle twenties never quite out of death's shadow; and Theodore, staying put like a stone in the loneliest village he could find to write his archetypal allegories. He goes from one to the other not chapter by chapter but almost paragraph by paragraph, so that their comments on one another's doings can be reported.

For all that they were different, their rectory upbringing had brought them common problems. First, there was God. John

Cowper's answer was simple: he *became* God by creating a succession of increasingly fantastic worlds and a religion from a series of private rituals. Llewelyn was an uncompromising Rationalist-Press atheist, pitting the glory of life against more ghostly and problematic comforts, and travelling to the Holy Land to make sure there was nothing there. For Theodore, God was 'wold Jar' [Jehovah] or the white-haired Mr Weston, bringing fearful retribution to the wicked, yet Himself appearing as 'the only penitent' on the charge of making the world.

Then there was death. John Cowper hardly bothered about it; dangerously ill in hospital, he went on planning his next book. For Theodore it had a Gothic repulsion, yet beckoned as the end of all worldly vanity ('Who would wish to give another tongue to a woman, and another greedy belly to a man?'). But for Llewelyn the thought of extinction was unforgettable ('cold nights, cold years, cold centuries, alone in a cold elm-wood coffin'), while also heightening his awareness of physical existence and making the duty of self-fulfilment more compelling. He was the first to die, slowly and painfully, at 55; Theodore succumbed serenely at 78, while the nonagenarian John Cowper sang 'D'ye Ken John Peel?' on his last day on earth.

And finally there was sex. Nothing emerges more strongly from their lives and works than the sense of powerful sexual instinct refracted by character and convention. Llewelyn, as so often, was the most straightforward; intensely susceptible to women, he was torn between his natural desires and his 'Powys caution', in later years suffering anguished division of affection. His constant advocacy of sexual freedom recalls D. H. Lawrence (his junior by a year), yet there is no evidence that he ever read, for instance, 'Lady Chatterley's Lover', which he would surely have liked. John Cowper was very different. To him, sex was 'a world of intense absorption, a world of maniacal exclusiveness, of delirious exaction, of insane pursuit' – a world, in short, of auto-erotic fantasies fuelled by sadistic pornography, an obsession that lasted till he was 80. Theodore's writings are instinct with a comparable preoccupation with what Llewelyn called '*very young* girls' ('She be growing a big maid, and t'ain't proper for she to show so much,' etc.) who are raped and murdered, or have ambiguous relations with old men. Between them the brothers exhibit virtually the whole gamut of sexual feeling.

One would like to know more about this, for love and death were principal Powys subjects (Llewelyn's novel of that title is one of his best books, although Mr Graves does not think so), and all their experience of them would be relevant. What precisely did the aged John Cowper mean by 'in our big family of six boys and five girls we were all of us constantly making love to each other! The idea that such *incest* was wrong ... never entered our heads' (quoted elsewhere by Colin Wilson)? In his introduction Mr Graves admits that his book must be 'treated in some respects as a work in progress'; documents have not been withheld, but permission to quote has been refused. It seems a pity that a work of such authority should be confessedly incomplete. It also badly needs a family tree such as Belinda Humfrey supplied in her essential *Recollections of the Powys Brothers*.

What it demonstrates is the curious Powys *modernity*; Victorians by birth and upbringing, and often comically at a loss in the twentieth century, they were none the less harbingers of the great shift in morals that took place in it. To read them is to enter a world of fantasy, fable and fabrication; but it is a world where sudden stunning truths are told. Start with Llewelyn, who, according to Somerset Maugham, 'by living so long cheek by jowl with death alone of them learnt to be honest'. Start with *Skin for Skin*.

Observer, 27 March 1983

Bubble Reputation

To read a sequence of 135 reviews of Auden from *Poems* (1930) to the posthumous *Thank You, Fog* is a more exciting experience than the weighty sub-title would suggest. First and foremost, it is a blow-by-blow account of the rise and fall of a major and controversial reputation. This gives it the quality of a radio documentary; voice cuts across voice, eager contentions and sour scepticisms surface and submerge.

At times there is a conflict of evidence, as in a court of law: 'compared to Eliot, he has no dramatic imagination,' complains John Updike; 'he dramatizes everything he touches,' counters Louise Bogan. Towards the end, longer retrospections range as prosecution or defence. And behind it all, the tow-haired moled impassive face weathers slowly to that last incredible relief map, webbed with a thousand ironies. 'Auden', runs Dr Haffenden's first sentence, 'paid little heed to reviews of his own work.'

By and large, the story is what we know already: the blinding explosion, the fierce ten-year flare, the sudden American extinction, the protracted guttering twilight. What fascinates is watching it happen, at times a little differently from how we thought. Auden's success was immediate and genuine; he was not bunked up by similarly-inclined friends. 'This fellow is about the best poet that I have discovered in several years,' exclaimed Eliot uncharacteristically. 'The six odes and epilogue [in *The Orators*] justify his being named in the same breath as Lawrence,' asserted Graham Greene.

In fact his actual friends were far from uncritical: 'at present he suffers from an extreme sensitiveness to the impact of ideas combined with an incapacity to relate them to any scheme of values,' said Day-Lewis in 1934. 'Much of his later work seems to

Review of *W. H. Auden: The Critical Heritage*, edited by John Haffenden (Routledge and Kegan Paul, 1983)

show a drying up of inspiration,' said John Lehmann in 1936, a premature burial if there ever was one.

What did people think so good about him? They found him exciting, but the excitement was not entirely literary. 'The country is not going to the dogs after all,' exulted Naomi Mitchison over *Poems*, surely the most overwhelming tribute ever paid to a first collection; there was a good deal of *Zeitgeist* about Auden's popularity, as with the Beatles'. They liked his aggression, his disrespect (writer after writer approves the vulgar doggerel 'Beethameer, Beethameer, bully of Britain', even Leavis), his high spirits, his menacing obscurities. They seem to have been less appreciative of his seamless wide-angled vision ('The summer holds, upon its glittering lake/Lie Europe and the islands'), the resourcefulness that in a simple jobbing poem such as 'Night Mail' threw up image after effortless image ('In a farm she passes no one wakes/But a jug in a bedroom gently shakes') that are instinct with the cinema he was writing for.

A lot of space is taken up by Auden's forays into poetic drama, which seem in retrospect to have been a terrible waste of time and obscured the virtues of his real poems. Nobody thought the plays much good even at the time, except Harold Hobson who claimed that *The Dance of Death* was a literary innovation equal to Scott's historical novels; when Spender wrote that they were inferior to both Auden's poems and Isherwood's novels he had said it all. But they confirmed Auden's reputation as a left-wing propagandist, which worried Cyril Connolly: 'Literature is something which is just as good in ten years' time, propaganda is not,' he wrote of 'Spain'. The *Daily Worker* was all for Auden up to this point, but dropped him over *Journey to a War*.

The first American books show Auden being dropped more comprehensively by the whole English literary establishment. 'When a poet has the will to write poetry and poetry does not come,' began Herbert Read ominously in his review of *New Year Letter*, 'he has two alternatives before him: he can relapse into silence, or he can find a substitute for poetry.' 'He cannot resist being mysteriously impressive when it would be in the end more impressive to try to be clear,' ruled Desmond MacCarthy of *For the Time Being*. 'The loss, as revealed in these American poems,' even Spender lamented, 'is ... a growing inability to experience things in his poetry.'

Such views were prevalent through the decade; it was with *The Shield of Achilles* (1951) that the tide seemed to turn. By then Auden had been taken up by American critics, always kinder to flatulent abstractions than their British counterparts. 'Don't let anyone tell you that your recent work isn't your best,' Edmund Wilson assured him, and Louise Bogan gave the 1945 *Collected Poems* what Auden himself called 'a swell write-up' in the *New Yorker*; in this book the poems were arranged in alphabetical order of first lines to conceal chronological decline, and given silly titles. But there were vigilantes: John Whitehead, in one of the most valuable pieces in the book, reports the findings of J. W. Beach on Auden's excisions, abridgements and alterations ('The question of "dishonesty" must inevitably arise').

The last contributions grow more charitable. Certainly Auden became less unreadable as his subject-matter reverted from the literary-mythological stew to his own feelings and circumstances, and this was met with increased benevolence from reviewers. 'Are these recent poems as good as the ones he wrote in the 1930s?' asks C. B. Cox. 'Perhaps not, but does it matter?' Clive James provides a paradoxical encomium: 'It has been a movement away from excitement and towards satisfaction ... [*Epistle to a Godson*] is flat champagne, but it is still champagne.' In the closing pages, Irving Ehrenpreis insists that 'It was by a profound act of imagination that he brought the terrible events of four decades into his moral and psychological schemes. It was through high art that he mastered verse forms of pyrotechnic variety and matched them to his meanings.'

Dr Haffenden's long introduction supplies many fascinating sidelights. Christopher Isherwood went to the first night of *The Dance of Death* with Unity Mitford. W. B. Yeats thought the figure on the summit of F6 ought to be Britannia. It does not, however, offer to summarize what the multiple chorus he has so skilfully orchestrated amounts to. I should say that the critical heritage, at least as presented here, was fairly reliable. Auden had a lot of praise when he was young, and deserved it, but it was sometimes for the wrong things. After 1940 he declined badly, and most reviewers said so. No wonder he didn't bother about them.

Observer, 11 September 1983

Point of No Return

Man's most remarkable talent is for ignoring death. For once the certainty of permanent extinction is realized, only a more immediate calamity can dislodge it from the mind, and then only temporarily. Yet on all sides people are booking foreign holidays, applying for permission to build sun-parlours, joining the Social Democratic Party. Truly, as Anatole France said, ignorance – in the sense of ignoring – is the necessary condition of life itself.

All the same, coming to terms with death has taken up a good deal of our time. Primarily in the form of religion: for if what distinguishes religion from ethics is the miraculous, the only miracle worth talking about is immortality. But there is also literature, where death is still the only possible end to a story, except marriage. Unfortunately, nothing is quite real in literature, not even death; either we are left feeling that in some indefinable way it is *all right*, or that the characters will get up unharmed and advance bowing to the footlights. This is not how death affects us in reality.

In this most audacious of Oxford anthologies, Dr Enright surveys what has been said on this colossal subject. In his introduction he touches on the theory that death has replaced sex as the forbidden topic, and is inclined to scout it; if death is not talked about, he says, it is because it is not worth talking about, or because life 'being so much shorter deserves to be given priority.' His method is to divide and conquer, grouping his material under fourteen headings with titles such as 'Suicide', 'Children', 'Revenants', and so on. This is not to dodge the issue: by far the longest section is 'The Hour of Death' (and the next longest 'Hereafters'), but it is noticeable how the pressure eases once attention shifts from them. Only very few people commit suicide, after all; most children grow up. The inescapability of death retreats.

Review of *The Oxford Book of Death*, chosen and edited by D. J. Enright (Oxford University Press, 1983)

Within these groupings, the diversity of reference is staggering. Ecclesiastes, Pascal, and Claudio in *Measure for Measure* jostle with Gavin Ewart, George Orwell and Flann O'Brien, and are interleaved with Japanese newspapers, letters to *The Times* about the price of coffins, and an open letter from a dying student nurse to her fellow nurses appealing for more sympathy ('all I want to know is that there will be someone to hold my hand when I need it'). In time we range from 2000 BC to Woody Allen ('I'm not afraid to die. I just don't want to be there when it happens'), in space from Pueblo Indians to Virginia Woolf, in mood from Sylvia Plath to Justice Shallow. Like all good anthologies, it seems less like a commissioned job than the work of a lifetime. How unexpected is the passage about African elephants:

> In a case where an animal is mortally wounded and cannot rise, the other members of the herd circle it disconsolately several times, and if it is still motionless they come to an uncertain halt. They then face outwards, their trunks hanging limply to the ground. After a while they may prod and circle again, and then again stand facing outward.

How serendipitous the remark from *Dr Who* ('Who was it said the living are the dead on holiday?'), how poignantly precise J. C. Hall's poem 'Twelve Minutes', ending

> We say the last amen.
> A button's pressed, and then
>
> To canned funeral strains
> His dear dead remains,
>
> Eighty-four years gone by,
> Sink with a whirring sigh.
>
> I tip and say goodbye.

There is nothing didactic in Enright's approach: he does not tell us what to think or feel. Nevertheless, several recognizable attitudes emerge from his chorus of voices. First, of course, death isn't going to happen ('One short sleep past, we wake eternally'). Or, if it does happen, it is by definition something we needn't worry about ('so long as we exist, death is not with us; but when death comes, then we do not exist'). Or, if it does happen, it is jolly nice and comfortable ('in a sleep deeper and calmer than that of infancy, wrapped in the finest and softest dust'). Or, finally, life would be very dull without death ('it is immeasurably heightened'), to me a view that fails to grip even more conspicuously than the others. It was thoroughly torpedoed by Kingsley Amis in 'Lovely' ('Look thy last on all things lovely/Every hour, an old shag said'), a poem I am sorry not to see included.

What might with some justice be called the majority view, however – death is the end of everything, and thinking about it gives us a pain in the bowels – is poorly represented. This is no doubt due to Dr Enright's tact as an anthologist. Unlike the Fat Boy, he doesn't want to make our flesh creep; slide after slide is whisked deftly away, with no chance to make a lasting impression. Nervous people need not be afraid of his pages. All the same, it may be wondered who will buy them. The volume hardly qualifies for the guest room, much less as a birthday or Christmas present. Whoever dreamed it up ('The Oxford Book of *Death!* How *marvellous!*') may have commercially miscalculated.

If so, serve them right. For in the last analysis the intrusion of death into our lives is so ruthless, so irreversible, so rarely unaccompanied by pain, terror and remorse, that to 'anthologize' it, however calmly, quizzically and compassionately, seems at best irrelevant, at worst an error of taste. 'Death and the sun are not to be looked at steadily,' says La Rochefoucauld, and by their nature anthologies do not look steadily, nor do they explain or console: they entertain. And death is not entertaining. The chapter on 'Care of the Dying' in any nursing manual makes this point more clearly.

Observer, 24 April 1983

Inner Horizons

This is a lop-sided book. The first section is an account (126 pages) of Connolly's life up to 1930, when he was 27. The second is Connolly's journal from 1928 to 1937 (148 pages). Finally there is a section 'Epilogue' which bundles up into 20 pages the rest of his life till his death in 1974. In other words, Mr Pryce-Jones spends nine-tenths of his space telling us what for the most part we either know already from *Enemies of Promise* or the Blakiston letters, or what Connolly is about to tell us, and very little on the Forties, Fifties and Sixties, which would have been comparatively fresh ground. Moreover, since Mr Pryce-Jones first met Connolly in 1953 when he was still at school, one jibs a little at the word 'memoir', which has overtones of personal knowledge, but perhaps it can be justified by his access to the papers held by Connolly's widow and in the University of Tulsa and Huntington libraries.

The journal material is not altogether new. Mr Pryce-Jones points out that part of it was reproduced ('clipped and manicured'), as 'One of my Londons' in *Previous Convictions* (1963), and another part as 'Conversations in Berlin' in *The Condemned Playground* (1945). Even more appeared in the latter book as 'England Not My England', including passages dated 1927 from another journal altogether. What is printed here for the first time, therefore, might be called all the author did not wish to preserve. This is unpromising, but in fact nearly every page is interesting. Connolly was a good journal-writer; self-absorbed, as one has to be, but ready to record other people's jokes, incidents, weather and scenery. And the journal picks up his life at an interesting point. He is beginning to notice women, and to try to write.

Up till then, thanks to Eton, the friendship of Maurice Bowra and the patronage of Logan Pearsall Smith, his emotions had expressed themselves in protracted romantic attachments to male friends

Review of David Pryce-Jones, *Cyril Connolly: Journal and Memoir* (Collins, 1983)

such as Robert Longden and Noel Blakiston. Now he is wondering 'if I am likely to be attractive to women and what one should do to please them'. There were 'Nancy whom I hate, Peggy who is a bore, Rachel whose shares go neither up nor down, Alex whom I have forgotten altogether ... and now Racy, divinely English, unawakened, staid'. This was a serious attachment, at least on his side, but he seems to have been politely warned off by her parents (her father was the formidable Sir William Fisher) with much consequent anguish. Then he met the eighteen-year-old American art student Jean Blakewell in Paris in 1928, and married her in 1930. She was potentially very rich, which was just as well since the Wall Street crash dried up Logan Pearsall Smith's allowance of £8 a week (this continued after Connolly had stopped working for him).

Many of the journal pages are concerned with this relation, but oddly enough they lack resonance. When he met her, Jean Blakewell was pregnant and posing as a lesbian; a subsequent abortion damaged her health and led ultimately to sterility. They travelled extensively with their pet ferrets, then settled in King's Road, where they entertained a good deal and Connolly wrote *Enemies of Promise*. Maddeningly, nothing is said about *The Rock Pool* except for its rejection by Fabers in what must be 1934 (the paucity of dates in the journal is also maddening). Slowly the marriage faded. Even in 1930, however, a long paragraph provoked by seeing in *The Times* the engagements of both Racy and Noel Blakiston ends with the reflection that he has escaped the heart-breaking distress they would have caused him in the past by skipping, like a bull-fighter, 'behind the slim partition – in this case Jean —'. To be someone's slim partition is not flattering. Soon Connolly was listing the ingredients for a successful marriage, with the implication that his did not contain them ('Wife must try to follow husband in his spiritual peregrinations'). In the end (1945) she was writing what are arguably the most moving sentences in the book:

> And don't please have fevers or be so ill. Sleep well and dream pleasures. You are a great successful man now. Not for you a middle-aged, poorish American expatriate on-the-town girl, romantic, insufferable. You are well out of it.

Despite her third sentence, Connolly's writing was not really much consolation. His hilarious novel *The Rock Pool* was not published in England till 1947 because of its matter-of-fact acceptance of sexual inversion ('Oh, he sticks around with her because she's got a very attractive husband'); *Enemies of Promise* (1938), dedicated with some irony to Logan Pearsall Smith, is a rich and multifaceted study of modern literature, of literary failure, of Connolly's failure, of Connolly himself (Mr Pryce-Jones calls it, rather curiously, 'one of the case-books of the century' dealing with loss of will-power and failure of nerve among the English), but it is hard to think of anyone reading it who is neither a writer nor an Old Etonian. *The Unquiet Grave* (1944), though respectfully received, staggered alarmingly between the pretentious and the ludicrous ('The object of Loving is to end Love', etc.). 'His books,' as Mr Pryce-Jones says,

> were offered as evidence of how much more he might have done, ought to have done. Guilt was one thing, though, and blame another. Circumstances had conspired against him. Nobody could argue the if-only case more plausibly. If only he had been born in another age he might have been an elegiac Roman poet, a classical English wit and essayist, a French *philosophe* or *poète maudit* – if only he had inherited an estate and a fortune to free him from drudgery – if only he were handsomer, lived elsewhere . . .

It could be argued that Connolly, at least in his younger days, never stayed long enough in one place to write anything. Travelling he defined, characteristically, as 'a search for a home'; in the first half of 1929, for instance, he visited, among other places, Paris, Valencia, Granada, Tangier, Gibraltar, Nice, Marseilles, Berlin and Paris again. The flesh creeps. He seems to have been impelled by an almost Lawrentian dislike for England and the English: 'Newspaper-fed ignorance, wistful cannon-fodder, larvae, they trail round whining out their days' ration of bromides as if cringing from somebody who was going to hit them' – someone should study this attitude, so common between the wars, and try to explain it.

But his journal is never coherent autobiography or reasoned advocacy; its pleasure is its anecdotes, its *aperçus*, its sheer irrelevant farce. Did Berenson think he missed anything by not going to the theatre? 'As much as by not seeing a blubber fight in Alaska.' 'The essence of country life is waiting for the post . . . Love in a cottage, agony in the garden.'

> Logan said of Hardy's second wife that she had tried first to get off with George Moore – or so he said. 'George Moore would have said that of the Virgin Mary,' said B.B., 'if he's ever heard of her.'

Harold Nicolson is reported as saying that when Gladstone was warned that a certain Canon of Windsor whom he was proposing to make a bishop was homosexual, he replied:

> I have learnt that the pagan qualities to which you refer are frequently possessed by men with the greatest erudition, the most absolute integrity and the deepest religious convictions.

Connolly's father, Major Matthew Connolly, thought we should give Germany her colonies back ('Except Tanganyka. That's the only one that's worth anything') and was impatient with his grandfather:

> Spent £50,000 on restoring Bath Abbey. The damned old fool. I hate him. I hate him. When you realise what we might have had.

Connolly's admiration for *Ulysses* breaks through frequently ('Moment of wild white city, sea city, of Margate, the wind streaming'), and a meeting with Joyce in 1930 is recorded (a footnote says he was 42, but Joyce was born in 1882):

> He wore a white cricketing blazer and blue trousers and at once began to ask me about my family, very very interested in Clontarf – he said he had mentioned Brian Boru's sword in the last bit of his book, and that it belonged to the Vernons. 'I am afraid I am more interested in little things like that,' he said, 'than in the problems of the solar system.'

His example, both reproachful and monitory, of the great writer living in silence, exile and cunning, was never far from Connolly's mind: 'O to be more like Daedalus and less like Bloom!' But,

> At Eton with Orwell, at Oxford with Waugh,
> He was nobody afterwards and nothing before.

Of course, the depiction of himself as some sort of royal failure, as Mr Pryce-Jones puts it, was largely bunk. He spent most of his life doing what he wanted. He found a rich patron, a rich wife, a rich backer (Peter Watson). The nearest he got to work was writing literary journalism. He liked travelling, and did a lot of it. He liked women, and had a lot of them. He liked celebrated and influential people; his diary is full of lists of their names. First as editor of *Horizon*, then as principal reviewer on the *Sunday Times*, he had literary authority. It is greatly to be doubted if he would have changed his life for anyone else's.

Above all, as a writer he was in a different league from the MacCarthys and Nicolsons. He was a master of the piercing pronouncement: anyone doubting this should read the 58 entries from his works in *The Penguin Dictionary of Modern Quotations* (Waugh has 57). His sense of the blackly depressing coupled with his sense of the comic make him a strangely consoling companion; I cannot think of any author I find more sympathetic while being indifferent or hostile to most of his interests. For years I carried *The Rock Pool* with me whenever I had anything unpleasant to face, such as an interview for a job; provincial hotel bedrooms were made less bleak by sentences such as 'He escaped three hundred francs to the bad, the equivalent of two women and an indecent cinema.' Even today there is comfort to be gained from 'If you have to be lumped, you don't need to be liked' or 'There are about forty-nine masochists to every sadist.' Misery and the ridiculous are constant human preoccupations; awareness of them, rather than any loftier cultural or intellectual ingredient, is what preserves his work.

Spectator, 9 July 1983

On Familiar Ground

Perhaps because I've never been there, I think of America as an old-fashioned place where you salute the flag, stand up when a lady comes in, and call your father Sir. This may resemble the Muscovite conviction that London is perpetually enveloped in thick fog and the surrounding countryside full of fox-hunters and starving peasantry, but equally I suspect there is an awful lot of historical coexistence in America, in the sense that the past takes a long while to be over. And here is Joseph Epstein writing a book of essays to prove it.

I say that because in England the essay, as a literary form, is pretty well extinct. It belonged to an age when reading – reading almost anything – was the principal entertainment of the educated class; this called for a plethora of dailies, weeklies, monthlies and quarterlies, all having to be filled. And what filled them, a lot of the time, was essays – not critical essays, or polemical essays, but what Mr Epstein calls *familiar* essays: on not going to the movies any more, on forgetfulness, on books and their many properties, on letters one gets and the letters one would like to get. Of course we have Mr Levin and Mr Hattersley, but I doubt if they are *pure* essayists; Mr Levin is always liable to tell us what he thinks, and Mr Hattersley who he is. Cyril Connolly fathered the genre on Addison, and was rather dismissive about him: 'He was the apologist for the New Bourgeoisie who writes playfully and apologetically about nothing, casting a smoke screen over its activities to make it seem harmless, genial and sensitive in its non-acquisitive moments.' The typical opening was something like 'If it be a sin to be half in love with the old days, then I must aver . . .'

On the face of it, Epstein is nothing like this. Watching a double feature of *Straw Dogs* and *The Wild Ones* 'has all the allure of riding a whiplash roller coaster after having been in a sphaghetti-eating

Review of Joseph Epstein, *The Middle of My Tether* (W. W. Norton)

contest'; the task of banishing clichés from our thought and language 'resembles cleaning out the Augean stables without removing the horses'. He quotes a bewildering range of authors, including Amis, Mencken and James Agate. But underneath there are remarkable similarities. He tells us about his love of, nay mania for, fountain pens ('meanwhile I am building up quite a nice arsenal . . . I have the little dears on my desk before me. Let me take an inventory . . .') He is addicted to juggling ('No self-improvement, no end other than itself, sheer play, exquisitely useless'). He ruminates on faces ('I have been told by different people at different times that I resemble . . . the actors Sal Mineo, Russ Tamblyn and Kent Barry, the scholar Walter Kaufmann, the assassin Lee Harvey Oswald, and a now-deceased Yorkshire terrier called Max'). This is well in the Addisonian line of succession that Connolly saw petering out in *Punch* and the professional humorists.

Epstein is a great deal more sophisticated than they were, and a great deal more readable. His subjects are tossed up, turned round, stuck with quotations, abandoned and returned to, playfully inverted, and finally set back on their feet, as is the reader, a little breathless but quite unharmed. But it is essentially a merry-go-round, not a view to a death.

Why has it started up again in America? Can there still be legions of prairie-surrounded televisionless, with nothing to do in the long evenings but read under the oil-lamp by a hot stove? Perhaps it hasn't. The small print tells us that these pieces first appeared in an amiable quarterly named *The American Scholar* (under the pseudonym, if my memory serves me, of Aristides). Mr Epstein is editor of *The American Scholar*. The situation would seem to be one of supply rather than demand.

Times Literary Supplement, 13 January 1984

Lost Content

There was an element of overkill in Housman. When he put you down ('you have confused two utterly different stories, and missed the point of both'), you stayed down. Having failed Greats in 1881, he became a professor of Latin in 1892. A book of short poems published at his own expense was, two decades later, selling 16,000 copies a year. Housman never did things by halves.

The same was true of his emotional life. Anyone who thinks he has loved more than one person has simply never really loved at all, as he said late in life, and this summarized his own experience. Whether his affection for his fellow-undergraduate Moses Jackson (they shared rooms, along with Alfred Pollard, in their final year) brought about his calamitous schools result is a matter for conjecture, but it was unquestionably the key to his poetry, and to some extent to his career.

Degreeless, he followed Moses Jackson into the Patent Office and lodged with him and his brother Adalbert; when Moses took up an appointment in India, and later married, Housman was left with the knowledge that his love was not only unrequited but criminal. This made no difference. In 1922, when he heard that Jackson was dying in Canada, he wrote 57 pages of verses in less than a fortnight; they formed the basis of *Last Poems*, a copy of which reached Jackson before his death.

Housman's life was a curious mixture of utter domination by circumstances and utter domination of them, the latter seeming a desperate rearguard action against the former. It is certainly quite at odds with the image of him as 'a prim, old-maidish, rather second-rate, rather tired, rather querulous person' (the words are A. C. Benson's); he effected the transition from the Patent Office to the Chair of Latin at University College London by writing 25 scholarly papers in ten years, and his later work earned him the

Review of Norman Page, *A. E. Housman: A Critical Biography* (Macmillan, 1983)

offer of several honorary degrees and the Order of Merit, all of which he refused. Yet temperamentally he seems to have been always on the defensive, as only one who knows his own powerlessness in the face of emotion can be.

This is the second life of Housman to be published within five years; R. P. Graves's 1979 study was longer, more detailed and more speculative (Professor Page is edgy about books that are 'dropsical with fact'), but the present work brings out Housman's academic significance – how, as an undergraduate, he found himself totally opposed to Jowett's emphasis on philosophy and literary criticism as distinct from the proper establishment of texts, and how, when a scholar himself, he insisted on an eclectic approach to each problem rather than allegiance to a particular manuscript or method. Page enables the layman to understand Housman's passionate advocacy of 'moral integrity and intellectual vigilance' in classical studies, even if such language seems rather comically hyperbolic.

He is less inclined than Graves to accept Laurence Housman's assertion that his brother had a physical relation with Adalbert Jackson, and is sceptical of Graves's interpretation of the 'small document in Housman's handwriting' as a list of male prostitutes and their charges. But he underlines Laurence's reference to Housman's disappearance for a week in 1885 from the London lodgings he shared with the Jacksons, pointing out that this was the year when the Labouchère Amendment made all homosexual acts between males illegal, and he includes the Wilde case among the factors that produced the 'continuous excitement' of 1895 and *A Shropshire Lad*, the others being Moses's emigration, Adalbert's death, and the death of his own father. The French companion ('a nice young man, not much educated') is put forward as a more stable, though perhaps equally illicit, partner in Housman's foreign holidays.

Page has disinterred a number of references to Housman from A. C. Benson's diaries. Some of them are friendlier than others ('both genial and good-humoured when one knows him'), but the basic charge, oddly enough, is 'commonness':

> Housman is a common little soul, who thinks that the don-epicure is a gentlemanly thing – it is not; it's the worst development of snobbish greediness.

'As he got easier he got *vulgar*,' runs another comment, and ten years later Benson cannot abide Housman's French jokes ('not funny, only abominable'). The robustly tough-minded Housman clearly grated on the gentler nerves of the Master of Magdalene.

Consideration of Housman as a poet is left to the final chapter, which provides a dying fall since Page does not make much of him. He examines the seductive notion that *A Shropshire Lad* conceals a story, but rejects it, while admitting that there are internal series of poems. He spends some time demonstrating that the first poem in that book, '1887', is ironical in its conclusion 'And God will save the Queen', thus echoing Frank Harris's 'Yes, God will save her, the old bitch, until the many refuse to be fooled any longer', but omitting Housman's indignant protestation that this was an utter misreading (the story is in Hugh Kingsmill's Life of Harris). Page's final verdict ('his output is small, and the best of it much smaller') ignores Housman's unique and plangent enchantment of generations of readers, the narrow yet unforgettable metaphor he made of his own life.

Observer, 29 January 1984

Bridey and Basil

The journalism of a major writer can be revealing. It shows his talent encountering the world outside his own imagination; we learn what he is prepared to write about, and what other people hope he will write about. And the passage of years can change or confirm these things.

This substantial collection presents Evelyn Waugh as a case in point. On the face of it, no one was less like old Waugh than young Waugh, shamelessly soliciting the most trivial of newspaper assignments ('fix up anything that will earn me anything') and pandering to such concepts as the Younger Generation and Modern Marriage as keenly as Beverley Nichols or his own Mr Chatterbox. Young Waugh, according to his editor Mr Gallagher, was 'hypersensitive to new fads and fashions'. But was old Waugh so very different? At no time did he see anything wrong or even distasteful in writing for money; 'the important point for me is the tax-free expenses,' he emphasized when seeking a commission about St Francis of Assisi. And he was into granny glasses long before John Lennon.

If the figure of Mr Chatterbox lurks behind Waugh's Mayfair pieces, it is the *louche* shadow of Basil Seal that falls across the Thirties. Basil is remembered as a rake, but he was also a traveller and a bore about politics ('fundamentally it is an issue between the Arabs and the christianized Sakuyu'). Waugh was a dedicated traveller as well; for many years before the war he had no home at all. At first sight this seems out of character. He did not particularly like foreigners, nor the dirt and dishonesty inseparable from the remote places that he went to, but all the same he went. In later years he pretended everyone had done likewise, but as early as 1933 he was explaining his motives in the *Daily Mail*; they were to get away from 'friends', to experience danger, to study the

Review of *The Essays, Articles and Reviews of Evelyn Waugh*, edited by Donat Gallagher (Methuen, 1983)

inhabitants of strange places, and to relish the fascination of those places. 'The truth is that I am deeply interested in the jungle and only casually interested in Mayfair, and one has to write about what interests one.'

And preferably one has to be paid for it, which is why Waugh's best-known journeys were undertaken as special correspondent for *The Times* in 1930 to the coronation of Haile Selassie and for the *Daily Mail* in 1935 to the Italo-Abyssinian war. He sustained each role conscientiously, giving *Mail* readers 'sodden and shivering schoolchildren' and *The Times* a burst of Basil Seal at his best ('So far as Ethiopia can be said to have a constitution, the succession is regulated by royal proclamation, and there has rarely been a case of undisputed succession in recent Ethiopian history'). But he annoyed people by supporting Mussolini ('Abyssinian Realities: We Can Applaud Italy'), pointing out that 'throughout the greater part of the country the Abyssinians are just as much foreigners as the Italians.' Bernard Shaw took the same view.

Such pronouncements foreshadow the third of the spirits presiding over Waugh's journalism: Lord Brideshead, or at least that aspect of Bridey that had to turn ideas round till they fitted in for him, although by then they were upside down to everyone else (Waugh cut out this comment in the revised edition). The element of paradox in modern Catholic apologists may spring from having to believe, as the world sees it, six impossible things before breakfast, but there was nothing Waugh liked better than to argue the universally execrated. His article on the Wilberforce Centenary in 1933 concluded that Emancipation had been a mistake: 'the descendants of the Negro slaves in the British Empire are a thriftless and dissolute lot'. Hemingway was a good writer because he made left-wingers feel small, which was why they attacked *Across the River and Into the Trees*. 'Liberty and Equality are irreconcilable conceptions ... The organic life of society should be a continuous process of evolving an aristocracy.' At first a champion of the Roman Catholic Church, he became its critic. Editors thought of him, as Mr Gallagher puts it, as a writer who by brilliance and nerve could make snobbery and prejudice compellingly readable. They commissioned 'outrageous' articles, then got cold feet, paying but not printing.

The literary pieces are oddly unsatisfying – oddly, because Waugh might have been expected to see and communicate literary virtues with irresistible force. Many have a slightly routine air, being celebrations of Catholics or chums. When dealing with a writer who is neither (such as Hemingway) his conclusions seem contrived. He writes enthusiastically of Maugham ('his new novel is his best ... inimitable artistry'), but is talking about *Christmas Holiday*. His account of Wodehouse, whom he adores, makes the Drones' Club sound like *The Immortal Hour* ('their language has never been heard on human lips. Their desperate, transitory, romantic passions are unconnected with the hope or fear of procreation').

Mr Gallagher's excellent editing (bar a misquotation on page 298 that Waugh was 'so popular as to be unemployable as an officer': the word is *unpopular*) reminds us that the visual arts were Waugh's first love, and he was always ready to review books on calligraphy, Victorian furniture or interior decoration. His most relaxed pages evoke life just before 1914 ('Maids still sat up yawning and gossiping to drive back with their mistresses from parties') and the elegancies of Georgian architecture ('A lovely house where an aged colonel plays wireless music to an obese retriever'). Indeed, there was a streak of Betjeman in Waugh; their grumbles about such things as London's thoroughfares are almost indistinguishable ('Vast ashtrays for the stubs of a million typists').

But although Waugh's journalism is highly readable and revelatory, it entirely lacks the hilarity of his novels. His manner is four-square and frowning, his style hammer-hard; here and there facetiousness and irony flicker, but I can recall only one laugh in over 600 pages (from a Swedish lady interviewer: 'Mr Wog, you are a great satyr' – 'I assure you not'). Its virtues are the virtues of Waugh himself, and to some extent the vices too: literate, serious, combative, loyal to the point of prejudice, deliberately provocative. A preliminary page bears a quotation from Swift: 'Some people take more care to hide their wisdom than their folly', but the implication is unfair. What these pages hide, and what Waugh's plethoric persona hid, is the enchanting fancy that produced Captain Grimes and the Connollies and dinner with the Laird of Mugg. For this all is forgiven.

Observer, 5 February 1984

David Lodge's Period Piece

Small World is a hymn to the academic conference, more particularly the overseas academic conference, and while we begin with one such at the University of Rummidge ('They had glumly unpacked their suitcases in study-bedrooms whose cracked and pitted walls retained, in a pattern of rectangular fade marks, the traces of posters hastily removed'), the breadth of modern scholarship is soon defined:

> 'Right. As long as you have access to a telephone, a Xerox machine, and a conference grant fund, you're OK, you're plugged into the only university that really matters – the global campus. A young man in a hurry can see the world by conference-hopping.'

The speaker is Morris Zapp, touching down at Rummidge to proclaim 'Every decoding is another encoding'; we remember him from *Changing Places*, along with Philip Swallow (now into Hazlitt), Howard Ringbaum and maybe one or two others – to be honest, Lodge's characters are not especially memorable. The principal newcomer is Persse McGarrigle, an innocent from Limerick, who is immediately overwhelmed by the ravishing Angelica ('A. L. Pabst', as her badge primly announces). But these drab confines are soon transcended to admit the cosmopolitan host of Rodney Wainwright of North Queensland (who is struggling to finish a lecture on criticism), Fulvia Morgana of Padua, Siegfried von Turpitz of Baden-Baden, Michel Tardieu of the Sorbonne, Ronald Frobisher (a middle-aged Angry Young Man with a writer's block caused by having his novels computerized), Akira Sakazaki of Tokyo, who is translating Frobisher's novels ('Sweet fanny adams. Who is she?'), and finally Arthur Kingfisher ('the only man in academic history to have occupied two chairs simultaneously in different continents'). He, as chief assessor for the new UNESCO Chair of Literary

Review of David Lodge, *Small World* (Secker and Warburg, 1984)

Criticism (£100,000 a year and no duties except discretionary attendances at conferences), holds their fates in his hands.

So the action whirls away to Milan, to Ankara, to Amsterdam, to Lausanne, and finally to the three-ring MLA conference in New York. Persse searches vainly for the elusive Angelica, who seems to exist alternately as a heavyweight research student and a club stripper; Swallow meets a British Council wife whom he once slept with but has since believed killed in an air crash; Wainwright's unfinished lecture, when delivered, is abandoned at a false alarm of an epidemic; Zapp is snatched by Italian terrorists who try to shake down his feminist ex-wife for half-a-million dollars ('How much do I have to pay to make you keep him?'). It is all fast-moving and fairly funny, some of it in the historic present favoured by writers in this genre, and its many themes are resolved with increasing improbability in the manner of W. S. Gilbert or *The Importance of Being Earnest*.

But the 'romance' of the sub-title ('An Academic Romance') is not the literary convention Angelica is studying, nor even what Persse feels for her, but the author's sheer exultant delight in the whole academic conference racket itself. 'WheeeeEEEE!' Part IV begins (only rather more extendedly, an imitation of a jet-plane preparing for take-off):

> The whole academic world seems to be on the move. Half the passengers on transatlantic flights these days are university teachers ... it's a way of converting work into play, combining professionalism with tourism, and all at someone else's expense. Write a paper and see the world! I'm Jane Austen – fly me! Or Shakespeare, or T. S. Eliot, or Hazlitt. All tickets to ride, to ride the jumbo jets. Wheeeee!

To know the Greek for bus-stop, the Polish for scrambled eggs, to be able to compare Pan Am, Qantas, Swissair, El Al – this is the true joy of learning, zested of course with the beer cellars, twisting in discothèques, nude midnight bathing ('Nobody pays to get laid at a Conference') that make up the rediscovery of a youth thought to have been sacrificed to study. And it is all so easy: all you need to do is write one good book, on the strength of which you can get a grant to write a second; this brings promotion, when you can devise your own courses so that teaching is a way of doing research for your third:

> This productivity made you eligible for tenure, more generous and prestigious research grants, more relief from routine teaching and administration. In theory, it was possible to wind up being full professor while doing nothing except be permanently absent on some kind of sabbatical grant or fellowship.

Yes, it is fairly funny, but only fairly. Some twenty years ago I fancifully proposed that English society has always included a kind of sleeping-bag for those members of the educated middle class who didn't want to work; first it was the monasteries, then the Court, then the established Church and the Civil Service, and now the universities. These shifts were occasioned by the progressive reform or abolition of each refuge as it was detected. This, like the campus novel, seemed funny at the time, but with the present incipient demolition of our universities both might be said to have been overtaken by events. While granting Professor Lodge, and Professor Bradbury for that matter, their hilarious comedy, literate wit and satiric perceptions, could it be that we are approaching a time when it would be refreshing to have a novel about a lecturer trying to teach his students rather than ogling their breasts, and bringing off a research project that was some use to someone rather than freeloading at subsidized exotic jamborees? Or is the campus novel (together, of course, with what we read in the newspapers about students) really all there is to be said?

Listener, 29 March 1984

Lover-Shadows in the Flesh

H. G. Wells was a man of enormous energy. In 1940 he undertook a lecture tour of America, flying some 24,000 miles to present the British cause; he noted amusedly that his agent had arranged for 'accommodating young ladies' to appear wherever he went. He was then seventy-four.

For the energy carried with it a powerful sexual appetite. Wells seems always to have acted on Wilde's dictum that the way to behave to a woman is to make love to her if she is pretty, and to someone else if she is plain. He threw himself at them ('with an increasing confidence of method'), and they threw themselves at him. He saw nothing unusual in this. 'To make love periodically, with some grace and pride and freshness, seems to be, for most of us, a necessary condition to efficient working', was his retrospective conclusion after a lifetime diversified and even disorganized by affairs outside marriage. For anyone under the impression that sexual intercourse began with Carnaby Street, *H. G. Wells in Love* will be a considerable revelation.

It is tempting to write Wells down, or even off, in this respect as a man for whom such exercise was a constant physical need, accompanied by no special spiritual or emotional commitment, but Wells did not see himself like this. 'I was never a great amorist,' he maintains, adding, 'though I have loved several people very deeply.' He regarded his incessant love-making as 'the restless dangerous unsatisfying search for temporary assuagement of the underlying desire for the Lover-Shadow' (his own odd term for the imaginary someone who will fulfil his longings, both sexual and social), at the same time being rather dismissive about 'incidental infidelities' and more so about 'Venus Meretrix'. In this he resembles a man who, while insisting that he must have only the best butter, is frequently found settling for margarine or even

Review of *H. G. Wells in Love*, edited by G. P. Wells (Faber and Faber, 1984) and Anthony West, *H. G. Wells: Aspects of a Life* (Hutchinson, 1984)

lard. At a loose end in Washington in 1906, after lunching with Theodore Roosevelt, he takes a cab, not to a museum, art gallery or bookshop, but to a brothel. His experience there is tender and memorable, which is why he mentions the incident; if it hadn't been, it would presumably have stayed unrecorded.

Whatever the nature and motivation of his womanizing, it existed by courtesy of his wife's tolerance. When Amy Catherine (whom Wells called Jane, an odd parallel with the habit of giving servants 'house' names rather than using their own) had borne their first son, Wells went off on a bicycle trip for two months without saying why or where he was going. When at last he was findable, Jane Wells wrote to him, not to give him the telling-off of his life, but to say that she was sorry to have driven him away by being over-possessive, and that he would always be free to come and go as he pleased. From then on, Wells had it made, as he sets out in the section 'Modus Vivendi' in *Experiment in Autobiography*. A loving and faithful wife and mother, a capable housekeeper and hostess, Jane shared Wells's enthusiasm for amateur theatricals as well as being something of a writer herself. 'She stuck to me so sturdily that in the end I stuck to myself,' he says rather comically, but in his fashion he stuck to her in return. There was never any question of his leaving her.

The main section of *H. G. Wells in Love* is a document written by Wells in 1934, as a *Postscript* to his autobiography. He was insistent that it should be published, if at all, 'not by itself but bound up with the rest'. From time to time he added to it, up to 1942; it remained in typescript simply because people it mentioned were still alive. The narrative is in many ways a strange one. After an initial windy section 'On Loves and the Lover-Shadow', and an account of a few early exploits (Dorothy Richardson 'was most interestingly hairy on her body'), it develops into a detailed exemplification of Cyril Connolly's remark that the punishment of continual philandering resides in the successes even more than in the failures.

There was Amber Reeves ('Give me a child!'), who had to be set up at Le Touquet and whose father made a fearful fuss. Still pregnant by Wells, she married Rivers Blanco White, then refused to let him touch her, expecting to carry on with Wells as usual ('I will not detail here ... the tensions and exasperations of everyone concerned'). There was Elizabeth von Arnim ('Little e', Jane called her), 'who had a teasing disposition and liked to vex me.... She developed a queer hostility to Jane.' There was Rebecca West ('she demanded to be my lover'), who also had a baby, and had to be set up and visited in the teeth of her family's disapproval; this led to such subterfuges as pretending he was the boy's uncle and she was his aunt ('Neither of us knew where we were ... we trailed a web of nervous irritation that twisted about us'). There was a young woman 'with a face like the Mona Lisa', who turned up at his Westminster flat and cut her wrists with a razor ('My carpet looked like three suicides'); Wells persuaded Beaverbrook and Rothermere to muzzle the papers, but the *Star* got hold of it, and the *New York Times* followed suit. Finally there was the appalling Odette Keun, whom even Wells called 'a thoroughly nasty and detestable person', for whom he built a house in the South of France but found it hard to persuade her to stay there ('I paid her bill at the Berkeley'). Fortunately none of their existences had to be kept from Jane, but sometimes they had to be kept from each other.

To contemplate these liaisons, some of which lasted for years, is to wonder how he could ever have endured them. One explanation is that Wells found it difficult to get rid of women ('"This must end," said I, "this must end" – allowing myself to be dragged upstairs'). It is hard to believe that if by pressing a button he could have permanently transported Rebecca West and Odette Keun to the moon (without, of course, harming them) he would not have done so, but lacking this expedient there was nothing to be done but continue the placatory visits and deflect the recriminations as best he could. 'He could be intensely kind', one of his own female characters is made to say,

> yet he didn't seem to care for you. There was a sort of dishonesty in his kindness. He would not let you have the bitter truth. He would not say that he did not love you.

Another explanation is that he enjoyed what he got from them enough to make it all worth while – from Amber, intense physical pleasure ('in a few days I could be clutching Amber's fuzz of soft black hair'); 'from Little e', absurdity and laughter ('she was Irish'); from Rebecca West, 'the warmest, liveliest and most irreplaceable of fellowships'; even the vindictive and hysterical Odette, apart from 'sensual gratification', gave him a base to work in, which after Jane's death in 1927 he found consoling. Both she and Rebecca West thought, with varying degrees of confidence, that now Wells was free to marry them, he could. But by this time there was Moura.

He had met Moura Budberg ('I shall call her Countess Bedbug,' declared Odette wittily: Wells was not amused) in Gorky's flat in 1920, and had an affair with her. In 1929 they met again in Berlin, and later she came to England. 'By the end of 1932', Wells writes, 'I was prepared to do anything and overlook anything to make Moura altogether mine.' There was a certain amount to overlook; she confessed to five other lovers, and he had no reason to 'suspect her of an extreme physical fastidiousness'. Though possessed of great charm, she was not beautiful; she drank and smoked excessively, and was badly dressed. But her biggest fault was that she did not want to marry him ('I'd be a bore if you had me always'). Ironically, Wells seems to have met someone rather like himself: 'She was content with the fun and pleasure of our association, and she was fundamentally indifferent to my dream.' In 1934 there was a major quarrel; Wells found out that when Moura had said she was in Estonia she was actually in Russia, seeing Gorky. Wells was filled with anguish (a portrait of him at this time is given in C. P. Snow's *Variety of Men*). He stormed and pleaded, she shrugged and prevaricated. On this note the narrative peters out in a delta of jottings on a year-to-year basis. Wells still dreamed of a wife and home ('Jane plus Moura plus fantasy'), but seems to have known he would never attain it. He remained a widower.

One writes this kind of book at one's own peril. In theory it is easy to rig evidence that will not be presented until no one can answer it. In practice it is a question of tone, of avoiding self-justification and retrospective recrimination. Wells comes out of it fairly well, partly because of his quasi-scientific approach. 'I have never been able to discover whether my interest in sex is more than normal', he writes (how he would have loved the Kinsey Report!), and is inclined to believe that what he had was not more interest but more opportunity. 'Except insofar as affection put barriers about me [the book gives few instances of this], I have done what I pleased.' He is without shame: when Odette threatens to publish his letters to her, he tells her to get on with it (a marked contrast to Shaw's response to Mrs Patrick Campbell in similar circumstances), believing they would have little interest except to those 'under-exercised in cheerful normality'.

But what was normal? If Wells did not set out, or choose to set out, the contradictions in his story, they none the less existed. Whatever the vagaries of his personal circumstances, Wells believed that both in his writings and his behaviour he was fighting what he called 'the open sex-war of 1900–1914', by which the nineteenth-century taboos and restrictions and restraints on relations between men and women were to be wiped out. His attempt to persuade the Fabian Society to add 'public support and education of the young' to its programme was a disastrous failure, older members seeing it as letting Free Love in at the back door, but in opposing the numerous political, economic and social sanctions against women he was on firmer ground. The trouble was that Wells could never quite free himself of the notion that when women were the equals of men they would become like men. Thanks to modern contraception, no one need have children if they didn't want to, and the whole business of sex would become just another agreeable way of passing the time, like golf or cards, something one did in the intervals of writing books or going on lecture tours.

H. G. Wells in Love, while plangently demonstrating the erroneousness of this view, fails to recognize the double inconsistency on which it rests. In the first place, his own radical sexual conduct depended on the remarkable complaisance of Jane; it was supported, that is, by the most Victorian of concepts, the wife required to be chaste, supportive and tolerant of the husband's infidelities which he could therefore indulge without fear of marital disharmony. Secondly, if radical conduct in this context meant anything, it was the creation of a single standard of sexual behaviour for men and women, sauce for both goose and gander. And when it came to the point, with Moura, Wells found he did not like this. 'I became exacting because now I was suspicious and jealous. I have always denounced this ugly condition of mind in theory, but that did not prevent my suffering continuously.' Had Odette Keun felt like that? Had Rebecca West?

To do Wells justice, he half-acknowledged this in his *Autobiography*. When 'a tiresome and obstructive accumulation of obsolete restraints' had been cleared out of the way, the 'Woman Problem' remained, 'an almost infinite series of variations of the problem of association between men and women, and an infinitude of opportunities for mutual charity'. He certainly contributed more than his share to the variations; it is to his credit that he took some of the opportunities they provided to be charitable. He paid bills, made settlements, bought or rented houses, arranged holidays, supported children, devoted weeks and months of his time. This is brought out in Anthony West's *Aspects of a Life*, from which some details in the above account have been taken.

It is a difficult book to review. West was the child of Wells and Rebecca West, and has been working on this life since 1948 with the express intention of setting the record straight – more precisely, the record of the relations between his parents. Few biographies scatter their subject's ashes on page 154, and announce his birth fifteen pages later; West starts the book with his own birth, in order to get at his main topic as soon as possible. This is not, as might be imagined, to defend his mother against his father; quite the reverse. He accuses her of producing 'a body of source material documenting her side of the story of their relationship and her view of his character', to the point, he implies, of fabricating letters and diaries in support of her claims. All this is consonant with his characterization of her as both self-dramatizing and dishonest, almost paranoiacally so. Worse, her fictions have begun to be accepted by reputable biographers.

All this may be true, but it is presented, perhaps unavoidably, in a muffled way. West paraphrases his sources instead of quoting from them – presumably permission to do so was refused – but even the reputable biographers are referred to as 'an American authority' and the like. Nor do the untruths in question seem of major importance – Rebecca West does not claim that in fact Wells was a bigamist, having secretly married her, or that Anthony West was not Wells's son at all; the distortions concern whether or not Wells snubbed a future Mayor of Croydon in Amalfi, or whether on another occasion he was 'actually out of his mind' or (as reported by Arnold Bennett) 'in the greatest form'. No doubt they are irritating to the author, but to the reader they seem either insufficiently authenticated or insufficiently momentous. West senses this when at the end of the book he mounts a final arraignment of his mother about her conduct during an illness he had in 1928, and how she subsequently distorted the facts to 'a distinguished American academic' (presumably Professor Gordon N. Ray): such matters 'can only seem on a first showing to be small beer'. The persistent discrediting of Rebecca West is obsessive:

obsessive, too, is the reference to Wells throughout as 'my father', which, when it leads to saying that 'my father spent the summer with my grandfather', instead of saying that Wells spent it with his father, becomes slightly absurd.

The other side of this, of course, is a highly appropriate wish to dispel the common image of Wells as a pushy journalistic philandering little cad, and show him as a warm-hearted visionary, generous in his dealings and human in his failings. On the whole he succeeds, but without suppressing absurd or damaging incident. Wells's disappearance after the birth of his first son is from West's pages; when the birth of his second son was approaching, Wells took to his bed, 'flattened by one of the disabling physical collapses that had been his stock response to stress throughout his early years'. Recovering, he spent Jane's eighth month on a walking tour in the Swiss Alps with Graham Wallas, who was moved to protest against Wells's propositioning of every eligible young woman they encountered. Another later revelation is that, instead of withdrawing with dignity from the villa he had built for Odette Keun in the South of France ('It needed an effort', wrote Wells, 'but once more the liberating influence was the stronger'), he was in fact 'sent packing'. Odette had discovered his affair with Moura, and saw all the difference in the world between playing second fiddle to Jane (who was now dead), and playing it to anyone else. Wells found this hard to understand.

But for the most part Wells emerges as a likeable man who wanted to be happy himself, and was prepared to assuage the difficulties of others he involved in this innocent aim. He cajoled and comforted, but at bottom he was stubborn: he was not going to pretend that any affair undertaken in a spirit of erotic hedonism on both sides could deflect his life's purposes. On less personal issues, the same principle of honesty prevailed. He had no more time for the later James than he had for the later Joyce ('Your last two works have been more amusing and exciting to write than they will ever be to read'). He went to America and met Franklin D. Roosevelt, and to Russia and met Stalin; he liked one and distrusted the other, thereby incurring the fury of the British left. As well as being happy himself, he wanted everyone else to be happy, to bring into being 'the new big-scale life' he felt was within mankind's grasp if only knowledge and wisdom would combine. He did all he could, by writing and lecturing, to realize this vision, but it was not enough. In the context of such an attempt, and such a failure, the vicissitudes of his personal life – no more ludicrous than many another's, and perhaps less reprehensible – seem of small account. It will be a pity if, in the reawakened interest in Wells these books will bring about, he is judged by them.

Times Literary Supplement, 28 September 1984

An Unofficial Life

To contemplate writing a life of T. S. Eliot is to face the fact at the outset that Eliot did not want his life to be written, and that his friends and relations are loyally cooperating by not giving permissions in order to make it as difficult as possible for anyone who tries. The retort scholarly is that although Eliot was a great poet, he was a notoriously enigmatic one, and that if by writing his biography these enigmas can be solved we are surely in honour bound to make the attempt. But here we come up against Eliot himself: 'the more perfect the artist, the more completely separate in him will be the man who suffers and the mind which creates'. Whoever has the temerity to proceed, therefore, is triply engaged: to disinter and disentangle the life, without the assistances normally afforded; to relate it, in the teeth of an explicit denial by its subject that such relation is possible, to the impenetrable poems; and to justify these audacities by rendering them less impenetrable than they otherwise would be.

Many would give up at this point – some, even, feeling it indelicate to persist in something that those most nearly concerned did not want done. Others, more practically, might argue that to write a biography with one hand tied behind you will lead to failure and is not worth doing. To be forbidden to quote from unpublished writings, or even from published ones 'except for the purpose of fair comment in a critical context', makes it impossible to say, for instance, 'Compare this unpublished letter with that published poem', and in such circumstances what becomes of the defence that an unauthorized life is all right if it elucidates the hitherto-obscure work? Subsidiary excuses may be called in to shore it up: 'Got to be a life some time'; 'Been dead nearly twenty years'; 'Only be muck-raking otherwise'; trailing off into disaffected mutterings such as 'Why are they so cagey – must be something there' and 'Bound to go like a bomb.'

Review of Peter Ackroyd, *T. S. Eliot* (Hamish Hamilton, 1984)

A tall order; but whatever the magnitude, or the enormity, of the task, Peter Ackroyd has done it, and it must be said at the outset that Eliot could not have had a more respectful biographer. There is no seeking after sensation; even when relating something surprising (such as that Eliot powdered his face green in 1922, or that Mary Trevelyan proposed marriage to him in 1949), Ackroyd does so in a way that suggests that, all things considered, it was only what might have been expected. The manuscript sources he acknowledges are extensive, as is the list of individuals who have helped him; the thoroughness of his method is impressive. Yet the life he outlines is not substantially different from what we already know: the serious, intellectually dandiacal young American philosopher, the disastrous marriage and its painful, long-drawn-out consequences, the retreat into drab and penitential Anglicanism, and the finale of international acclaim, the fashionable theatre, happiness in a second marriage. For despite the justifiable claim this book can make to be the most detailed account so far of Eliot's life, it is by no means the first; Ackroyd's appendix of biographies, memoirs, reminiscences and the like underlines how much has been said already. Truly it is not much use trying to put people off.

Even though there are advantages in being an 'unauthorized' biographer, therefore, in that one is not committed to any 'official' viewpoint, Ackroyd's account brings out what such a viewpoint would entail. Despite his well-known evasiveness, Eliot had a determined toughness that enabled him to give up both his country and his family, though sincerely attached to both; however bitter his misfortunes, he never contemplated returning to either. He was an enormously hard worker, even if it made him ill; first as a full-time bank employee, then as a publisher, in both cases coming home in the evening to edit *The Criterion* (1922–39), write articles and reviews, and somehow produce his own poems. The illness, indeed, seems to have been almost a chronic condition: Eliot was never completely well. If it was not influenza or bronchitis, it was various manifestations of stress, producing symptoms of tachycardia, or phobias about lifts or large dogs. But the hard work was evidence of another trait: responsibility. Knowing that his inheritance from his father (who died in 1919) would revert at his own death, he remained in his Lloyds Bank job even when it became insupportable through other commitments because it would provide a pension for his wife. He paid her many doctors' bills, and presumably all or part of her keep at the sanatorium to which she was committed in 1938. Though they were separated, he remained faithful to her. She died in 1947.

At the same time, he was curiously indecisive, or bad at knowing what was best for him. 'I have never been wise,' he said late in life. He persisted as an academic philosopher throughout his twenties, abandoning his Harvard doctorate in 1916. His marriage to Vivien Haigh-Wood within a few weeks of meeting her in 1915 was not only an appalling blunder but completely out of character, although Ackroyd makes out a case that Eliot had reached a state of mind when something of the sort was inevitable (one remembers his remark quoted in Lyndall Gordon's excellent *Eliot's Early Years* to the effect that it is better to do wrong than to do nothing). He shrank from discharging disagreeable personal obligations – instructing Ezra Pound to write to his father after the unannounced wedding; serving a notice of separation on Vivien while he himself was in America (she had decorated their flat against his return); deserting his flatmate John Hayward virtually without warning when he married again in 1957 (Ackroyd analyses the relation at length, without excusing the desertion). Eliot learned to handle people in his own way, but it was an aloof and uncommitted way; divesting oneself of the love of created beings naturally appealed to one who had experienced what love of them could lead to, and he tended to keep such created beings as he knew separate from each other and even from himself.

But there were compartments in Eliot too: 'A company of actors inside one suit', was V. S. Pritchett's description of him, a telling one that Ackroyd quotes twice; Edmund Wilson, meeting him in 1933, concluded that his personality was 'really rather incoherent', and calls him 'a self-invented character'. Ackroyd sees him as 'a master of protective camouflage'. Bertrand Russell commented, after teaching a class that included Eliot in 1914, that 'window-dressing seems irresistible to Americans', which might be applied to the array of references that make up the notes to *The Waste Land*, designed to impress rather than illuminate, a technique Eliot sometimes employed in his earlier criticism. Philosopher, scholar; to these personae can be added the English clubman, the church-warden (which Eliot himself likened to a practical joke), and the reputation for a kind of rarified piety that provoked, in a competition for 'dull BBC radio programmes', the prize-winning entry '*11.0–11.15: Mr T. S. Eliot will meditate in the studio.*'

All this falls into place if we consider one of Ackroyd's most striking comments: 'it may emerge that Eliot's poetry was the real English drama of the twentieth century'. For the oddest thing about an admittedly odd life was his turning from poetry in order to write what he clearly hoped would be popular West End plays; if we buy his collected works, we find that nearly two-thirds of it is in dramatic form, and his first two major poems were dramatic monologues. Clearly the drama, for Eliot, was not only a way of life but a way of literature. His best lines have the dramatic projection that he excitedly discovered in Shakespeare's contemporaries, like brilliant film-shots. Of course, in a sense all good literature is drama – 'Dramatize, dramatize,' said Henry James – in so far as it is designed to produce a deliberate effect on the reader; but the montage of Eliot's method was more deliberate than most. Indeed, his besetting temptation, as Ackroyd points out, was to make drama of drama – to assimilate the impression of other writers' forms and language within an original design. A case could be made for calling Eliot a synthetic writer, and his mind 'a piece of elaborate machinery run on a very rare and expensive fuel' – that fuel being all that had been written up to the moment of his own creations.

This is the nearest Ackroyd gets to establishing a connection between the life and the work, and it is perhaps not very near. His last paragraphs restate the contradictions and paradoxes of Eliot's life and temperament that in his Prelude he sets out to solve (in his end, one might say, is his beginning); he has documented them, described them, prowled round them with endless patience, but in the last analysis he has not explained them.

Is it ungrateful to feel relieved? If Eliot wished to live quietly, succeeding in avoiding notice, living and partly living, without making his life a continual allegory, then he had a right to. There was pain, there was dignity, finally there was happiness. Let it go at that.

Encounter, December 1984

Solitary Walker

At his best, Andrew Young is a lonely eye, a level voice, an ingenious fancy. He stares at a haystack, a line of washing in the wind, a wall, a wood, a dead rat, seeing them briefly but with intense sharpness that is a kind of parallax, so that the haystack becomes a cottage without windows or doors, the washing a set of clothes being tried on by ghosts. There are no people; to read him is like walking all day without meeting a soul. The silence, the absence are in the end intimidating.

The bones of his life, here articulated by his editors (his daughter and son-in-law), are simple indeed. Graduating in arts from Edinburgh in 1907, he wanted to become a barrister, but an elder brother got into trouble in Singapore and disappeared, and Andrew entered a theological college in deference to his father's wishes. The editors suggest a connection between these events. In 1914 he was appointed to his first ministry, in Scotland, and married; after the war he moved to Sussex, and 'after much mental conflict' (nature not stated) became an Anglican, eventually dying in 1971 at Chichester, where he was a canon of the cathedral.

He wrote poems, and books about wild flowers; his parishioners found him likeable though reserved, but wished he wouldn't keep referring to death in his sermons. The portrait is so ordinary that it invites questions. Can one become a priest in such circumstances without the deliberate suppression of part of one's nature? Why did he erase his errant brother so completely from his mind, almost to the point of refusing to admit his existence? After graduating, and before becoming an ordinand, Young lived for a while in Paris, and saw Strauss's *Salome* five times. His early poems were Swinburnian ('the ancient flame/Of lust and shame/ Within fierce lips of courtezans and kings'); in later years he destroyed as many copies of them as he could find.

Review of *The Poetical Works of Andrew Young*, edited by Edward Lowbury and Alison Young (Secker and Warburg, 1985).

Yet poetry was his devotion. Between 1920 and 1931 he published seven collections; the Meynells praised and eventually published him; he caught the perspicacious attention of Rupert Hart-Davis. The attempted obliteration of his early work was not only self-criticism; he cannibalized them ruthlessly. 'The buds in glistening varnish dripped' on page 8 reappear on page 96; 'low-shouldered coffins' are on pages 74 and 131; the hoof-slung 'divots at the sky' on page 70 are culled from page 146 (the poems are not printed in chronological order). His manuscripts are illegibly minuscular, as if coding a secret dedication.

> When day dawned with unusual light,
> Hedges in snow stood half their height,
> And in the white-paved village street,
> Children were walking without feet.

It looks easy to do, but the double refinement – first of vision, then of language – comes to few, and came to Young only after years of practice. In the Thirties, when Eliot had shown that it was still possible to write religious verse and drama (if you were Eliot), he produced a short verse play, *Nicodemus*, and later two long and confusing poems about the afterlife for which large claims were made, but which, as Martin Seymour-Smith said, lack the compact power of the earlier work.

This year marks the centenary of his birth. His work is in no danger of being forgotten, but it is appropriate to have it presented again in a way that shows its development and its less-known facets. Whether it will extend his reputation, as the publishers seem to hope, is doubtful. Some years ago, Kingsley Amis wrote a poem ('Here is Where') which said in effect that while nature poetry was all very well in its way, in the end one wants humanity and human emotions. It is an apt comment on Young's work. To walk all day without meeting a soul can be refreshing and restoring. But at last one is glad to get back to humankind again.

Observer, 13 January 1985

The Missing Thou

Like all biographies, this book claims to redraw 'the old picture' of its subject; but what was the old picture of Edward FitzGerald? An orientalist voluptuary? Gosse's 'unobtrusive' author, who 'by the force of his extraordinary individuality gradually influenced the whole face of English *belles-lettres*'? Or Tennyson's 'my Fitz', vegetarian, with doves perching all over him?

In fact he was not unlike a kind of reverse Tennyson. Both came from large eccentric families ('all mad,' as FitzGerald said of his own). Both had East Anglian connections. Both went to Trinity College, Cambridge, where they met. Both were melancholy. And finally, both by completely different routes, became overwhelmingly popular poets.

Anyone who wishes he had been born rich, and so freed from external compulsion to earn a living, might well ponder FitzGerald's life. In 1818 his mother inherited her father's money, bringing her personal estate to well over a million pounds, and her husband, not unnaturally, changed his name (Purcell) to hers. In consequence their seven children (FitzGerald was the youngest of three sons) were never less than comfortably off, and when FitzGerald went down from Cambridge (106th in the pass degrees) he had no idea what to do.

He drifted indecisively from lodging to lodging, spending long periods with a married sister in Norfolk, and slowly disentangling himself from his striking ancestrally-Irish mother who expected him to squire her about London, an expectation enthusiastically supported by his vague Irish Inner Temple father, who preferred living at Boulge Hall in Suffolk, one of their several family estates. Mrs FitzGerald had no liking for country life: she gave dinners on gold plate in Portland Place, and drove about in a yellow carriage with four black horses. FitzGerald hated this kind of thing, and

Review of Robert Bernard Martin, *With Friends Possessed: A Life of Edward FitzGerald* (Faber and Faber, 1985)

had shabby rooms in Charlotte Street when a spell of squiring was unavoidable.

He was not without resources. He loved music – Purcell, Handel, Mozart – and played the piano and organ; he bought pictures (sometimes 'improving' them himself); and of course he read, and at times tried to write, though the sense of his two Trinity contemporaries Tennyson and Thackeray looking over his shoulders must have been inhibiting. But what was he to do? Should he have a house? Should he marry? 'How you would hate to stay with me and my spouse,' he told Thackeray, 'dining off a mutton chop, and a draught of sour thin beer.' Whatever Thackeray thought of the prospect, it was clearly uninviting to FitzGerald.

Yet in the end he did both these things, first living in a cottage on the Boulge estate, then finally, when over 60, buying a farmhouse ('a rotten Affair') at Woodbridge. Here he recreated a sort of Cambridge existence, a muddle of books and sheet music to hand, smoking till midnight with a glass within reach; only the intellectual stimulus was lacking ('a Man is going to lecture on the Gorilla in a few weeks. So there is something to look forward to'). His solace was his friends, visiting them, and above all writing to them. FitzGerald was an enchanting correspondent. It is his letters that build up his popular image, garden-tending, book-of-verse, flask-of-wine.

And Thou? At the age of 47, when his mother's will had bequeathed him £50,000, he married the daughter of a friend who when dying had asked him to look after her. The predictably disastrous episode lasted less than a year. It aroused in FitzGerald a totally uncharacteristic caddishness; on passing a Fat Lady booth, he remarked 'I can see my own wife any hour.' After their separation in 1857, he settled £300 a year on her, and there is no evidence of lingering bitterness on either side. FitzGerald ascribed the break to the inability of two fixed characters to alter their habits: 'they may lay nine-tenths of the Blame on me. I don't want to talk more of the matter, but one must say something.'

His reaction was to throw himself into the task of translating the rubaiyat (quatrains) of the Persian poet Omar Khayyam. These had been transcribed in the Bodleian by Edward Cowell, a remarkable Ipswich man who had learnt Persian when fourteen, and whom FitzGerald had known for over a dozen years, since Cowell was eighteen.

The translation was no scholarly exercise; his brief excursion into altruism had set him up to receive the full impact of Omar's hedonism, and he fiercely resisted Cowell's pious contention that Omar meant wine as the Godhead, and drunkenness as divine love: 'Omar was too honest of Heart as well as of Head for this.' And so there came into being not only the most powerful expression of *carpe diem*, but one of the most popular poems in the English language.

It was published in 1859 (along with *Origin of Species*) in an anonymous edition of 250 copies at a shilling. Two years later Quaritch put the residue outside his shop in a penny box. It is estimated that by 1929 over 300 editions had been issued. On his deathbed, Thomas Hardy asked for a verse of it to be read to him. Far from being a celebration of sensual indulgence, it is a poignant utterance of *lacrimae rerum*, of transience, of things having gone wrong:

> Ah Love! could thou and I with Fate conspire
> To grasp this sorry Scheme of Things entire,
> Would we not shatter it to bits – and then
> Remould it nearer to the Heart's Desire!

It is ironic that this sudden apotheosis of FitzGerald's temperament should have arisen from his friendship with the eighteen-year-old Cowell. Not all his friendships were as rewarding. As well as for his Apostolic Cambridge contemporaries, he had a liking for uncomplicated young men. There had been the sixteen-year-old William Kenworthy Browne he met at Tenby in 1832, handsome, unintelligent, with whom he spent many idyllic summer holidays fishing. When Browne (who had got married) died in the year the *Rubaiyat* was published, FitzGerald started going down to the shore at Lowestoft at night, armed with a bottle of rum, to talk to sailors. He was looking, as he wrote to, of all people, Browne's mother, for 'some fellow who might give promise of filling up a very vacant place in my heart'.

His choice ultimately fell on handsome broad-shouldered Joseph Fletcher (nicknamed 'Posh'), who for seven or eight years seems to have magnetized his imagination. He built Posh a boat ('Meum et Tuum'), following him in his own ('Scandal'), and backed his losses. He had him painted by Samuel Laurence, and hung the result alongside portraits of Tennyson and Thackeray.

The absurd relation came to an end when FitzGerald tired of subsidizing the feckless (and rather drunken) Fletcher's improvidence, but he was always 'the Greatest Man I have ever known.'

His last ten years, like all last ten years, were sad, but not unbearably so. True, his eyes went, and he had to be read to by barely literate boys; friends died – Carlyle, Spedding, Donne – and his brother John and sister Andalusia too ('the funeral Bell has been at work all this winter'), but new friends wrote from America, and he was active enough to visit Cambridge, and to drop in at the Lyceum to see Irving's *Hamlet* (he walked out in disgust). He died in his sleep in 1883, having arrived at a friend's house the night before.

Professor Martin is concerned to show that FitzGerald was not simple but complex. His engrossing narrative develops this contention. FitzGerald was idle yet industrious, committed to friends yet kept them at arm's length, an indifferent poet who in one instance became a superb translator.

His life could be depicted as a failure, but the judgment cannot be sustained. Apart from squiring his mother, and getting married, he did little he did not want to. His one poem will last as long as any of Tennyson's. And his friendships, which, as he said, 'are more like loves', did not perish insofar as they gave rise to his letters, 'witty, picturesque and sympathetic,' as Gosse called them, and still a monument to a puzzling, unpretentious and wholly individual temperament.

Observer, 17 February 1985

Index

Abercrombie, Lascelles 95, 230
Ackerley, J. R. 11
Ackroyd, Peter, *T. S. Eliot* 372–5
Adcock, Fleur 331, 332
AE *see* Russell, George
Agate, James 354
Akhmatova, Anna 275
Allen, Woody 346
Alvarez, A. 20, 259
  The New Poetry 30
Amichai, Yehuda 275
Amis, Kingsley 14, 32, 33–4, 36, 50, 276, 306, 310, 347, 354, 377
  A Case of Samples 176
  Lucky Jim 19
  The James Bond Dossier 257–8
  The New Oxford Book of Light Verse xiv, 291–5
Amory, Mark, *The Letters of Evelyn Waugh* 301–3
Aragon, Louis 144
Arbuthnot, John 304
Archer, William, *Real Conversations* 190
Ardizzone, Edward 248
Armstrong, Louis 103, 319
Arnim, Elizabeth von 365
Arnold, Matthew 310
Arnold, Thomas 92
Auden, W. H. xiv, xv, 14, 19, 28, 29–30, 40–41, 52, 54, 55, 95, 108, 119, 160, 161, 184, 202, 207, 224, 237, 241, 244, 246, 275, 291, 294, 295, 296–8, 299, 311, 317–19, 342–4
  The Age of Anxiety 183
  Another Time 168
  Collected Poems 344
  The Dance of Death 343
  Epistle to a Godson 344
  For the Time Being 343
  Journey to a War 343
  Look, Stranger! 319
  New Year Letter 343
  Nones 168
  'On the Circuit' 40
  The Oxford Book of Light Verse 292, 336
  Paul Bunyan 317
  Poems 342, 343
  The Shield of Achilles 168–73
  Thank You, Fog 342
Austin, Alfred 287

Bailey, J. O., *Thomas Hardy and the Cosmic Mind* xiv, 190–91
Barnes, William 14, 19, 60, 259, 260, 275
Barrie, J. M. 269, 310
Basie, William 'Count' 54
Baudelaire, Charles 193, 239
Bayley, John, *The Romantic Survival* 183–4
Beach, J. W. 344
Bechet, Sidney 54
Beecham, Thomas 110
Beerbohm, Max 252
Beethoven, Ludwig van 11
Belloc, Hilaire 306
Bennett, Alan 294
Bennett, Arnold 10, 45, 339, 369
Benson, A. C. 355, 356, 357
Berenson, Bernard 350
Berry, Francis, *Poetry and the Physical Voice* 36n
Berryman, John 275
  Homage to Mistress Bradstreet 219
Betjeman, John xiv, 14, 29, 47, 52, 53, 95, 119, 195, 230, 246, 251–2, 275, 294, 302, 306, 321, 334–7, 360
  Collected Poems 200–202, 206–16, 334
  Continual Dew 160
  A Few Late Chrysanthemums 160–64, 200
  New Bats in Old Belfries 160
  Old Lights in New Chancels 160
  A Ring of Bells 248–50
  Selected Poems 160
  Summoned by Bells 112
  Uncollected Poems 325–7
Birkenhead, Earl of 200, 216

Birkett, Norman 134
Bishop, Elizabeth 184
Blackburn, Thomas 28
Blake, William 205, 263
Blakewell, Jean 349
Blakiston, Noel 348, 349
Bloomfield, B. C. xv
Blunden, Edmund 119
Bogan, Louise 342, 344
Booth, James xvi
Bottomley, Gordon 230
Bowra, C. M. 254, 348
Bradbury, Malcolm 363
Bradman, Donald 8
Brecht, Bertolt 319
Brett, John 162
Britten, Benjamin 297, 317–19
Brooke, Jocelyn, *Ronald Firbank and John Betjeman* 251–2
Brooke, Rupert 29, 229, 276
Browne, William Kenworthy 380
Browning, Elizabeth Barrett 310
Browning, Robert 293
Budberg, Moura 367, 368, 370
Bunting, Basil 95
Burne-Jones, Edward 310
Butler, Samuel 10
Byron, George Gordon, Lord 293, 305, 306

Calverley, Charles Stuart 293
Campbell, Mrs Patrick 367
Campbell, Roy 186, 306
  Collected Poems 239
Cannan, May Wedderburn 98
  'Rouen 1915' 97
Carey, Henry 306
Carlyle, Thomas 310, 381
Carr, A. W. 7
Carr, John Dickson 115, 131
Carroll, Lewis 293
Carter, John 121
Causley, Charles 120
  Union Street 186
Cayley, Charles Bagot 253
Chambers, Harry: *An Enormous Yes* xv
Chaucer, Geoffrey 52, 103, 259, 293
Chesterton, G. K. 10
Church, Richard 244
Churchill, R. C., *The Powys Brothers* 251
Churchill, Winston 299
Clare, John 259, 275
Clark, Kenneth 252
Clark, Leonard 228
Claudel, Paul 193
Clough, Arthur Hugh 294
Cobbett, William 259
Cocteau, Jean 144
Coleman, Terry 281
Coleridge, Samuel Taylor, 'Dejection: an ode' 120
Collins, William 259
Collinson, James 253
Connery, Sean 256
Connolly, Cyril xvi, 155, 274, 301, 343, 348–52, 353, 354, 365
  The Condemned Playground 142–6, 348
  Enemies of Promise 144, 348, 349, 350
  Previous Convictions 348
  The Rock Pool 144, 349
  The Unquiet Grave 143, 350
Connolly, Major Matthew 351
Conquest, Robert, *New Lines* 20, 330
Coolidge, Albert Sprague 267
Coward, Noel 295
  'The Boy Actor' 98
Cowell, Edward 379, 380
Cowper, William 338
Crabbe, George 259
Cranmer, Thomas 181
Crispin, Edmund *see* Montgomery, Bruce
Crozier, Eric 319
cummings, e. e. 184
Curzon, Lord 287

Dali, Salvador 297
Davie, Donald 20, 54, 101
  The Forest of Lithuania 233–5
Day-Lewis, C. 47, 224, 299–300, 342
  The Buried Day 243–4
Day-Lewis, Sean, *C. Day-Lewis: An English Literary Life* 299–300
de la Mare, Walter 47, 243
de Selincourt, Ernest 120
De Tabley, Lord 276
de Vere, Aubrey 204
Deacon, Lois 281
  Providence and Mr Hardy 261
Deloney, Thomas 147
Deutsch, Babette, *This Modern Poetry* 184
Dickens, Charles 10
Dickinson, Emily 52, 263
Dickinson, Patric 263
Disraeli, Benjamin 287

Donne, John 54, 274, 276, 338, 381
Douglas, Keith 119
Dowson, Ernest 29, 275
Dryden, John 293, 304
Duffy, Gavan 204
Dunbar, William 293
Duncan, Ronald 318
Dunn, Douglas, *A Rumoured City* xv, 136
Durrell, Lawrence, *Selected Poems* 176–8
Dutton, Geoffrey xiv
Dutton, Geoffrey, *Antipodes in Shoes* 223–5
Dyer, Lady Catherine 276

Ehrenpreis, Irving 344
Elgar, Edward 109
Eliot, George 45
Eliot, T. S. 19, 29, 44, 49, 52, 54, 95, 96, 108, 134, 145, 188, 207, 229, 335, 336, 342, 377
  The Waste Land 120, 374
Ellington, Edward 'Duke' 110
Elwin, Malcolm 150
Engel, Paul 17
Enright, D. J. xii, 241, 322, 345–7
  The Oxford Book of Death 345–7
Epstein, Joseph, *The Middle of My Tether* 353–4
Ewart, Gavin xiv, 295, 306, 346
  Collected Poems 320
  The New Ewart 320–24
  Pleasures of the Flesh 323

Farnes, Kenneth 7
Fenton, James 332
Ferguson, Milton J. 266
Fisher, Sir William 349
FitzGerald, Edward 203, 313, 315, 378–81
  The Rubaiyat of Oma Khayyam 334, 379–80
Fleming, Ian 256–8
  Casino Royale 257
  The Living Daylights 256
  Octopussy 256
Fletcher, Joseph 380
Ford, Ford Madox 218
Forster, E. M. 45, 104
France, Anatole 345
Francis, Dick
  Banker 328–9
  Blood Sport 307
  Bonecrack 308, 329
  Flying Finish 308
  For Kicks 308
  Forfeit 307, 308
  In the Frame 308
  Knock Down 307, 329
  Nerve 308
  Odds Against 307
  Rat Race 308
  Reflex 307–9, 328
  Trial Run 329
  Twice Shy 329
  Whip Hand 309, 328
Francis of Assisi, St 358
Frost, Robert 14, 67
Fry, Christopher 252
Fuller, Roy 28, 119, 300

Gallagher, Donat, *The Essays, Articles and Reviews of Evelyn Waugh* 358–60
Galsworthy, John 10, 143
Gardiner, Raymond 53
George III, King 305–6
Gibson, James 39
Gibson, Wilfrid 96, 109
Gide, André 144
Gilbert, W. S. 293, 321, 362
Gittings, Robert, *Young Thomas Hardy* 277–81
Goethe, Johann Wolfgang von 40, 47
Gogarty, Oliver St John 204
Goldschmidt, Eva M. 266
Goldsmith, Oliver 203
Goodman, Benny 108
Gordon, Lyndall, *Eliot's Early Years* 374
Gorky, Maxim 367
Gosse, Edmund 261, 277, 279, 285, 310, 378, 381
Grahame, Kenneth, *The Wind in the Willows* 128, 130
Gransden, Richard Perceval 356
  The Brothers Powys 338–41
Graves, Robert 52, 197–9, 204, 275, 276, 300
  Collected Poems 217–20
  Steps 197–9
Green, F. Pratt 98
  'The Old Couple' 98
Green, Henry 32, 49
Greene, Graham 45, 342
Greenwell, John 6
Gregory, Alyse 148

Grigson, Geoffrey
The Faber Book of Love Poems 274–6
The Oxford Book of Satirical Verse 304–6
Poems and Poets 259–60
Guinness Book of Poetry 1958–59 240–41
Gunn, Thom 20
Gunner, Colin xv, 127–30
Adventures with the Irish Brigade 127–30

Haeckel, Ernst 190
Haffenden, John 47–62
W. H. Auden: The Critical Heritage 342–4
Haigh-Wood, Vivien 374
Hall, J. C. 241
Hall, Julian
The Senior Commoner 32–3
Two Exiles 33
Hallam, Arthur 314
Hamilton, Ian 19–26, 38, 51
Hammond, Walter 7
Handel, George Frederick 110
Hardy, Emma 278–9, 280, 285, 286
Hardy, Evelyn, *One Rare Fair Woman: Thomas Hardy's Letters to Florence Henniker 1893–1922* 269–73
Hardy, Thomas xiv, 19, 22, 29, 42, 45, 51–2, 60, 76–7, 95, 96, 105, 120, 184, 215, 236, 259, 260, 261–2, 269–73, 274, 276, 293, 310, 380
Collected Letters of Thomas Hardy: Volume I, 1840–1892 285–90
The Dynasts xiv, 190–91, 262
Far from the Madding Crowd 279, 286, 287
A Group of Noble Dames 287
The Hand of Ethelberta 278
Jude the Obscure 272, 277
A Pair of Blue Eyes 262
The Poor Man and the Lady 278
The Return of the Native 286, 287, 289
Satires of Circumstance 164
Tess of the d'Urbervilles 285, 287, 288
'The Unplanted Primrose' 76–7
The Trumpet Major 191
Under the Greenwood Tree 262, 286, 287
Winter Words 289
The Woodlanders 287
Harris, Frank 357
Harrison, Tony xii, 332
Hart-Davis, Rupert 377
Hartley, George xiv, 12, 13
Hartmann, Eduard Von, *The Philosophy of the Unconscious* 190–91
Hassall, Joan 228
Hattersley, Roy 353
Hayward, John 374
Heaney, Seamus 331, 332
Heath-Stubbs, John 275
A Charm Against the Toothache xii, 158–9
Hecht, Anthony 26
Heguri, Lady 275
Hemingway, Ernest 156, 360
Across the River and Into the Trees 359
Henniker, Florence 269–73, 278, 285
Herbert, A. P. 98
Herrick, Robert 274
Hewitt, John 204, 332
Hill, Geoffrey xii
Hillier, Bevis 325
Hitchcock, Alfred 131
Hoare, Peter 43
Hobson, Harold 343
Hodges, Johnny 110
Hodgson, Ralph, *The Skylark and Other Poems* 231–2
Hoggart, Richard 12
Holbrook, David 276
Hölderlin, Friedrich 259
Holiday, Billie 109–10
Holloway, John, *The Minute and Longer Poems* 185–6
Homer 316
Hood, Thomas 293, 294
Hopkins, Gerard Manley 14, 184, 260
Horace 239
Horovitz, Michael 330
Housman, A. E. 29, 47, 106, 294, 310, 355–7
Last Poems 355
A Shropshire Lad 334, 356, 357
Housman, Laurence 356
Howard, Brian 144
Hughes, Ted 119, 323
Crow 100–101
Hulme, T. E. 188
Humfrey, Belinda, *Recollections of the Powys Brothers* 341
Huxley, Aldous 10, 104, 144
Huysmans, J. K. 252
Hynes, Samuel 300

Innes, Michael *see* Stewart, J. I. M.
Isherwood, Christopher 98, 317, 343, 344

Jackson, Adalbert 355, 356
Jackson, Moses 355, 356
Jacobson, Dan xv
Jaffe, Rhoda 297
James, Clive 306, 318, 344
James, Henry 40, 310, 375
James, M. R. 11
Jarrell, Randall 65–9, 189
'La Belle au Bois Dormant' 66–7
'The Face' 66
'Money' 67–9
Selected Poems 65
Jennings, Elizabeth, *A Sense of the World* 192–3
John of the Cross, St 239
Johnson, Lionel 204
Johnson, Samuel 167
Jowett, Benjamin 314, 356
Joyce, James 145, 180, 370
Finnegans Wake 167
Ulysses 167, 351
Justice, Donald 26

Kavanagh, P. J., *One and One* 234–5
Keats, John 28–9, 184, 259
Kelly, Thomas
Books for the People (with Edith Kelly) 282–4
History of the Public Libraries in Great Britain 1845–1965 283
Kendall, May 205
Kendon, Frank 230
Kenner, Hugh 167
Kermode, Frank, *Romantic Image* 188–9
Keun, Odette 366, 368, 370
Kierkegaard, Sçren 40
Killen, Louis 104
Kingsmill, Hugh 357
Kinsella, Thomas 204
Kipling, Rudyard 26, 95, 252, 295, 306, 310
Barrack-Room Ballads 334
Knebworth, Anthony 225

La Rochefoucauld, François, duc de 347
Lancaster, Osbert 160
Landor, Walter Savage 259, 275
Langbaum, Robert, *The Poetry of Experience* 188–9
Langland, Joseph 17
Langland, William 224
Latimer, Hugh 181
Laurence, Samuel 380
Lawrence, D. H. 10, 42–6, 53, 143, 184, 229, 236, 260, 263, 282
Aaron's Rod 43
Kangaroo 45
Lady Chatterley's Lover 44, 53, 340
Letters 45
Sea and Sardinia 43
Women in Love 44, 45
Lawrence, Frieda 43
Lawrence, T. E. 299
Lear, Edward 314
Leavis, F. R. 45, 343
Ledwidge, Francis 230
Lee, Gypsy Rose 297
Lehmann, John 4, 19, 343
Lehmann, Rosamond 300
Lennon, John 358
Lerner, Laurence, 'A Wish' 98
Levi, Peter, *The Gravel Ponds* 241–2
Levin, Bernard 353
Lewis, Alun 275
Lewis, Percy Wyndham 188, 205
Lewis, Ted 245
Linklater, Eric 143
Locker, Frederick 287, 294
Lodge, David, *Small World* 361–3
Logue, Christopher, *Songs* 219
Longden, Robert 349
Longley, Michael 331
Lorca, Federico García 239
Lowbury, Edward 376
Lowell, Robert 241, 275
Life Studies 26, 218–19
Luce, Claire 303
Lucie-Smith, Edward 330
Lytton, Lord 287, 314

MacCaig, Norman 331
MacCarthy, Desmond 142, 343, 352
McCarthy, Justin, *Reminiscences* 273
McCarthy, Mary 213
MacDiarmid, Hugh 184
MacDonagh, Donagh 241
The Oxford Book of Irish Verse 203–4
McFadden, Roy 204
McGough, Roger 333
McGuckian, Medbh 331
McKinley, William 266
MacLeish, Archibald xiv

MacLeish, Archibald, *Champion of a Cause* 266–8
MacNeice, Louis xv, 52, 193
Autumn Journal 18
The Burning Perch 18
Visitations 185, 187
Malraux, André 144
Mansfield, Katherine 10, 104
Mante-Proust, Mme Gérard 124
Marshall, Arthur 200
Martial 275
Martin, Robert Bernard
Tennyson: The Unquiet Heart 310–16
With Friends Possessed: A Life of Edward FitzGerald 378–81
Marvell, Andrew 136
Masefield, John 229
Masters, Edgar Lee 304
Matthews, Stanley 193
Mattocks, Jimmy 128
Maugham, W. Somerset 10, 104, 147, 151, 341
Christmas Holiday 360
Melba, Nellie 245
Meleager 275
Mencken, Ada 162
Mencken, H. L. 268, 354
Merwin, W. S., *Green with Beasts* 174
Mickiewicz, Adam, *Pan Tadeusz* 233
Millay, Edna St Vincent, *Collected Poems* 182
Millay, Norma 182
Miller, Henry 287
Miller, Karl xiii
Millgate, Michael 285
Thomas Hardy: His Career as a Novelist 261, 262
Milne, A. A. 291, 293
Milton, John 188, 259
Mitchell, Adrian 275
Mitchell, Donald, *Britten and Auden in the Thirties: The Year 1936* 317–19
Mitchell, Gladys 14, 115
Mitchell, Matthew 241
Mitchison, Naomi 343
Mitford, Nancy 301
Mitford, Unity 344
Monro, Harold 230
Montale, Eugenio 321
Montgomery, Bruce ['Edmund Crispin'] xvi, 307
The Case of the Gilded Fly 131
Fen Country 131–2
Holy Disorders 131
The Moving Toyshop 131
Montherlant, Henri de 53
Moore, T. Sturge 99
Moore, Thomas 305
Moore, W. G. 132
Morris, William 29
Morrison, Blake xi
Morrison, Blake, *The Penguin Book of Contemporary British Poetry* 330–33
Mortimer, Raymond 142
Motion, Andrew, *The Penguin Book of Contemporary British Poetry* 330–33
Moule, Horace 278–9, 281
Muir, Edwin 119
Collected Poems 241
'A Late Wasp' 71–2
One Foot in Eden 71
Muir, Willa 241
Muldoon, Paul 331
Munro, H. H. ['Saki'] 252
Murphy, Richard 241
Murry, John Middleton 29
Mussolini, Benito 359

Neruda, Pablo 275
New Poems 240
Newton, Frankie 108
Nichols, Beverley 358
Nicholson, Norman 160
Nicolson, Harold 311, 351, 352
Nott, Kathleen, *Poems from the North* 174–5

O'Brien, Flann 346
O'Grady, Standish 204
Orwell, George 346
Osborne, Charles, *W. H. Auden: The Life of a Poet* 296–8
Owen, Wilfred 19, 29, 47, 98, 229
'The Calls' 120

Packer, Lona Mosk 253–5
Christina Rossetti 253
The Rossetti-Macmillan Letters 253, 254
Page, Norman, *A. E. Housman: A Critical Biography* 355–7
Palmer, Richard xiii
Pascal, Blaise 346
Patmore, Coventry 275, 310
Patten, Brian 101, 333
Paulin, Tom 332
Péguy, Charles 193

Philips, Ambrose 306
Picasso, Pablo 180
Pinion, F. B., *One Rare Fair Woman: Thomas Hardy's Letters to Florence Henniker 1893–1922* 269–73
Pinto, Vivian de Sola 42
Plath, Sylvia 346
Plomer, William 119, 241
Collected Poems 245–7
Plomley, Roy 103–11
Pollard, Alfred 355
Pope, Alexander 236, 293, 305, 306
Pound, Ezra 19, 26, 54, 96, 120, 163, 188, 197, 207, 336, 374
Section: Rock Drill 182
Powell, Anthony xi, 14
Afternoon Men 155–7
Agents and Patients 155
A Buyer's Market 155
From a View to a Death 155, 157
Venusberg 155
What's Become of Waring? 155
Powell, Neil 27–34
Powys, Charles Francis 147, 338
Powys, John Cowper 147–8, 149, 251, 338–41
Autobiography 339
Powys, Littleton, *The Joy of It* 339
Powys, Llewelyn xvi, 147–51, 251, 338–41
Apples Be Ripe 148
Black Laughter 148, 338
Confessions of Two Brothers (with John Cowper Powys) 148
Earth Memories 147–51
Ebony and Ivory 148, 338
Glory of Life 149
Love and Death 150
Natural Happiness 149
Natural Worship 149
Now That The Gods are Dead 149
Skin for Skin 341
Powys, T. F. 147, 148, 251, 264, 338–41
Black Bryony 338
The Left Leg 338
Powys, Sir Thomas 338
Powys, Willie 148
Praed, William Mackworth 14, 293, 294
Praz, Mario 188
Press, John 241
The Chequer'd Shade 195–6
Pritchett, V. S. 374
Proust, Marcel 124
Pryce-Jones, Alan, *Georgian Poets* 229–30
Pryce-Jones, David, *Cyril Connolly: Journal and Memoir* 348–52
Pudney, John 98
'Johnny Head-in-Air' 97
'Missing' 97
Purdy, Richard Little 285
Pym, Barbara xiii–xiv, xvi, 14, 137–41
Excellent Women 139
A Glass of Blessings 140
Jane and Prudence 139
Less Than Angels 132
No Fond Return of Love xi, 138, 139
Quartet in Autumn 138
Some Tame Gazelle 140
The Sweet Dove Died 138
An Unsuitable Attachment 137–41

Raine, Craig 331
Raine, Kathleen xii, 72–6
Collected Poems 72, 165–6
'Night Thoughts' 72–3
'Spell against Sorrow' 74
'Spell to Bring Lost Creatures Home' 74
'Two Invocations of Death' 74–6
'The Unloved' 73
Randall, David A. 124
Ray, Gordon N. 369
Read, Herbert 252
Reading, Peter 333
Redgrove, Peter, *The Collector and Other Poems* 237–8
Reeves, Amber 365
Reid, Christopher 331
Reid, Forrest 79, 243
Richardson, Dorothy 365
Ricks, Christopher 314
Ridler, Anne 181–2
A Matter of Life and Death 227–8
The Trial of Thomas Cranmer 181
Ridley, Nicholas 181
Rike, Rainer Maria 40
Robinson, Lennox 203–4
Rochester, John Wilmot, Earl of 274, 275, 293
Rodgers, W. R. 160, 204
Roethke, Theodore 28, 275
Roosevelt, Franklin D. 266, 370
Roosevelt, Theodore 365
Rosenberg, Isaac 229
Ross, Alan 15, 186

To Whom It May Concern 193
Rossetti, Christina 14, 19, 47, 253–5, 275
Rossetti, Dante Gabriel 255
Rossetti, Maria 255
Rossetti, William Michael 253
Rota, Bertram 122, 124
Rumens, Carol 331
Russell, Bertrand 374
Russell, George ['AE'] 227, 230

Saki *see* Munro, H. H.
Samuel, Viscount 195
Sassoon, Siegfried 14, 112
Sequences 177–8
The Weald of Youth 177
Scannell, Vernon, *The Masks of Love* 236–7
Schopenhauer, Arthur 190
Scott, Sir Walter 343
Scott, William Bell 253–4
Scovell, E. J. 69–71, 275
The River Steamer 69
'The River Steamer' 71
'Sorrows of Childhood' 70–71
'The Swan's Feet' 70
Seal, Basil 358–9
Selassie, Haile 359
Selwood, Emily 312
Seymour-Smith, Martin 377
Shakespeare, William 29, 42, 52, 65, 103, 110, 120, 245, 260, 272, 314, 375
Shapiro, Karl 184
Shaw, George Bernard 10, 110, 310, 359
Shelley, Percy Bysshe 305
Shuttle, Penelope 331
Silkin, Jon xii
Simmons, James 333
Sitwell, Edith 186, 239, 241, 302
Skelton, John 293
Slade, Irene 248–50
Slater, Montagu 319
Smart, Christopher 259
Smith, Bessie 107–8
Smith, Logan Pearsall 348, 350
Smith, Stevie, *Scorpion and Other Poems* 263–5
Snow, C. P., *Variety of Men* 367
Southerington, F. R., *Hardy's Vision of Man* 261–2
Sparks, Olive 336
Sparks, Tryphena 261, 280
Sparrow, John 160, 216, 325
Spender, Stephen 52, 160, 297, 298, 300, 343
Sprigge, Elizabeth, *Gertrude Stein: Her Life and Work* 179–80
Squire, J. C. 95, 96
Collected Poems of Sir John Squire 230–31
Stalin, Joseph 370
Stallworthy, Jon, *The Penguin Book of Love Poetry* 274–6
Stein, Gertrude 179–80
Stanzas in Meditation and Other Poems 1929–1933 179
Stephen, Leslie 164, 278, 279, 288
Stevens, Wallace 28
Stevenson, Anne 331, 332
Stevenson, Robert Louis 294
Stewart, J. I. M. ['Michael Innes'], *Hamlet, Revenge!* 132
Stow, Randolph xiv
Stow, Randolph, *Act One* 221–3
Sutherland, Donald 179
Swift, Jonathan 293, 305, 306, 360
Swinburne, Algernon Charles 162
'Duriesdyke' 120
Sykes, Christopher 302
Symonds, J. A. 289
Synge, J. M. 204

Tallis, Thomas 106
Tanner, Jack 246
Taylor, Rex, *Poems* 219–20
Taylor-Martin, Patrick, *John Betjeman: His Life and Work* 334–7
Teagarden, Jack 108
Tennyson, Alfred Lord xiv, 163, 205, 236, 275, 293, 310–16, 378, 379, 380, 381
The Idylls of the King 310
In Memoriam 313
Maud 310, 313
The Princess 313
Tennyson, Sir Charles 311, 312
Tennyson, Emily 315
Tennyson, Hallam 315
Thackeray, William Makepeace 294, 379, 380
Thomas, Dylan 21, 29, 36, 52, 60, 95, 96, 100, 101, 119, 183, 184, 195, 202, 207, 227, 259
Thomas, Edward 14, 220, 229
Thomas, R. S., *Poetry for Supper* 194
Thwaite, Anthony 25, 94–102

Trevelyan, Mary 373
Turner, W. J. 99

Updike, John 342
Urquhart, Sir Thomas 147

Vaughan-Thomas, Wynford 294

Wain, John 20, 25
Walpole, Horace 303
Walpole, Hugh 143
Walsh, Ernest 184
Warburg, Jeremy, *The Industrial Muse* xiv, 205
Watkins, Vernon 28, 119, 322
Cypress and Acacia 226–7
Watson, Peter 351
Waugh, Evelyn xiv, 252, 301–3, 352, 358–60
Brideshead Revisited 48
Decline and Fall 48, 155
Webb, William xii
Weill, Kurt 319
Wellesley, Dorothy 99
Wells, G. P., *H. G. Wells in Love* 364–8
Wells, H. G. 364–71
Wells, Jane 365–6, 370
Wesley, Samuel 293
West, Anthony, *H. G. Wells: Aspects of a Life* 364, 369–71
West, Rebecca 366, 368, 369
White, John xiii
White, Rivers Blanco 365
Whitehead, John 344
Whitman, Walt 14, 26, 260
Wilberforce, William 359
Wilbur, Richard, *Poems 1943–56* 186–7
Wilde, Oscar 10, 26, 33, 200
The Importance of Being Earnest 362
Wilkinson, Louis, *Welsh Ambassadors* 339
Williams, William Carlos 184
Wilson, A. N. 112–16
Wilson, Colin 341
Wilson, Edmund 202, 207, 219
Wilson, Teddy 110
Woddis, Roger 306
Wodehouse, P. G. 294–5
Wolfe, Humbert 101
Woolf, Virginia 32, 49, 346
The Waves 69
Woolley, Frank 7
Woolsey, Gamel 150
Wordsworth, William 14, 45, 51, 52, 184, 259, 306
The Prelude 120
Wyatt, R. E. S. 7

Yeats, W. B. 21, 27, 28–9, 50, 92, 95, 96, 98, 102, 108, 159, 163, 183–4, 204, 227, 276, 344
'Lapis Lazuli' 36
Young, Alison 376
Young, Andrew 119, 376–7
Nicodemus 377
The Poetical Works of Andrew Young 376–7
Quiet as Moss 228